VOLUME FIFTY TWO

ADVANCES IN
CHILD DEVELOPMENT
AND BEHAVIOR

ADVANCES IN CHILD DEVELOPMENT AND BEHAVIOR

Series Editor

JANETTE B. BENSON
Department of Psychology,
Morgridge College of Education,
University of Denver,
Denver, CO, United States

VOLUME FIFTY TWO

Advances in
CHILD DEVELOPMENT
AND BEHAVIOR

Edited by

JANETTE B. BENSON
Department of Psychology,
Morgridge College of Education,
University of Denver,
Denver, CO, United States

ELSEVIER

ACADEMIC PRESS
An imprint of Elsevier
elsevier.com

ISBN: 978-0-12-812122-1
ISSN: 0065-2407 (Series)

For information on all Academic Press publications
visit our website at https://www.elsevier.com/books-and-journals

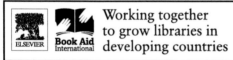

Working together
to grow libraries in
developing countries

www.elsevier.com • www.bookaid.org

Publisher: Zoe Kruze
Acquisition Editor: Kirsten Shankland
Editorial Project Manager: Hannah Colford
Production Project Manager: Magesh Kumar Mahalingam
Cover Designer: Alan Studholme

Typeset by SPi Global, India

CONTENTS

CONTRIBUTORS

M.L. Allen
Lancaster University, Lancaster, United Kingdom

E. Armitage
AQA, Manchester, United Kingdom

A. Baimel
University of British Columbia, Vancouver, BC, Canada

S.A.J. Birch
University of British Columbia, Vancouver, BC, Canada

A.J. Bremner
Goldsmiths, University of London, London, United Kingdom

P. Brosseau-Liard
École de Psychologie, Faculté des Sciences Sociales, Université d'Ottawa, Ottawa, ON, Canada

N. Cowan
University of Missouri, Columbia, MO, United States

S.R. Damiano
School of Psychology and Public Health, La Trobe University, Melbourne, VIC, Australia

L.L. Emberson
Princeton University, Princeton, NJ, United States

S.E. Ghrear
University of British Columbia, Vancouver, BC, Canada

T. Haddock
University of British Columbia, Vancouver, BC, Canada

V. Li
University of British Columbia, Vancouver, BC, Canada

S.J. Paxton
School of Psychology and Public Health, La Trobe University, Melbourne, VIC, Australia

S. Perone
Washington State University, Pullman, WA, United States

R.A. Settersten Jr.
Hallie E. Ford Center for Healthy Children & Families, College of Public Health & Human Sciences, Oregon State University, Corvallis, OR, United States

V.R. Simmering
University of Wisconsin–Madison, Madison, WI, United States

C. Spence
University of Oxford, Oxford, United Kingdom

T.D. Warner
University of Nebraska-Lincoln, Lincoln, NE, United States

M. Whyte
University of British Columbia, Vancouver, BC, Canada

PREFACE

Since the founding of this series in 1963, each volume has comprised an interesting and wide-ranging assortment of theoretical and research perspectives that typify the important issues in developmental psychology at that time. I am honored to continue the tradition of the *Advances in Child Development and Behavior* series as founded by coeditors Lew Lipsett and Charles Spiker, and then subsequently nurtured for over 30 years under the editorship of Hayne Reese and those editors who subsequently followed in his footsteps.

In the preface to Volume 1 of this series (1963), Lipsett and Spiker wrote,

The serial publication of Advances in Child Development and Behavior is intended to provide scholarly reference articles in the field and to serve two purposes. On the one hand, it is hoped that teachers, research workers, and students will find these critical syntheses useful in the endless task of keeping abreast of growing knowledge in areas peripheral to their primary focus of interest. There is currently an indisputable need for technical, documented reviews which would facilitate this task by reducing the frequency with which original papers must be consulted, particularly in such secondary areas. On the other hand, the editors are also convinced that research in child development has progressed to the point that such integrative and critical papers will be of considerable usefulness to researchers within problem areas of great concern to their own research programs.

This vision and the original intent of this series are as relevant today as it was over 60 years ago.

Volume 52 contains eight invited chapters that underwent a rigorous review and revision before final publication. These chapters illustrate the current range and diversity of theory and research in developmental psychology and provide insight into current and future trends in developmental science. The first three chapters of this volume focus on important empirical and theoretical questions concerning basic perceptual and cognitive developmental processes that span several periods of development. Lauren Emberson crafts a compelling argument for the role of experience in the early development of top–down perceptual processes that help to account for phenomena that bottom–up perceptual processes, by themselves, cannot explain, and she so does so by reviewing an impressive body of literature, including neuroimaging data. Perone and Simmering remind us of the many applications of dynamic systems theory to a wide range of developmental phenomena, including cognitive and perceptual processes that focus on the key developmental question of the emergence of new behavioral forms. The third chapter focuses on the development of working memory as Nelson Cowan tackles two classic challenges for the study of development: Researchers may focus their work on a specific process (i.e., working memory) but cannot ignore contributions of parallel processes that are developing at the same time (e.g., processing efficiency, attentional processes), and the persistent problem of how to study the same behavior across different periods of development with different tasks. Together, these three chapters also highlight the importance of studying development across multiple levels of analyses, including the neural, physiological, and behavioral.

The next three chapters share a broader behavioral focus and level of analysis that emphasizes the importance of context on development. Warner and Settersten provide a comprehensive view of the influence of the neighborhood context on adolescent development; they go well beyond existing research on "neighborhood effects" to highlight how neighborhoods encompass social stratification forces that can have positive and negative influences. Allen and Armitage discuss how children gain an understanding of the meaning conveyed in pictures by exploring both the context of the artist's intention and different picture types, such as drawings vs photographs. Birch and colleagues provide a detailed review of children's perspective-taking abilities and extend their analysis beyond the context of the classic *false belief* task to a wide range of naturally occurring social contexts that require the understanding of others' minds, such as faux pas situations and understanding irony.

The final two chapters share a common focus by offering new insights and intriguing possibilities that should generate future research activity, but for two very different areas of behavioral development. Bremner and Spence draw attention to the surprising lack of attention that has been paid to the development of tactile perception, which they distinguish from the development of touch. They make a convincing case for a new area of research by arguing that tactile perception plays an important role across the lifespan and for both social and cognitive domains. Paxton and Damiano review the existing literature on body image throughout childhood and make an critical distinction between factors that influence the development of body image attitudes directed at the self (e.g., body satisfaction and dissatisfaction) vs those generated by others (e.g., weight bias). They conclude by drawing attention to the need for future prevention research on body image attitudes for both girls and boys from an ecological framework.

This eclectic collection of chapters reflects the broad range of topics, their critical synthesis and integration, and the sophisticated approaches of today's developmental scholars. In the vision articulated over 60 years ago by founding editors Lew Lipsett and Charles Spiker, these chapters continue to honor the intent and the impact of the *Advances in Child Development and Behavior* series.

October 15, 2016

J.B. BENSON

Department of Psychology,

Morgridge College of Education,

University of Denver, Denver, CO, United States

How Does Experience Shape Early Development? Considering the Role of Top-Down Mechanisms

L.L. Emberson[1]
Princeton University, Princeton, NJ, United States
[1]Corresponding author: e-mail address: lauren.emberson@princeton.edu

Contents

Abstract

Perceptual development requires infants to adapt their perceptual systems to the structures and statistical information of their environment. In this way, perceptual development is not only important in its own right, but is a case study for behavioral and neural plasticity—powerful mechanisms that have the potential to support developmental change in numerous domains starting early in life. While it is widely assumed that perceptual development is a bottom-up process, where simple exposure to sensory input modifies perceptual representations starting early in the perceptual system, there are several critical phenomena in this literature that cannot be explained with an exclusively bottom-up model. This chapter proposes a complementary mechanism where nascent top-down information, feeding back from higher-level regions of the brain, helps to guide perceptual development. Supporting this theoretical proposal, recent behavioral and neuroimaging studies have established that young infants already have the capacity to engage in top-down modulation of their perceptual systems.

Advances in Child Development and Behavior, Volume 52
ISSN 0065-2407
http://dx.doi.org/10.1016/bs.acdb.2016.10.001

1

1. INTRODUCTION

How does experience support development? This is not a question about the trajectory of development (e.g., "what happens when"), nor the relative importance of experience vs innate capacities. This is a question about the means or mechanisms by which one factor, experience, shapes a developing brain. To investigate *how* experience supports development, most accept that experience plays some important role and that assumption is well supported in perceptual development. Building perceptual systems that adaptively reflect an individual's environment forms the foundation of more complex perceptual-cognitive abilities, such that language comprehension is supported by changes in speech perception; and social development is supported through the development of face perception. Regardless of what balance of innate or experience-driven mechanisms is at play in perceptual development, it is widely accepted that an infant's *individual* experience plays some crucial role. For example, infants adapt themselves to their native language and the faces of their communities, but babies of English-speaking parents are not more prepared to speak English. Thus, perceptual systems must adapt themselves to the structures and statistical information that infants experience. In this way, perceptual development is not only an important topic in its own right, it is a case study for behavioral and neural plasticity—those powerful mechanisms that have the potential to support developmental change broadly starting early in life.

Thus, on one hand, perception is a domain that readily lends itself to studying how experience shapes development because it is uncontroversial that experience plays *some* crucial role. On the other hand, perceptual development is a difficult domain in which to investigate these questions because developmentalists have strong, preexisting assumptions about how experience shapes perception. Specifically, there are long-held beliefs that experience supports perceptual development through a passive accumulation of experience. That is, the type of sensory input that a developing individual receives helps to solidify internal perceptual representations. This is a *bottom-up* view of perceptual development as part of the foundation upon which research in this area has been built.

This chapter proposes a complementary mechanism by which experience can shape perceptual development and development in general. Specifically, a thesis of this chapter is to propose that experience can shape perceptual development in a *top-down* fashion. Experience with patterns and structures in the environment allows the engagement of high-level cognitive systems, such as learning and memory and attentional/executive function systems, and these higher-level systems can exert a top-down influence on perception. These top-down connections can shape the pattern of activity and responses in perceptual systems and, thus, are part of the mechanism by which experience affects perceptual development. In addition, establishing these top-down connections can also start to create the larger networks in the developing brain that will support the development of cognitive function more broadly.

In this chapter, I will start by briefly addressing the widely held but largely implicit assumption that perceptual development is bottom-up. Then, I will present evidence for why a bottom-up model is not sufficient to explain a number of behavioral phenomena, nor the organization of mature perceptual systems seen in adults. I propose that the presence of nascent top-down influences on developing perceptual systems will better explain these key behavioral phenomena and provide new insight into how experience is shaping perceptual development. In addition, I will survey the current evidence, both behavioral and neural, that young infants already have the capacity to engage in top-down modulation of their perceptual systems.

2. AN (IMPLICIT) BOTTOM-UP MODEL OF PERCEPTUAL DEVELOPMENT

Perception is not a single ability and is often considered a range of abilities from low-level (e.g., visual acuity) to high-level functions (e.g., face perception). In this chapter, I focus on the perception of high-level stimuli such as speech sounds and faces because the role of experience is quite clear compared to lower-level perception. The discovery of *perceptual narrowing* of faces (Kelly et al., 2007; Pascalis et al., 2005) and speech (Werker & Tees, 1984) with important parallels in multisensory processing (Lewkowicz & Ghazanfar, 2006) has sparked great interest. Very young infants have the capacity to equally perceive all faces (e.g., human and nonhuman primate faces) and all speech sounds (i.e., those of many different languages), and with development, infants lose their ability to discriminate both faces and speech sounds that are not present in their environment. In other words, young infants are initially better at perceiving than adults, because adults exhibit diminished perceptual abilities for faces and speech that are not present in their environment vs those that are. The investigation of these phenomena has resulted in a strong case that experience matters for the development of face and speech perception. This may simply be because experience with faces and speech is not uniform across all infants. Infant A who will learn language A will be surrounded by speech sounds that differ markedly from infant B who will go on to learn language B. Thus, it is easier to see when the perception of infant A differs from infant B and attribute that difference to their differential experiences. It has been well documented that infants change their perception to fit their specific environments starting after 6 months (for reviews across domains see Maurer & Werker, 2014; Scott, Pascalis, & Nelson, 2007). Knowledge of the developmental time course of these effects has allowed researchers to manipulate the types of experience that infants receive during this period and demonstrate experience-dependent effects on perceptual narrowing (Scott & Monesson, 2009).

Compare this to the question of whether visual experience is important for the development of lower-level perceptual abilities, for example, visual acuity. The developmental trajectory of increases in visual acuity has been a focus for decades and is relatively well determined (Arteberry & Kellman, 2016), but it is difficult to uncover the role of early experience because infants have, by-and-large, similar experiences (e.g., with objects in the world, natural images). Thus, tackling the question of how experience matters for the development of lower-level perceptual abilities is much more difficult: Daphne Maurer and her research team have recruited adults affected by cataracts early in life to investigate the effects of early visual deprivation on visual development (Maurer, Lewis, & Mondloch, 2005), Helen Neville and colleagues investigate adults who are blind or deaf to examine perceptual plasticity (Neville & Bavelier, 2002), and a number of groups are starting to investigate these questions with premature infants to determine whether additional weeks of *extra uterine* experience affect perceptual development (Bosworth & Dobkins, 2009; Dobkins & Mccleery, 2009; Peña, Pittaluga, & Mehler, 2010). Animal models are well suited to addressing these scientific questions. In their classic work, Hubel and Weisel found striking evidence that typical experience is necessary for the development of receptive fields in early visual cortex (Wiesel & Hubel, 1963). However, asking how experience supports development of low-level perceptual abilities in humans has been difficult both pragmatically and interpretively, and thus the role of experience is less clear. For these reasons, this chapter will focus on high-level perceptual abilities, such as face and speech perception and the phenomenon of perceptual narrowing.

There is strong empirical evidence that experience shapes face and speech perception, yet there is little evidence as to *how* experience shapes the development of these perceptual abilities. There are, however, strong and often implicit assumptions that experience shapes perceptual development through bottom-up processes. What do I mean by bottom-up processes? In this context, *bottom-up refers to a passive accumulation of experience.* Perceptual development is entirely stimulus-driven without the requirement of any cognitive engagement from the infant. In this view of perceptual development, sensory experience strengthens or solidifies internal perceptual representations starting from the lowest levels of the perceptual system and moving to higher levels. Relatedly, the information flow of bottom-up processing is unidirectional starting from the lowest levels of the visual hierarchy and moving upward toward cognitive systems without any feedback of information from these higher-level systems to lower-level systems (see Table 1, left panel; Fig. 1).

This bottom-up model is well reflected in Hubel and Weisel's classic studies demonstrating that the development of the visual system is affected by early visual experience. By manipulating whether kittens received normal

Table 1 Characteristics of Bottom-Up and Top-Down Models of Perceptual Development

Bottom-Up	Top-Down
Passive: experience supports changes through the simple accumulation of experience	*Active*: certain types of experience produce engagement in higher-level systems which can change perception
Same sensory experience = same changes in perception	Same sensory experience can yield different changes in perception depending on structural/cognitive/task context
Unidirectional, *feedforward* flow of information from lowest levels of perception to cognitive systems	*Feedback* creates a bidirectional flow of information across the levels of perception and cognition
Experience changes perception in a feedforward, hierarchical fashion (i.e., lower levels before higher levels)	Higher-level cognitive abilities (e.g., learning/memory, attention, reward, executive function) can influence perception at any level
Experience changes perceptual representations/sensitivity	Experience may change the interpretations of perceptual information but not necessarily perceptual sensitivity

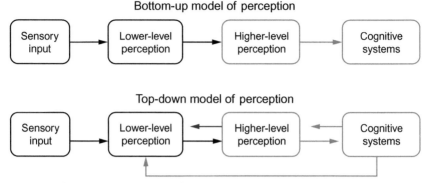

Fig. 1 Boxological representation of bottom-up vs top-down models of perception.

or substantially altered experience, they found that sensory input, as opposed to maturation, shapes the receptive fields of the lateral geniculate nucleus (LGN, the first location of visual processing in the brain after the retina) and then the receptive fields of the early visual regions of the cortex (i.e., V1 or striate cortex). This is a classic bottom–up model where development is presupposed to occur through the amount and type of sensory input. It also catalogs development starting from the periphery of the nervous system where experience is first encountered and onward up the visual hierarchy. Another important feature of this bottom–up model is that representation or sensitivity to sensory input is being shaped (i.e., kittens with substantially altered visual input exhibit reduced neural sensitivity to certain types of sensory input). This model assumes that no engagement is required by any system or region of the brain beyond the lowest levels of the visual system where receptive field changes are occurring. Sensory input shapes the LGN then V1 and does not require the engagement of higher-level systems such as attention or learning/memory. Finally, this bottom–up model also heavily relies upon the notion of critical periods where early sensory input results in changes in the visual system but later sensory input does not result in changes. Thus, the classic model of perceptual development suggests a highly inflexible adult visual system where sensory input no longer shapes perceptual function.

This model of how experience shapes perceptual development has become the implicit assumption of developmental psychology regardless of what type of perceptual ability is being considered (e.g., low level as was investigated by Hubel and Weisel vs high level that is the topic of this paper). This assumption of a bottom–up model of perceptual development can be seen in the framing of how experience leads to perceptual narrowing. Researchers will often characterize the structure of the infant's environment as the *cause* for perceptual narrowing. For example, researchers often state that infants become attuned to the more *frequent* perceptual exemplars in their environment (Scott et al., 2007). In this way, they have assumed that the infant's perceptual system is simply a reflection of the biases that are present in experience that they receive. Perceptual narrowing occurs as infants soak up sensory input, and it just so happens that their experiences are biased toward some exemplars over others (e.g., their native language), so their perceptual abilities will naturally reflect that. Similarly, researchers often point to the raw amount of experience overall as being the main way that experience can contribute to changes in perception. For example, Maurer and Werker (2014, p. 171) point to the "simple accrual of experience" as being the candidate way that experience can result in perceptual narrowing.

Overall, there is an assumption that infants are passively soaking up their perceptual experience, and in this way their perceptual systems come to reflect the structure of their environment. This assumption reflects a view of perceptual development as a bottom-up process where experience shapes development by simple exposure, whereby perceptual systems become a kind of summary of early sensory experiences. This bottom-up view is attractive for a number of reasons. First, it follows from a key historical model (i.e., put forward by Hubel and Weisel). Second, it broadly fits the pattern of perceptual narrowing where biases in environmental exposure result in biases in perceptual abilities (e.g., language A vs language B). A logical leap is that it is this heterogeneity in sensory experience alone that drives changes in perceptual experience (i.e., it is bottom-up or entirely stimulus-driven). Third, it is parsimonious and requires information flow in only a single direction. However, there are empirical findings that cannot be accounted for by a purely bottom-up model of perceptual development. I review these challenges to a bottom-up model next.

3. CHALLENGES TO THE BOTTOM-UP VIEW OF PERCEPTUAL DEVELOPMENT

Several findings are not readily accommodated by a bottom-up model of how experience shapes the development of perception. These findings suggest that infants are not simply passively soaking up their experience and their developing systems are not simply a summary of their sensory input, as is predicted by a bottom-up model. Further, the understanding of the adult perceptual system has shifted radically in the last decade. There is a renewed focus on how top-down processes enable effective perceptual systems that are highly attuned to the environment. Given that earlier views of the adult perceptual system were also dominated by bottom-up accounts, this shift in the understanding of the developed system begs a corresponding reconsideration of perceptual development and the role of top-down processes within it.

3.1 Infants Do Not Passively Absorb Sensory Experience

A bottom-up model is committed to the fact that if sensory input is the same, then the perceptual outcomes will also be the same. That is, if two infants see the same distribution of faces (i.e., which ones are frequent and which ones are infrequent), then they will develop the same perceptual abilities. The commitment follows directly from the view that sensory input is driving perceptual development without the involvement of any other system (see Table 1). However, there have been influential demonstrations that the same sensory input does not result in the same perceptual outcomes. In the seminal study by Scott and Monesson (2009), 6-month-old infants were given the same visual experience with monkey faces (via a storybook read by their parents), while some infants received variations to the linguistic context. Over 3 months, one group of infants simply saw the pictures, another group saw the pictures labeled with the category label "monkey," and the last group saw the pictures but each monkey had their own name (i.e., the individuation group). According to a bottom-up model of perceptual development, these infants should all have the same outcomes as they all viewed the monkey faces during the same period of time, and yet only infants in the individuation group, where each monkey had its own name, maintained their discrimination of monkey faces. In other words, having parents give proper names for each monkey pictured somehow affected infants' visual development beyond their visual experience.

Similar examples have been found in audition for speech perception. Yeung and Werker (2009) found that 9-month-old infants were able to discriminate between two nonnative speech sounds but only when each sound type was paired with its own novel object. Infants used lexical context to perform this difficult auditory discrimination when auditory experience alone was not enough. Similarly, Thiessen (2007) examined word learning in a well-known context where infants were able to discriminate two speech sounds when the sounds were presented in isolation (daw/taw) but failed to make use of this auditory information in a word-learning task (e.g., cannot learn that one object is a daw and the other object is a taw; see Stager & Werker, 1997). Thiessen (2007) found that when infants were familiarized with this distinction in combination with a perceptually salient distinction (daw-bow/taw-goo), they were able to use this structural or distributional information to perform the difficult word-learning task even when the daw/ taw distinction was again presented in isolation. Thus, in both of these examples simple auditory experience with speech contrasts is not sufficient to drive changes in perception or the use of perceptual information, but the augmentation of this auditory input with additional structural information supported better perception.

There are some suggestions that the nature of perceptual processing after perceptual narrowing may not be consistent with a purely bottom–up model. Specifically, because a bottom–up model affects the lowest levels of the perceptual system first and is believed to shape perceptual representations, it is predicted from this model that a perceptual narrowing should result in a reduction of perceptual sensitivity of nonnative or infrequent stimuli. Perceptual narrowing reduces behavioral performance in recognition tasks, and there have been a number of findings that show perceptual narrowing might affect the efficacy of the interpretation of nonnative stimuli (i.e., later stages of perceptual processing) as opposed to a reduction in perceptual sensitivity. As reviewed in Scott et al. (2007), researchers reported that in the absence of behavioral demonstrations of perceptual discrimination infants demonstrate neural discrimination. Specifically, in circumstances where infants do not reliably respond to changes in face or speech identity for nonnative categories (e.g., faces from nonexperienced groups), there remain systems in their brain that are sensitive to changes (however, see Grossmann, Missana, Friederici, & Ghazanfar, 2012 for a contrary example in cross-modal face-voice matching). Wu et al. (2015) found evidence in adults of intact early ERPs after perceptual narrowing but altered late ERP components. While there are a number of possible explanations for these results, these studies do establish that the absence of behavioral responses is not necessarily indicative of an absence of perceptual representations or a reduction in perceptual sensitivity to nonnative stimuli as would be predicted by a bottom–up model of perceptual development.

Similarly, Markant, Oakes, and Amso (2016) investigate whether selective attention may play a role in the decline of perception for other-race faces. These researchers used an ingenious attentional manipulation, relying on inhibition of return, to control the neural engagement of attentional systems of infants. Inhibition of return is a phenomenon where a reflexive or automatic shift of attention to a particular spatial location (e.g., orienting toward a sudden flash on a screen) is followed by an internal inhibition to return attention to that spatial location and a tendency to turn attention to a new location. Using this attentional phenomenon allowed these researchers to ensure that infants were perceiving native and nonnative stimuli with the same attentional processes, and they found that when selective attention is controlled this way, the other-race effect disappears. Convergent with the neural results presented earlier, Markant et al. (2016) suggest that the other-race effect may not be exclusively driven by declines in perceptual sensitivity or perceptual representations but differential engagement of high-level systems such as selective attention. Finally, intriguing results by Hadley, Pickron, and Scott (2014) suggest that the effects of perceptual training are not stimulus specific and that sensory input during development is not simply fine-tuning specific representations but permits infants to develop higher-level perceptual skills. Infants who received experience with non-native visual categories (monkey faces or strollers) with individual, proper names (as in Scott & Monesson, 2009) were followed up at 4 years to examine how this early experience affected their neural processing of human faces and the nonnative visual categories for which they received training. Surprisingly, these children had more mature neural responses to *human* faces but did not exhibit any differences to the nonnative categories that they were exposed to during training. Infants who received individuation training for a nonnative perceptual category became better at processing human faces years later but did not retain better individuation for the nonnative categories for which they received. These findings suggest that the additional, early perceptual experience, which has lasting impacts on perception during infancy, is not affecting perceptual representations for the nonnative stimuli but is building more generalizable perceptual *skills*. Hadley et al. (2014) suggest that this additional training boosts infants' abilities to individuate faces and does not directly affect infant perceptual representations.

Taken together these findings are difficult for a bottom-up model of perceptual development to accommodate, and suggest that additional, complementary models should be considered. A bottom-up model requires that the specifics of the sensory experience be the essential factor that is driving changes in perception. However, research has shown that sensory experience with the relevant stimuli (e.g., faces or speech) on its own is not sufficient to drive changes in perceptual development. Instead, infants are sensitive to the structure of the environment that supports these perceptual distinctions (Scott & Monesson, 2009; Thiessen, 2007; Yeung & Werker, 2009). Moreover, a bottom–up model is committed to experience affecting perceptual representations and not other processes, and these representations should be at the lowest possible level of perceptual processing. Again, there are strong counterexamples. There are cases where infants retain neural sensitivity but lose behavioral sensitivity, suggesting that their lower-level perceptual representations are unaffected. Similarly, recent findings suggest that selective attention may partly explain perceptual narrowing (Markant et al., 2016) and that perceptual experience might not affect perceptual representations per se but broader, general perceptual skills (Hadley et al., 2014).

3.2 Top-Down Processes Support Effective Perception in Adults

Another reason to revisit a purely bottom–up account of perceptual development is that the adult perceptual system is highly affected by top–down information.

Historically, adult perception was studied as a bottom–up, feedforward system where information is processed hierarchically. The dominant view was also that the perceptual system was inflexible in adulthood and does not change based on sensory input later in life (i.e., the critical period hypothesis). However, the last two decades of research has uncovered the myriad of ways in which adult perceptual systems continue to be shaped by experience (both in the short term and over longer periods of time) and how permeable perception is to the influence of top–down connections from other systems. This research has amounted to a recharacterization of adult perception as being relatively plastic or changeable and the nexus of both bottom–up and top–down information. This shift of understanding of adult perception begs the question: How and when does a highly top–down, adult perceptual system develop? If experience supports changes in perception in a strictly bottom–up fashion during development, why does the adult system readily employ top–down mechanisms to shape perception in response to experience and task demands? This section summarizes recent findings of top–down influences on perception in adults (also see Gilbert & Li, 2013).

Consider the primary visual cortex (V1, the earliest cortical visual area). This region has been viewed as the canonical bottom–up perceptual region as it is the first in the cortex to receive incoming visual information ascending from the retina. Yet, the *majority* of the neural information arriving at the primary visual cortex is *not* bottom–up sensory input but rather is top–down or feedback pathways from the rest of the brain. V1 receives five to eight times more excitatory feedback or top-down connections than it receives in feedforward information (i.e., 45% feedback vs 6–9% feedforward from LGN; see Latawiec, Martin, & Meskenaite, 2000).

Fig. 2 provides a visualization of the bottom-up, feedforward visual system classically studied along with the myriad of feedback connections received by the adult visual system. Some of these feedback connections are within the visual system itself with higher-level areas feeding back to lower-level areas but also from regions and systems far beyond the visual system such as the frontal cortex. As summarized by Gilbert and Li (2013, p. 350), "[f]or every feedforward connection [in the adult visual system], there is a reciprocal feedback connection that carries information about the behavioral context." Thus, from a purely neuroanatomical perspective, top-down information is a significant factor influencing the activity of the adult visual system.

In addition to the neuroanatomical argument for the importance of top-down information, it has been well documented that these feedback

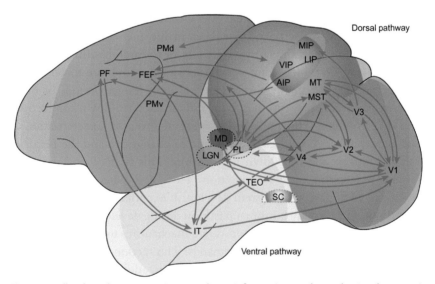

Fig. 2 Feedback pathways carrying top-down information to the early visual system in the adult brain. *Blue arrows* represent the feedforward, bottom-up connections across the hierarchy of visual regions. *Red arrows* represent feedback, top-down connections. Information from diverse cortical regions and systems is conveyed in top-down fashion to the visual system: Motor/efference copy, attention, expectation, and executive functions. *Reproduced from Gilbert, C. D., & Li, W. (2013). Top-down influences on visual processing.* Nature Reviews Neuroscience, 14, 350–363 with permission.

connections have functional significance. Top-down influences in perception take a variety of forms, including the effects of attention, expectation, learning/memory, and other more general task demands. While all of these types of top-down influences have the potential to play a role in perceptual development, this chapter will focus on effects of expectation and learning/memory. For an excellent review highlighting the potential role of attention in visual development, see Amso and Scerif (2015).

Experimental task and prior experience have broad effects on behavior, and often these effects are attributed solely to the feedforward modulations of higher-level systems. However, there are many circumstances in which aspects of either prior experience or task modulate behavior by directly affecting perception. For example, in a continuous flash suppression paradigm, Lupyan and Ward (2013) found that linguistic labels (e.g., "chair") boosted sensory input that was below a perceptual threshold to conscious awareness. This is a clear example where a memory or piece of learned information about the world (e.g., what the visual features of a chair are) is being used in a top-down fashion in the adult brain to change what is being perceived. This is simply one of many examples where predictions about future sensory input or learned information about the world has an affect on perception (see Hutchinson & Turk-Browne, 2012; Lupyan, 2015; Panichello, Cheung, & Bar, 2013; Summerfield & Egner, 2009 for reviews on impacts of top-down predictions and memory on perception).

Since expectations about the environment bias perceptual processing, where do these signals come from? One possibility is that what has been learned about the environment has simply shifted the representations in the perceptual system, and in this way, these effects of learning or expectation could be entirely consistent with a bottom-up model.

However, data strongly suggest that this is not the case and that these predictive signals that change perception originate from outside the visual system. Summerfield et al. (2006) found that when adults make decisions about ambiguous sensory input, these decision signals originate in the frontal cortex. Specifically, they found that the presentation of a given stimulus (e.g., a face) modulates bottom-up connections within the visual system and that expectation for a specific stimulus (e.g., being in a block with many face stimuli that results in a face expectation) strengthens top-down connections from the frontal cortex to the visual system (see Fig. 3). Similarly, Bar et al. (2001) found that adults activate their frontal cortex when experiencing unclear or difficult to process perceptual information (see Bar, 2003 for a

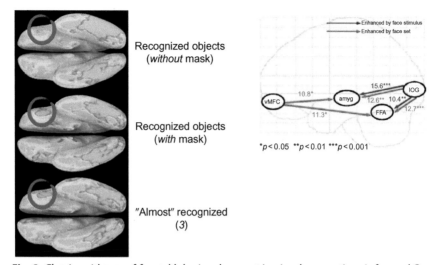

Fig. 3 Classic evidence of frontal lobe involvement in visual perception. *Left panel,* Bar et al. (2001) found increased frontal lobe activity when visual images were masked (i.e., are difficult to perceive) but not when stimuli were unmasked (i.e., easy to perceive). *Right panel,* Summerfield et al. (2006) found that when the probability of seeing a certain type of stimulus (e.g., a face in a block when there were a high proportion of faces presented), there are increases in the top-down connections from the frontal lobe to the visual system. *Figures reproduced with permission.*

specific theory as to how these prefrontal cortex signals may be biasing visual perception and Fig. 3).

In line with Bar et al. (2001), it is important to note that these top-down effects are clearest when bottom-up or sensory information is weak or ambiguous. When there are reasons to doubt or have uncertainty about bottom-up sensory input, and there is a strong top-down source of information, it is rational for an individual to rely on the top-down signal. However, this does not mean that top-down signals are only effective during these specialized laboratory tasks. Some have argued that, given the complexity of sensory input in combination with the highly structured nature of the environment, perception in the natural environment is most like these ambiguous laboratory contexts (Summerfield & de Lange, 2014).

In addition, consider the circumstances where there is strong, unambiguous bottom-up sensory information that is in conflict with top-down signals or expectations. In this case, the difference between top-down and bottom-up signals can be highly informative and could effectively guide learning. Predictive coding, a prominent theory of cortical processing, proposes that top-down connections are ubiquitous and are essential to the functioning of the brain. Predictive coding proposes that cortical activity is the relation between incoming sensory input and top-down expectations where expectations arise from each level of the cortex are conveyed to previous levels of the system (e.g., color expectations in V4, a region sensitive to color information, are sent back to regions that provide bottom-up input to V4). Then, each incoming sensory input is compared to the expectations and the difference between these signals is propagated forward (Friston, 2005; Rao & Ballard, 1999). There has been some support for predictive coding (though mostly in imaging studies, see den Ouden, Daunizeau, Roiser, Friston, & Stephan, 2010; Emberson, Richards, & Aslin, 2015; Kok, Failing, & de Lange, 2014; Summerfield et al., 2006; Summerfield & Koechlin, 2008; Summerfield, Trittschuh, Monti, Mesulam, & Egner, 2008). While future work is needed to support this specific theory of the brain, predictive coding has sparked widespread interest in the role of expectation or prediction in cognition and perception as many researchers have argued that prediction explains a wide variety of phenomena (see reviews by Clark, 2013; Lupyan, 2015).

Thus, there is strong evidence that adults can use previously learned information and expectations about future sensory input to exhibit top-down control on perception. These are examples of the role of top-down information influencing perception in adulthood. Moreover, neuroimaging studies have demonstrated that the origin of these top-down signals is beyond the visual system often originating in the frontal cortex.

Researchers have found that top-down effects on perception function more than to exert transient or trial-by-trial effects, but can also guide perceptual learning over longer timescales. For example, researchers in the field of perceptual learning have investigated how experience can result in changes in perception in adulthood (also called visual plasticity). Typically, these changes in perception are low level and specific to given stimuli and even regions of the visual field (e.g., a given retinotopic region of the cortex). While traditional perceptual learning was seen as a bottom-up process by which additional experience with a given stimulus shapes specific perceptual representations, a few decades of work has established that perceptual learning is highly sensitive to top-down factors. For example, Seitz, Watanabe, and colleagues have found that amount of perceptual experience is only one factor that drives perceptual learning, and reward and attention are extremely important in modulating whether experience results in changes in low-level perception (Roelfsema, van Ooyen, & Watanabe, 2010;

Seitz, Nanez, Holloway, Tsushima, & Watanabe, 2006; Seitz & Watanabe, 2005). Providing convergent findings to this behavioral work, Li, Piëch, and Gilbert (2004) examined functional properties in early visual cortex of monkeys trained on novel objects in two different tasks. They found changes in functional properties in these neurons as a result of experience, and that learning was highly sensitive to the task that the monkeys were engaged in. This finding again demonstrates that bottom–up sensory input is not the only factor affecting how experience changes perception. Similar findings have been documented in the auditory system (Polley, Steinberg, & Merzenich, 2006). Ahissar and Hochstein (2004) have proposed the Reverse Hierarchy hypothesis and argued that perceptual learning occurs in a top-down fashion with a preference for shifts at the highest possible levels of the visual system and only affects lower levels when changes to higher levels are insufficient.

Recent work has demonstrated that, in addition to experimental task, reward and attention, learning and memory systems can also spark changes in perception. Emberson and Amso (2012) gave adults' experience with novel visual stimuli. Through the integration of variable visual experiences, participants would be able to create a novel object representation to change their perception. Despite receiving the same sensory experiences, strong individual differences were found in roughly half of the individuals who were studied when they changed their perception and the other half persisting with their initial, prestudy percepts. fMRI recordings during these new experiences also revealed that activity in multiple learning and memory systems differentiated those who changed their percept with experience from those who did not. This finding further demonstrates that bottom–up sensory input is not sufficient to produce changes in perception and higher-level systems play a role in changing perception as a result of experience (see similar findings by Stokes, Atherton, Patai, & Nobre, 2012).

Overall, these findings challenge classic, bottom–up models of perception in several ways. First, demonstrations of perceptual learning in adulthood challenge the view that, after early development, perceptual systems are inflexible and largely resistant to change as a result of new experiences. Second, in adulthood, perception and perceptual learning are highly influenced by top-down information. While these sensory experiences are necessary for perceptual learning to take place, they are not necessary and *sufficient*. Instead, top-down processes, such as attention, reward, and learning/memory systems, are responding to this experience and helping to adaptively shape adult perceptual systems. Third, demonstrations that top-down information influences visual perception at the behavioral level and the neural activity in these regions also suggest that the adult perceptual system readily takes advantage of top-down information to boost perceptual capacities. Finally, the anatomical organization of the adult brain is highly bidirectional with the bottom-up connections complemented with numerous top-down connections both within a given perceptual system and far beyond.

4. COULD TOP-DOWN INFORMATION SHAPE PERCEPTUAL DEVELOPMENT?

In the previous section, two broad challenges to an exclusively bottom-up model of perceptual development were presented: First, findings from the developmental literature that are not compatible with an exclusively bottom-up model of perceptual development; Second, evidence for the pervasive influence of top-down processes in the adult perceptual system and that top-down information guides how experience changes perception later in life. Focusing on the latter, since top-down information has been established to adaptively shape adult perception in response to the environment, this raises a distinct possibility that these same top-down processes are involved in helping to shape perceptual development early in life. Moreover, it could be the presence of these top-down mechanisms that account for the discrepancy between an exclusively bottom-up view of perceptual development and the findings reviewed previously where perceptual experience is necessary but not sufficient to explain changes in infant perception. Infant perceptual development is sensitive to the structure of the environment in which this sensory experience is embedded (Scott & Monesson, 2009; Thiessen, 2007; Yeung & Werker, 2009). So too has adult perceptual learning been found to be sensitive to context in which this information is provided (though in adult perceptual learning "task" is typically studied rather than structural context; Li et al., 2004; Seitz et al., 2006).

Yet key questions remain to be resolved: What *is* the top-down model of development? What commitments does it make? What phenomena (behavioral or neural) should we expect to observe if top-down processes are affecting development? These are difficult questions to answer in part because the definition of top-down is being debated. At one extreme, top-down mechanisms are defined as volitional, available to consciousness, goal-directed, and must originate entirely outside any perceptual system (i.e., the feeding back of higher levels to lower levels within the visual system is not considered top-down in this view; Firestone & Scholl, 2016). This is consistent with a modular view of perception and is largely grounded in behavioral evidence. At the other extreme, any feedback between any cortical regions (e.g., from V2 to V1) could be considered top-down as it entails some amount of feedback. This is consistent with predictive coding, a largely neuroanatomically based theory of cortical function (Friston, 2005; Rao & Ballard, 1999). Moreover, the most successful contemporary computational model of human vision is described as an entirely feedforward system in that it does not explicitly incorporate feedback connections or information about cognitive task (Yamins et al., 2014). However, this model does employ supervised learning algorithms that provide a clear feedback signal to the model. Interestingly, the model is trained to match a picture to its word referent (e.g., to predict the word bunny when seeing a picture of a bunny). It is unclear whether this model is exclusively bottom-up, in line with the classic models outlined in this chapter as the method of training is surprisingly similar to the behavioral study by Scott and Monesson (2009) that involved providing infants with individual names of monkeys. Thus, the models (Yamins et al., 2014) seem different from the passive, stimulus-driven models discussed here despite their claim that they are exclusively bottom-up. Overall, the line between bottom-up and top-down processes can be unclear, and the definition of what is top-down is currently under debate.

The definition of top-down employed here plots a middle course between the two extremes and is meant to guide future work into the developmental origins of top-down processing. Specifically, I broadly divide the hierarchy of processing into three parts: lower-level perception, higher-level perception, and cognitive. Information can be considered to be top-down if it jumps between these parts (Fig. 1). For example, the feedback from demonstrable cognitive processes such as learning and memory or reward systems to perception at either level would be considered top-down (e.g., from Emberson & Amso, 2012, the influence of the hippocampus and basal ganglia in shifting object representations in adults). If higher-level representations within a perceptual system (or information across perceptual systems) feed back to lower-level representations, this would also be considered top-down (e.g., Lupyan & Spivey, 2008 found that processing novel stimuli as familiar categories of visual objects such as letters affected their low-level visual processing of these objects). These individual parts are not precisely defined (e.g., Where is the boundary between high-level vs low-level perceptual processing? Why is reward considered cognitive?), and, instead, the focus here is, first, on the *direction* of the information flow where top-down is going from a point that is clearly further along the processing hierarchy and affecting processing earlier in the hierarchy. Second, the division into these parts is meant to shift the emphasis toward top-down processing which is of greater distance than predictive coding where *distance* can be defined anatomically or representationally. The inclusion of anatomical distance highlights the fact that for systems such as the frontal cortex and learning and memory systems to influence perceptual regions, they have large anatomical distance to cover, and the developing brain starts out with very few of these long-range connections and with a bias toward local processing.

What commitments does a top-down model of development make? Table 1, right panel, presents the corresponding characteristics of a top-down model to the bottom-up model already discussed. Importantly, while a bottom-up model requires that the same sensory input results in the same changes in perception, a top-down model allows that the same sensory input can result in differences in perceptual outcomes if there are differences in the structural/cognitive/task context in which the sensory input is received. A top-down model allows that experience can shape perception not only through tuning perceptual representation or sensitivity but also through shifts in the interpretation of this sensory input. Finally, while bottom-up models are passive and only require the simple accumulation of experience, top-down models are active and require the engagement of systems beyond the relevant perceptual region.

One of my goals is to argue that the investigation of top-down processes in early development is an important topic for future research. However, in the remainder of this section, I will review the literature for existing evidence that infants can engage in top-down modulation of their perceptual systems with particular emphasis on what pieces of evidence are suggestive but do not yet require invoking top-down mechanisms.

4.1 Neuroimaging Evidence for Top-Down Modulation in Infancy

The burgeoning field of developmental cognitive neuroscience is providing neuroimaging evidence for the availability of top-down mechanisms in infants. These findings support the early operation of systems that can exhibit a top-down influence (e.g., the frontal lobe) as well as evidence that perceptual systems are receiving and being modulated by top-down signals.

4.1.1 Prediction/Expectation Modulates Neural Activity in Perceptual Systems

Recent neuroimaging studies with infants provide convergent evidence that stimulus predictability is likely exerting a top-down influence on perceptual processing. Emberson et al. (2015) used functional near-infrared spectroscopy (fNIRS, an optical method of recording the hemodynamic response in the surface of the infant cortex that provides an alternative to fMRI for young developmental populations) to examine responses in the visual systems of 6-month olds when they predicted a visual stimulus. Specifically, infants were provided with a brief familiarization to learn that auditory cues predicted visual events. After this familiarization, infants were presented with a small number of trials where the auditory cue was not followed by a visual event (20% of trials). These *unexpected visual omission trials* provided an avenue for disentangling responses in relation to visual prediction and visual error without the confounding effect of presenting a novel stimulus. Consistent with the view that top-down mechanisms are available early in development, infants exhibited robust visual cortex responses to the auditory cue when the visual stimulus was unexpectedly omitted. Thus, the visual system responded when no visual stimulus was presented, indicating that top-down signals are modulating the visual system as early as 6 months of age and after only a couple of minutes of experience (see Fig. 4).[a]

Other researchers (Kouider et al., 2015) report similar findings that expectation modulates perceptual processing where infants learned audiovisual pairings and visual events were either presented to be inconsistent or consistent with the preceding auditory event. Twelve-month-old infants exhibited differences in both early and late ERP components when the visual event was incongruent vs congruent with the preceding auditory cue. Specifically, there was a facilitation of the early ERP component when the visual event was congruent, suggesting top-down facilitation of visual

---

[a] Nelson, Ellis, Collins, and Lang (1990) also examined infant neural responses to missed or unexpectedly omitted stimuli in a cross-modal cueing paradigm where an auditory event predicts a visual event. This study employed ERPs with 6-month olds and found that in trials where the predicted visual stimulus was unexpectedly omitted, there was no evidence of a surprise component but ERPs were modulated to the presented visual stimulus in the subsequent trial. There are a number of differences between these paradigms that might explain the discrepancy in the findings. For example, the Emberson et al.'s (2015) procedure has auditory cues overlapping with the start of the visual presentation which will likely produce stronger cross-modal learning and may provide more opportunity for top-down signals to be produced and detected. Moreover, it is possible that there are differences in the detection of top-down signals in ERPs and fNIRS; however, similar responses to an unexpected auditory omission have been reported using intracranial ERPs in adults (Hughes et al., 2001). These are important avenues for future investigation.

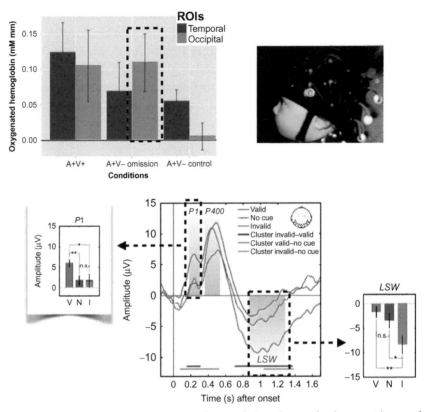

Fig. 4 Emberson et al. (2015) and Kouider et al. (2015) provide direct evidence of top-down effects of expectation and feedback on perceptual processing in young infants. *Top panel,* functional near-infrared spectroscopy (fNIRS) recordings of the temporal and occipital cortex of 6-month-old infants revealed expected sensory cortex responses to both audiovisual stimuli (A+V+) and occipital lobe activity during the presentation of an auditory cue, but the unexpected omission of the visual stimulus (A+V− omission). This occipital cortex response is not a response to auditory only stimuli when infants are not expecting the visual stimulus (A+V− control, Emberson et al., 2015). *Bottom*: Twelve-month-old infants were presented with visual stimuli that were either validly predicted by an auditory cue or invalidly predicted. The validity of the cue modulated two components of the event-related potentials (ERPs, Kouider et al., 2015). *Figures reproduced with permission.*

processing as a result of cross–modal associations and prediction. The opposite pattern was observed for the late ERP component where incongruent visual events exhibited a stronger late slow–wave response, suggesting a difference in error processing or perceptual consciousness (Kouider et al., 2013).

Turning to the auditory system, Nakano, Homae, Watanabe, and Taga (2008) found that sleeping 3-month-old infants exhibit anticipatory cortical activation after experience with auditory events that demonstrate the presence of these effects in the auditory modality. Although the use of unimodal stimuli here makes the argument for top-down mechanisms less conclusive, these results are suggestive of similar top-down modulation, especially in combination with findings by Emberson et al. (2015) and Kouider et al. (2015).

Overall, these results suggest that the infant brain is exquisitely sensitive to patterns of sensory input and rapidly modulates perceptual systems in the face of new experiences. Indeed, Basirat, Dehaene, and Dehaene-Lambertz (2014) suggest that young infants encode expectations in computationally sophisticated ways. Consistent with findings from adults (Wacongne et al., 2011), infants were exposed to temporal sequences with both local and global structures or expectancies. The authors found differences in infant ERPs to violations of local vs global expectancies, suggesting that error processing occurs in a hierarchical fashion by 3 months of age. Similarly, researchers have investigated responses to odd-ball stimuli in infancy and found evidence for sophisticated responses to novel or deviant stimuli in young infants (Ackles, 2008).

In sum, a number of neuroimaging studies with young infants have suggested that early in development, perceptual system is being modulated by top-down signals. Specifically, the top-down signals being received are in the context when infants are given a chance to predict or expect future input. In these cases, perceptual systems respond differently depending on the expectancy of that stimulus input in a way that cannot be explained by low-level adaptation effects (e.g., repetition suppression). Moreover, these studies have revealed sophisticated neural responses by young infants to structure in the environment and suggest that early learning systems exert top-down influences on perceptual systems starting early in life.

4.1.2 Availability of Frontal Systems Early in Development

The previous section reviewed direct evidence for top-down modulation of perceptual systems. The field of developmental cognitive neuroscience has also revealed the early availability of higher-level systems in young infants. Activity in these higher-level systems, often assumed to be silent or inactive early in development, suggests the possibility that these systems have the potential to be the origin of top-down information that is fed back to perceptual systems.

The higher-level system that has received the most focus in infants is the frontal lobe. This is in part because of the ease of recording this area using fNIRS as opposed to regions that are out of the field of view of this imaging modality (e.g., learning and memory systems: hippocampus, basal ganglia). Moreover, fNIRS recordings are particularly important because they allow spatial localization akin to fMRI that ERPs do not.

The investigation of frontal lobe function in infancy using fNIRS has revealed the surprisingly early involvement of this slow developing system. A long-held belief is that the frontal lobe is the last cortical system to develop as research has shown that changes occur into late adolescence and early adulthood (Conklin, Luciana, Hooper, & Yarger, 2007; Gogtay et al., 2004). There is support for this view as some executive functions show developmental changes into these later ages (for a review see Grossmann, 2013). However, these findings have led to the assumption that the frontal lobes are largely silent early in development and only come online later in life. In vivo neuroimaging with children and infants has challenged this view (see Stuss & Knight, 2013 for a number of excellent chapters on the development of the frontal lobes). Neuroimaging studies instead provide ample evidence that the frontal lobes are functioning early in life. Numerous experiments across a number of domains have found that the frontal lobe is very active in young infants (Grossmann, 2013). Here I focus on studies within domains that are most connected to experience-based perceptual development (i.e., prediction, learning/memory, modulating perceptual responses) and will review evidence that the infant frontal lobe could be the source of top-down information early in development.

A number of studies have found evidence that the infant frontal lobe is involved in processing stimulus novelty. Nakano, Watanabe, Homae, and Taga (2009) examined the temporal and frontal cortices of 3-month-old sleeping infants while they habituated to a single auditory stimulus (e.g., "ba") and then when this stimulus was changed (e.g., "pa"). They found dishabituation/novelty responses in the frontal lobe. Interestingly, there are no significant differences in response to habituated and nonhabituated auditory stimuli in the temporal lobe where it would be expected in adults (Zevin, Yang, Skipper, & McCandliss, 2010). This finding suggests that the frontal lobe is involved in novelty responses and change detection in infants, while perceptual cortices might be responsible for these functional responses later in development.

Similar findings were presented by Emberson, Cannon, Palmeri, Richards, and Aslin (in press) who examined frontal and perceptual cortex responses to repeated vs variable sensory input in both the auditory and visual modalities. Six-month-old infants exhibited repetition suppression, the attenuation of sensory cortex responses after repetition of a stimulus, but only in the auditory modality. This repetition suppression was found in both the frontal cortex and the temporal cortex where auditory perceptual processing occurs.

No changes in response to repetition were found for visual stimuli in either the frontal lobe or the occipital cortex where visual perceptual processing occurs. These findings provide direct evidence that the frontal lobe is tracking repetition and novelty in young infants, similar to the findings reported by Nakano et al. (2009), and provide indirect evidence that the frontal lobe might be involved in modulating perceptual systems in response to these changes in the environment.[b]

Overall, these findings suggest that young infants are employing their frontal lobes to track structure or novelty in the environment; however, the tasks that the infant frontal lobes engage in might be different than the tasks that engage the frontal lobe later in development. The activity in this classic higher-level system has been shown to be source of top-down information that modulates perceptual functions in adulthood (Bar et al., 2001; Summerfield et al., 2006). The involvement of the frontal lobe early in development in these types of circumstances provides the possibility that this higher-level region could be a source of top-down information in infants as well. However, future work is needed to more directly link activity in the infant frontal lobe with changes in perceptual systems.

4.2 Behavioral Evidence for Top-Down Modulation in Infancy

One of the major families of findings that has raised questions as to whether perceptual development is entirely bottom-up is that the *structure* underlying sensory input changes the way that perceptual experience shapes infant behavior either in the short term (Thiessen, 2007; Yeung & Werker, 2009) or long term (Hadley et al., 2014; Scott & Monesson, 2009). Learning about the structure of the environment (e.g., word-object associations)

---

[b] It is unclear why Emberson et al. (n.d) and Emberson et al. (2015) found evidence of perceptual system modulation during repetition/variability and unexpected omissions, respectively, and Nakano et al. (2009) did not. One possibility is that the 3-month olds studied by Nakano et al. (2009) are too young to engage in this kind of top-down modulation or sleeping infants are unable to do so. It could be that the task does not sufficiently encourage infants to predict upcoming sensory input so top-down signals are not communicated back to the temporal lobe. Future work is needed to investigate these possibilities.

involves systems at a higher level than the kinds of perceptual processes being affected (e.g., speech perception). Demonstrations that infants are using their expanding knowledge about the structure of the environment to shape their perceptual processing are evidence for top-down influences on perceptual development. A complementary finding by Feldman, Myers, White, Griffiths, and Morgan (2013) suggests that infants can use their emerging knowledge of words (i.e., the lexicon) to change their perception of speech sounds. As articulated in Swingley (2008), it has been traditionally viewed that language development proceeds in a bottom-up fashion as infants learn the sounds of their native language, then use these sounds to learn words, and then use these words to learn syntax. However, it has long been known that these developmental stages are not discrete. Infants have knowledge of words well before they have solidified their perception of speech sounds (Bergelson & Swingley, 2012). If language development is not purely bottom-up in this way, how does it proceed? Findings like those presented by Feldman et al. (2013) suggest that infants may utilize knowledge of the structure of the environment to shape changes in their perceptual abilities. Building on findings presented earlier, this section will review and evaluate a number of other related studies showing that infants have the capacity for top-down modulation of their perceptual systems early in development.

4.2.1 Generalization From Prior Experience Supports Changes in Perception: Auditory

Research shows that infants can use prior experience to change their perceptual processing, but is this evidence that infants have employed top-down mechanisms? An excellent example of work in this area is in speech segmentation. The segmentation of fluent speech is one of the most difficult developmental tasks facing infants as they start to learn their native language. Natural speech does not have pauses at the word boundaries, and yet, we perceive each word as temporally distinct. Numerous mechanisms have been proposed to help infants with this difficult task. Bortfeld, Morgan, Golinkoff, and Rathbun (2005) found that 6-month-old infants can use a familiar name to segment a novel word from continuous speech. Specifically, they found that if infants were familiarized with a word they did not know (e.g., "bike") and it was consistently paired with either their name or the moniker used for their mother (e.g., "Mommy" or "Mama"), they showed evidence of segmenting and representing that word. However, this did not occur if a novel word was paired with another name or a word similar to, but not the same as, their mother's referent (e.g., "Tommy" vs "Mommy").

Is the ability to use a familiar word to segment fluent speech evidence that infants are employing top-down information to affect auditory processing? Bortfeld et al. (2005) present compelling work in contrast to those claiming that only bottom-up cues are used for speech segmentation in infancy (e.g., prosody). In the field of psycholinguistics, the use of lexical representations to affect speech perception is seen as a top-down effect because lexical representations are thought of as higher-level representations built from speech sounds. Thus, the flow of information across levels of representation contains feedback from a higher level (i.e., words, the lexicon) to a lower level (i.e., speech sounds).

Bortfeld et al. (2005) define top-down speech segmentation as "…using stored knowledge of the phonological forms of familiar words to match the portions of the speech stream and forecast locations of word boundaries" (p. 298).

However, is this the same meaning of top-down mechanisms that have been proposed in this chapter? I have presented accounts of how the use of a familiar word(s) to segment speech could be consistent with both bottom-up and top-down models of perception. One bottom-up explanation is that infants have discrete and relatively strong representations for their name and familiar words, such as mommy by 6 months (Mandel, Jusczyk, & Pisoni, 1995). These representations could have been created purely from the greater frequency of their occurrence in sensory input similar to the stronger representations of vertical lines in kittens exposed exclusively to vertical lines (Wiesel & Hubel, 1963). These stronger, frequency-produced representations might *pop-out* of subsequent sensory input, providing a type of bottom-up segmentation cue. Indeed, the attentional pop-out effect has traditionally been seen as a classic example of bottom-up attentional processes. Moreover, Bortfeld et al. (2005) make a clear parallel between their findings with infants and the cocktail party effect, where adults reflexively shift their attention when they hear their name. In this case, representations were created based on the simple frequency or amount of sensory input (i.e., does not require higher-level learning and memory systems to integrate across experiences), and that these memories result in what is effectively a bottom-up cue during perception (i.e., a pop-out effect) both would suggest a bottom-up explanation of this phenomenon.

However, there are alternative explanations that are consistent with the involvement of top-down processes. First, it could be that the use of familiar references is a top-down process of matching perceptual templates to incoming sensory input. However, for this to be a top-down process there must be some kind of expectation to hear one's name that is applied to the input. Such an expectation could very well have occurred for infants in this study as their names were repeated along with a novel word, across several sentences (e.g., "Maggie's bike had big, black wheels." or "The girl rode Maggie's bike." or "The boy played with Maggie's bike."). In this case, infants were not experiencing a pop-out effect of their names but rather they heard their name in each sentence and were using this representation to initiate an expectation or perceptual template that helped them segment speech by exerting a top-down influence on the lower levels of auditory processing.

A second, mutually exclusive, top-down explanation is that infants do experience a pop-out effect of their names, but this pop-out effect is only possible through the previous interaction of higher-level systems and the auditory system. Recent work with adults has challenged the view that all pop-out effects are purely bottom-up. Specifically, pop-out effects can be readily triggered by previous experience that involves the reward system (e.g., pairing a stimulus with a previous reward; Hutchinson & Turk-Browne, 2012) or structure in the environment (e.g., experiencing a familiar scene triggers higher-level learning systems that provide feedback information to direct attention and perception; Awh, Belopolsky, & Theeuwes, 2012; Stokes et al., 2012). Applying this logic to the case of infants' using their name to segment speech, the question becomes how did the representations of the infants' name and their mothers' moniker arise in the first place, and did the creation of these representations depend on higher-level systems? If the answer is yes (i.e., it is not purely about the frequency of experience of their names), then the use of these familiar words to segment fluent speech would be an example of top-down processes supporting language development.

4.2.2 Generalization From Prior Experience Supports Changes in Perception: Vision

In the domain of visual perception, Quinn, Bhatt, Needham, and colleagues have investigated the role of object knowledge and perceptual categories on visual perception. This literature does focus on lower-level visual processes (as opposed to faces and speech, the primary focus of this chapter), but nevertheless provides some direct evidence for top-down processes in the development of infant vision. Overall, these studies demonstrate that variable visual experience can overcome bottom-up visual processes starting very early in development (3–4 months). These paradigms often require infants to generalize from familiarization to test trials. In addition to these behavioral findings, convergent evidence from computational models and adult neuro-imaging studies also suggests that top-down processes are required for these effects.

Quinn, Schyns, and colleagues conducted a series of studies examining bottom-up Gestalt perceptual-grouping principles in young infants to ask whether object knowledge is sufficient to override bottom-up, perceptual cues. At a young age (3–4 months), infants use perceptual-grouping princi-ples to disambiguate novel sensory input. For example, in the top, middle panel of Fig. 5, the sensory input is consistent with either a closed circle

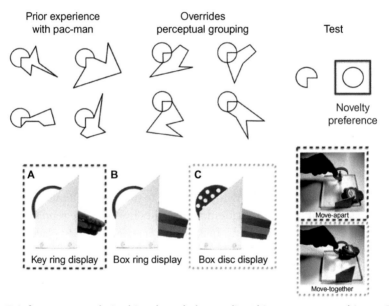

Fig. 5 Infants can use their object knowledge to disambiguate perceptual input. *Top panel*, Quinn and Schyns (2003) gave 3- to 4-month-old infants' experience with a pac-man shape (*left*). After this experience, infants used this pac-man knowledge to override their Gestalt perceptual-grouping principles when receiving ambiguous expe-rience (*middle*) as evidenced by infants exhibiting a novelty preference for the circle at test. This novelty preference is a marked departure from looking preferences without that prior pac-man experience. *Bottom panel*, 8.5-month-old infants were able to employ their object knowledge of a key ring to generalize to an ambiguous display as evidenced by longer looking to the "move-apart" event compared to the "move-together" event. Consistent with the view that infants are using their object knowledge to disambiguate this scene, when a similar object is presented that does not fit the category of a key ring, infants looked longer at the "move-together" event. *Figures reproduced with permission.*

or a pac-man shape present in the upper right of each of these figures. Consistent with Gestalt perceptual-grouping principles, infants perceive the circle and not the pac-man (Quinn, Brown, & Streppa, 1997). Given this finding, Quinn and Schyns (2003) provided infants with unambiguous experience with the pac-man shape (see top, left panel of Fig. 5) and then provided infants with this ambiguous experience. Across two experiments, infants showed evidence of using their new knowledge of the pac-man shape to override the bottom–up perceptual-grouping principles.

Specifically, this was exhibited by a novelty preference for the circle but only in the presence of the prior experience with the pac-man shape.

Similar to the findings in the context of speech segmentation (Bortfeld et al., 2005), these results suggest that infants are able to apply previously formed knowledge to change their bottom–up perception of their sensory input. Again, the bottom–up alternative explanation for this result is that simple repetition or increased frequency results in biases in bottom–up perception. Quinn, Schyns, and Goldstone (2006) conducted a follow-up study to address this alternative explanation by providing equal experience of the pac-man and the circle shapes, and continued to find evidence suggesting that infants were using their object knowledge to change their bottom–up perceptual propensities. Moreover, this work is supported by a computational model (Goldstone, 2000) that requires top–down influences from the categorization layer to the perceptual (detector) layer in order for these effects to occur.

Similar findings on the effect of object knowledge and categorization on vision have been presented by Needham and colleagues. Across numerous studies using the same task shown in Fig. 5, this group has demonstrated that 4.5-month-old infants are able to use prior experience and object knowledge to segment an ambiguous visual scene. Young infants used this knowledge even 24 h after initial exposure, in a different context (Needham & Baillargeon, 1998), to generalize from variable experience with different perceptual characteristics to the ambiguous scene (Needham, Dueker, & Lockhead, 2005). Infants were also able to generalize when the recent experience was of the box in a different orientation as shown in Fig. 5 (Needham & Modi, 1999). Finally, Needham, Cantlon, and Ormsbee Holley (2006) showed that older infants (8.5 months) use the features of a familiar category (keys) to disambiguate novel exemplars of this category. Specifically, the more similar the novel visual scene was to keys, the longer infants looked when the ring was moved independently from the keys, demonstrating that they are segmenting the scene consistent with the familiar category (see Fig. 5).

These results demonstrate that infants are able to use their object knowledge to disambiguate new visual input, which is similar to findings that infants can use a familiar word to segment fluent speech (Bortfeld et al., 2005). As supported by additional research that controls for differences in the frequency of sensory experience with each exemplar, both Quinn et al. (2006) and computational models point to a role of top–down processes in these phenomena (Goldstone, 2000). These studies provide convergent evidence that infants can employ top–down processes when using visual experience to support changes in perception.

4.2.3 Generalizing From Variable Perceptual Experience

An interesting detail in Needham's work on how experience supports changes in infants' scene segmentation is that variability of experience is essential to infants' generalization of their past experience (Needham et al., 2005; Needham & Modi, 1999). This finding is relevant to mediating between bottom–up and top–down accounts. If infants were using bottom–up mechanisms, prior experience could work as a prime where previously activated representations of a given object in prior experience would lead to better processing of that object in the future. In this case, perceptual similarity between previous experience and future input would be essential, and Needham and Modi (1999) reported that if infants are familiarized with a single box before test that this box must be extremely similar to the box used during test. This finding is consistent with what would be expected by bottom–up mechanisms. However, Needham et al. (2005) reported that when infants were exposed to three different boxes, none of these boxes needed to be as similar as the box needed in the single-exposure case. This is consistent with top–down models where a broader, higher-level representation is being formed through variable experience and is feeding back to affect perceptual processing. Since variability of prior experience seems to free infants from the constraints of perceptual similarity, this suggests that infants could employ either bottom–up or top–down mechanisms, and the characteristics of their experience (e.g., how variable it is) help determine which strategy is used.

Specifically, in the case where infants have prior experience with a single box and require strong perceptual similarity, they are likely employing a bottom–up method. However, when infants are permitted variable experience, they do not have the same rigid need for perceptual similarity and are likely employing a top-down method. Variable experience is likely allowing infants to form a higher-level perceptual category of the box that can be generalized to more dissimilar test instances.

Similar findings have been reported by Quinn and Bhatt (2005). These authors examined a type of Gestalt grouping principle, grouping by similarity, that is beyond the reach of 3- to 4-month-old infants. Across three experiments, these researchers investigated three different types of scenes, each composed of different elements that infants could distinguish and yet, infants consistently failed at this perceptual task (Fig. 6, left panel). However, the authors found that exposing infants to a combination of all three scene types resulted in successful perceptual performance (Fig. 6, right panel). In this case, variability allows infants to perceive a higher-level representation in the scene that longer exposure to a single scene type did not allow. This finding can be explained by both bottom-up and top-down accounts, and the authors did not provide any additional evidence to support either view, but the strong parallel with Needham's findings supports a top-down account in this case as well. As infants receive this variable exposure, they are able to form a higher-level representation. In the top-down account, this higher-level representation would feedback to earlier perceptual areas to change infants' perceptions of future sensory input.

In both of these examples it is not known what systems are integrating across these variable experiences to give rise to changes in perception.

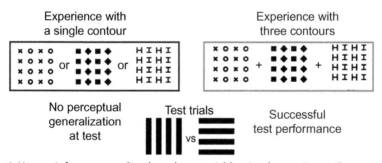

Fig. 6 Young infants generalize based on variable visual experience. For example, Quinn and Bhatt (2005) found that when 3- to 4-month-old infants experienced one of three contours constructed from different elements (i.e., requiring infants to use the Gestalt perceptual-grouping principle of similarity), they could not generalize this experience to an unambiguous contour at test. This indicates that they could not perceive the contour using these elements. However, if infants were exposed to all three of these contours, they could generalize at test. Thus, variable experience supported better perception than more experience with a single type of stimulus. *Figures reproduced with permission.*

However, convergent findings from adult learning studies suggest that higher-level learning and memory systems might be involved. The role of these higher-level systems provides additional evidence that the use of variable experiences to change future perception might be mediated by top-down mechanisms. As reviewed previously, Emberson and Amso (2012) presented adults with variable experience with a novel object. At the start of the experiment, adults were not able to perceive the novel object in an ambiguous scene. After familiarization to this object when it was embedded into three additional scenes, half of the adults changed their perception and detected the novel object, and the other half persisted with their initial percept. fMRI recordings taken during exposure revealed that the systems which differentiated the adults who used their variable experience to learn and those who did not were higher-level learning and memory systems. Specifically, those adults who changed their perception activated the hippocampus and the caudate (basal ganglia) during their variable experiences, suggesting that these systems are involved in building the object representation necessary to change future perception of this object. While it is possible that infants employ different neural systems to do this compared to adults, it is unlikely that their perceptual systems have the memory capacity to compare across the numerous experiences necessary to make these comparisons. Future methodological advances that will allow more sophisticated neuroimaging with infants will be helpful in answering these questions.

Finally, while there are no clear auditory analogues to these visual findings, there is some suggestion that infants can assimilate across variable experience to learn about the structure of their environment and again, the amount of variability matters. Specifically, *more* variability produces greater learning. Graf Estes and Lew-Williams (2015) found that infants can perform statistical learning across variable speakers but fail if there are only a couple of speakers present during familiarization. Gómez (2002) found that infants can learn from nonadjacent dependencies in an artificial grammar when the non-relevant items are highly variable. While it is not known whether these instances of learning from auditory variability result in top-down changes in perception, this is an interesting area for future research.

4.3 Neuroanatomical Evidence for Top-Down Modulation in Infancy

While there is strong evidence from both behavioral and neuroimaging studies that young infants have the capacity for top-down modulation of perceptual systems based on learning, experience, and expectation, infants have remarkably poor overall neural connectivity. Neural connectivity is the means by which information is transmitted between systems of the brain. The clear presence of top-down neuroanatomical connections throughout in the mature, adult brain (e.g., within perceptual systems and between cognitive and perceptual systems) is a strong piece of evidence in favor of top-down mechanisms later in life (see Fig. 2). However, these connections are remarkably weak early in development. Though it must be noted that investigations into neural connectivity are both much sparser in young developmental populations and more difficult to ascertain as the long-range connections in the brain are not yet myelinated, which is a necessary precondition for the detection of these connections using popular, noninvasive techniques, such as diffusion tensor imaging (DTI). However, there are three major sources of information about neural connectivity early in development: two types of noninvasive measures in humans: (1) structural connectivity using DTI, (2) functional connectivity (using fMRI), and (3) results from animal models of development. This section reviews each of these literatures in turn.

Studies of structural and functional connectivity in human infants reveal large developmental changes in the connectivity of the brain through the first years of life. In general, the brain starts out less interconnected and becomes more connected with age (Ball et al., 2014; Fair et al., 2009; Gao et al., 2011; Sasai et al., 2012; Smyser et al., 2010; Tymofiyeva et al., 2013; Yap et al., 2011). However, there is controversy with respect to how connected or disconnected the young brain is (i.e., how local or global). Some researchers claim that large-scale networks, similar to adults, exist at birth (Ball et al., 2014; Doria et al., 2010), while others report evidence of only local, proximity-driven networks in young infants (Fransson, Aden, Blennow, & Lagercrantz, 2011; Fransson et al., 2007; Gao et al., 2011; Sasai et al., 2012; Smyser et al., 2010; Tymofiyeva et al., 2013; Yap et al., 2011). Regardless of how interconnected or local the young brain is, there is clear evidence of a dramatic increase in the connectivity of the brain with development with the brain becoming more interconnected and creating more long-range, global connections. There are convergent findings in the measures of both functional connectivity and structural connectivity of this direction of development (Fig. 7).

Animal models of neural connectivity early in development are also relatively sparse. However, existing research on the development of cortico-cortical interactions in nonhuman primates suggests that, within the occipital lobe, there exist both feedback and feedforward connections

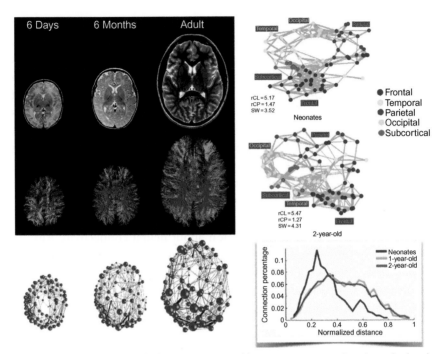

Fig. 7 Increases in both global connectivity and long-range connections in early development. *Left panel* from Tymofiyeva et al. (2013) presents (*top row*) structure MR images of neonates, 6-month olds, and adults, (*middle row*) images of long-range fiber tracks identified using diffusion tensor imaging (DTI) with notable differences in connection density between age groups, and (*bottom row*) brain networks represented as weighted graphs. Each size of each node represents the proportional node degree, or how many connections this area of the brain has. A large node will be a network hub. Again, there are notable differences in the relative size of the nodes and the distribution of connections between the nodes. *Right panel* from Gao et al. (2011) presents a graphical representation of the neonate and 2-year-old brain with nodes shaded by lobes. Neonate connections are largely local and nodes within each lobe are clustered together; however, by age 2 there are networks that span lobes as seen by less clear clustering by lobes. Moreover, there is a clear increase in the distance between connections as visualized in the graph. Distance is normalized to the size of the brain at each age. *Figures reproduced with permission.*

early in development. However, whereas some aspects of a visual hierarchy exist early, there is a dominance of feedforward connections. With visual experience, the balance of these types of connections shifts with both an increase in feedback connections and a decrease in feedforward connections (Price et al., 2006).

Interestingly, the development of long-range connections within the occipital lobe, in cats, emerges from the more local connections present early in development (Kaschube, Schnabel, Wolf, & Löwel, 2009). Findings like these again suggest that early in development neuroanatomical connections are readily available for feedforward, bottom-up processing and there is a development of feedback, top-down, and global connections.

Even though there is a clear developmental bias toward local, feedforward connections early in development compared with adults, and the development of global connections occurs well into adolescence (Fair et al., 2009), this does not mean that young infants cannot use their relatively weak global connections to exert top-down influences on their perceptual systems. It is possible that contexts where top-down influences are seen in neuroimaging and behavioral studies are part of the developmental mechanism by which these global connections are built. Neuroimaging work with adults suggests that learning and predictability can rapidly modify connectivity (in this case functional) between disparate brain regions (den Ouden et al., 2010).

5. CONCLUSIONS AND FUTURE DIRECTIONS

Perception is where cognition and reality meet (Neisser, 1976). What is the nature of that meeting? According to a bottom-up view of perception and perceptual development, it is a unidirectional meeting where reality walks through a passive perceptual system, and perception is simply a turnstile to the rest of the brain. Alternatively, perception could be the place where cognition and sensory input rendezvous. It could be a place where cognition makes guesses about the nature of reality, and reality reveals itself.

This latter characterization of perception, as a nexus of bottom-up information coming from the external world and top-down information coming from the rest of the brain, is receiving a great deal of support and interest by those studying mature perceptual systems. Top-down processes have been found to affect adult perception and guide perceptual learning. However, the possible role of top-down processes in the development of perception has received little attention. Instead, it has been largely assumed that experience supports perceptual development in a purely bottom-up fashion.

In this chapter I have argued that a strictly bottom-up model is not sufficient to explain known phenomena in perceptual development nor how a highly top-down adult perceptual system develops. Moreover, there is already evidence that infants as young as 3 months engage in top-down modulation of their perceptual systems when they are given the opportunity to predict or learn from sensory input. While this chapter argues for the early availability of top-down processes, further work is needed to investigate the extent and efficacy of these abilities.

It is also clear that even if top-down information is available early, these abilities are not mature early in life. However, that immaturity does not mean that top-down influences cannot play a role in shaping development. It has been well established that some types of top-down processes are developing well into adolescence (Hwang, Velanova, & Luna, 2010). This is one sense of the term top-down (i.e., inhibiting responses to salient stimuli), and other types of top-down information with other functions or involving other systems (e.g., learning/memory systems) could have different developmental time courses, be available earlier, and be more ecologically relevant for younger developing populations.

Certainly, the higher-level systems that would be the origin of a top-down influence are developing themselves (e.g., attention, memory, executive function), so either the nature or the efficacy of the information they can feedback will change across development. Moreover, neural connections between regions of the brain exhibit a protracted developmental trajectory and better connections will enable more effective feedback. Even though both higher-level systems that can originate top-down signals and the connections between higher- and lower-level systems are developing, this does not mean that top-down information is not exhibiting feedback control over earlier systems. It could be the use of these nascent, top-down connections that help to establish the highly top-down adult perceptual system and global, distributed networks that characterize the adult brain.

Finally, it is also likely that top-down and bottom-up processes are highly interdependent within development. Amso and Scerif (2015) hypothesize that "with visual development, there is an increase in feedforward information competing for attention allocation in higher-level regions, thus linking top-down visual attention development with visual experience. In turn, these regions, now engaged, send top-down signals to begin to tune local visual areas, setting the hierarchical loops in motion from very early in the first postnatal year" (p. 609). For this reason, it is important for future work to balance the general assumption of bottom-up models of perceptual development with investigations into the role of top-down processes in perceptual development.

ACKNOWLEDGMENTS

This work was supported by NICHD 4R00HD076166-02.

REFERENCES

Ackles, P. K. (2008). Stimulus novelty and cognitive-related ERP components of the infant brain. *Perceptual and Motor Skills, 106*(1), 3–20.

Ahissar, M., & Hochstein, S. (2004). The reverse hierarchy theory of visual perceptual learning. *Trends in Cognitive Sciences, 8*(10), 457–464. arXiv: 9605103 [cs].

Amso, D., & Scerif, G. (2015). The attentive brain: Insights from developmental cognitive neuroscience. *Nature Reviews. Neuroscience, 16*(10), 606–619.

Arteberry, M. E., & Kellman, P. J. (2016). *Development of perception in infancy: The cradle of knowledge revisited.* New York: Oxford University Press.

Awh, E., Belopolsky, A. V., & Theeuwes, J. (2012). Top-down versus bottom-up attentional control: A failed theoretical dichotomy. *Trends in Cognitive Sciences, 16*(8), 437–443.

Ball, G., Aljabar, P., Zebari, S., Tusor, N., Arichi, T., Merchant, N., ... Counsell, S. J. (2014). Rich-club organization of the newborn human brain. *Proceedings of the National Academy of Sciences of the United States of America, 111*(20), 7456–7461.

Bar, M. (2003). A cortical mechanism for triggering top-down facilitation in visual object recognition. *Journal of Cognitive Neuroscience, 15*(4), 600–609.

Bar, M., Tootell, R. B. H., Schacter, D. L., Greve, D. N., Fischl, B., Mendola, J. D., ... Dale, A. M. (2001). Cortical mechanisms specific to explicit visual object recognition. *Neuron, 29*(2), 529–535.

Basirat, A., Dehaene, S., & Dehaene-Lambertz, G. (2014). A hierarchy of cortical responses to sequence violations in three-month-old infants. *Cognition, 132*(2), 137–150.

Bergelson, E., & Swingley, D. (2012). At 6–9 months, human infants know the meanings of many common nouns. *Proceedings of the National Academy of Sciences of the United States of America, 109*(9), 3253–3258.

Bortfeld, H., Morgan, J. L., Golinkoff, R. M., & Rathbun, K. (2005). Mommy and Me: Familiar names help launch babies into speech-stream segmentation. *Psychological Science, 16*(4), 298–304.

Bosworth, R. G., & Dobkins, K. R. (2009). Chromatic and luminance contrast sensitivity in fullterm and preterm infants. *Journal of Vision, 9*(13), 1–16.

Clark, A. (2013). Whatever next? Predictive brains, situated agents, and the future of cognitive science. *The Behavioral and Brain Sciences, 36*(3), 181–204.

Conklin, H. M., Luciana, M., Hooper, C. J., & Yarger, R. S. (2007). Working memory performance in typically developing children and adolescents: Behavioral evidence of protracted frontal lobe development. *Developmental Neuropsychology, 31*(1), 103–128.

den Ouden, H. E. M., Daunizeau, J., Roiser, J., Friston, K. J., & Stephan, K. E. (2010). Striatal prediction error modulates cortical coupling. *The Journal of Neuroscience: The Official Journal of the Society for Neuroscience, 30*(9), 3210–3219.

Dobkins, K. R., & Mccleery, J. P. (2009). Effects of gestational length, gender, postnatal age, and birth order on visual contrast sensitivity in infants. *Journal of Vision, 9*(10), 1–21.

Doria, V., Beckmann, C. F., Arichi, T., Merchant, N., Groppo, M., Turkheimer, F. E., ... Edwards, a. D. (2010). Emergence of resting state networks in the preterm human brain. *Proceedings of the National Academy of Sciences of the United States of America, 107*(46), 20015–20020.

Emberson, L. L., & Amso, D. (2012). Learning to sample: Eye tracking and fMRI indices of changes in object perception. *Journal of Cognitive Neuroscience, 24*(10), 2030–2042.

Emberson, L. L., Cannon, G., Palmeri, H., Richards, J. E., & Aslin, R. N. (in press). Using fNIRS to examine occipital and temporal responses to stimulus repetition in young infants: Evidence of selective frontal cortex involvement. *Developmental Cognitive Neuroscience*. arXiv:1011.1669v3. http://dx.doi.org/10.1016/j.dcn.2016.11.002.

Emberson, L. L., Richards, J. E., & Aslin, R. N. (2015). Top-down modulation in the infant brain: Learning-induced expectations rapidly affect the sensory cortex at 6-months. *Proceedings of the National Academy of Sciences of the United States of America*, *112*(31), 9585–9590.

Fair, D. A., Cohen, A. L., Power, J. D., Dosenbach, N. U. F., Church, J. A., Miezin, F. M., … Petersen, S. E. (2009). Functional brain networks develop from a "local to distributed" organization. *PLoS Computational Biology*, *5*(5), 14–23.

Feldman, N. H., Myers, E. B., White, K. S., Griffiths, T. L., & Morgan, J. L. (2013). Word-level information influences phonetic learning in adults and infants. *Cognition*, *127*(3), 427–438.

Firestone, C., & Scholl, B. (2016). Cognition does not affect perception: Evaluating the evidence for 'top-down' effects. *Behavioral and Brain Sciences*, *39*, 1–77. http://dx.doi.org/10.1017/S0140525X15000965.

Fransson, P., Aden, U., Blennow, M., & Lagercrantz, H. (2011). The functional architecture of the infant brain as revealed by resting-state fMRI. *Cerebral Cortex (New York, N.Y.: 1991)*, *21*(1), 145–154.

Fransson, P., Skiöld, B., Horsch, S., Nordell, A., Blennow, M., Lagercrantz, H., & Aden, U. (2007). Resting-state networks in the infant brain. *Proceedings of the National Academy of Sciences of the United States of America*, *104*(39), 15531–15536.

Friston, K. (2005). A theory of cortical responses. *Philosophical Transactions of the Royal Society of London. Series B, Biological Sciences*, *360*(1456), 815–836.

Gao, W., Gilmore, J. H., Giovanello, K. S., Smith, J. K., Shen, D., Zhu, H., & Lin, W. (2011). Temporal and spatial evolution of brain network topology during the first two years of life. *PLoS One*, *6*(9)e25278.

Gilbert, C. D., & Li, W. (2013). Top-down influences on visual processing. *Nature Reviews. Neuroscience*, *14*, 350–363.

Gogtay, N., Giedd, J. N., Lusk, L., Hayashi, K. M., Greenstein, D., Vaituzis, a. C., … Thompson, P. M. (2004). Dynamic mapping of human cortical development during childhood through early adulthood. *Proceedings of the National Academy of Sciences of the United States of America*, *101*(21), 8174–8179.

Goldstone, R. L. (2000). A neural network model of concept-influenced segmentation. In *Proceedings of the twenty-second annual conference of the cognitive science society* (pp. 172–177).

Gómez, R. L. (2002). Variability and detection of invariant structure. *Psychological Science*, *13*(5), 431–436.

Graf Estes, K., & Lew-Williams, C. (2015). Listening through voices: Infant statistical word segmentation across multiple speakers. *Developmental Psychology*, *51*(11), 1–12.

Grossmann, T. (2013). Mapping prefrontal cortex functions in human infancy. *Infancy*, *18*(3), 303–324.

Grossmann, T., Missana, M., Friederici, A. D., & Ghazanfar, A. A. (2012). Neural correlates of perceptual narrowing in cross-species face-voice matching. *Developmental Science*, *15*(6), 830–839.

Hadley, H., Pickron, C. B., & Scott, L. S. (2014). The lasting effects of process-specific versus stimulus-specific learning during infancy. *Developmental Science*, *5*, 1–11.

Hughes, H. C., Darcey, T. M., Barkan, H. I., Williamson, P. D., Roberts, D. W., & Aslin, C. H. (2001). Responses of human auditory association cortex to the omission of an expected acoustic event. *NeuroImage*, *1089*, 1073–1089.

Hutchinson, J. B., & Turk-Browne, N. B. (2012). Memory-guided attention: Control from multiple memory systems. *Trends in Cognitive Sciences*, *16*(12), 576–579.

Hwang, K., Velanova, K., & Luna, B. (2010). Strengthening of top-down frontal cognitive control networks underlying the development of inhibitory control: A functional magnetic resonance imaging effective connectivity study. *Journal of Neuroscience, 30*(46), 15535–15545.

Kaschube, M., Schnabel, M., Wolf, F., & Löwel, S. (2009). Interareal coordination of columnar architectures during visual cortical development. *Proceedings of the National Academy of Sciences of the United States of America, 106*(40), 17205–17210. arXiv: 0801.4164.

Kelly, D. J., Quinn, P. C., Slater, A. M., Lee, K., Ge, L., & Pascalis, O. (2007). The other-race effect develops during infancy: Evidence of perceptual narrowing. *Psychological Science, 18*(12), 1084–1089.

Kok, P., Failing, M. F., & de Lange, F. P. (2014). Prior expectations evoke stimulus templates in the primary visual cortex. *Journal of Cognitive Neuroscience, 26*(7), 1546–1554.

Kouider, S., Long, B., Stanc, L. L., Charron, S., Fievet, A. C., Barbosa, L. S., & Gelskov, S. V. (2015). Neural dynamics of prediction and surprise in infants. *Nature Communications, 6*, 1–8.

Kouider, S., Stahlhut, C., Gelskov, S. V., Barbosa, L. S., Dutat, M., de Gardelle, V., ... Dehaene-Lambertz, G. (2013). A neural marker of perceptual consciousness in infants. *Science, 340*(6130), 376–380.

Latawiec, D., Martin, K. A. C., & Meskenaite, V. (2000). Termination of the geniculocortical projection in the striate cortex of macaque monkey: A quantitative immunoelectron microscopic study. *Journal of Comparative Neurology, 419*(3), 306–319.

Lewkowicz, D. J., & Ghazanfar, A. A. (2006). The decline of cross-species intersensory perception in human infants. *Proceedings of the National Academy of Sciences of the United States of America, 103*(17), 6771–6774.

Li, W., Piëch, V., & Gilbert, C. D. (2004). Perceptual learning and top-down influences in primary visual cortex. *Nature Neuroscience, 7*(6), 651–657.

Lupyan, G. (2015). Cognitive penetrability of perception in the age of prediction: Predictive systems are penetrable systems. *Review of Philosophy and Psychology, 6*(4), 547–569.

Lupyan, G., & Spivey, M. J. (2008). Perceptual processing is facilitated by ascribing meaning to novel stimuli. *Current Biology, 18*(10), R410–R412.

Lupyan, G., & Ward, E. J. (2013). Language can boost otherwise unseen objects into visual awareness. *Proceedings of the National Academy of Sciences of the United States of America, 110*(35), 14196–14201.

Mandel, D. R., Jusczyk, P. W., & Pisoni, D. B. (1995). Infants' recognition of the sound patterns of their own names. *Psychological Science, 6*(5), 314–317.

Markant, J., Oakes, L. M., & Amso, D. (2016). Visual selective attention biases contribute to the other-race effect among 9-month-old infants. *Developmental Psychobiology, 58*(3), 355–365.

Maurer, D., Lewis, T. L., & Mondloch, C. J. (2005). Missing sights: Consequences for visual cognitive development. *Trends in Cognitive Sciences, 9*(3), 144–151.

Maurer, D., & Werker, J. F. (2014). Perceptual narrowing during infancy: A comparison of language and faces. *Developmental Psychobiology, 56*(2), 154–178.

Nakano, T., Homae, F., Watanabe, H., & Taga, G. (2008). Anticipatory cortical activation precedes auditory events in sleeping infants. *PLoS One, 3*(12), e3912.

Nakano, T., Watanabe, H., Homae, F., & Taga, G. (2009). Prefrontal cortical involvement in young infants' analysis of novelty. *Cerebral Cortex, 19*(2), 455–463.

Needham, A., & Baillargeon, R. (1998). Effects of prior experience on 4.5-month-old infants' object segregation. *Infant Behavior & Development, 21*(1), 1–24.

Needham, A., Cantlon, J. F., & Ormsbee Holley, S. M. (2006). Infants' use of category knowledge and object attributes when segregating objects at 8.5 months of age. *Cognitive Psychology, 53*(4), 345–360.

Needham, A., Dueker, G., & Lockhead, G. (2005). Infants' formation and use of categories to segregate objects. *Cognition, 94*(3), 215–240.

Needham, A., & Modi, A. (1999). Infants' use of prior experiences with objects in object segregation: Implications for object recognition in infancy. *Advances in Child Development and Behavior*, *27*, 99–133.

Neisser, U. (1976). *Cognition and reality: Principles and implications of cognitive psychology*. New York: WH Freeman & Co.

Nelson, C. A., Ellis, A. E., Collins, P. F., & Lang, S. F. (1990). Infants' neuroelectric responses to missing stimuli: Can missing stimuli be novel stimuli? *Developmental Neuropsychology*, *6*(4), 339–349.

Neville, H., & Bavelier, D. (2002). Human brain plasticity: Evidence from sensory deprivation and altered language experience. *Progress in Brain Research*, *138*, 177–188.

Panichello, M. F., Cheung, O. S., & Bar, M. (2013). Predictive feedback and conscious visual experience. *Frontiers in Psychology*, *3*, 620.

Pascalis, O., Scott, L. S., Kelly, D. J., Shannon, R. W., Nicholson, E., Coleman, M., & Nelson, C. A. (2005). Plasticity of face processing in infancy. *Proceedings of the National Academy of Sciences of the United States of America*, *102*(14), 5297–5300.

Peña, M., Pittaluga, E., & Mehler, J. (2010). Language acquisition in premature and full-term infants. *Proceedings of the National Academy of Sciences of the United States of America*, *107*(8), 3823–3828.

Polley, D. B., Steinberg, E. E., & Merzenich, M. M. (2006). Perceptual learning directs auditory cortical map reorganization through top-down influences. *Journal of Neuroscience*, *26*(18), 4970–4982.

Price, D. J., Kennedy, H., Dehay, C., Zhou, L., Mercier, M., Jossin, Y., … Molnár, Z. (2006). The development of cortical connections. *European Journal of Neuroscience*, *23*(4), 910–920.

Quinn, P. C., & Bhatt, R. S. (2005). Learning perceptual organization in infancy. *Psychological Science*, *16*(7), 511–515.

Quinn, P. C., Brown, C. R., & Streppa, M. L. (1997). Perceptual organization of complex visual configurations by young infants. *Infant Behavior & Development*, *20*(1), 35–46.

Quinn, P. C., & Schyns, P. G. (2003). What goes up may come down: Perceptual process and knowledge access in the organization of complex visual patterns by young infants. *Cognitive Science*, *27*(6), 923–935.

Quinn, P. C., Schyns, P. G., & Goldstone, R. L. (2006). The interplay between perceptual organization and categorization in the representation of complex visual patterns by young infants. *Journal of Experimental Child Psychology*, *95*(2), 117–127.

Rao, R. P. N., & Ballard, D. H. (1999). Predictive coding in the visual cortex: A functional interpretation of some extra-classical receptive-field effects. *Nature Neuroscience*, *2*(1), 79–87.

Roelfsema, P. R., van Ooyen, A., & Watanabe, T. (2010). Perceptual learning rules based on reinforcers and attention. *Trends in Cognitive Sciences*, *14*(2), 64–71.

Sasai, S., Homae, F., Watanabe, H., Sasaki, A. T., Tanabe, H. C., Sadato, N., & Taga, G. (2012). A NIRS-fMRI study of resting state network. *NeuroImage*, *63*(1), 179–193.

Scott, L. S., & Monesson, A. (2009). The origin of biases in face perception. *Psychological Science*, *20*(6), 676–680.

Scott, L. S., Pascalis, O., & Nelson, C. a. (2007). A domain-general theory of the development of perceptual discrimination. *Current Directions in Psychological Science*, *16*(4), 197–201.

Seitz, A. R., Nanez, J. E., Holloway, S., Tsushima, Y., & Watanabe, T. (2006). Two cases requiring external reinforcement in perceptual learning. *Journal of Vision*, *6*(9), 966–973.

Seitz, A., & Watanabe, T. (2005). A unified model for perceptual learning. *Trends in Cognitive Sciences*, *9*(7), 329–334.

Smyser, C. D., Inder, T. E., Shimony, J. S., Hill, J. E., Degnan, A. J., Snyder, A. Z., & Neil, J. J. (2010). Longitudinal analysis of neural network development in preterm infants. *Cerebral Cortex (New York, N.Y.: 1991)*, *20*(12), 2852–2862.

Stager, C. L., & Werker, J. F. (1997). Infants listen for more phonetic detail in speech perception than in word-learning tasks. *Nature*, *388*(6640), 381–382.

Stokes, M., Atherton, K., Patai, E. Z., & Nobre, A. C. (2012). Long-term memory prepares neural activity for perception. *Proceedings of the National Academy of Sciences of the United States of America*, *109*(6), E360–E367.

Stuss, D. T., & Knight, R. T. (2013). Principles of frontal lobe function. In (2nd ed.). New York: Oxford University Press.

Summerfield, C., & de Lange, F. P. (2014). Expectation in perceptual decision making: Neural and computational mechanisms. *Nature Reviews. Neuroscience*, *15*(October), 745–756.

Summerfield, C., & Egner, T. (2009). Expectation (and attention) in visual cognition. *Trends in Cognitive Sciences*, *13*(9), 403–409.

Summerfield, C., Egner, T., Greene, M., Koechlin, E., Mangels, J., & Hirsch, J. (2006). Predictive codes for forthcoming perception in the frontal cortex. *Science*, *314*(November), 1311–1314.

Summerfield, C., & Koechlin, E. (2008). A neural representation of prior information during perceptual inference. *Neuron*, *59*(2), 336–347.

Summerfield, C., Trittschuh, E. H., Monti, J. M., Mesulam, M. M., & Egner, T. (2008). Neural repetition suppression reflects fulfilled perceptual expectations. *Nature Neuroscience*, *11*(9), 1004–1006.

Swingley, D. (2008). The roots of the early vocabulary in infants' learning from speech. *Current Directions in Psychological Science*, *17*(5), 308–312.

Thiessen, E. D. (2007). The effect of distributional information on children's use of phonemic contrasts. *Journal of Memory and Language*, *56*(1), 16–34.

Tymofiyeva, O., Hess, C. P., Ziv, E., Lee, P. N., Glass, H. C., Ferriero, D. M., … Xu, D. (2013). A DTI-based template-free cortical connectome study of brain maturation. *PLoS One*, *8*(5), 1–10.

Wacongne, C., Labyt, E., van Wassenhove, V., Bekinschtein, T., Naccache, L., & Dehaene, S. (2011). Evidence for a hierarchy of predictions and prediction errors in human cortex. *Proceedings of the National Academy of Sciences of the United States of America*, *108*(51), 20754–20759.

Werker, J. F., & Tees, R. C. (1984). Cross-language speech perception: Evidence for perceptual reorganization during the first year of life. *Infant Behavior & Development*, *7*(1), 49–63.

Wiesel, T. N., & Hubel, D. H. (1963). Single-cell responses in striate cortex of kittens deprived of vision in one eye. *Journal of Neurophysiology*, *26*, 1003–1017.

Wu, R., Nako, R., Band, J., Pizzuto, J., Ghoreishi, Y., Scerif, G., & Aslin, R. N. (2015). Rapid attentional selection of non-native stimuli despite perceptual narrowing. *Journal of Cognitive Neuroscience*, *27*(11), 2299–2307. arXiv: 1511.04103.

Yamins, D. L. K., Hong, H., Cadieu, C. F., Solomon, E. A., Seibert, D., & DiCarlo, J. J. (2014). Performance-optimized hierarchical models predict neural responses in higher visual cortex. *Proceedings of the National Academy of Sciences of the United States of America*, *111*(23), 8619–8624. arXiv: 0706.1062v1.

Yap, P. T., Fan, Y., Chen, Y., Gilmore, J. H., Lin, W., & Shen, D. (2011). Development trends of white matter connectivity in the first years of life. *PLoS One*, *6*(9), e24678.

Yeung, H. H., & Werker, J. F. (2009). Learning words' sounds before learning how words sound: 9-Month-olds use distinct objects as cues to categorize speech information. *Cognition*, *113*(2), 234–243.

Zevin, J. D., Yang, J., Skipper, J. I., & McCandliss, B. D. (2010). Domain general change detection accounts for "dishabituation" effects in temporal-parietal regions in functional magnetic resonance imaging studies of speech perception. *Journal of Neuroscience*, *30*(3), 1110–1117.

CHAPTER TWO

Applications of Dynamic Systems Theory to Cognition and Development: New Frontiers

S. Perone*,[1], V.R. Simmering†,[1]

*Washington State University, Pullman, WA, United States
†University of Wisconsin–Madison, Madison, WI, United States
[1]Corresponding author: e-mail address: sammy.perone@wsu.edu; simmering@wisc.edu

Contents

Abstract

A central goal in developmental science is to explain the emergence of new behavioral forms. Researchers consider potential sources of behavioral change depending partly on their theoretical perspective. This chapter reviews one perspective, dynamic systems theory, which emphasizes the interactions among multiple components to drive behavior and developmental change. To illustrate the central concepts of dynamic systems theory, we describe empirical and computational studies from a range of domains, including motor development, the Piagetian A-not-B task, infant visual recognition, visual working memory capacity, and language learning. We conclude by advocating for a broader application of dynamic systems approaches to understanding cognitive and behavioral development, laying out the remaining barriers we see and suggested ways to overcome them.

Advances in Child Development and Behavior, Volume 52
ISSN 0065-2407
http://dx.doi.org/10.1016/bs.acdb.2016.10.002

1. DYNAMIC SYSTEMS THEORY

Dynamic Systems Theory (DST) is a set of concepts that describe behavior as the emergent product of a self-organizing, multicomponent system evolving over time. This chapter reviews the progress DST has made in the domain of cognitive and behavioral development, the promise we see in further applications of this perspective, and our vision of how the field may meet challenges that are yet unmet. The application of DST to human behavior that we describe here is rooted in Thelen and Smith's (1994) book, *A dynamic systems approach to the development of cognition and action*, in which they proposed a bold rethinking of human cognition, behavior, and development. They took inspiration from at least two sources. One source was the complex models of other physical systems that did not reduce them to their elementary parts but embraced their complexity as an interactive whole. Such physical models span domains, including chemical phenomena such as crystal growth, oscillating movements of a spring or pendulum, flow patterns in water and air, cloud formation, and more. Thelen and Smith (1994; see also Fogel & Thelen, 1987) recognized a remarkable parallel between complex physical systems and human behavioral development, and sought to formally apply the same concepts across these domains.

Another source of inspiration was the theoretical climate in developmental psychology in the 1980s and 1990s (for an example see Haith, 1998). In the domain of cognitive development in particular, historical views of infant cognition as being constructed from sensorimotor origins were being replaced with the view of the infant as a precocious learner with, perhaps, inborn competencies (e.g., Spelke, 1985). For example, measures of infant looking behavior were beginning to be interpreted as reflecting conceptually based cognition about objects and events rather than the perceptual and memory processes more characteristic of interpretations espoused throughout the 1960s and 1970s (see Perone & Ambrose, 2015; Perone & Spencer, 2013b). These views were often built upon faulty empirical foundations (for example, see Baillargeon, 1987; and critiques by Cashon & Cohen, 2000; Rivera, Wakeley, & Langer, 1999; Schöner & Thelen, 2006), leading Thelen and Smith (1994) to advocate for bringing sophisticated theory and methodological rigor into research on child development.

The goal of this chapter is to illustrate the application of DST concepts to cognitive and behavioral development. This chapter is divided into four sections. In the first section, we provide a review of several foundational DST concepts. In the second section, we describe a formal instantiation of DST concepts into a computational framework called the Dynamic Field Theory that we and our colleagues have used as a tool to understand cognition, behavior, and development. We will illustrate how formal models that simulate behavioral and cognitive dynamics have yielded new insights and advanced the application of DST to human behavior. Although our own "home territory" is the application of computational tools, there are many excellent noncomputational applications of DST as well, which we describe in the third section. In the last section, we sketch a road map for advancing DST in the domains of cognition and development, broadly defined.

1.1 Foundational Concepts

DST has been applied to human cognition and development both as a conceptual framework and as a literal description of a dynamic system. We contend that both approaches are valuable and enrich our understanding. Our review of DST concepts is not an exhaustive list but instead focuses on those most foundational to the study of cognitive development. DST applications within psychological science have not been unitary. At the 2009 biennial meeting of the Society for Research in Child Development, a panel discussion of dynamic systems as a metatheory presented four "camps" of DST (see Witherington, 2007 for similar discussion). These camps all adopt the foundational concepts that we review here, but differ in the domains of application, the relative emphasis on different features of DST, and the philosophical perspective on what can (or cannot) be understood about the mental structures that underlie behavior (for further discussion see, e.g., Fogel, 2011; Hollenstein, 2011; Lewis, 2011; Spencer, Perone, & Buss, 2011; van Geert, 2011; van Geert & Steenbeek, 2005; Witherington & Margett, 2011). We come from the "Bloomington camp" associated with Thelen and Smith, and therefore primarily present examples from this "family" of researchers. Although we acknowledge the differences between camps as meaningful and consequential for research programs, we see great value in integrating conceptual and methodological variants across camps to achieve our ultimate goal: to understand how development happens. In the context of explaining cognition and development, we consider three concepts to be central: multicausality, self-organization, and the nesting of timescales.

The foundational DST concept of *multicausality* refers to the convergence of multiple forces to create behavior. The contributions to behavior in the moment include a person's body, age, mental state, emotional state, social context, personal history, and more. Furthermore, in dynamic systems no single factor is more important than any other—only through the combination of all factors together does causation occur, so it is illogical to consider any given factor in isolation. Proponents of DST emphasize an appreciation for mutual, bidirectional dependencies between brain and behavior, rather than considering behavior to be driven primarily by a single component (i.e., the brain). This aspect of DST has sometimes been criticized as making research intractable, as it is impossible to measure or control every potential contributing factor. As we illustrate in subsequent sections, however, we contend that multicausality can inform research design, implementation, and interpretation through the questions we ask with our studies, the way in which we gather information, and how we extrapolate from our results.

A second foundational concept is *self-organization*. The behavior of a system is an emergent product of multiple components interacting through time, interactions that are context dependent. Self-organization is related to a collection of additional DST concepts. Systems organize into what are called *attractor states*, which are ways in which the components of a system reliably interact (e.g., crawling, walking, and running are different attractor states for locomotion). Systems are *historical*, which means that their organization in an attractor state in the moment biases them to revisit those attractor states at a future point in time (Spencer & Perone, 2008). These states become increasingly *stable* through experience, which means that they are resistant to perturbations from internal and external forces. Systems are *open* to the environment, which means that external forces can shift the components of a system into a new way of interacting, which can often be *nonlinear*.

The last foundational concept is the *nesting of timescales*. The timescale of neural firing is nested within the timescale of cognition, which is nested within the timescale of behavior over learning and development. The strong claim of DST is that these timescales create each other. Consider a prevalent example from developmental science. Typically, we study children's behavior in the lab at one point in time and then at another point in time. This provides good insight into developmental differences. Developmental change, however, happens in between lab visits via massive quantities of real-time processes that occur across multiple levels. How do the neural processes, brain-wide dynamics, and movement that are involved in the behavioral decisions children make on a daily basis create developmental change? This is a central challenge for DST. This is illustrated in a case study described in a subsequent section that uses a computational model of infant looking behavior.

The three central concepts we described here—multicausality, self-organization, and nesting of timescales—are each interconnected in the empirical phenomena that illustrate them. Thelen's early application of DST concepts to development was in the motor domain, considering changes in infants' stepping, reaching, and posture (see Spencer, Clearfield, et al., 2006 for review). But this subdomain of developmental psychology had become increasingly distant from the study of infant cognition, as researchers began to posit more complex and mature "concepts" that supported infant behavior. A critical challenge for DST was to move from the mechanics of motor development—where analogies to physical systems were easier to understand and appreciate—into the domain of human thought, which is often treated as qualitatively different from motor behavior. A first step in this direction was taken as Thelen, Smith, and colleagues applied DST concepts to Piaget's A-not-B task, purported to index the concept of object permanence in infants. This work illustrated the parallel between motor and cognitive development and, critically, their inseparability. Thus, we turn to a discussion of the Piagetian A-not-B error as an influential and historically important application of DST.

1.2 The Piagetian A-Not-B Error

The classic A-not-B paradigm can be used to illustrate the central concepts of DST explanations of cognition and development. In this task, an infant is seated in front of a box with two lids covering wells to hide a toy; an experimenter hides a toy in one well (the A location) and the infant retrieves it. Following a few repetitions at the A location, the experimenter hides the toy in the other well (the B location). When allowed to reach for the toy after a short delay, infants younger than 10–12 months of age will erroneously search at A, whereas older infants will search correctly at B. Two types of explanations dominated the literature prior to the DST conceptualization. First was Piaget's interpretation that this "A-not-B error" indicated a lack of object permanence—a qualitative developmental change, the acquisition of a new cognitive structure, explained older infants' success (Piaget, 1954). This perspective was challenged by evidence that infants' behavior could be modulated through changes in the task structure. Thus, a second class of explanations emerged in which young infants' errors were attributed to limitations in basic cognitive processes, such as attention, inhibition, and/or memory (e.g., Diamond, 1985; Marcovitch & Zelazo, 1999; Munakata, 1998). Critically, these theories posited that these processes were present in younger infants, but merely ineffective under the demands of the task: the change in behavior arose through quantitative improvements in existing processes rather than a new cognitive ability.

As a new view on the A–not–B error, Thelen and Smith (1994; see also Smith & Thelen, 2003; Smith, Thelen, Titzer, & McLin, 1999) presented a DST account in which multiple causal components came together in the context of the task (self-organized) to produce the characteristic error. In contrast to Piaget, they argued that there was no specific concept that supported successful performance in this task, but rather infants' actions in the task emerged from the confluence of components (Smith et al., 1999). To understand developmental change in behavior, then, required studying how reaching decisions were made in the specific task context. Thus, it was not only the case that individual components of the system were improving developmentally, but also how these components were brought to bear on the task at hand. In addition to attention, inhibition, and memory (processes highlighted independently in previous explanations; Diamond, 1985; Marcovitch & Zelazo, 1999; Munakata, 1998), Thelen, Smith, and colleagues showed how behavior was influenced by motor planning, posture, and features of the task space (see Smith & Thelen, 2003 for review). Most critically, no single process or component was central in their theory; rather, behavior depended on the convergence of all components together, and the manner in which they combine may vary according to task demands.

Smith et al. (1999) argued that we should focus on describing and explaining what we can measure—behavior—and not conflate that with the underlying knowledge we aim to understand. They demonstrated, for example, that the error occurs in the absence of objects: cueing infants to reach only by lifting the lid showed the same developmental transition from perseveration to correct reaching on B trials; without hidden objects, a concept of object permanence could not explain this change. An infant's reach on any given trial (whether the A or B side was cued) was influenced by the infant's history of reaches in the task and the direction of their visual attention in the moment. Thus, where an infant looked and reached before, and where they looked right before reaching, all contributed to their reaching behavior on a trial-by-trial basis.

Additional analyses of reaching trajectories showed how the history of reaches built up across trials, with a more stable reach in the moment leading to a stronger influence on future reaches (Diedrich, Thelen, Smith, & Corbetta, 2000). Further studies connected this behavior in the moment of the task to developmental changes in task performance. Very young infants, with immature reaching abilities, do not perseverate in the A–not-B task; rather, stable reaching on A trials is necessary to form the memory traces that produce errors on B trials (Clearfield, Smith, Diedrich, & Thelen, 2006). These studies illustrated that the history of reaching in the task is not independent of those specific reaches: unstable reaches leave weak traces that exert little influence on future reaches. Longer-term experience with reaching increases the stability of reaching, which first allows for the emergence of the error (Clearfield et al., 2006) and later allows infants to overcome the error by maintaining a stable plan to reach to the B location (described further later; Thelen, Schöner, Scheier, & Smith, 2001). These findings, along with many others (some of which are described later), provide a compelling demonstration of how the self-organization of multiple components produces behavior in the moment, connections across timescales, and the many sources of change over development.

Although this line of work uncovered a vast range of influences on infants' and older children's search abilities, the illustration of dynamic systems concepts through the A–not-B error has been a double-edged sword: it allows for clear description and manipulation of the many factors that will influence infants' behavior, but it also led to the erroneous impression that systems perspectives are best suited to explanation of fairly simple sensorimotor tasks and development during infancy. An inherent challenge in the application of DST to cognition and brain processes is that one cannot directly observe and measure them in the way sensorimotor behaviors can be. Tackling this challenge requires an application that connects cognitive and brain processes to behavior as a dynamic system. This was a driving force behind the application of computational models to explain cognitive and behavioral processes in development, which we turn to next.

2. THE DYNAMIC FIELD THEORY AND DYNAMIC NEURAL FIELDS

Our own research programs incorporate a style of computational modeling that formally implements cognitive, neural, and behavioral processes as dynamic systems. These types of models are called dynamic neural fields (DNFs) and embody a set of concepts from the Dynamic Field Theory. The Dynamic Field Theory extends DST to neural population dynamics to bridge brain and behavioral dynamics (Spencer & Schöner, 2003). The overarching goals of this approach have been detailed in an edited volume entitled *Dynamic thinking: A primer on dynamic field theory* (Schöner, Spencer, & The DFT Research Group, 2015). The volume includes a collection of chapters that each describe a particular computational model architecture and its application(s), with exercises to explore the model using interactive simulators provided with the book. Here we provide examples from a subset of these applications within visuospatial cognitive development to illustrate central characteristics of the approach, to highlight the models as formally implementing the concepts of DST. A key benefit of this computational approach is the formalization of not only the processes that support the central cognitive processes such as encoding, maintenance, and comparison of items in memory but also the specific types of behavior measured in each task. This allows for a systematic analysis of what types of memory processes might be necessary and sufficient for specific behavioral patterns to emerge in a task.

We provide a brief introduction to DNFs and then describe three case studies that illustrate the use of DNFs to implement key DST concepts. Because these concepts are necessarily interrelated, each case study can be used to illustrate multiple concepts, but we chose to emphasize specific concepts that are particularly salient in each case.

2.1 Introduction to DNF Models

DNFs belong to a larger class of bistable attractor networks (Amari, 1977; Wilson & Cowan, 1972). DNFs simulate neural populations tuned to represent a continuous dimension, such as space or color. DNFs represent these populations through functional topography such that neurons representing similar feature values (e.g., shades of blue) are next to one another within the field. The unit of cognition in DNFs is the "peak," which is a real-time neuronal representation of a stimulus that supports behavioral decisions. For example, a working memory representation of a blue stimulus emerges from the excitation of neurons selectively tuned to its hue. This, in turn, leads to the excitation of neighboring, similarly tuned neurons (i.e., representing other shades of blue) and inhibition of more distant, dissimilarly tuned neurons (i.e., representing red, orange, and yellow). The result is a localized peak of activation that is a dynamically stable attractor state. Multiple fields (also called layers) can be coupled together in a variety of ways to create more complex model architectures to simulate different neurocognitive functions (e.g., movement planning, attention, memory), as described in the case studies in the following section.

DNFs are dynamic systems, and thus, a key feature of these models is that they are influenced by their own history. The cases we will consider include a simple mechanism of learning, the laying down of memory traces by active nodes that facilitate activation of those same nodes in the future. Peaks leave memory traces that strengthen activity among active neurons in a Hebbian fashion (Perone & Ambrose, 2015; Perone & Spencer, 2013a). This primes those neurons to respond more strongly to a similar stimulus at a future point in time. For example, a peak representing a blue item leaves a memory trace associated with the color blue that, in turn, facilitates the formation of a peak associated with the color blue if it is presented again. This simple memory trace mechanism enables real-time experience to be carried forward in time to influence cognitive and behavioral dynamics across a longer timescale. This feature can shift DNFs into qualitatively different modes of operating and have a big impact on behavior by, for instance, enabling DNFs to remember more items simultaneously (see Perone, Simmering, & Spencer, 2011; Simmering, 2016; Simmering, Miller, & Bohache, 2015).

A unique feature of DNF models is that they can be situated in the same task context as participants to simulate self-organization. For example, a DNF model can be presented with objects that vary along color and shape dimensions, that are presented in different locations, and that are associated with different labels. Memory along any of these dimensions (features, locations, labels) can then be probed through different types of behavioral responses (e.g., selecting one from a set of choices, explicitly judging "same" or "different," fixating, estimating a feature or dimension) depending on the task demands. This feature of DNFs has yielded numerous novel insights about the connection between cognition and behavior across tasks (for specific examples of different response types in the same system, see Samuelson, Schutte, & Horst, 2009; Simmering, 2016; Spencer, Simmering, & Schutte, 2006).

2.2 DNFs Are Dynamic Systems: Three Applications

DNFs have been applied to a diverse range of phenomena. We selected three examples from our own repertoire that illustrate how DNFs embody DST concepts, foster understanding of the link between cognitive and behavioral dynamics in a theoretically rigorous fashion, and provide a tractable road map to guide empirical research. Within each of these examples, the same underlying concepts can be found, but the relative emphasis on each concept varies. We highlight one concept within each of the sections, but do not intend to imply that the concepts can be separated entirely.

2.2.1 Multicausality in the Piagetian A-Not-B Error

As a first example, we consider model simulations of performance in the classic A–not–B task and variants that have followed to test specific predictions. As described earlier, the A–not–B task was proposed by Piaget (1954) to assess object permanence, whereas other researchers argued that task failures reflected immature cognitive processes like attention, memory, and/or inhibition (e.g., Diamond, 1985; Marcovitch & Zelazo, 1999; Munakata, 1998). Thelen et al. (2001) proposed a model that focused on movement planning (cf. Erlhagen & Schöner, 2002). Movement direction was instantiated as a continuous DNF, and activation on a given trial was influenced by the discrete hiding locations of the A–not–B task, the specific hiding event (toy at A or B), and the history of reaches on prior trials. Integration of these internal and external contributions showed concretely how a plan to reach evolved over the timescale of each trial in the task. The output on each trial was the location (A or B) that corresponded to the movement direction with maximal activation. Over time, within and across trials, activation in the motor planning field left a memory trace, which influenced subsequent activation (as described earlier). These characteristics together allowed the model to perform the A–not–B task: task input at the beginning of each trial represented the hiding locations, a specific input signaled the hiding event, then activation in the field propagated throughout the delay, and with the most active location at the end of the trial read out as the reach direction. Over repeated trials as experience accumulated, the memory trace from activation within the field served as another source of input, reflecting the history of planned and executed reaches in the task.

With a DNF model constructed to incorporate the important details of the task that influences performance, the final step was to consider potential sources of developmental change. In contrast to invoking a new cognitive construct to account for the transition from failure to success in the A–not–B task (such as object permanence; Piaget, 1954), Thelen et al. (2001) implemented a continuous change in the cooperativity of the movement planning field to simulate development. Specifically, they modified functional interactions among neighboring nodes by increasing the resting level of the field. With a higher resting level, the same magnitude of inputs to the model created stronger effects, with more robust formation and maintenance of peaks reflecting memory of the hidden object (see Simmering, Schutte, & Spencer, 2008 for an alternative instantiation of this concept in a more complex architecture). Thelen et al. showed how this DNF model could account for perseverative reaching early in development and correct reaching later in development, as well as the fact that perseveration only occurs with a delay between hiding and search (cf. Gratch, Appel, Evans, LeCompte, & Wright, 1974). They also simulated the effects of changing target distinctiveness, in which infants are less likely to perseverate when the lid for the B location is highly distinct from the A location and background (Diedrich, Highlands, Thelen, & Smith, 2001). The model architecture and simulations illustrate the multiple influences on infants' performance in A–not–B tasks, combining the structure of the task (lids, objects, delay), the internal dynamics of movement planning, and the history of reaches in the task, to predict reaching on a given trial.

Beyond the simulations presented by Thelen et al. (2001), this formalization (and subsequent adaptations of the model architecture) led to a number of specific predictions and new explanations of infants' behavior in the A–not–B task. For example, Clearfield, Dineva, Smith, Diedrich, and Thelen (2009) showed the interaction between the salience of the reaching locations and the delay implemented in the task. With the lowest and highest salience of the lid at B, perseveration was uniformly high or low, respectively, regardless of the delay between hiding and search. With a moderate level of salience, however, perseveration after no delay was low, but increased when a delay was added. Thus, the influence on reaching was not affected solely by salience or delay, but rather by the nonlinear combination of these factors.

A similar model was applied to results from another lab seeking to test the influence of social cues on A–not–B performance. Topál, Gergely, Miklósi, Erdőhegyi, and Csibra (2008) tested infants in three conditions of the A–not–B task with varying levels of social engagement by the experimenter. Perseveration decreased with reduced social engagement, which the authors interpreted as evidence that the social pragmatics of the task induced perseveration. In particular, they argued that infants misinterpret the social cues from the experimenter as indicating the object will continue to be found at the A location even after it is hidden at B. Spencer, Dineva, and Smith (2009) simulated these results in a DNF model, showing that the difference across conditions could be explained through the relative strength of encoding the hiding event: with high (typical) social engagement, the hiding event was encoded weakly (due to competition for attention), and the strength of encoding increased as social engagement decreased. Spencer et al. argued that the results from Topál et al. add to the broad range of conditions the DNF model could account for, and further illustrate the importance of considering how multiple factors contribute to performance in laboratory tasks.[a]

Beyond infancy and the A–not-B task, the general notion that spatial responses in a task are influenced by memory traces from past trials has been extended much later in development. Spencer and colleagues showed that toddlers and older children make A–not-B-type errors in a continuous space: searches for a toy hidden in a sandbox showed influence of past searches (Schutte, Spencer, & Schöner, 2003; Spencer, Smith, & Thelen, 2001) as well as memory for other locations even in the absence of past reaches (Spencer & Schutte, 2004). Spencer and colleagues also developed a similar task in which targets are presented on a large homogeneous table (rear-projection surface) and participants point or use a mouse to click on the remembered location. In this task, 3- to 11-year-old children and adults also show the influence of previous responses (Hund & Spencer, 2003; Lipinski, Simmering, Johnson, & Spencer, 2010; Schutte & Spencer, 2002; Spencer & Hund, 2002, 2003) as well as visual feedback (Lipinski, Spencer, & Samuelson, 2010). Note that, across these various studies of spatial cognition and development, some predictions and explanations have been derived from quantitative model simulations, whereas others have been motivated solely by the conceptual features of the theory (e.g., Simmering & Spencer, 2007). Thus, although formalization in a model can provide quantitative predictions, it is also possible to use the concepts embodied in such formalizations to generate qualitative predictions as well.

---

[a] Topál, Tóth, Gergely, and Csibra (2009) responded to Spencer, Dineva, et al.'s (2009) alternative explanation by testing a fourth condition, in which the social engagement from the experimenter was high on A trials and low on B trials. Infants in this study showed high perseveration, which Topál et al. argued contradicted the DNF model. However, they did not consider the fact that the sudden change in engagement between A and B trials likely drew the infants' attention more strongly to the experimenter (cf. the "still-face paradigm" by Tronick, Als, Adamson, Wise, & Brazelton, 1978), which would predict weaker encoding on B trials leading to high perseveration. This example highlights the importance of considering the full task context not only in the influence of the history of reaches but also in the history of the experience in the task more generally.

2.2.2 Self-Organization in Visual Working Memory Capacity

Our second example is a bridge between work with infants and later development, moving from the sensorimotor foundations that are apparent in reaching studies to higher-level cognition: working memory. Working memory has been identified as a vital cognitive skill that underlies many complex behaviors (Baddeley, 1986). In this section, we focus on studies of visual working memory (which is at least partially separable from verbal working memory in early childhood; Alloway, Gathercole, Willis, & Adams, 2004), as it can be studied over the life span (including infancy) and it predicts higher cognitive skills both longitudinally (e.g., Rose, Feldman, & Jankowski, 2012) and concurrently (e.g., Cowan, Fristoe, Elliott, Brunner, & Saults, 2006). We specifically consider capacity limits for nonspatial visual information (the "visual cache" described by Logie, 1995) and how they are estimated from lab tasks.

The concept of self-organization is most apparent when considering how performance differs across variations in task details. Simmering and Perone (2013) surveyed the literature on working memory development and found that estimates of capacity varied dramatically across studies, even when the general structure of the task and age group was the same. One way to address the variation due to task structure is through the use of DNF models, which allows researchers to situate the same cognitive system in different tasks and then to "look inside" to see how cognitive functioning compares between tasks. Simmering (2016) took this approach to understand an apparent contradiction in the literature on visual working memory capacity estimates. In particular, prior studies suggested that capacity increased from one item at 6 months to four items by 10 months (Ross-Sheehy, Oakes, & Luck, 2003), but was limited to only two or three items during the preschool years (Riggs, McTaggart, Simpson, & Freeman, 2006; Simmering, 2016). These inconsistent estimates were presumed to arise from the different behavioral tasks used across age groups (Cowan, 2007; Riggs et al., 2006), but no theoretical account had been proposed to explain precisely how and why estimates differed across tasks.

Simmering (2016) proposed that the same memory processes supported performance over tasks and development, and that understanding how the tasks relate could be achieved through formalizing the tasks into the same DNF model. The paradigm used to assess visual working memory capacity in young children and adults was the change-detection task (see Vogel, Woodman, & Luck, 2001 for task development), shown in Fig. 1A. On each trial in this task, a small number of simple items (i.e., colored squares, white

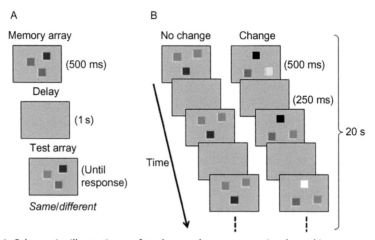

Fig. 1 Schematic illustrations of tasks used to assess visual working memory in (A) children and adults vs (B) infants; both present examples of set size three. *Adapted from Simmering, V. R., & Perone, S. (2013). Working memory capacity as a dynamic process.* Frontiers in Developmental Psychology, 3, 567. http://doi.org/10.3389/fpsyg.2012.00567.

shapes, oriented bars) are presented briefly in a memory array. After a short delay, a test array is presented and the participant is asked to judge whether the items in the test array are "same" or "different" compared to the items in the memory array. Across trials, the set size (number of items per memory array) may vary, and performance typically declines as set size increases. Capacity can be estimated from this task using a formula proposed by Pashler (1988), in which K is the estimated number of items held in memory, calculated from the proportion of hits (i.e., correct "different" responses) relative to the total number of items in the memory array (set size) with correction for "guessing" (i.e., incorrect "different" responses).

Ross-Sheehy et al. (2003) developed a task for infants motivated by the design of the change-detection task. Because infants cannot explicitly judge arrays as "same" or "different," Ross-Sheehy et al. capitalized on infants' tendency to prefer looking to novel displays (e.g., Fagan, 1970) in a preferential looking paradigm. For this change-preference task, shown in Fig. 1B, infants viewed two displays that each contained a small number of colored squares that blinked on (for 500 ms) and off (for 250 ms) repeatedly throughout the duration of a 20-s trial. On the no-change display, the colors remained the same across presentations; on the change display, one randomly selected color changed to a new color following each blank delay. The amount of time infants spent looking to each display was tabulated across the trial, and the proportion of time that was directed toward the change display was used to calculate a change-preference score. Mean change-preference scores that were reliably above chance (0.50) were interpreted as evidence of memory for the items in the array: if the infants could remember the colors, they would be able to detect that one color was changing in the change display and it would appear more novel than the no-change display. Ross-Sheehy et al. used this task to estimate infants' capacity by comparing performance across multiple set sizes, varying the number of items in each display, and assuming capacity for the highest set size at which the age group showed a robust change preference. Estimates of capacity during infancy suggested a rapid increase, from remembering only a single item at 6 months to remembering four items at 10 months (Ross-Sheehy et al., 2003); follow-up studies indicated that infants could remember at least three items (no higher set sizes were tested) by 7.5 months (Oakes, Messenger, Ross-Sheehy, & Luck, 2009; Oakes, Ross-Sheehy, & Luck, 2006).

The estimates derived from the infant change-preference task were seemingly inconsistent with estimates derived from early childhood using the change-detection task, which indicate capacity of less than two items between ages 3 years (Simmering, 2012) and 5 years (Riggs et al., 2006). As potential explanations for this inconsistency, Riggs et al. (2006) hypothesized that the change-preference task might rely on a more passive type of memory than the change-detection task. Cowan (2007) proposed that estimates may differ across tasks due to different attentional demands. Simmering (2016), by contrast, examined how the same processes of formation, maintenance, and use of memory representations self-organized to produce different behaviors across tasks. Building from the type of model architecture developed to explain spatial working memory development (Spencer, Simmering, Schutte, & Schöner, 2007), Simmering and colleagues used a three-layer DNF architecture to account for performance across these two visual working memory tasks (Johnson, Simmering, & Buss, 2014; Perone et al., 2011; Simmering, 2016).

This architecture, shown in Fig. 2, includes two excitatory layers coupled to a shared inhibitory layer (see Johnson & Simmering, 2015 for review). The excitatory layers correspond to the perceptual processing vs working memory representation of information relevant to the task through different strength of connections. Weaker excitation and inhibition in the perceptual layer produces input-driven representations, that is, activation that remains above threshold only in the presence of input; this reflects

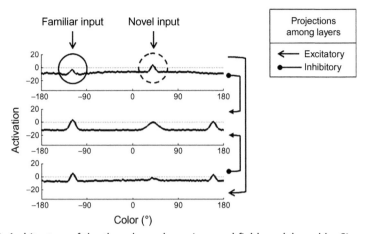

Fig. 2 Architecture of the three-layer dynamic neural field model used by Simmering and colleagues. This simulation shows two items held in the working memory field (WM; *bottom*) with two inputs projected into the perceptual field (PF; *top*), labeled as familiar vs novel. As described in the text, perceptual processing of the familiar item is suppressed due to shared inhibition (Inhib; *middle*). *Dashed horizontal lines* in each layer indicate the activation threshold for interactions among nodes.

perceptual processing of incoming visual information. Stronger excitation and inhibition in the working memory layer allows self-sustaining representations, with peaks maintaining above-threshold activation after input has been removed. Activation within and between layers interacts continuously throughout the task, with excitation projecting from the perceptual layer to the inhibitory and working memory layers, as well as from the working memory layer to the inhibitory layer, with inhibition projecting back into both excitatory layers (see Johnson & Simmering, 2015 for further details).

Fig. 2 shows a simulation of this architecture to illustrate the basic mechanisms of recognizing familiar feature values vs detecting novelty. In this simulation, color is the feature dimension represented along the horizontal axis; peaks in the bottom field represent two different color values that have been encoded into working memory. In the context of the change-detection task, this would be the case if two items had been presented in the memory array and were remembered throughout the delay. The middle inhibitory layer in this figure shows how coupling among layers can provide an emergent comparison process: when a peak is present within an excitatory field, activation projects to similarly tuned nodes within the inhibitory layer, which produces an inhibitory bump (note that the difference between "peak" and "bump" reflects the presence vs absence, respectively, of local excitatory interactions within the field). The inhibitory bumps project inhibition to the similarly tuned nodes in both excitatory layers, which slightly suppresses activation at these locations. When two inputs are presented in this simulation, as in the test array of a change-detection trial, one is a familiar value (i.e., a color held in working memory) and the other is novel. The peak in working memory that corresponds to the familiar item has an associated inhibitory bump, which leads to suppressed processing of this item in the perceptual field (see circle in Fig. 2). The input from the novel item, by contrast, projects into the perceptual field at a point where activation is closer to threshold (0, marked with a dashed line), which allows a peak to build. This above-threshold activation in the perceptual field serves as a signal of novelty, which can then be used to support task-relevant behavior.

In the change-detection task, the required "same" or "different" response has been implemented as a simple decision system that is coupled to the excitatory layers, such that activation in the perceptual layer projects to the "different" node and activation in the working memory layer projects to the "same" node (see Johnson et al., 2014 for further details). The decision nodes include self-excitation and mutual inhibition such that only one can achieve above-threshold activation, yielding a single response on each trial. For the change-preference task, a rudimentary fixation system can be linked to the perceptual layer (see Perone et al., 2011 for further details). This system includes nodes representing fixation of the left vs right display in a paired comparison task, as well as nodes representing central fixation and fixating away from the displays. The fixation system is reciprocally coupled to the perceptual layer, allowing it to serve as a perceptual "gate," such that input associated with a display only projects into the three-layer architecture when the corresponding fixation node activation is above threshold. When activation in the perceptual layer is above threshold, this activation projects back to the fixation system to support continued fixation. When combined with the mechanism for detecting novelty shown in Fig. 2, this leads the model to "prefer" looking at novel stimuli, similar to infants (see also Perone & Spencer, 2014).

Implementing both change-detection and change-preference tasks into the same model architecture allowed Simmering (2016) to analyze the causes and consequences of memory formation in these different task contexts. Model simulations revealed two important characteristics of the change-preference and change-detection tasks to help explain the apparent discrepancy in estimates across tasks. First, the different behaviors required by each task led to different relations between the underlying memory representations and the behavioral estimates. In particular, simulations of change-detection performance across multiple age groups and data sets have shown that capacity estimates using Pashler's (1988) K underestimate the number of items that must be held in memory to generate that level of behavioral performance. Three-year-old children's mean K_{max} estimates (i.e., maximum K across set sizes for each child; Simmering, 2012) were 1.90 items. Analysis of the number of peaks held in the working memory field on simulations that produced a comparable level of performance (K_{max} estimate of 1.99 across 20 simulations) showed an average of 3.23 peaks per trial. Across two studies, adults' mean K_{max} estimates were 4.58 (Johnson et al., 2014) and 4.62 (Simmering, 2016), and simulations fitting that performance revealed (respectively) averages of 5.79 peaks in set size six and 4.99 peaks in set size five. Thus, simulations of behavior suggest that K may underestimate the number of items held in memory (Johnson et al., 2014; Simmering, 2016). This is because the processes that generate behavior are not free of errors: there may be cases in which the items were held correctly in memory, but did not lead to accurate responses (see Johnson et al., 2014 for example).

In contrast to the change-detection simulations, behavior in the change-preference task appears to overestimate the number of items held in working memory. In particular, the same model architecture used to generate simulations of children's change-detection performance was also tested in the change-preference task (Simmering, 2016). Behavioral estimates indicated memory for at least six items in 3- to 5-year-old children and adults, reflected in robust preferences for the change display in set size six (the highest set size tested). Analysis of the contents of the working memory field, however, showed that the significant preferences in set size six could be supported by holding fewer items in memory (see Perone et al., 2011 for analogous results simulating infants' performance). In particular, Simmering calculated the mean number of peaks held in working memory in the final delay period of each change-preference trial (i.e., after 26 presentations of each display, with autonomous looking between displays). In set size six, where all age groups showed significant change preferences, the mean number of peaks ranged from 4.38 to 5.58 across parameter sets tuned to children's vs adults' performance. Thus, remembering a portion of the items presented was sufficient to support a preference for the change display, and the capacity assumed from this preference overestimated the contents of memory.

These simulations of change-preference and change-detection tasks demonstrated that capacity is not independent of the task, but rather emerges through self-organization of the memory system in the particular task context. Specifically, the structure of the task allowed the exact same memory system—computationally specified in a neural network model—to hold more items in memory in a more supportive context (i.e., the change-preference vs change-detection tasks; Simmering, 2016). This formalization provided an alternative to the explanations generated in the literature, in which the looking task was considered to possibly measure a more passive type of memory (Riggs et al., 2006), relative rather than absolute capacity (Ross-Sheehy et al., 2003), or rely on long-term memory or habituation rather than short-term memory (Oakes, Baumgartner, Barrett, Messenger, & Luck, 2013). Rather, capacity limits in visual working memory arise dynamically in the context or particular task structures, and estimates of capacity depend on the type of behavior required (see also Simmering & Perone, 2013). The dynamic systems explanation of capacity limits emerging through the constraints of the specific task and the developing cognitive system can provide a more comprehensive and parsimonious explanation of developmental change than prior theories.

2.2.3 Connecting Real and Developmental Timescales in Infant Looking

A central claim of DST is that there is nothing but real-time process: all further changes along longer timescales (i.e., learning and development) are created from the real-time scale. There is no governing agent in development, no road map telling development where to go, only real-time process and the history it creates (Smith & Thelen, 2003). This claim is bold, and a concrete theoretical understanding of how the real and developmental timescales are connected has remained elusive. To appreciate why this is so, consider just one common context in which most infants are situated on a daily basis—sitting among a cluttered array of toys. For simplicity, let us just consider a very short period of time, 1 min or less. In that snippet of time, an infant may look at a toy, switch gaze to mom, then to the dog, and then to a new toy. Next, the television may capture the infant's attention and gaze before switching gaze to yet another new toy, then to a sibling, and then back to the toy. How does this chaotic world create any sort of systematic developmental change?

Perone and Spencer (2013a) sought to answer this question in a series of simulations in the same three-layer model described in the preceding section. At issue is the robust observation that infants exhibit highly predictable changes in looking behavior in visual memory tasks over the course of the first year. For example, with age, infants' looking to a visual stimulus habituates more quickly (Colombo & Mitchell, 1990), they exhibit faster gaze switching, shorter look durations, and stronger visual recognition (Rose, Feldman, & Jankowski, 2001), discrimination becomes more precise (Brannon, Suanda, & Libertus, 2007; Perone & Spencer, 2014), and memory for visual stimuli endures over longer delays (Fagan, 1977; for review, see Rose, Feldman, & Jankowski, 2004). These predictable changes appear consistent across infant populations. For example, infants who were born preterm also show predictable developmental changes in gaze switching, look duration, and visual recognition, but at a delayed rate that can linger well into adolescence (Rose et al., 2012). If we can attain a theoretical understanding of how real-time processes create developmental change in these cognitive and behavioral systems, we can play on those real-time processes to push those systems along a positive developmental trajectory.

The three-layer model integrates second-to-second dynamics of looking behavior, encoding, and working memory formation with the longer timescale of long-term memory formation via the memory trace mechanism (Hebbian learning) described earlier. As illustrated in Fig. 3, Perone and Spencer (2013a) situated this model in a virtual world in which it was free to explore objects distributed over a dimension (e.g., several objects that differ in color), much like infants sitting and switching gaze among an array of objects. Periodically, one object was swapped out for a new one in order to provide the model experience with a variety of objects distributed along an entire dimension (i.e., many objects of different colors, such as blues, purples, reds, and oranges). While the model was exploring its virtual world, it was occasionally situated in a laboratory task, the "processing speed" task developed by Rose, Feldman, and Jankowski (2002). The purpose was to probe the influence of the history the model was accumulating over a series of real-time instances of fixating, encoding, and remembering objects on cognition and looking behavior as we measure them in the laboratory, that is, in a constrained task context in a cross-sectional fashion.

The Rose et al.'s (2002) processing speed task is based on the fact that infants look less at remembered items than novel items. Infants were presented with a pair of items, one designated as the familiar and the other as the novel, as shown in Fig. 4. On every trial, the novel item was replaced with a new item and the familiar remained the same, with the side of the display that contained the familiar item changing randomly across trials. Processing speed was defined as the number of trials it took for the infant to display a

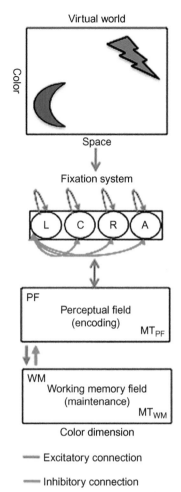

Fig. 3 DNF model architecture situated in the "virtual world" used by Perone and Spencer (2013a). At the *top* is a virtual world at which the model looks. The virtual world consists of two objects at *left* and *right* locations distributed over a continuous feature dimension (e.g., color). The presence of items at *left* and *right* locations biases the fixation system to look at those locations (see *green arrow* from space to fixation system). The fixation system interacts in a winner-take-all fashion such that fixating a location suppresses fixation to all other locations (see *red arrows* between nodes). Fixating a location acts like a perceptual gate into the cognitive system, which consists of a perceptual field (PF) and working memory (WM) field. PF and WM are reciprocally coupled to a shared layer of inhibitory interneurons (Inhib; not show). Activity in PF supports fixation (*green* bidirectional *arrow* between PF and fixation). Activity in WM suppresses PF via a strongly tuned connection from WM to Inhib (*red arrow* from WM to PF). Activity in PF and WM is influenced by activity in Hebbian layers, HLPF and HLWM, respectively, which accumulates over learning and facilitates encoding in PF and memory formation in WM. *Adapted from Perone, S., & Spencer, J. P. (2013a). Autonomous visual exploration creates developmental change in familiarity and novelty seeking behaviors. Frontiers in Cognitive Science, 4, 648. http:/doi.org/10.3389/fpsyg.2013.00648.*

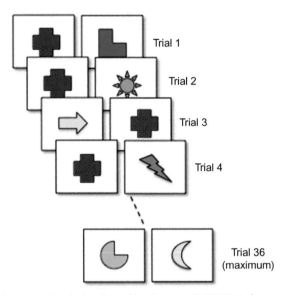

Fig. 4 Processing speed task developed by Rose et al. (2002). Infants were presented with a pair of different stimuli on each trial. Across trials, one stimulus remained unchanged (familiar) and one changed (novel). On each trial, infants were required to accumulate 4 s of looking. Infants met a learning criterion once they looked at the novel stimulus more than 55% of the time on the three consecutive trials or 36 trials had passed. There were 19 stimuli, one designated as the familiar and 18 designated as novel. If 18 trials had passed before infants met the criteria, the 18 novel stimuli were re-presented. *Adapted from Perone, S., & Spencer, J. P. (2013a). Autonomous visual exploration creates developmental change in familiarity and novelty seeking behaviors. Frontiers in Cognitive Science, 4, 648. http://doi.org/10.3389/fpsyg.2013.00648.*

reliable novelty preference (i.e., three consecutive trials in which infants looked at the novel item at least 55% of the time). With age, infants required fewer trials to meet this criterion. What did the DNF model do as it accumulated experience over "development"? It performed similarly to infants. As the DNF model accrued stronger memory traces over a dimension (e.g., color), the model more quickly processed objects sampled from that dimension. Why did this happen? Perone and Spencer (2013a) found that as the long-term memory traces built up via exploration of objects in the virtual world, the model formed working memory representations of the familiar item in the lab-based processing speed task more quickly. This highlights the reciprocal causality of dynamic systems: the real-time scale (i.e., fixating, encoding, and remembering objects) was structuring the developmental timescale (i.e., accumulation of memory traces) just as the developmental timescale constrained the real-time scale (i.e., the formation of working memory representations). This also highlights how the historical nature of systems enables them to create developmental change in themselves.

Rose et al. (2002) found that preterm infants exhibited a delayed developmental trajectory relative to full-term infants. Perone and Spencer (2013a) were able to capture this delay by simply initializing the DNF model with slightly weaker strength of the excitatory and inhibitory connections that governed the cognitive processes in the model. This preterm infant version of the model accumulated memory traces via exploration of the virtual world that were comparable in strength to the full-term infant model. However, the weaker connectivity of the preterm infant model led it to form working memory representations for familiar items more slowly than the full-term infant model did. Perone and Spencer tested whether a simple intervention might alter the developmental trajectory of the preterm infant model. Specifically, they situated an algorithmic "parent" in the virtual world with the preterm infant model. The role of the parent was to maintain the preterm infant model's gaze on the object it was looking at, much like a parent would tap or hold up an object to keep their baby interested in looking at it. Encouraging this type of parental behavior is a common component of early interventions for preterm infants (e.g., Landry, Smith, & Swank, 2006). This simple manipulation led the preterm infant model to accumulate very strong memory traces that in turn enabled it to form working memory representations more rapidly in the lab-based processing speed task. The preterm infant model now exhibited a developmental trajectory much like the full-term infant model. This set of simulations nicely showed that understanding the real-time processes of an historical system can be a powerful tool for practitioners and parents to help nudge development along a positive path. Such interventions could be greatly facilitated by a firm foundational appreciation of the link between the real-time processes and developmental change like that specified by the DNF model.

3. NONCOMPUTATIONAL APPLICATIONS OF SYSTEMS CONCEPTS

The preceding section showcased applications of DST to cognition and development using neural process models, but computational approaches only represent a small proportion of research conducted under the umbrella of DST. In this section, we highlight noncomputational applications of DST that embrace the complexity of cognition, behavior, and development. We selected three applications that have yielded unique insights using a variety of innovative methodologies. First, we review research examining the connection between motor and language development to illustrate the interdependency and inseparability of systems that are traditionally considered unrelated. Second, we describe the emergence of the shape bias in early word learning. This research illustrates nesting of timescales in developmental change and highlights the type of rigorous methodology used to apply DST to the study of development. Last, we discuss research demonstrating the importance of zooming in on development to understand developmental trajectories.

3.1 Coupled Motor and Language Systems

Systems approaches have often led to the discovery of nonobvious connections between systems, which in turn have led to a deep understanding of how the behavior of one system can propel development in another domain forward (see Spencer, Blumberg, et al., 2009). One excellent example is the connection between motor and language systems. Iverson (2010) proposed that language development should be viewed within the context of the body in which it develops. The motor system can provide children practice generating behaviors in the movement domain that mimic those in the linguistic domain. There is good evidence that motor movements and language are tightly coupled over development. Rhythmic motor behaviors (e.g., shaking) emerge at the same time as, or just precede, reduplicated babble—vocalizations that are organized into a rhythmic sequence, like "bababa" (e.g., Eilers et al., 1993). One possible connection is that rhythmic motor behaviors provide infants the opportunity to practice and master rhythmically organized behaviors. A collection of longitudinal studies have shown that shaking was low in prebabbling infants, increased as infants began to babble, and then declined when infants became experienced babblers (for review, see Iverson, 2010).

The motor system can also shape language by providing the child new opportunities to explore the environment and communicate with others, as illustrated by Walle and Campos (2014). Their first study utilized a longitudinal design that followed infants from 10 to 14 months of age, a time when infants in the United States typically transition from crawling to walking (Adolph, Tamis-LeMonda, & Karasik, 2010). Walle and Campos found that this transition in locomotor skill was associated with an increase in infants' receptive and expressive language. Their second study, using an age-held–constant design, showed that walking infants had larger vocabularies than same-aged crawling infants. They also observed same-aged crawling and walking infants in a free play session with caregivers and found that acting and communicating in the social environment predicted infants' language. For example, parents' vocalizations toward their infants and infants' own movements positively predicted receptive vocabulary, after controlling for locomotive status (i.e., cràwler vs walker). Interestingly, they found an interaction between parents' vocalizations and locomotor status, such that greater vocalizations predicted receptive vocabulary only for walking infants. They also found an interaction between parental movement around the space and locomotor status, such that less parental movement predicted greater receptive vocabulary for walking infants. This finding may reflect the reorganization of the dyadic system, induced by the child learning to walk. For instance, parents may need to frequently communicate with their newly walking infant at greater distances as they explore the space. This can help the infant build a receptive vocabulary and free the parent from moving about the space to communicate.

Parladé and Iverson (2011) also investigated the link between motor and language development using DST concepts as a concrete guide to experimental design. These researchers were interested in transition points in vocabulary development. The premise of their research was that transition points provide a window into the processes of change. During transition points, systems become less stable as they reorganize. For this reason, Parladé and Iverson expected that the stable link between gesture, affect, and communication would temporarily become decoupled as children direct effort toward building their first vocabulary. The vocabulary spurt, a period during which children's vocabulary can double in as little as one month's time, typically occurs around 16–18 months of age in US English-speaking children. Parladé and Iverson examined the coupling between communicative behaviors (i.e., gestures, affect, vocalizations) during this transitional period. They expected a change in coordination among communicative behaviors during the vocabulary spurt, reasoning that language during this time is effortful, so coordination among systems would be disrupted. They identified children who exhibited a vocabulary spurt and examined their behavior before, during, and after their spurt in naturalistic interactions with caregivers and structured interactions with toys. Results showed that children who did vs did not go through a vocabulary spurt showed different developmental patterns in the coordination of communicative behaviors (e.g., gesturing and vocalizing close in time). Children who did not show a spurt showed a gradual increase in coordinated behaviors. For those children who did show a spurt, the coordination varied at this point, with a decrease in coordinated communication during the spurt relative to their own pre- and postspurt periods. These individual differences in developmental trajectories illustrate how systems interact and influence each other through time.

The literature examining how motor and language systems are connected highlights how dynamic systems can propel themselves forward. This might involve the production of rhythmic behaviors in the motor domain that bootstrap rhythmic behaviors in the language domain. This might involve emergent consequences of locomotion, such as communicating over a distance that can foster receptive vocabulary growth. This literature also highlights innovative methodologies, such as zooming in on transition points (cf. microgenetic method; Siegler & Crowley, 1991) and analyzing individual developmental trajectories in detail that can provide unique insights into the processes of change.

3.2 Shape Bias in Word Learning

The shape bias is a word-learning bias that young word learners exhibit in which they generalize new labels (e.g., ball) to novel objects that share the same shape (e.g., round) rather than other properties like color or material. This bias helps children rapidly acquire a vocabulary of count nouns, which are words that generally refer to categories organized by shape (e.g., apple, shoe, ball; see Samuelson & Smith, 1999). There is some debate about the origins of the shape bias. For example, Markson, Diesendruck, and Bloom (2008) proposed a shape-as-cue account that posits that the shape bias reflects children's explicit understanding that count nouns and object shape are a cue to object "kind," a concept that is independent of language experience. Samuelson and colleagues (e.g., Samuelson, 2002; Samuelson & Smith, 1999) have proposed an attentional learning account that is grounded in DST. Their research has demonstrated that the emergence of the shape bias reflects a history of word learning that creates change in and propels the language system forward. One of the key insights from Samuelson and colleagues' research is that the emergence of the shape bias depends on the structure of the early vocabulary. Among English-learners in the United States, the statistics of children's early vocabulary are typically dominated by nouns that refer to categories of solid objects organized by shape (e.g., ball, cup; Samuelson & Smith, 1999). A number of training studies have shown that the language system is open to external forces that alter vocabulary structure. For example, Samuelson (2002) taught young word learners (15- to 20-month-olds) 12 nouns from the natural statistics of the early vocabulary, which is dominated by solid objects in shape-based categories (e.g., shoe, ball, bucket). Relative to nontrained children, these children exhibited a precocious shape bias after only 9 weeks and, remarkably, continued rapid vocabulary growth 1 month after the training ended.

The acquisition of the shape bias also depends on the particular category exemplars children experience. Perry, Samuelson, Malloy, and Schiffer (2010) taught two groups of 18-month-old children the same set of 12 nouns, but manipulated the similarity among exemplars. For example, one group of children was taught the word "bucket" for three very different buckets (e.g., spherical, short cylindrical, tall cylindrical) and one group of children was taught the same word for three similar buckets (e.g., tall cylindrical). These two groups of children exhibited different word-learning trajectories. Children who were trained with more variable exemplars acquired a discriminating shape bias (i.e., generalizing differently for solid vs nonsolid items) and greater vocabulary growth than children who were trained with less variable examples of solid, shape-based categories.

The shape bias studies we reviewed are tied to several DST concepts. For example, the studies illustrate that the language system is open to variants in input (e.g., category exemplars), which can nudge the emergence of the shape bias for an individual child along a unique trajectory. The studies showed that the shape bias emerges from the accumulation of real-time word-learning experiences over time, and in this way exemplifies how an historical system can propel itself forward. The shape bias literature has also illustrated another important DST concept that the language system self-organizes in context. A classic example of the context dependency of a self-organizing system is the stepping reflex. Very young infants will lift their feet in alternation when held up with their feet touching a hard surface. Around 5 months of age, this reflex "disappears": infants no longer lift their legs when held upright, a change that had been explained as a developmental shift from reflexes to voluntary (cortical) control of movement. Thelen, Fisher, and Ridley-Johnson (1984) showed that the "stepping reflex" disappears as infants' legs gain fat and their muscles are not strong enough to lift their legs against the force of gravity. However, when infants are placed in a fish tank filled with water, their legs become buoyant and the stepping reflex reappears. Thelen et al. proposed that the appearance of stepping in the fish tank reflected the assembly of motor system components in context. Perry, Samuelson, and Burdinie (2014) showed that children's early word-learning biases similarly self-organize in context. In particular, when young word learners (16-month-olds) were situated in a high chair, they were more likely to generalize novel names by material than by shape. When at a table, by contrast, children showed no systematic biases. Why would this be so? Perry et al. (2014) proposed the intriguing idea that mealtime is a unique word-learning context in which children are exposed to many nonsolid substances with categories organized by material (e.g., applesauce, yogurt). Thus, the most relevant information for generalizing names differs based on context—a regularity that toddlers can learn to use for learning new words.

3.3 Sampling Development

The literatures on the coupling between language and motor development and the shape bias focus on the process of change. These literatures nicely highlight that a system's approach to understanding developmental change requires "zooming in" on the real-time processes that shape trajectories over the course of months and years. Adolph, Robinson, Young, and Gill-Alvarez (2008) argued that understanding the shape of trajectories and why they progress the way they do requires a unique methodology (see also Adolph & Robinson, 2011). Indeed, they propose that understanding such trajectories requires sampling behavior in a much more fine-grained fashion than is typical in developmental science. A good example is physical growth. Observing growth yearly, monthly, daily, or hourly tells us something very different about growth trajectories, as well as the process that leads children to grow. Growth is usually described as spurts during infancy and adolescence. When measured every day, however, growth appears to be more episodic throughout childhood, with children growing quite a bit in a single day interspersed with longer periods without growth. Large temporal gaps in sampling, such as on an annual basis, artificially make growth appear smooth and continuous when it is not.

Sampling development frequently is critically important for the application of DST to development and can provide a powerful window into individual trajectories. Adolph et al. (2008) demonstrated this in a study on motor skill acquisition during infancy. They asked parents to record daily observations of their infants' motor behavior (32 gross motor and balance skills) for several months. When mapping trajectories using daily data, the key finding was that infants rarely exhibited stage-like transitions, for instance, a period of never walking followed by a period of always walking.

Stage-like transitions were only observed about 15% of the time across all infants and skills. Instead, infants typically went through periods of variability in which they exhibited motor skills on some days and not others, vacillating through time as they acquired the skill. Sampling periodically from the daily observations, Adolph et al. could compare the trajectories implied by different rates of sampling using the same infants' data. Specifically, when sampled weekly, the percentage of transitions that appeared stage-like increased to about 50%, and when sampled monthly it increased to about 90%. Furthermore, not only did the less frequent sampling rate make skill transitions appear more stage-like than the more frequent sampling rate, the estimated age of acquisition was delayed with less frequent rates of sampling. Thus, both the timing and nature of skill transitions appeared different based on sampling rates, and these differences may lead theorists to propose different underlying mechanisms of change.

One of the most intriguing findings from the daily diaries was that infants exhibited about 13 transitions either way (i.e., from not showing a skill to showing it, or from showing a skill to not) for each motor skill. From a DST perspective, such variability arises from the interaction among components that make up the individual infant organizing in a new way once, twice, and so on, creating a new attractor state for the system to organize around. Entering an attractor state creates a history that, in turn, biases the system to reenter that state at a future point in time. Eventually, this pattern of organization will become a stable state that is the dominant behavior (see Spencer & Perone, 2008). The application of Adolph et al.'s (2008) methodology to other domains, such as cognition, may provide equally unique insights into what sources may move development along the trajectory it travels.

4. MOVING DYNAMIC SYSTEMS THEORY FORWARD

The goal of the current chapter was to illustrate the application of DST concepts to cognitive and behavioral development. DST emerged in developmental science in the early 1990s. In 1994, an issue of the *Journal of Experimental Child Psychology* focused on dynamic modeling of cognitive development, which stressed the computational application of the ideas embodied in DST. A quote from Bogartz (1994) regarding the future of DST stands out as particularly apropos in the context of our current review:

*On the basis of history, current proclivities of active researchers, and current quan-
titative training of psychology students, my bet would have to be that this
approach will probably fade from the scene or at best remain a little island of activity restricted to a small group of interested parties. (This is the kind of remark that
gets quoted and snickered at 20 years later when the approach is flourishing)
(p. 314).*

In developmental science, DST may currently be the island Bogartz
predicted. Indeed, Howe and Lewis (2005) stated that "dynamic systems
approaches to development remain a clear minority" (p. 250) and our survey
of the literature more than a decade later reconfirmed this point. Although
DST is not flourishing in the way we would like to see in the 20 years since
Bogartz's comments on the application of this approach, neither has it
faded from the scene. Our review shows that there are many applications
of DST, suggesting growth along a trajectory that we believe is poised to
continue upward.

We recognize that there are still significant barriers that stand in the way
of DST becoming more widely applied to developmental science. These
barriers must be overcome in order to go beyond the metaphorical chain
of islands we have described here. We have identified four such barriers.
First, as Bogartz (1994) so keenly noted, current (and prior) training of students does not equip them to handle the computational rigor of dynamic
modeling. These computational demands include explicit simulation of cognitive processes and behavior, as we outlined in the modeling section earlier,
but also sophisticated analytic tools that describe the dynamics of behavior
via analysis of various time series data (e.g., recurrence quantification analysis). A deep discussion of such analytic methods is beyond the scope of the
current chapter, but we want to highlight that methods are available to analyze coordination across levels (e.g., behavioral, cognitive, physiological)
within individuals (e.g., van Orden, Holden, & Turvey, 2005), between
conversation partners (e.g., Richardson, Dale, & Kirkham, 2007), or even
among groups participating in social rituals (Konvalinka et al., 2011). These
tools provide a different level of analysis than typical methods that treat the
individual as the fundamental unit of measure. To our knowledge, these
analytic tools have not been applied to development but would likely provide valuable insights into development as a dynamic system. Until such
methods are taught as part of a typical curriculum in psychology or developmental science, their application will remain a narrow specialization.
A recent increase in the resources available for scholars to learn different
computational techniques is promising. This includes Schöner et al.'s

(2015) primer, workshops, and summer schools to learn DNF modeling, or workshops, courses, and web books in nonlinear methods offered by the University of Cincinnati and the University of Connecticut.

Second, the application of the DST framework requires rethinking the very nature of human thought, behavior, and development relative to our theoretical predecessors. Most psychology researchers have been trained (implicitly or explicitly) to seek single-cause explanations for behavior, or assume that multiple causal factors will interact linearly. The empirical paradigms taught in psychological science, in which we seek to control whatever factors we can and/or use random assignment to try to isolate the contribution of a single factor, are inherently contrary to the notion of multicausality. Knowing that human behavior is determined by the interaction of multiple factors (some of which combine nonlinearly) should lead us away from depending solely on these methods for drawing inferences and making predictions. This is not to say such studies have no place in psychological science—by analogy, the science of physics has benefitted from studying artificial environments like a vacuum—but we must be mindful that these approaches are removing meaningful variance by design, and temper our generalizations accordingly.

Third, a related limitation in the typical psychological perspective is the notion that only closely related experiences and behaviors may be "relevant" to the behavior of interest (see Spencer, Blumberg, et al., 2009 for discussion). The earlier examples of motor and language development provide a clear demonstration of how broadly relevant experience can be: how infants move their bodies through space and time influences what they hear (as well as what they see; Kretch, Franchak, & Adolph, 2014), which affords and elicits different opportunities for learning. A striking example of the need to consider learning in the context of the body comes from the groundbreaking studies of toddlers' visual perspective during naturalistic interactions with parents. Smith, Yu, and colleagues used head-mounted cameras to capture the view of objects by both the parent and toddler as they played with and talked about objects (e.g., Yu & Smith, 2012). Although the view from the parents' perspectives appeared unstructured for the purpose of word learning, analysis of parents' actions, toddlers' views, and the timing of naming events showed a great reduction in ambiguity: because toddlers' arms are short, when they hold objects in their hands, the proximity to their eyes makes the held object take up nearly the entire view. This example illustrates that a dimension that seems entirely irrelevant to language (body size) provides critical structure in the moment of learning.

Last, it is essential for researchers to understand behavior across time-scales. We cannot explain how behavior changes over development without explaining how behavior emerges in the moment of a task. As our examples have illustrated, a careful analysis of the structure provided from the task context (as in the studies of visual working memory capacity) and an individual's history within and beyond the task (as in studies on the shape bias) can provide insights that are not apparent from theories that neglect these details. Although we believe this attention to task details is most transparently accomplished through computational modeling, such approaches are not strictly necessary. Careful analysis of what abilities are minimally required to perform a task can provide new insights into contributions to change (see, e.g., analysis of the A-not-B task by Smith et al., 1999).

In conclusion, adopting a DST approach to conducting developmental research is difficult, but ultimately worth the effort because it can provide a more complete explanation of how behavior emerges across task contexts over development. In the three decades since Fogel and Thelen (1987) introduced these ideas as a way to understand development, and especially since Thelen and Smith (1994) advocated for the broad application to the fields of cognitive and developmental psychology, we can chart remarkable growth in the appreciation of this perspective. Through our compilation and explanation of the range of applications reviewed, we hope to pave the way for continued expansion of these ideas into new and exciting frontiers in psychological science.

REFERENCES

Adolph, K. E., & Robinson, S. R. (2011). Sampling development. *Journal of Cognition and Development, 12*(4), 411–423. http://doi.org/10.1080/15248372.2011.608190.

Adolph, K. E., Robinson, S. R., Young, J. W., & Gill-Alvarez, F. (2008). What is the shape of developmental change? *Psychological Review, 115*(3), 527–543. http://doi.org/10.1037/0033-295X.115.3.527.

Adolph, K. E., Tamis-LeMonda, C. S., & Karasik, L. B. (2010). Motor skills. In M. H. Bornstein (Ed.), *Handbook of cultural developmental science* (pp. 61–88). New York: Psychology Press.

Alloway, T. P., Gathercole, S. E., Willis, C., & Adams, A.-M. (2004). A structural analysis of working memory and related cognitive skills in young children. *Journal of Experimental Child Psychology, 87*, 85–106.

Amari, S. (1977). Dynamics of pattern formation in lateral-inhibition type neural fields. *Biological Cybernetics, 27*, 77–87.

Baddeley, A. D. (1986). *Working memory.* Oxford: Oxford University Press.

Baillargeon, R. (1987). Object permanence in 3.5- and 4.5-month-old infants. *Developmental Psychology, 23*, 655–664.

Bogartz, R. S. (1994). The future of dynamic systems models in developmental psychology in the light of the past. *Journal of Experimental Child Psychology, 58*(2), 289–319. http://doi.org/10.1006/jecp.1994.1036.

Brannon, E. M., Suanda, S., & Libertus, K. (2007). Temporal discrimination increases in precision over development and parallels the development of numerosity discrimination. *Developmental Science, 10*(6), 770–777. http://doi.org/10.1111/j.1467-7687.2007.00635.x.

Cashon, C. H., & Cohen, L. B. (2000). Eight-month-old infants' perception of possible and impossible events. *Infancy, 1*(4), 429–446. http://doi.org/10.1207/S15327078IN0104_4.

Clearfield, M. W., Dineva, E., Smith, L. B., Diedrich, F. J., & Thelen, E. (2009). Cue salience and infant perseverative reaching: Tests of the dynamic field theory. *Developmental Science, 12*, 26–40.

Clearfield, M. W., Smith, L. B., Diedrich, F. J., & Thelen, E. (2006). Young infants reach correctly on the A-not-B task: On the development of stability and perseveration. *Infant Behavior & Development, 29*(3), 435–444.

Colombo, J., & Mitchell, D. W. (1990). Individual differences in early visual attention: Fixation time and information processing. In J. Colombo & J. Fagen (Eds.), *Individual differences in infancy: Reliability, stability, and prediction* (pp. 193–227). Hillsdale, NJ: Lawrence Erlbaum.

Cowan, N. (2007). What infants can tell us about working memory development. In L. M. Oakes & P. J. Bauer (Eds.), *Short- and long-term memory in infancy and early childhood: Taking the first steps toward remembering* (pp. 126–152). New York: Oxford University Press.

Cowan, N., Fristoe, N. M., Elliott, E. M., Brunner, R. P., & Saults, J. S. (2006). Scope of attention, control of attention, and intelligence in children and adults. *Memory & Cognition, 34*(8), 1754–1768. http://doi.org/10.3758/BF03195936.

Diamond, A. (1985). Development of the ability to use recall to guide action, as indicated by infants' performance on AB. *Child Development, 56*, 868–883.

Diedrich, F. J., Highlands, T., Thelen, E., & Smith, L. B. (2001). The role of target distinctiveness in infant perseverative reaching errors. *Journal of Experimental Child Psychology, 78*, 263–290.

Diedrich, F. J., Thelen, E., Smith, L. B., & Corbetta, D. (2000). Motor memory is a factor in infant perseverative errors. *Developmental Science, 3*, 479–494.

Eilers, R. E., Oller, D. K., Levine, S., Basinger, D., Lynch, M. P., & Urbano, R. (1993). The role of prematurity and socioeconomic status in the onset of canonical babbling in infants. *Infant Behavior and Development, 16*(3), 297–315. http://doi.org/10.1016/0163-6383(93)80037-9.

Erlhagen, W., & Schöner, G. (2002). Dynamic field theory of movement preparation. *Psychological Review, 109*, 545–572.

Fagan, J. F. (1970). Memory in the infant. *Journal of Experimental Child Psychology, 9*(2), 217–226.

Fagan, J. F. (1977). Infant recognition memory: Studies in forgetting. *Child Development, 48*(1), 68. http://doi.org/10.2307/1128883.

Fogel, A. (2011). Theoretical and applied dynamic systems research in developmental science: Dynamic systems research. *Child Development Perspectives, 5*(4), 267–272. http://doi.org/10.1111/j.1750-8606.2011.00174.x.

Fogel, A., & Thelen, E. (1987). Development of early expressive and communicative action: Reinterpreting the evidence from a dynamic systems perspective. *Developmental Psychology, 23*(6), 747–761. http://doi.org/10.1037/0012-1649.23.6.747.

Gratch, G., Appel, K. J., Evans, W. F., LeCompte, G. K., & Wright, N. A. (1974). Piaget's stage IV object concept error: Evidence of forgetting or object conception? *Child Development, 45*(1), 71. http://doi.org/10.2307/1127751.

Haith, M. M. (1998). Who put the cog in infant cognition? Is rich interpretation too costly? *Infant Behavior and Development, 21*(2), 167–179. http://doi.org/10.1016/S0163-6383(98)90001-7.

Hollenstein, T. (2011). Twenty years of dynamic systems approaches to development: Significant contributions, challenges, and future directions: 20 Years of dynamic systems. *Child Development Perspectives, 5*(4), 256–259. http://doi.org/10.1111/j.1750-8606.2011.00210.x.

Howe, M. L., & Lewis, M. D. (2005). The importance of dynamic systems approaches for understanding development. *Developmental Review, 25*(3–4), 247–251. http://doi.org/10.1016/j.dr.2005.09.002.

Hund, A. M., & Spencer, J. P. (2003). Developmental changes in the relative weighting of geometric and experience-dependent location cues. *Journal of Cognition and Development, 4*(1), 3–38.

Iverson, J. M. (2010). Developing language in a developing body: The relationship between motor development and language development. *Journal of Child Language, 37*(2), 229. http://doi.org/10.1017/S0305000909990432.

Johnson, J. S., & Simmering, V. R. (2015). Integrating perception and working memory in a three-layer dynamic field architecture. In G. Schöner, J. P. Spencer, & The DFT Research Group (Eds.), *Dynamic thinking: A primer on dynamic field theory* (pp. 151–168). New York: Oxford University Press.

Johnson, J. S., Simmering, V. R., & Buss, A. T. (2014). Beyond slots and resources: Grounding cognitive concepts in neural dynamics. *Attention, Perception, & Psychophysics, 76*(6), 1630–1654. http://doi.org/10.3758/s13414-013-0596-9.

Konvalinka, I., Xygalatas, D., Bulbulia, J., Schjødt, U., Jegindø, E.-M., Wallot, S., ... Roepstorff, A. (2011). Synchronized arousal between performers and related spectators in a fire-walking ritual. *Proceedings of the National Academy of Sciences of the United States of America, 108*(20), 8514–8519. http://doi.org/10.1073/pnas.1016955108.

Kretch, K. S., Franchak, J. M., & Adolph, K. E. (2014). Crawling and walking infants see the world differently. *Child Development, 85*(4), 1503–1518. http://doi.org/10.1111/cdev.12206.

Landry, S. H., Smith, K. E., & Swank, P. R. (2006). Responsive parenting: Establishing early foundations for social, communication, and independent problem-solving skills. *Developmental Psychology, 42*(4), 627–642.

Lewis, M. D. (2011). Dynamic systems approaches: Cool enough? Hot enough? Dynamic systems approaches. *Child Development Perspectives, 5*(4), 279–285. http://doi.org/10.1111/j.1750-8606.2011.00190.x.

Lipinski, J., Simmering, V. R., Johnson, J. S., & Spencer, J. P. (2010). The role of experience in location estimation: Target distributions shift location memory biases. *Cognition, 115*, 147–153.

Lipinski, J., Spencer, J. P., & Samuelson, L. K. (2010). Biased feedback in spatial recall yields a violation of delta rule learning. *Psychonomic Bulletin & Review, 17*(4), 581–588.

Logie, R. H. (1995). *Visual-spatial working memory*. Hove, UK: Erlbaum.

Marcovitch, S., & Zelazo, P. D. (1999). The A-not-B error: Results from a logistic meta-analysis. *Child Development, 70*, 1297–1313.

Markson, L., Diesendruck, G., & Bloom, P. (2008). The shape of thought. *Developmental Science, 11*(2), 204–208. http://doi.org/10.1111/j.1467-7687.2007.00666.x.

Munakata, Y. (1998). Infant perseveration and implications for object permanence theories: A PDP model of the AB task. *Developmental Science, 1*(2), 161–184.

Oakes, L. M., Baumgartner, H. A., Barrett, F. S., Messenger, I. M., & Luck, S. J. (2013). Developmental changes in visual short-term memory in infancy: Evidence from eye-tracking. *Frontiers in Psychology, 4*, 697. http://doi.org/10.3389/fpsyg.2013.00697.

Oakes, L. M., Messenger, I. M., Ross-Sheehy, S., & Luck, S. J. (2009). New evidence for rapid development of color-location binding in infants' visual short-term memory. *Visual Cognition, 17*, 67–82.

Oakes, L. M., Ross-Sheehy, S., & Luck, S. J. (2006). Rapid development of feature binding in visual short-term memory. *Psychological Science, 17*(9), 781–787.

Parladé, M. V., & Iverson, J. M. (2011). The interplay between language, gesture, and affect during communicative transition: A dynamic systems approach. *Developmental Psychology, 47*(3), 820–833. http://doi.org/10.1037/a0021811.

Pashler, H. (1988). Familiarity and visual change detection. *Perception and Psychophysics, 44*, 369–378. http://doi.org/10.3758/BF03210419.

Perone, S., & Ambrose, J. P. (2015). A process view of learning and development in an autonomous exploratory system. In G. Schöner, J. P. Spencer, & The DFT Research Group (Eds.), *Dynamic thinking: A primer on dynamic field theory* (pp. 271–296). New York: Oxford University Press.

Perone, S., Simmering, V. R., & Spencer, J. P. (2011). Stronger neural dynamics capture changes in infants' visual working memory capacity over development. *Developmental Science, 14*, 1379–1392. http://doi.org/10.1111/j.1467-7687.2011.01083.x.

Perone, S., & Spencer, J. P. (2013a). Autonomous visual exploration creates developmental change in familiarity and novelty seeking behaviors. *Frontiers in Psychology, 4*, 648. http://doi.org/10.3389/fpsyg.2013.00648.

Perone, S., & Spencer, J. P. (2013b). Autonomy in action: Linking the act of looking to memory formation in infancy via dynamic neural fields. *Cognitive Science, 37*, 1–60. http://doi.org/10.1111/cogs.12010.

Perone, S., & Spencer, J. P. (2014). The co-development of looking dynamics and discrimination performance. *Developmental Psychology, 50*(3), 837–852. http://doi.org/10.1037/a0034137.

Perry, L. K., Samuelson, L. K., & Burdinie, J. B. (2014). Highchair philosophers: The impact of seating context-dependent exploration on children's naming biases. *Developmental Science, 17*(5), 757–765. http://doi.org/10.1111/desc.12147.

Perry, L. K., Samuelson, L. K., Malloy, L. M., & Schiffer, R. N. (2010). Learn locally, think globally: Exemplar variability supports higher-order generalization and word learning. *Psychological Science, 21*(12), 1894–1902. http://doi.org/10.1177/0956797610389189.

Piaget, J. (1954). *The construction of reality in the child.* New York: Basic Books.

Richardson, D. C., Dale, R., & Kirkham, N. Z. (2007). The art of conversation is coordination common ground and the coupling of eye movements during dialogue. *Psychological Science, 18*(5), 407–413. http://doi.org/10.1111/j.1467-9280.2007.01914.x.

Riggs, K. J., McTaggart, J., Simpson, A., & Freeman, R. P. J. (2006). Changes in the capacity of visual working memory in 5- to 10-year-olds. *Journal of Experimental Child Psychology, 95*, 18–26. http://doi.org/10.1016/j.jecp.2006.03.009.

Rivera, S. M., Wakeley, A., & Langer, J. (1999). The drawbridge phenomenon: Representational reasoning or perceptual preference? *Developmental Psychology, 35*(2), 427–435.

Rose, S. A., Feldman, J. F., & Jankowski, J. J. (2001). Attention and recognition memory in the 1st year of life: A longitudinal study of preterm and full-term infants. *Developmental Psychology, 37*(1), 135–151. http://doi.org/10.1037/0012-1649.37.1.135.

Rose, S. A., Feldman, J. F., & Jankowski, J. J. (2002). Processing speed in the 1st year of life: A longitudinal study of preterm and full-term infants. *Developmental Psychology, 38*, 895–902. http://doi.org/10.1037/0012-1649.38.6.895.

Rose, S. A., Feldman, J. F., & Jankowski, J. J. (2004). Infant visual recognition memory. *Developmental Review, 24*, 74–100.

Rose, S. A., Feldman, J. F., & Jankowski, J. J. (2012). Implications of infant cognition for executive functions at age 11. *Psychological Science, 23*(11), 1345–1355. http://doi.org/10.1177/0956797612444902.

Ross-Sheehy, S., Oakes, L. M., & Luck, S. J. (2003). The development of visual short-term memory capacity in infants. *Child Development, 74*, 1807–1822.

Samuelson, L. K. (2002). Statistical regularities in vocabulary guide language acquisition in connectionist models and 15-20-month-olds. *Developmental Psychology, 38*(6), 1016–1037. http://doi.org/10.1037/0012-1649.38.6.1016.

Samuelson, L. K., Schutte, A. R., & Horst, J. S. (2009). The dynamic nature of knowledge: Insights from a dynamic field model of children's novel noun generalization. *Cognition, 110*, 322–345. http://doi.org/10.1016/j.cognition.2008.10.017.

Samuelson, L. K., & Smith, L. B. (1999). Early noun vocabularies: Do ontology, category structure and syntax correspond? *Cognition, 73*(1), 1–33. http://doi.org/10.1016/S0010-0277(99)00034-7.

Schöner, G., Spencer, J. P., & The DFT Research Group. (2015). *Dynamic thinking: A primer on dynamic field theory*. New York: Oxford University Press.

Schöner, G., & Thelen, E. (2006). Using dynamic field theory to rethink infant habituation. *Psychological Review, 113*(2), 273–299.

Schutte, A. R., & Spencer, J. P. (2002). Generalizing the dynamic field theory of the A-not-B error beyond infancy: Three-year-olds' delay- and experience-dependent location memory biases. *Child Development, 73*, 377–404.

Schutte, A. R., Spencer, J. P., & Schöner, G. (2003). Testing the dynamic field theory: Working memory for locations becomes more spatially precise over development. *Child Development, 74*(5), 1393–1417.

Siegler, R. S., & Crowley, K. (1991). The microgenetic method: A direct means for studying cognitive development. *American Psychologist, 46*(6), 606–620. http://doi.org/10.1037/0003-066X.46.6.606.

Simmering, V. R. (2012). The development of visual working memory capacity in early childhood. *Journal of Experimental Child Psychology, 111*, 695–707. http://doi.org/10.1016/j.jecp.2011.10.007.

Simmering, V. R. (2016). Working memory capacity in context: Modeling dynamic processes of behavior, memory, and development. *Monographs of the Society for Research in Child Development, 81*, 1–168. http://doi.org/10.1111/mono.12202.

Simmering, V. R., Miller, H. E., & Bohache, K. (2015). Different developmental trajectories across feature types support a dynamic field model of visual working memory development. *Attention, Perception, & Psychophysics, 77*(4), 1170–1188. http://doi.org/10.3758/s13414-015-0832-6.

Simmering, V. R., & Perone, S. (2013). Working memory capacity as a dynamic process. *Frontiers in Psychology, 3*, 567. http://doi.org/10.3389/fpsyg.2012.00567.

Simmering, V. R., Schutte, A. R., & Spencer, J. P. (2008). Generalizing the dynamic field theory of spatial cognition across real and developmental time scales. *Brain Research, 1202*, 68–86. http://doi.org/10.1016/j.brainres.2007.06.081.

Simmering, V. R., & Spencer, J. P. (2007). Carving up space at imaginary joints: Can people mentally impose spatial category boundaries? *Journal of Experimental Psychology Human Perception and Performance. 33*, 871–894. http://doi.org/10.1037/0096-1523.33.4.871.

Smith, L. B., & Thelen, E. (2003). Development as a dynamic system. *Trends in Cognitive Sciences, 7*(8), 343–348. http://doi.org/10.1016/S1364-6613(03)00156-6.

Smith, L. B., Thelen, E., Titzer, R., & McLin, D. (1999). Knowing in the context of acting: The task dynamics of the A-not-B error. *Psychological Review, 106*, 235–260.

Spelke, E. S. (1985). Perception of unity, persistence, and identity: Thoughts on infants' conceptions of objects. In J. Mehler & R. Fox (Eds.), *Neonate cognition: Beyond the blooming buzzing confusion* (pp. 89–113): Lawrence Erlbaum.

Spencer, J. P., Blumberg, M. S., McMurray, B., Robinson, S. R., Samuelson, L. K., & Tomblin, J. B. (2009). Short arms and talking eggs: Why we should no longer abide the nativist-empiricist debate. *Child Development Perspectives, 3*(2), 79–87. http://doi.org/10.1111/j.1750-8606.2009.00081.x.

Spencer, J. P., Clearfield, M., Corbetta, D., Ulrich, B., Buchanan, P., & Schöner, G. (2006). Moving toward a grand theory of development: In memory of Esther Thelen. *Child Development, 77,* 1521–1538.

Spencer, J. P., Dineva, E., & Smith, L. B. (2009). Comment on "Infants' perseverative search errors are induced by pragmatic misinterpretation". *Science, 325*(5948), 1624. http://doi.org/10.1126/science.1172759.

Spencer, J. P., & Hund, A. M. (2002). Prototypes and particulars: Geometric and experience-dependent spatial categories. *Journal of Experimental Psychology. General, 131,* 16–37.

Spencer, J. P., & Hund, A. M. (2003). Developmental continuity in the processes that underlie spatial recall. *Cognitive Psychology, 47*(4), 432–480.

Spencer, J. P., & Perone, S. (2008). Defending qualitative change: The view from dynamical systems theory. *Child Development, 79*(6), 1639–1647. http://doi.org/10.1111/j.1467-8624.2008.01214.x.

Spencer, J. P., Perone, S., & Buss, A. T. (2011). Twenty years and going strong: A dynamic systems revolution in motor and cognitive development. *Child Development Perspectives, 5*(4), 260–266.

Spencer, J. P., & Schöner, G. (2003). Bridging the representational gap in the dynamical systems approach to development. *Developmental Science, 6,* 392–412.

Spencer, J. P., & Schutte, A. R. (2004). Unifying representations and responses: Perseverative biases arise from a single behavioral system. *Psychological Science, 15*(3), 187–193.

Spencer, J. P., Simmering, V. R., & Schutte, A. R. (2006). Toward a formal theory of flexible spatial behavior: Geometric category biases generalize across pointing and verbal response types. *Journal of Experimental Psychology. Human Perception and Performance, 32,* 473–490.

Spencer, J. P., Simmering, V. R., Schutte, A. R., & Schöner, G. (2007). What does theoretical neuroscience have to offer the study of behavioral development? Insights from a dynamic field theory of spatial cognition. In J. M. Plumert & J. P. Spencer (Eds.), *The emerging spatial mind* (pp. 320–361). New York: Oxford University Press.

Spencer, J. P., Smith, L. B., & Thelen, E. (2001). Tests of a dynamic systems account of the A-not-B error: The influence of prior experience on the spatial memory abilities of 2-year-olds. *Child Development, 72,* 1327–1346.

Thelen, E., Fisher, D. M., & Ridley-Johnson, R. (1984). The relationship between physical growth and a newborn reflex. *Infant Behavior & Development, 7,* 479–493.

Thelen, E., Schöner, G., Scheier, C., & Smith, L. B. (2001). The dynamics of embodiment: A field theory of infant perseverative reaching. *Behavioral and Brain Sciences, 24,* 1–86.

Thelen, E., & Smith, L. B. (1994). *A dynamic systems approach to the development of cognition and action.* Cambridge: MIT Press.

Topál, J., Gergely, G., Miklósi, A., Erdőhegyi, A., & Csibra, G. (2008). Infants' perseverative search errors are induced by pragmatic misinterpretation. *Science, 321*(5897), 1831–1834. http://doi.org/10.1126/science.1161437.

Topál, J., Tóth, M., Gergely, G., & Csibra, G. (2009). Response to comment on "Infants' perseverative search errors are induced by pragmatic misinterpretation". *Science, 325*(5948), 1624. http://doi.org/10.1126/science.1173024.

Tronick, E., Als, H., Adamson, L., Wise, S., & Brazelton, T. B. (1978). The infant's response to entrapment between contradictory messages in face-to-face interaction. *Journal of the American Academy of Child Psychiatry, 17*(1), 1–13. http://doi.org/10.1016/S0002-7138(09)62273-1.

van Geert, P. (2011). The contribution of complex dynamic systems to development: Contribution of complex dynamic systems to development. *Child Development Perspectives, 5*(4), 273–278. http://doi.org/10.1111/j.1750-8606.2011.00197.x.

van Geert, P., & Steenbeek, H. (2005). Explaining after by before: Basic aspects of a dynamic systems approach to the study of development. *Developmental Review, 25*(3–4), 408–442. http://doi.org/10.1016/j.dr.2005.10.003.

van Orden, G. C., Holden, J. G., & Turvey, M. T. (2005). Human cognition and 1/f scaling. *Journal of Experimental Psychology. General, 134*(1), 117–123. http://doi.org/10.1037/0096-3445.134.1.117.

Vogel, E. K., Woodman, G. F., & Luck, S. J. (2001). Storage of features, conjunctions, and objects in visual working memory. *Journal of Experimental Psychology Human Perception and Performance, 27*, 92–114.

Walle, E. A., & Campos, J. J. (2014). Infant language development is related to the acquisition of walking. *Developmental Psychology, 50*(2), 336–348. http://doi.org/10.1037/a0033238.

Wilson, H. R., & Cowan, J. D. (1972). Excitatory and inhibitory interactions in localized populations of model neurons. *Biophysical Journal, 12*, 1–24.

Witherington, D. C. (2007). The dynamic systems approach as metatheory for developmental psychology. *Human Development, 50*(2–3), 127–153. http://doi.org/10.1159/000100943.

Witherington, D. C., & Margett, T. E. (2011). How conceptually unified is the dynamic systems approach to the study of psychological development? Conceptual unification in dynamic systems. *Child Development Perspectives, 5*(4), 286–290. http://doi.org/10.1111/j.1750-8606.2011.00211.x.

Yu, C., & Smith, L. B. (2012). Embodied attention and word learning by toddlers. *Cognition, 125*(2), 244–262. http://doi.org/http://dx.doi.org/10.1016/j.cognition.2012.06.016.

CHAPTER THREE

Mental Objects in Working Memory: Development of Basic Capacity or of Cognitive Completion?

N. Cowan[1]

University of Missouri, Columbia, MO, United States
[1]Corresponding author: e-mail address: cowann@missouri.edu

Contents

Abstract

Working memory is the small amount of information that we hold in mind and use to carry out cognitive processes such as language comprehension and production, problem solving, and decision making. In order to understand cognitive development, it would be helpful to know whether working memory increases in capacity with development and, if so, how and why. I will focus on two major stumbling blocks toward understanding working memory development, namely that (1) many potentially

Advances in Child Development and Behavior, Volume 52
ISSN 0065-2407
http://dx.doi.org/10.1016/bs.acdb.2016.12.001

relevant aspects of the mind change in parallel during development, obscuring the role of any one change; and (2) one cannot use the same test procedure from infancy to adulthood, complicating comparisons across age groups. With regard to the first stumbling block, the parallel development of different aspects of the mind, we discuss research in which attempts were made to hold constant some factors (knowledge, strategies, direction of attention) to investigate whether developmental differences remain. With regard to the second stumbling block, procedural differences in tests for different age groups, I suggest ways in which the results might be reconciled across procedures. I highlight the value of pursuing research that could distinguish between two different key hypotheses that emerge: that there is a developmental increase in the number of working memory slots (or in a basic resource that holds items in working memory), and that there is a developmental increase in the amount of detail that each of these slots can hold.

1. INTRODUCTION

A young child who is upset that an older sibling has two cookies to her one can be appeased if the one cookie is broken in half to make two. How does this happen in the young child's mind? How is it that a child just beginning school would be intellectually lost in a classroom slightly more advanced, or an elementary school child lost in a high school environment? An ancient, naïve assumption might have been that it just takes time for a child to learn, but it might have become evident that some children learn more quickly than others in a comparable environment, so that there would appear to be a biological component. A more sophisticated concept, therefore, is of the readiness to learn. For a child to learn some concepts the brain must mature, with a capability to understand more complex concepts as the neural system grows. Here I consider some possibilities and then focus attention on two hypotheses about cognitive growth that seem worthy of further investigation.

I have worked on the growth of the mind with respect to one of its most fundamental properties, the number of items retained in working memory (e.g., Cowan, 2016). The term *working memory* in psychology refers to the small amount of information that is held in mind in order to carry out cognitive tasks (Baddeley & Hitch, 1974; Miller, Galanter, & Pribram, 1960). In learning language, a child has to hold onto a spoken word while considering what object or event it refers to. Without working memory, there could be no possibility of issuing instructions for a child to follow. There would be no possibility of retaining a partial result in mind while carrying out an arithmetic problem. Understanding a new concept involves combining its elements in working memory (Halford, Cowan, & Andrews, 2007). For example, in folk terms a tiger is essentially a large cat with stripes. If one forgets that it is a cat, the concept is not differentiated from a zebra; if one forgets that it is large, one has a striped house cat; or if one forgets that it is striped, it could be a lion instead.

Clearly, what is needed for maturation of the brain is an increase in the ability to retain usable elements in working memory and to combine them or use them in the right way. Cowan (2016) recently reviewed various ways that this ability could increase with age. Some of these ways involve learning. For example, elements that have already been combined in memory are called chunks (Miller, 1956). If a child already knows about big cats, then the concept of a tiger reduces from three separate ideas or chunks (big, cat, striped) down to two (big-cat, striped). Although it is pedagogically important to know what information is typically learned by children of different ages, I do not examine that topic here because I define our task as trying to figure out what development is possible and what is not possible in development, leaving the task of figuring out what children actually know to educators and parents.

In what follows, I first provide some evidence that certain very important developmental changes taking place outside of the working memory system are not enough to explain developmental increases in mental capability. The general possibilities that I consider, but ultimately rule out, include possibilities that developmental growth occurs entirely through knowledge coming from experience, through the efficiency of attention, through increased encoding efficiency, or through mnemonic strategies. I then discuss an apparent developmental increase in working memory capacity and what processes might explain that increase consistently across the life span, from infancy onward, despite apparent inconsistencies between the infant and child literatures. Before I discuss the childhood development of working memory, though, it is necessary first to examine how capacity can be measured in some of the procedures that I highlight.

2. THE MEASUREMENT OF WORKING MEMORY CAPACITY

Pashler (1988) and Cowan (2001) provided some simple tools that will be used throughout this chapter to describe performance on tasks in which an array of objects is presented for study and is then followed by a probe array or a single-item probe to be judged as the same as, or different from, the studied array. These tools have been validated extensively (Rouder et al., 2008; Rouder, Morey, Morey, & Cowan, 2011) although they possibly may only be approximations if memory in fact occurs as a fluid resource rather than a fixed number of items on each trial (Fougnie, Cormiea, Kanabar, & Alvarez, 2016; Ma, Husain, & Bays, 2014). Here I provide just brief explanations to allow the rest of the chapter to be clear. Suppose an array of S items is followed by another, probe array that is the same or differs in the nature of one object in the array. The task is to indicate if the arrays are the same. Assume that the participant has k items in working memory and that the goal of the model is to estimate k. If one item in fact changes, the likelihood that the participant has that item in working memory and therefore notices the change is k/S. If the participant does not notice a change, he or she is assumed to guess that there was a change with probability g. Thus,

$$P(\text{respond ``change''}|\text{change}) = P(\text{hits}) = k/S + (1 - k/S)g$$

When no change has occurred, the participant is assumed to be in the same guessing state, hence

$$P(\text{respond ``change''}|\text{no change}) = P(\text{false alarms}) = g$$

One can combine these equations to show that

$$k = S[P(\text{hits}) - P(\text{false alarms})]/[1 - P(\text{false alarms})]$$

In another circumstance (Cowan, 2001), the probe shows which item may have changed, so only a single decision has to be reached. In that case, if the item in question is in working memory, the participant will know whether a change has occurred or not. The difference from the previous situation is in the false alarms:

$$P(\text{respond ``change''}|\text{no change}) = P(\text{false alarms}) = (1 - k/S)g$$

One can show that now, in this situation, by combing equations for hits and false alarms,

$$k = S[P(\text{hits}) - P(\text{false alarms})]$$

The value of k typically increases as the set size increases, reaching a level or asymptote at between three and four items in adults (but with individual differences ranging usually between two and six items). Sometimes, when the array sizes are very large, such as 10 items, k begins to decrease as the array size increases (e.g., Cusack, Lehmann, Veldsman, & Mitchell, 2009). I use k

to describe the number of items in working memory in the developmental studies in childhood. The number of items in working memory may be smaller than capacity (when there are few array items), but it is limited by the participant's capacity.

3. SOURCES OF CHILDHOOD DEVELOPMENT OF WORKING MEMORY: IS THERE A FUNDAMENTAL INCREASE IN CAPACITY?

There are a number of processes that could account for developmental increases in working memory performance from the early elementary school years through adulthood. I next consider these one at a time to make the case that it is reasonable to suspect that there is a fundamental increase in capacity, in addition to other important factors.

3.1 Childhood Working Memory Development Is Probably Not Entirely Based on Learning

One thing that is important from my point of view is to establish that there is an implication of brain growth for cognitive development that cannot just be attributed to increasing knowledge across ages coming from experience. One might build a case that, indeed, knowledge growth is enough to explain the maturation of the mind. In one approach showing the dramatic role of knowledge, Chi (1978) examined the ability of six children in third through eighth grade, and adults, to remember both lists of digits and the positions of pieces on a chess board. These, however, were not just any children and adults. The adults were somewhat familiar with chess, but the children were chess experts. The finding was that although the adults substantially out-performed the children on digits as in many previous studies, the children dramatically outperformed adults on remembering chess configurations. Clearly, knowledge plays a key role in working memory so it is worth asking: if adults and children can be equated on knowledge, will an age difference still be found?

Case, Kurland, and Goldberg (1982) further showed that knowledge affects processing efficiency. In one experiment, participants were to remember and then immediately repeat each list of spoken words and, in a separate task, listen to isolated words and repeat each one as quickly as possible. Young children repeated items slower than adults and remembered commensurately fewer of these items. When adults were given a different set of items, nonsense words, their repetition rate slowed to match the children's rate with real words, and the adults' working memory performance was accordingly reduced to match the children. Thus, there is no question that knowledge is an important factor in working memory development.

Cowan, Ricker, Clark, Hinrichs, and Glass (2015) examined working memory with knowledge varied, in children in the United States ranging from first through seventh grades and adults, using briefly presented arrays of English letters and arrays of unfamiliar characters for which the contribution of knowledge should be greatly diminished (illustrated in Fig. 1A). The goal was to determine whether equating knowledge across age groups would eliminate age differences in working memory performance.

Each array was followed by a single character that was to be judged present in the array or absent from it. This kind of task becomes more difficult as the number of items in the array increases (Luck & Vogel, 1997). Cowan et al. (2015) found that performance was especially low in children in the first grade, the youngest age group tested, because some children did not know the letters very well. These children were excluded from the study, which also included older children and adults. Performance on the letters was much better than it was on the characters, showing a robust role of knowledge, but the rate of developmental change was nevertheless very similar for letters and unfamiliar characters. (Using z scores to examine the relative performance levels of different participants in each task, the

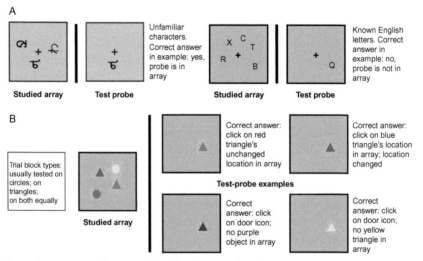

Fig. 1 Illustrations of the procedures used in visual working memory tasks with children. The *dark vertical bar* in each case represents a delay between the end of the materials to be remembered and the beginning of the probe item. (A) Cowan et al. (2015) and (B) Cowan, Morey, AuBuchon, Zwilling, and Gilchrist (2010).

developmental growth curves for letters and familiar characters fell on top of one another.) This result suggests that there is a fundamental development of the capacity of working memory that cannot be attributed to the increase in knowledge. In this task, knowledge was equated across age groups by making the materials very similar and excluding children who did not know their English letters well. If knowledge had accounted for the developmental growth, there should have been a faster rate of improvement across age groups for letters than for unfamiliar characters as knowledge accrued. If knowledge is all there is and it was equated across age groups, there should have been no remaining developmental growth in this experiment, yet in fact there was a dramatic developmental improvement in z scores that was almost identical for letters and unfamiliar characters.

Another approach to the same issue was taken by Gilchrist, Cowan, and Naveh-Benjamin (2009). Series of short, unrelated sentences were orally presented for oral, verbatim recall (e.g., *our neighbor sells vegetables; we welcomed the family; my temper causes trouble; the birds circled above*). This procedure allows for a measure of items in working memory (the number of sentences for which at least one substantive word was recalled) and a measure of knowledge (the number of words per sentence recalled given that at least one word was recalled). In 7–year-old children through adults, the measure of knowledge was about 80% of the words in the sentences that were at least partly recalled; but the measure of items in working memory increased steadily with age despite this apparent success in equating for linguistic knowledge needed to perceive these simple sentences.

It still remains possible that, as the brain grows, it is able to apply knowledge even in cases in which unknown material is presented. A particular unfamiliar character might be recoded in a way that is mnemonically helpful (e.g., as a wavy squiggle resembling a sign for the ocean, with a periscope sticking out of it). It should, however, be easier to use knowledge in a situation in which the elements are well known. Some of the letters in an array might be put together to resemble a known English word, for example. Still, a case can be made that more research is needed to show the full contribution of knowledge.

3.2 Childhood Working Memory Development Is Probably Not Entirely Based on Increases in the Efficiency of Attention Allocation

Another hypothesis about cognitive growth that can be suggested, this time based on research on individual differences in adults, is that differences in capacity might occur because less-capable individuals are not as efficient in focusing on the important items in the environment. Research by Vogel, McCollough, and Machizawa (2005) examined this possibility. They asked that participants examine an array in which some items were to be attended and other items were to be ignored. Their participants were to attend to a field with two targets (e.g., the spatial orientations of two red bars) or four targets (e.g., four red bars). Sometimes, two targets were interspersed with two distractors that were to be ignored (e.g., two blue bars). An event-related potential brain signal was used to indicate the memory load that the individual held in mind. Those with high spans were able to limit their performance to the relevant bars, and therefore their brain signals indicated a considerably larger memory load with four targets than with two targets. Other individuals were limited to fewer items in working memory and thus showed a smaller brain difference between two- and four-target trials. Notably, when these lower-capacity individuals were presented with two targets and two distractors, their brain responses suggested that they were trying to retain both targets and distractors in working memory, making the process of using the contents of working memory more difficult. The hypothesis that lower-span individuals do not inhibit memory for distractors also has been put forward as an explanation for the decline in working memory that occurs with cognitive aging (Stoltzfus, Hasher, & Zacks, 1996).

Not all findings have been favorable to the hypothesis that lower-capacity individuals fail to filter out less-relevant items as well as higher-capacity individuals. Gold et al. (2006) examined this hypothesis in a comparison of adults with and without schizophrenia using a procedure in which there were more- and less-often-tested items. In one experiment, for example, the colors of items of one particular shape were tested on 75% of the trials and the colors of items of another shape were tested on only 25% of the trials. The tendency to remember more of the items that are tested more often was found not only in participants without schizophrenia but to a similar extent in those with schizophrenia. What distinguished best between the groups was simply how many of the objects were remembered, summed across the more- and less-often-tested shapes. Similarity, Mall, Morey, Wolf, and Lehnert (2014) recorded eye movements to show that low-span participants tended to look at task-relevant items more than task-irrelevant items, to the same extent as higher-span individuals.

Cowan et al. (2010) examined this issue of filtering in elementary school children and adults using a procedure modeled after Gold et al. (2006). In their procedure, illustrated in Fig. 1B, each array involved a grid with colored circles and triangles. In the most important condition, there were two colored circles and two colored triangles in an array, with a unique color for each object in the array. In the cover story that was used to make the task more interesting for the children, these objects were "students" in a "classroom." The array of four objects was followed by a single probe object that was presented at the correct location (in the cover story, sitting at the right desk), or that was sitting at a location that had been occupied by a different object (in the cover story, sitting at the wrong desk), or that was not found in the array at all (in the cover story, a student that did not belong in the classroom). The response was to use the mouse to click on the location where the student belonged; if the student belonged nowhere in the classroom (i.e., items absent from the array), the correct response was to click on a door icon to send the student to the principal.

Cowan et al. (2010) used different instruction conditions in different trial blocks but the most critical trial block was one in which memory for items of one shape (e.g., circles) were tested on 80% of the trials, whereas items of the other shape (triangles) were tested on the remaining 20% of trials. The youngest participant group, with children as young as 7 years, remembered far fewer items than the other groups (summed across the more- and less-often-tested items), but they did better on the more-often-tested items, to the same extent as the older groups. The adults remembered about 1.5 of the 2 items of the 80%-tested shape vs only about 1.0 of 2 of the 20%-tested shape (a 0.5-item drop; in all, ~2.5 items in memory), and the 7-year-olds similarly remembered about 0.8/2 vs 0.4/2 in these conditions (a comparable 0.4-item drop; but in all, only ~1.2 items in memory).

There was an age difference in the ability to favor the more-often-tested items, however, for larger arrays of three more- and three less-often-tested items. With that higher memory load, the youngest age group no longer favored more- over less-often-tested items. Cowan et al. (2010) concluded, therefore, that 7-year-olds allocate attention in this task as efficiently as adults unless their working memory is sufficiently overloaded. Attention apparently must be shared between storage and processing (Daneman & Carpenter, 1980; Kane, Bleckley, Conway, & Engle, 2001), and, with too much to store, the process of allocating attention becomes inefficient in these young children. Still, this age difference in efficiency for larger arrays cannot explain the age differences in capacity, which occurred even with smaller arrays for which all age groups allocated attention similarly.

3.3 Childhood Working Memory Development Is Probably Not Entirely Based on an Improved Efficiency of Encoding

Many studies have suggested that younger children have a slower speed of processing than older children or young adults (e.g., Kail & Salthouse, 1994). This slower speed of processing could come into play in several ways in working memory tasks. First, some have argued that what we take to be concurrently held items in working memory could result from a rapid circulation of attention between these items, one at a time (e.g., Cowan et al., 1998; Gaillard, Barrouillet, Jarrold, & Camos, 2011). Insofar as that happens, it simply suggests that what can be taken as a multiple-item capacity limit on a macroscopic timescale might be considered a speed limit on a microscopic timescale. There is, however, another way in which processing speed or efficiency could provide a more fundamental alternative to a capacity limit and that is with respect to encoding.

Cowan et al. (2010) presented the array of objects at a rapid pace, as is typical in this kind of change–detection experiment (e.g., Luck & Vogel, 1997). It seems possible that children would not be able to encode items into working memory at the same rapid pace that has been demonstrated in adults (Vogel, Woodman, & Luck, 2006). To pursue that possibility, Cowan, AuBuchon, Gilchrist, Ricker, and Saults (2011) conducted an experiment similar to the key conditions of Cowan et al. (2010), involving an array with two circles and two triangles of different colors on each trial, but with one critical difference. Instead of presenting all items briefly and concurrently, each item was presented individually at a slow rate of 1 s per item. The developmental result was the same as before: children as young as 7 years allocated attention to the shape tested on most trials as well as adults did, but they remembered considerably fewer items overall. Encoding speed cannot be the basis of the age differences observed by Cowan et al. (2010) after all.

3.4 Childhood Working Memory Development Is Probably Not Entirely Based on an Improved Use of Covert Rehearsal as a Mnemonic Strategy

One of the most often investigated bases of developmental changes in working memory has to do with the observation that it is possible to apply different strategies to carry out a particular task. Flavell, Beach, and Chinsky (1966) examined children's memory for lists of easily nameable objects and found developmental increases in the tendency to verbalize items as they were presented. Other work has shown developmental increases in the speed with which items can be named or identified (Case et al., 1982; Hitch, Halliday, & Littler, 1989) or recited (Hulme & Tordoff, 1989), and it is possible that covert verbal rehearsal could underlie improved performance, given that memory maintenance through covert verbal rehearsal has been proposed within standard theories of working memory (e.g., Baddeley & Hitch, 1974; Baddeley, Thomson, & Buchanan, 1975).

Articulation can be suppressed through the repetition of a word during the presentation of items to be remembered or during a retention interval (e.g., Baddeley et al., 1975). Morey and Cowan (2004) found that suppressing articulation had no effect on the memory for nonverbal arrays in adults. Nevertheless, to investigate the role of rehearsal developmentally, Cowan et al. (2011) included three conditions that differed in what participants had to do following the presentation of each successive array item. In one condition, they said nothing; in another, they said "wait" to suppress articulation of the presented item; and in the third condition, they named the color of the object just presented, to encourage covert rehearsal. The results of these conditions differed in the overall level of performance, but the developmental pattern was the same in each condition, and still supported the finding that there was an age difference in the number of items retained from four-item arrays of circles and triangles, but no age difference in the allocation of attention to the more- vs less-often-tested shape. These results suggest that rehearsal cannot account for the capacity findings.

3.5 The Estimated Rate of Childhood Working Memory Development Appears to Depend on the Test Procedure

The procedures discussed in the previous section that show increases in working memory capacity, with some confounding factors controlled, indicate steady increases throughout the elementary school years. Other findings, however, indicate earlier maturity.

Finding a long developmental course with a simple procedure, Cowan, Elliott, et al. (2005, experiment 2) used a simple array-comparison procedure with arrays of colored squares, in which only one color can change between the array and probe displays. That experiment showed developmental growth in children from second to fourth to sixth grades. Riggs, McTaggart, Simpson, and Freeman (2006) found a similar trend, but with younger ages, with improvement between 5, 7, and 10 years of age. The developmental trend was similar in a very different procedure in which lists of spoken digits were unattended at the time of their presentation, with occasional lists attended and recalled following a postlist cue (Cowan, Nugent, Elliott, Ponomarev, & Saults, 1999). In that procedure, the assumption is that capacity limited the amount that could be retrieved from a fading sensory trace into the focus of attention when the postlist cue arrived. Using a wide variety of typical working-memory procedures, Gathercole, Pickering, Ambridge, and Wearing (2004) found steady increases in working memory performance from 4 to 15 years.

Riggs, Simpson, and Potts (2011) examined memory for the orientation alone or both orientation and color of objects in an array. Developmental increases from 7 to 10 years to adulthood were the same for both kinds of test. This result suggests that the ability to remember both features, orientation and color, does not develop later than the ability to remember just one feature per object. It would have been helpful to see memory for color alone, as it is typically easier than either orientation-alone or orientation-plus-color (e.g., Hardman & Cowan, 2015).

Other researchers have suggested that under different test circumstances, capacity can reach maturity considerably earlier than the above results would indicate. Simmering (2012) used a modified array-comparison procedure with colored squares, designed to eliminate interference between trials (Shipstead & Engle, 2013) by presenting alternative trials on the left vs right sides of the field. That procedure produced performance that was not different from a standard array-comparison procedure. In both cases, performance increased between 3 and 7 years and by 7 years reached a mean of about 3.5 items, similar to what is typically found in adults. Unlike the other developmental studies just discussed, though, each color was allowed to occur only once per array (i.e., selection of colors for the array without replacement). This kind of procedure should allow the use of some kind of novelty-detection signal when a new color appears in the comparison array, unlike the usual procedure in which novelty may be absent if a color changes to the same color that already exists elsewhere in the array. Yet, when colors are selected without replacement in adults, the result is about the same, with capacity limited to about three-and-a-half objects (Rouder et al., 2008).

Perhaps, then, there is a developmental increase in how many different objects can be kept active at once, reaching an asymptote of between three and four objects on average by about 7 years of age, but with further developments after that age in the ability to keep in mind separate but identical tokens (e.g., discriminating a difference between a set of four objects that are *red, red, blue,* and *green,* respectively, vs *red, blue, blue,* and *green*). I will return to this possibility of the late development of object individuation after discussing the infant literature.

In a very different procedure, Pailian, Libertus, Feigenson, and Halberda (2016) also suggested developmental change that reached an asymptote by about 7 years. Their measure of capacity was indirect; a flickering array of objects always included one changing object, and it was assumed that the search through the array to find the changing object occurred k objects at a time for an individual with a capacity of k objects. Therefore, the reaction times revealed the capacity. The estimated capacity by 8 years equaled the capacity in adults. This result provides further support for the notion of some basic capacity that is mature early in the elementary school years, but with abilities of object individuation needed only in some tasks and maturing later in childhood.

3.6 Summary of Child Research

The observations on children's development of working memory have fit a consistent pattern. Development is difficult to decipher given that many aspects of development co-occur. I have described a series of experiments in which various possible developmental factors have been highlighted, one at a time: knowledge, attention allocation, encoding efficiency, and the use of covert rehearsal. For each one, I have shown that when the factor is equated across age groups, developmental improvements in working memory remain. These findings are summarized in Table 1 (see also Cowan, 2016, Fig. 1). In the various procedures I have discussed, the number of items held in working memory increases with age between 7 years and adulthood. In each case, this developmental increase in capacity was observed with a reasonable measure of the efficiency of processing (relevant knowledge, attention allocation efficiency, or effects of rehearsal) equated across groups.

Yet, the skills involved in these tasks may involve not only holding a certain number of objects in mind but also distinguishing between those objects and allowing the possibility of multiple identical objects. Under certain circumstances, mature behavior may occur by 7 or 8 years, so further investigation is needed. Hold that thought until we can examine what happens in infancy and how it seems to conflict with the results from children, calling for careful thought about how the results with different procedures from different age groups might be reconciled and integrated.

Table 1 Chunks in Working Memory and Processing Efficiency Measures in Four Experiments

Experiment/Type of Materials	Chunks in Working Memory		Processing Efficiency	
	7–9 Years	College	7–9 Years	College
Gilchrist et al. (2009) Lists of short sentences	2.5 (0.25)	3.1 (0.25)	0.79 (0.02)	0.80 (0.02)
Cowan et al. (2015, 1-s) Arrays of English letters	1.89 (0.22)	4.41 (0.16)	0.68 (0.05)	0.70 (0.01)
Cowan et al. (2010) Arrays of colored shapes	1.50 (0.10)	3.00 (0.13)	0.60 (0.06)	0.58 (0.03)
Cowan et al. (2011) Temporospatial sequences of colored shapes	1.99 (0.13)	3.15 (0.09)	0.58 (0.04)	0.52 (0.02)
			0.57 (0.03)	0.57 (0.01)

Note. Data from four experiments show age differences in the estimated number of chunks in working memory, when processing efficiency has been equalized across ages. The first row of results reflects memory for at least one content word from each simple, spoken sentence indicating access to that sentence within four-sentence lists; the second row, letters in a briefly presented spatial array; the third row, colored objects in a brief spatial array; and the fourth row, colored objects in a slower, spatiotemporal array. The measures of processing efficiency are, in the first row, the proportion of words recalled from accessed sentences for which at least one content word was recalled; in the second row, memory for letters divided by the sum of memory for letters and unfamiliar characters; in the next two rows, memory for the colors of the more-relevant shape divided by that for both shapes together, for four-item arrays in the silent condition; and in the fifth row of numbers, another efficiency measure for Cowan et al. (2011), memory for colors from trials with silence divided by memory for colors from the sum of the silent and speak-an-irrelevant-word conditions.

4. DEVELOPMENT OF WORKING MEMORY CAPACITY IN INFANCY

Research in infancy has profoundly changed the common perception of development in many areas, including the area of working memory. A common view is that many skills that appeared to develop only at some point in childhood, as seen, for example, in Jean Piaget's theory of cognitive development, prove to have beginning forms earlier, at some point in infancy. The research on working memory in infancy seems to fit this rule. A number of studies, taken together, appear to have been interpreted as indicating that infants already acquire the ability to keep about three items in working memory (for review, see Cowan, 2016). This finding is remarkable because it seems to suggest that the infants know more than children early in the elementary school years! I assume that this cannot be the case, and therefore that the theoretical question of interest is which particular differences in the infant vs child working memory task procedures account for the apparent drop in capacity between infancy and childhood.

A few of the infant studies taken together illustrate where the field has gone and how I believe it might be interpreted. Ross-Sheehy, Oakes, and Luck (2003) presented in each trial successive arrays of colored spots on the left and right sides of a screen. During each trial, with each array presentation an item on one side of the screen changed color compared to the last array, whereas there was no change on the other side. The experimental logic exploited babies' general preference for novelty. The expectation was that babies would prefer to look more at the changing side of the array if the changes were noticed, as that side would then provide more novelty than the unchanging side. Ten-month-old infants looked longer at the changing side for four-item arrays, but not for five-item arrays. This would appear to indicate a capacity of four items in infants, as in adults, but the capacity estimate should not be taken at face value; an infant would not have to encode all array items in order to notice some of the changes, so this repeated-presentation procedure cannot provide a capacity estimate. Oakes, Baumgartner, Barrett, Messenger, and Luck (2013) eliminated the repeated-presentation aspect of the procedure and replaced it with a one-shot procedure, but the larger set sizes necessary to estimate a capacity limit were not included in the experiment.

Another procedure that has been used to examine working memory capacity in slightly older infants is one in which items are placed into a box and infants have the opportunity to retrieve items from a box. The best performance has been obtained when the items are all different (Zosh & Feigenson, 2015). Infants 13 months old will search for the first two items and often will search for a third item. If, however, four items are placed in a box, the infants' predominant response is to search for three objects and then stop looking.

On the surface, this response pattern suggests that 13-month-olds often have three items in working memory. Notice, though, that by chance, on most trials the first three objects that the infant retrieves will not be the same as the three objects that are held in working memory. Cowan (2016) noted that this pattern of responding can occur in two ways. The calculations show that if the infants held specific items in mind and withdrew objects from the box until finding matches for the specific items in working memory, then capacity would appear to be about two because holding about two items in mind would result in about three items being drawn on average before those two specific items are found. Alternatively, it is possible that an infant holds about three items in mind, but without comparing specific feature information so that any three items withdrawn from the box would presumably displace the ones in working memory and the infant would be happy with those new three items, inasmuch as working memory is full.

The evidence with this procedure favors the latter hypothesis. Zosh and Feigenson (2012) arranged a switch so that three items hidden in the box (e.g., a cat, a shoe, and a bus) were not the same ones that were there to be retrieved from the box (e.g., a car, a duck, and a brush), yet these changes did not increase the time 18–month–olds spent looking in the box. The switches did make a difference when only one or two items were hidden in the box, so it appears that the feature information was lost (or at least, not usable in the same way) when too many items were added to working memory.

Kibbe and Leslie (2013), on the other hand, suggest that infants are able to keep track of the specific shapes presented at two locations by the age of 9 months and are able to keep track of the shapes presented at three locations by 12 months. This conclusion is based on a task in which two or three simple shapes (triangle, square, or circular disc) are placed behind barriers and then one of these is revealed, with looking time as the dependent measure. Looking time should increase if a switch is noticed and at 12 months of age it was noticed for three simple shapes. Keeping track of the binding between shape and location is difficult even for adults (e.g., Cowan, Blume, & Saults, 2013), so much so that this finding suggests near–adult–like performance by 12 months unless the difference can be attributed to differences between the procedures used in the infant and adult studies. One potential limitation of the Kibbe and Leslie (2013) finding is that infants were always tested on the second of three locations. It is possible that infants allocated most of their attention to that location after the first trial, and therefore did not have to store in mind all three locations in order to notice many of the changes in the second location.

The notion that infants have objects in working memory but do not completely include all of the features of those objects is consistent with several kinds of adult studies. Work by Kahneman, Treisman, and Gibbs (1992) supports the notion of an object file, which is a marker that an item exists whether or not the object is complete with all of the important features. The notion of an object file with only some features bound to it, or with the need for attention to maintain binding, can result in errors of feature binding (e.g., Wheeler & Treisman, 2002), such as forgetting which shape went with which color. At one time, it was believed that adults' working memory representations of objects include all of the objects' physical features, inasmuch as participants could attend to four features of the objects with the same performance level as a preselected one feature of those same objects (Luck & Vogel, 1997). However, several studies have failed to replicate that finding, instead showing that memory of features is somewhat independent (Wang, Cao, Theeuwes, Olivers, & Wang, 2016) or that memory of any one kind of feature from multifeatured objects in an array (e.g., color) comes at the expense of memory for another kind of feature (e.g., shape) (Cowan et al., 2013; Hardman & Cowan, 2015; Oberauer & Eichenberger, 2013).

It would be theoretically possible that infants do not encode all of the features of objects, or that the features are encoded but then not tightly bound to the objects in working memory, so that it would be possible for an infant to be content to retrieve the correct number of objects without caring about the details of the objects. The results of Zosh and Feigenson (2015) favor the latter account. Previous work combined with that of their 2015 paper showed that when the objects are all identical, fewer of them are retrieved than when the objects differ, suggesting that infants process the differences between objects. When the objects retrieved do not match the ones hidden, it is possible that the infants even realize that something has changed, but are not committed to the specific features of the objects hidden when working memory is overwhelmed because their attention has shifted to using the limited available working memory to keep track of the *number* of items retrieved, with not enough capacity left to keep track of *which* objects have been retrieved. Some such account would help to explain why Zosh and Feigenson (2012) found that 18-month-old infants appeared to care about the switch given one or two hidden items but were unconcerned about the switch given three hidden items.

4.1 Summary of Infant Research

The infant studies leave many issues yet to be resolved but on the whole seem consistent with the view that older infants in some basic sense have in mind about three objects, rather like adults, but with the amount of detail in each object increasing with age both within and beyond infancy.

5. RECONCILIATION OF THE INFANT AND CHILD LITERATURES

Let us emphasize at this point some fundamental limitations in developmental research. First, it is clear that many processes change together in development, so it is difficult to identify which changing process is critical to the improvement of any one function at a macroscopic level, such as working memory and how it is used. Second, we lack techniques that can be applied without modification throughout the developmental life span, so it is not easy to track the fate of any particular process. Respecting these limitations, we nevertheless can propose a hypothesis regarding developmental change from infancy through childhood.

The extant data seem consistent with a view in which the number of items in working memory is not the whole story. To be sure, there are studies suggesting an increase with age in the number of items stored in infancy, and an increase with age in the number of items stored in childhood. Regarding the latter, much of the review was dedicated to research indicating that developmental changes in capacity cannot be explained away through the development of concomitant processes such as knowledge or strategies, even though development of those processes undoubtedly also occurs.

There is evidence, though, of developmental increase in the features bound to each object file, or the strength with which that binding takes place. In infancy, 18-month-olds acted as if they cared about the particulars of objects in working memory when one or two items were hidden and had to be stored in working memory, but were not concerned about particulars any more when three objects were hidden and had to be stored in working memory (Zosh & Feigenson, 2012).

Is there further evidence of a similar trend in childhood? In an ongoing study, we (Blume & Cowan, in preparation) have observed a striking difference between the apparent number of object files in working memory, which changes little across the elementary school years, vs the number of preserved objects with at least one informative feature, which changes markedly across the elementary school years. We tested working memory in a situation in which no binding between features was needed because each item had only a single relevant feature. Specifically, we examined children's memory for five-item arrays in which each item was a square of a single color. The array was followed by a single-square probe to be recognized as a color that was present in the array or absent from the array. Location information was not needed because the probe was centrally presented. Memory performance increased steadily as a function of age from about 7 years through adulthood. Probably because of a procedure that had some challenges for the participants (a 500-ms blank period after the array and then a mask presented for 4000 ms), performance increased steadily from only about one item in working memory in 7-year-olds to just under three items in adults. On some trials, moreover, a metamemory response was obtained during the 4000-ms masking period that preceded the memory probe. (Memory performance was only mildly affected by this added metamemory response.) In particular, when the fixation point of the masking array had a "?" symbol, the participant was to indicate how many array colors he or she still had in mind. Amazingly, children of all ages indicated on average about three colors held in mind, despite the fact that this was a dramatic over-estimate in the younger children.

Combining across the infant studies and this metamemory result in children, there may be a constant or relatively constant number of object files that are kept active in working memory, about three; but the ability to bind the informative features to each object file may increase with age in infancy and childhood, making the object files useful for increasingly challenging test situations.

Of course, this hypothesis raises a host of additional questions. Suppose the children had active memory for the colors but these active features (e.g., in the color-feature map of Wheeler & Treisman, 2002) were not bound to the object files. Would not the activation of the features themselves be enough to determine whether the probe was in the array or not? That might be the case on the first trial of the experiment, but across trials there is a buildup of proactive interference; the participant might not be able to tell whether "red" is active from the present trial or from a previous recent trial. It might take limited working memory capacity to overcome this proactive interference and determine whether the object files of the current trial are associated with particular active features in memory. Indeed, it has been proposed that a key function of working memory is to help overcome effects of proactive interference (Cowan, Johnson, & Saults, 2005) and it has been found that array performance is susceptible to proactive interference (Shipstead & Engle, 2013). In fact, when items are drawn from a new, meaningful set on each trial rather than drawn from a repeating set, the typical limit of working memory capacity does not apply (Endress & Potter, 2014).

What I propose, then, is a general developmental course across infancy and childhood in which the number of object files changes little but the

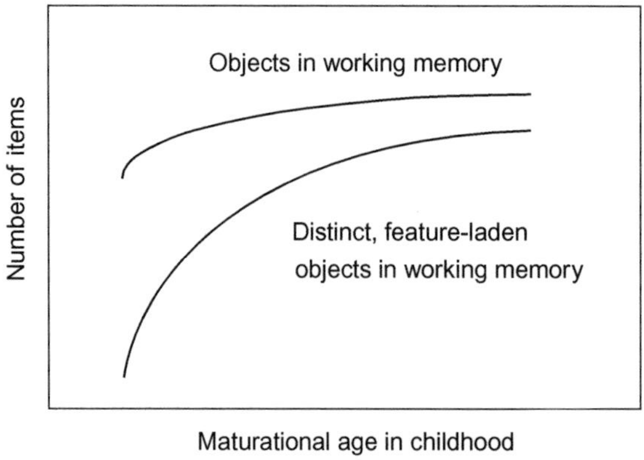

Fig. 2 A schematic diagram of how we might obtain different rates of development for different procedures. The number of objects in working memory (*top line*) might be larger than the number of distinct, feature-laden objects that can be discriminated from one another. In-between curves might also exist, for partly distinguished objects.

informativeness of those object files improves markedly with development. Fig. 2 depicts this developmental principle. In a recent review, Kibbe (2015) has provided more detail about how the featural information associated with each object improves in infancy, and there is as yet considerably less information on the distinction in childhood. Cowan et al. (2010) did find that memory for the simple feature of color developed earlier than the memory for the binding between color and shape or between color and location, but much more detailed information is needed.

If the furnishing or featural filling-in of objects in working memory improves across child development, what will the implications be for young children's experience and behavior? One could speculate based on the present chapter. Consider the young child at this chapter's opening who was upset that an older sibling had two cookies to her one. If the older sibling or adult breaks the child's cookie into two, this doubles the number of cookie–object files and the child may be satisfied because she now has two good things and does not take into consideration, or hold in working memory, the halving of mass within each cookie-object. Neither of the present half-cookies is compared to the original, glorious whole cookie. Yet, this kind of funny error will not prevent important learning by the child because the space in working memory is useful as a vehicle for new ideas. The child can have a working memory slot for the word dog and another for an actual dog, allowing the special moment when the word and animal are together in working memory concurrently and are successfully bound together; the word–referent pair is suddenly learned. Still, limitations in the child's use of working memory for careful comparison may contribute to typical errors like thinking that a horse is also a kind of dog (overextension), or that the word dog only applies to this one dog (undergeneralization). Until working memory matures further, it may be difficult for the child to distinguish a tiger from all three of its conceptual neighbors (striped house cats, stripeless lions, and zebras). Young children may remember and even repeat sequences of several events in a favorite book, but this kind of learning may not apply well to a situation in which several instructions must be followed, with each instruction carefully compared to the current state of affairs. So it is that putting away several toys upon request involves both remembering the instruction to do so and comparing that instruction to the actual room with still-scattered toys.

Regardless of the fate of the current evidence, discrepancies, hypotheses, and speculations, I look forward to a blossoming field in which the difficult problem of the transition between infancy and childhood is directly approached, a field in which there already is some growing interest (e.g., Pailian et al., 2016; Simmering, 2012).

ACKNOWLEDGMENTS

This is a draft of a paper for *Advances in Child Development and Behavior*. This work was completed with support from NIH Grant R01-HD21338. I thank Lisa Feigenson for helpful discussions.

REFERENCES

Baddeley, A. D., & Hitch, G. (1974). Working memory. In G. H. Bower (Ed.), *The psychology of learning and motivation: 8* (pp. 47–89). New York: Academic Press.

Baddeley, A. D., Thomson, N., & Buchanan, M. (1975). Word length and the structure of short term memory. *Journal of Verbal Learning and Verbal Behavior, 14*, 575–589.

Blume, C. L., & Cowan, N. (in preparation). The development of knowledge of the contents of working memory.

Case, R., Kurland, D. M., & Goldberg, J. (1982). Operational efficiency and the growth of short term memory span. *Journal of Experimental Child Psychology, 33*, 386–404.

Chi, M. T. H. (1978). Knowledge structures and memory development. In R. Siegler (Ed.), *Children's thinking: What develops?* Hillsdale, NJ: Erlbaum.

Cowan, N. (2001). The magical number 4 in short-term memory: A reconsideration of mental storage capacity. *Behavioral and Brain Sciences, 24*, 87–185.

Cowan, N. (2016). Working memory maturation: Can we get at the essence of cognitive growth? *Perspectives on Psychological Science, 11*, 239–264.

Cowan, N., AuBuchon, A. M., Gilchrist, A. L., Ricker, T. J., & Saults, J. S. (2011). Age differences in visual working memory capacity: Not based on encoding limitations. *Developmental Science, 14*, 1066–1074.

Cowan, N., Blume, C. L., & Saults, J. S. (2013). Attention to attributes and objects in working memory. *Journal of Experimental Psychology. Learning, Memory, and Cognition, 39,* 731–747.

Cowan, N., Elliott, E. M., Saults, J. S., Morey, C. C., Mattox, S., Hismjatullina, A., et al. (2005). On the capacity of attention: Its estimation and its role in working memory and cognitive aptitudes. *Cognitive Psychology, 51,* 42–100.

Cowan, N., Johnson, T. D., & Saults, J. S. (2005). Capacity limits in list item recognition: Evidence from proactive interference. *Memory, 13,* 293–299.

Cowan, N., Morey, C. C., AuBuchon, A. M., Zwilling, C. E., & Gilchrist, A. L. (2010). Seven-year-olds allocate attention like adults unless working memory is overloaded. *Developmental Science, 13,* 120–133.

Cowan, N., Nugent, L. D., Elliott, E. M., Ponomarev, I., & Saults, J. S. (1999). The role of attention in the development of short-term memory: Age differences in the verbal span of apprehension. *Child Development, 70,* 1082–1097.

Cowan, N., Ricker, T. J., Clark, K. M., Hinrichs, G. A., & Glass, B. A. (2015). Knowledge cannot explain the developmental growth of working memory capacity. *Developmental Science, 18,* 132–145.

Cowan, N., Wood, N. L., Wood, P. K., Keller, T. A., Nugent, L. D., & Keller, C. V. (1998). Two separate verbal processing rates contributing to short-term memory span. *Journal of Experimental Psychology. General, 127,* 141–160.

Cusack, R., Lehmann, M., Veldsman, M., & Mitchell, D. J. (2009). Encoding strategy and not visual working memory capacity correlates with intelligence. *Psychonomic Bulletin & Review, 16,* 641–647.

Daneman, M., & Carpenter, P. A. (1980). Individual differences in working memory and reading. *Journal of Verbal Learning & Verbal Behavior, 19,* 450–466.

Endress, A. D., & Potter, M. C. (2014). Large capacity temporary visual memory. *Journal of Experimental Psychology. General, 143,* 548–566.

Flavell, J. H., Beach, D. H., & Chinsky, J. M. (1966). Spontaneous verbal rehearsal in a memory task as a function of age. *Child Development, 37,* 283–299.

Fougnie, D., Cormiea, S. M., Kanabar, A., & Alvarez, G. A. (2016). Strategic trade-offs between quantity and quality in working memory. *Journal of Experimental Psychology. Human Perception and Performance, 42*(8), 1231–1240. http://dx.doi.org/10.1037/xhp0000211.

Gaillard, V., Barrouillet, P., Jarrold, C., & Camos, V. (2011). Developmental differences in working memory: Where do they come from? *Journal of Experimental Child Psychology, 110,* 469–479.

Gathercole, S. E., Pickering, S. J., Ambridge, B., & Wearing, H. (2004). The structure of working memory from 4 to 15 years of age. *Developmental Psychology, 40,* 177–190.

Gilchrist, A. L., Cowan, N., & Naveh-Benjamin, M. (2009). Investigating the childhood development of working memory using sentences: New evidence for the growth of chunk capacity. *Journal of Experimental Child Psychology, 104,* 252–265.

Gold, J. M., Fuller, R. L., Robinson, B. M., McMahon, R. P., Braun, E. L., & Luck, S. J. (2006). Intact attentional control of working memory encoding in schizophrenia. *Journal of Abnormal Psychology, 115,* 658–673.

Halford, G. S., Cowan, N., & Andrews, G. (2007). Separating cognitive capacity from knowledge: A new hypothesis. *Trends in Cognitive Sciences, 11,* 236–242.

Hardman, K., & Cowan, N. (2015). Remembering complex objects in visual working memory: Do capacity limits restrict objects or features? *Journal of Experimental Psychology. Learning, Memory, and Cognition, 41,* 325–347.

Hitch, G. J., Halliday, M. S., & Littler, J. E. (1989). Item identification time and rehearsal rate as predictors of memory span in children. *The Quarterly Journal of Experimental Psychology, 41A,* 321–337.

Hulme, C., & Tordoff, V. (1989). Working memory development: The effects of speech rate, word length, and acoustic similarity on serial recall. *Journal of Experimental Child Psychology, 47,* 72–87.

Kahneman, D., Treisman, A., & Gibbs, B. J. (1992). The reviewing of object files: Object specific integration of information. *Cognitive Psychology, 24,* 175–219.

Kail, R., & Salthouse, T. A. (1994). Processing speed as a mental capacity. *Acta Psychologica, 86,* 199–255.

Kane, M. J., Bleckley, M. K., Conway, A. R. A., & Engle, R. W. (2001). A controlled-attention view of working-memory capacity. *Journal of Experimental Psychology. General, 130,* 169–183.

Kibbe, M. M. (2015). Varieties of visual working memory representation in infancy and beyond. *Current Directions in Psychological Science, 24,* 433–439.

Kibbe, M. M., & Leslie, A. M. (2013). What's the object of object working memory in infancy? Unraveling 'what' and 'how many'. *Cognitive Psychology, 66,* 380–404.

Luck, S. J., & Vogel, E. K. (1997). The capacity of visual working memory for features and conjunctions. *Nature, 390,* 279–281.

Ma, W. J., Husain, M., & Bays, P. M. (2014). Changing concepts of working memory. *Nature Neuroscience, 17,* 347–356.

Mall, J. T., Morey, C. C., Wolf, M. J., & Lehnert, F. (2014). Visual selective attention is equally functional for individuals with low and high working memory capacity: Evidence from accuracy and eye movements. *Attention, Perception, & Psychophysics, 76,* 1998–2014.

Miller, G. A. (1956). The magical number seven, plus or minus two: Some limits on our capacity for processing information. *Psychological Review, 63,* 81–97.

Miller, G. A., Galanter, E., & Pribram, K. H. (1960). *Plans and the structure of behavior.* New York: Holt, Rinehart and Winston, Inc.

Morey, C. C., & Cowan, N. (2004). When visual and verbal memories compete: Evidence of cross-domain limits in working memory. *Psychonomic Bulletin & Review, 11,* 296–301.

Oakes, L. M., Baumgartner, H. A., Barrett, F. S., Messenger, I. M., & Luck, S. J. (2013). Developmental changes in visual short-term memory in infancy: Evidence from eye-tracking. *Frontiers in Psychology, 4,* 1–13.

Oberauer, K., & Eichenberger, S. (2013). Visual working memory declines when more features must be remembered for each object. *Memory & Cognition, 41,* 1212–1227.

Pailian, H., Libertus, M., Feigenson, L., & Halberda, J. (2016). Visual working memory capacity increases between ages 3 and 8 years, controlling for gains in attention, perception, and executive control. *Attention, Perception and Psychophysics, 78,* 1556–1573.

Pashler, H. (1988). Familiarity and visual change detection. *Perception & Psychophysics, 44,* 369–378.

Riggs, K. J., McTaggart, J., Simpson, A., & Freeman, R. P. J. (2006). Changes in the capacity of visual working memory in 5- to 10-year-olds. *Journal of Experimental Child Psychology, 95,* 18–26.

Riggs, K. J., Simpson, A., & Potts, T. (2011). The development of visual short-term memory for multifeature items during middle childhood. *Journal of Experimental Child Psychology, 108,* 802–809.

Ross-Sheehy, S., Oakes, L. M., & Luck, S. J. (2003). The development of visual short-term memory capacity in infants. *Child Development, 74,* 1807–1822.

Rouder, J. N., Morey, R. D., Cowan, N., Zwilling, C. E., Morey, C. C., & Pratte, M. S. (2008). An assessment of fixed-capacity models of visual working memory. *Proceedings of the National Academy of Sciences (PNAS), 105,* 5975–5979.

Rouder, J. N., Morey, R. D., Morey, C. C., & Cowan, N. (2011). How to measure working-memory capacity in the change-detection paradigm. *Psychonomic Bulletin & Review, 18,* 324–330.

Shipstead, Z., & Engle, R. W. (2013). Interference within the focus of attention: Working memory tasks reflect more than temporary maintenance. *Journal of Experimental Psychology. Learning, Memory, and Cognition, 39*, 277–289.

Simmering, V. R. (2012). The development of visual working memory capacity during early childhood. *Journal of Experimental Child Psychology, 111*(4), 695–707.

Stoltzfus, E. R., Hasher, L., & Zacks, R. T. (1996). Working memory and retrieval: An inhibition resource approach. In J. T. E. Richardson, R. W. Engle, L. Hasher, R. H. Logie, E. R. Stoltzfus, & R. T. Zacks (Eds.), *Working memory and human cognition* (pp. 66–88). New York: Oxford University Press.

Vogel, E. K., McCollough, A. W., & Machizawa, M. G. (2005). Neural measures reveal individual differences in controlling access to working memory. *Nature, 438*, 500–503.

Vogel, E. K., Woodman, G. F., & Luck, S. J. (2006). The time course of consolidation in visual working memory. *Journal of Experimental Psychology. Human Perception and Performance, 32*, 1436–1451.

Wang, B., Cao, X., Theeuwes, J., Olivers, C. N. L., & Wang, Z. (2016). Separate capacities for storing different features in visual working memory. *Journal of Experimental Psychology. Learning, Memory, and Cognition.* Epub ahead of print. http://dx.doi.org/10.1037/xlm0000295.

Wheeler, M. E., & Treisman, A. M. (2002). Binding in short term visual memory. *Journal of Experimental Psychology. General, 131*, 48–64.

Zosh, J. M., & Feigenson, L. (2012). Memory load affects object individuation in 18-month-old infants. *Journal of Experimental Child Psychology, 113*, 322–336.

Zosh, J. M., & Feigenson, L. (2015). Array heterogeneity prevents catastrophic forgetting in infants. *Cognition, 136*, 365–380.

CHAPTER FOUR

Why Neighborhoods (and How We Study Them) Matter for Adolescent Development

T.D. Warner*,1, R.A. Settersten Jr.†,1

*University of Nebraska-Lincoln, Lincoln, NE, United States
†Hallie E. Ford Center for Healthy Children & Families, College of Public Health & Human Sciences, Oregon State University, Corvallis, OR, United States
1Corresponding authors: e-mail address: twarner2@unl.edu; richard.settersten@oregonstate.edu

Contents

Abstract

Adolescence is a sensitive developmental period marked by significant changes that unfold across multiple contexts. As a central context of development, neighborhoods capture—in both physical and social space—the stratification of life chances and differential distribution of resources and risks. For some youth, neighborhoods are springboards to opportunities; for others, they are snares that constrain progress and limit the ability to avoid risks. Despite abundant research on "neighborhood effects," scant attention has been paid to how neighborhoods are a product of social stratification forces that operate simultaneously to affect human development. Neighborhoods in the United States are the manifestation of three intersecting social structural cleavages: race/ethnicity, socioeconomic class, and geography. Many opportunities are allocated or denied along these three cleavages. To capture these joint processes, we advocate a "neighborhood-centered" approach to study the effects of neighborhoods on adolescent development. Using nationally representative data from the National Longitudinal Study of Adolescent to Adult Health (Add Health), we demonstrate the complex ways that these three cleavages shape specific neighborhood contexts and can result in stark differences in well-being. A neighborhood-centered approach demands more rigorous and sensitive theories of place, as well as multidimensional classification and measures. We discuss an agenda to advance the state of theories and research, drawing explicit attention to the stratifying forces that bring about distinct neighborhood types that shape developmental trajectories during adolescence and beyond.

1. INTRODUCTION

Neighborhoods are central social settings for organizing and experiencing human life. In this chapter, we focus on youth, whose lives are constrained by the housing and neighborhood choices of their parents and are more geographically bound than adults. The growing need for autonomy during adolescence increases the amount of time adolescents spend outside of their home, typically with peers, and often in neighborhoods that provide the physical and social space within which much interaction occurs (Leventhal, Dupéré, & Brooks-Gunn, 2009). Extensive scholarship has linked neighborhood contexts—particularly their socioeconomic characteristics—to various domains of youth development and well-being: violence and delinquency, substance use, sexual activity, child-bearing, high school drop-out, educational attainment, employment, and physical and mental health (e.g., Dupéré, Leventhal, Crosnoe, & Dion, 2010; Leventhal et al., 2009; McBride Murry, Berkel, Gaylord-Harden, Copeland-Linder, & Nation, 2011).

Inequalities are readily observed in the physical properties of neighborhoods that reflect and reinforce the existing stratification of social groups whose members have differential access to resources, power, status, and prestige (McLeod, 2013; Squires & Kubrin, 2005; Sundstrom, 2003, p. 84).

Thus, the processes that occur in these settings generate—and are sometimes meant to compensate for—problems of social stratification. That is, the social and economic characteristics of youth and their families result in a set of risks and resources that can stem from or interact with their neighborhood environments. Youth and their families are changing over time, but so too are the neighborhoods in which they are located, creating a kind of "dynamism" of shifting opportunities and constraints. Neighborhoods are a primary setting within which life course transitions occur and life trajectories are situated.

US neighborhoods, our focus, are largely shaped by the intersection of three key structural "cleavages": race/ethnicity, social class, and geography.[a] Neighborhoods are where these cleavages are most visibly "etched in place" (Sampson, 2012, p. 19), resulting in complex neighborhood "types" defined by "profiles" of characteristics, such as those implied by the terms "distressed," "privileged," or "bad" neighborhoods (Leicht & Jenkins, 2007). Yet, traditional "neighborhood effects" research has generally focused on single items (e.g., percent Black) or indices (e.g., of concentrated disadvantage) related to the demographic and/or economic composition of neighborhoods.

Although this work has been instrumental in identifying some of the place-based characteristics that influence development, such a "variable-centered" (Weden, Bird, Escarce, & Lurie, 2011) approach treats the structural cleavages superficially and as if they are independent, thereby ignoring their intersections (Choo & Ferree, 2010) and neglecting how they are complex latent aspects of social structure (Diez Roux & Mair, 2010; Ferraro, Shippee, & Schafer, 2009). These three structural cleavages, independently and jointly, are already powerfully associated with individuals' life chances (McLeod, 2013), reflecting larger social forces such as discrimination, segregation, stratification, and inequality—processes that systematically put certain social groups at an economic or social disadvantage (Braveman, 2014). This is consistent with an "intersectionality" perspective, which underscores the need to probe the meaning and consequences of multiple categories of difference and disadvantage (McCall, 2005), divisions that are often enmeshed and not reducible to each other (Yuval-Davis, 2006).

---

[a] Although the most widely recognized means of stratification in the United States are social class, race/ethnicity, and gender (McLeod, 2013), physical/geographical space is less significantly structured by gender. Geography is also a factor in its own right (e.g., urban/rural), independent of social class and race/ethnicity. Together, these three factors heavily determine space-based risks, resources, and opportunities.

In this chapter, we aim to advance theories and measures of neighborhoods as a key developmental context, particularly for youth, via three primary goals. First, we briefly establish adolescence as a key developmental period that unfolds across multiple contexts, with neighborhoods being a focal context. We then provide an overview of the state of research on neighborhood effects and describe the advantages of bridging current approaches with more macrosociological stratification theories in order to illuminate the three structural cleavages noted earlier and to generate an integrated perspective.

Second, we outline how a "neighborhood-centered" approach offers an alternative and effective means for studying the effects of neighborhoods on adolescent development and trajectories into adulthood. This approach permits the simultaneous consideration of multiple forms of inequality and a relational, comparative investigation of neighborhoods.

Third, to demonstrate the power of a neighborhood-centered approach, we draw on data from the National Longitudinal Study of Adolescent to Adult Health (Add Health) to examine how trajectories of violent victimization during adolescence and into young adulthood differ across neighborhood types, and how neighborhoods shape victimization behaviors directly and indirectly.

2. ADOLESCENT DEVELOPMENT AND THE LIFE COURSE: AN ORIENTING NOTE

Adolescence is a sensitive developmental period marked by significant biological, physiological, psychological, and social changes. It is characterized by increasing independence from parents and family, salience of friendships and peer groups, exploration of identity, and experimentation with a wide range of behaviors, some of which can be risky (e.g., Smetana, Campione-Barr, & Metzger, 2006). Scholarship on adolescent development has been consistently attuned to matters of risk and resilience that accompany this period and to the early causes and later consequences of youth outcomes.

The evolution of the life course perspective in recent decades has been particularly influential in generating sensitivity to how individual lives unfold over time and within personal and social environments (for an overview, see Elder, Shanahan, & Jennings, 2015; Kohli, 2007; Mayer, 2004). It has especially turned attention to how social structure and historical time impinge on human lives, and how individuals orient themselves to the opportunities and constraints they face, expressing their "agency" within the confines of "structure" (Settersten & Gannon, 2005). In emphasizing the embeddedness of developmental experiences in time and place, the life course perspective resonates with developmental perspectives such as Bronfenbrenner's (1979) social ecological theory and relational developmental systems theories (e.g., Lerner, Lerner, & Benson, 2011), all of which underscore the fact that individual development is nested within multiple, mutually reinforcing, and transactional contexts.

Although neighborhoods have been acknowledged in both developmental and life course scholarship, they warrant much greater attention, as they are far more than background factors or simple stages on which lives unfold (Sampson, 1993). To that end, we first discuss the emergence of "neighborhood effects" research, tracing it to where it is today and advocating for methods that enhance and extend existing research.

3. THE NEIGHBORHOOD CONTEXT OF ADOLESCENCE: HOW NEIGHBORHOODS *WORK*

3.1 A Brief History of Sociological Scholarship on Neighborhood Effects

Serious attention to persons *in* places—and to the influence of place *on* human development—can be traced to the early contextual thinkers of the Chicago School (particularly, Burgess, 1925; Park, 1936; Wirth, 1945). These scholars were concerned with understanding everyday human life in relation to the social world, and they used human ecology as the guiding framework for identifying the social forces that organize persons and institutions in a given social space (Gross, 2004). In one of the earliest uses of the term "human ecology" in sociology, McKenzie (1924, p. 288) defined it as "a study of the spatial and temporal relations of human beings as affected by the selective, distributive, and accommodative forces of the environment... [it] is fundamentally interested in the effect of *position...*" (emphasis added), as place involves both geographic location and social station (Sundstrom, 2003, p. 84).

The Chicago School also recognized that individuals cannot be separated from the social structures and geographical locations of which they are part (Snell, 2010, p. 59). The clustering of social problems in a neighborhood or area was therefore interpreted as a sign of *concentrated* social disorganization. Several consistent risk factors emerged as common characteristics of urban neighborhoods plagued with high rates of various social problems, particularly crime and deviance: population size and density, racial/ethnic heterogeneity, socioeconomic status (SES), residential mobility, mixed land use, and dilapidation. The revelation was that social problems are not randomly distributed.

Among the early research linking place and risk specifically for youth was Shaw and McKay's (1942) study of juvenile delinquency rates in Chicago between 1927 and 1933. Much of the research on neighborhood effects in sociology and criminology owes its origins to this work. After observing the persistence of high juvenile delinquency rates in certain neighborhoods over time, Shaw and McKay (1942) concluded that neighborhood juvenile delinquency rates were caused by some properties of the neighborhood as a whole, not simply by the characteristics of individual residents. For both Blacks and Whites, juvenile delinquency rates declined with growing distance from the city center. One core explanation related to the invasion of industry into particular central city neighborhoods, which made these areas less desirable for residents and led to decreasing population as economically able residents migrated out. The loss of population undermined social order and social organization, thus leaving the neighborhood vulnerable to disorder and deviance. In what came to be known as the *theory of social disorganization*, Shaw and McKay argued that low SES, racial/ethnic heterogeneity, and residential mobility undermined social organization—and were the gateway to delinquent subcultures and behaviors.

3.2 A Shift to Processes and Mechanisms

The research of the Chicago School prompted a shift away from individual-based theorizing to place-based theorizing about social problems and other indicators of life chances, health, and well-being. Social disorganization theory has since been expanded by many scholars (e.g., Bursik, 1988; Sampson & Groves, 1989; Sampson, Morenoff, & Gannon-Rowley, 2002) and is now largely understood as capturing the inability of a community to realize the common values of its residents and maintain effective social control (Sampson & Groves, 1989). The urban ecologists of the Chicago School provided a critical foundation for current research in which neighborhoods are hypothesized to affect individual and group outcomes through positive and negative social mechanisms. Positive mechanisms include social capital, control, solidarity, cohesion, networks, resources, and a commitment to the "common good." Negative mechanisms include social disorder, isolation, and resource and opportunity deprivation.

Three additional theoretical developments since the Chicago School have been instrumental in advancing neighborhood effects research to its current state. These are exemplified in the work of William J. Wilson, Christopher Jencks and Susan Mayer, and Robert Sampson and his colleagues, respectively. First, Wilson's (1987) *The Truly Disadvantaged* has informed much research on how neighborhoods affect children, youth, and families—especially in identifying the concentration of poverty in urban areas as a major culprit and linking it to the outmigration of middle-income residents from mixed-income inner-city neighborhoods and the loss of manufacturing jobs in those areas. Remaining residents became trapped in highly impoverished neighborhoods with few or no opportunities or resources.

Second, Jencks and Mayer (1990) identified some of the processes through which neighborhoods are expected to exert their influence on residents, particularly children and adolescents. This research created a foundation for understanding how neighborhoods "work." Structural characteristics (e.g., neighborhood SES, racial/ethnic heterogeneity, residential mobility) influence development via processes captured in distinct models: collective socialization, institutional, social comparison, and epidemic/contagion.

Collective socialization or *social interaction models* focus on the presence (or absence) of prosocial adult role models for children—for instance, the protective effect of "old heads" who provide informal social control in the community (Anderson, 2013), or of parents' social networks and/or ties to children's friends and families that are critical for monitoring and supervising children (Coulton & Spilsbury, 2014). *Institutional models* emphasize both the quality and regulatory capacity of social institutions, such as schools and law enforcement agencies. They also capture how processes of economic and racial segregation deprive certain neighborhoods of resources needed for schools, child care centers, youth development programs, parks and recreational centers, medical care, social services, and other child-serving institutions (Coulton & Spilsbury, 2014). *Social comparison* models emphasize the detrimental consequences of (perceptions of) deprivation or competition relative to others, including more affluent neighbors, which may lead to subcultural adaptations and conflict (as observed in Anderson's (1999) account of inner city youth).

Epidemic/contagion models highlight the power of peers—youths' immediate friends and more distant age-mates—in the transmission of norms through networks and communities. Social isolation and neighborhood disorganization create a context within which certain norms and behaviors that counter those shared by the majority of residents develop and crystallize, creating a subculture that threatens social order (Anderson, 1999). The notion that disadvantaged neighborhoods foster problem behaviors by exposing youth to a greater number of peers who are engaged in and provide opportunities for problem behaviors is nicely illustrated in Osgood and Anderson's (2004) application of routine activities theory. They showed that adolescents who were exposed to environments where youth spent a majority of time engaged in unstructured socializing (away from shared parental and community monitoring) had more, and more significant, problem behaviors. Similarly, bridging the logic of institutional and epidemic models, Thomas and Shihadeh (2013) found that areas where youth were institutionally disengaged—not in school, the labor force, or the military—had higher crime rates because these idle youth (compared to those who were institutionally engaged) were freer to drift into deviance since they lacked the social bonds needed to keep them from acting on deviant opportunities or impulses.

Third, the work of Sampson and colleagues has explicitly targeted the capacity of adults to regulate the behaviors of children and youth in their community. Sampson's theorizing emphasizes the role of neighborhood organization in facilitating (or inhibiting) the development of social capital, control, and cohesion. Sampson, Raudenbush, and Earls (1997) further refined this by advancing the concept of "collective efficacy," which is comprised of cohesion among residents, social control of public space, and willingness to intervene for the common good. Thus, the role of the neighborhood transcends particular interpersonal ties because it reflects a larger *shared* commitment among residents. Accordingly, neighborhood characteristics, particularly neighborhood poverty, can be linked to neighborhood-level social problems because poverty undermines collective efficacy; that is, poverty undermines the *regulatory capabilities* of residents.

3.3 The Indirect Effects of Neighborhoods: The Role of Other Contexts

In addition to the direct effects of neighborhoods on development, neighborhoods also have indirect effects that operate through and/or interact with other key contexts (Cook, Herman, Phillips, & Settersten, 2002; Leventhal et al., 2009). In fact, the long-term consequences of community context may be largely indirect (Wickrama & Noh, 2010). Particularly relevant for adolescents are neighborhood effects on family, school, and peer domains. For instance, stress process research finds that neighborhood disadvantage leads to parents' physical, psychological, and emotional distress, which contributes to parental hostility, harsh parenting, and compromised parent–child relationships (Leventhal et al., 2009). Conflicting results exist regarding the effect of neighborhood context on parental monitoring, with some studies showing that disadvantage undermines monitoring, while others show that it increases monitoring (see Antonishak & Reppucci, 2008). Neighborhoods also shape and structure the types of peers to whom young people are exposed (Haynie, 2001). Youth who grow up in disadvantaged neighborhoods are more likely to be exposed to deviant peers, which increases their risk of engaging in risky behaviors themselves (Cantillon, 2006), particularly in neighborhoods with few opportunities for prosocial activity (Osgood & Anderson, 2004).

4. THE NEIGHBORHOOD CONTEXT OF ADOLESCENCE: HOW NEIGHBORHOODS *LOOK*

4.1 Shifting Back Upstream

Current research on neighborhoods as contexts of development remains largely grounded in a social disorganization framework and on the concepts, models, and mechanisms described previously. Although significant advancements have been made by researchers in these directions, one perhaps unintended result of this "social process turn" (Browning, Cagney, & Boettner, 2016) is the movement of neighborhoods research "downstream," away from the "upstream" macrolevel factors that shape neighborhoods in the first place (Berkman, Glass, Brissette, & Seeman, 2000). This hinders thinking about the extent to which neighborhoods represent different "ecological niches" or developmental contexts with respect to the distribution of risks and resources (Shinn & Toohey, 2003; Wilson, 1987), and any subsequent implications for development in adolescence or across the life course. That is, when we are attuned primarily to neighborhood processes (e.g., the "black box" of neighborhood effects), we are less able to conceptualize and capture neighborhoods as indicative of individuals' social location and position in the opportunity structure—as markers of intersecting social divisions. This also limits the ability to make comparisons *across* neighborhood types.

Concerns about the patterns and consequences of inequalities among social groups have dominated current research on the life course and stratification (e.g., Massey & Denton, 1993; O'Rand, 2001; Wilson, 1987). Yet, research tends to examine the effects of neighborhoods independent from the residential sorting or segregation processes that perpetuate significantly different neighborhood contexts for individuals according to their racial/ethnic and class group membership (Osypuk, 2013), as well as the actual geographic location of these neighborhoods.

Although individuals act independently, the possibilities they face and the decisions they make are constrained by their social positions (Merton, 1996) and their associated limitations, whether those are actual or perceived (Galster & Killen, 1995). With respect to neighborhoods specifically, individual choices and preferences are conditioned by opportunities and constraints—those of individuals, those of the market, and those that stem from larger social forces and policies (e.g., zoning and other land use practices; federal, state, and local housing policies; exclusionary housing ordinances; subsidized suburban development; discrimination, perceived/experienced harassment). All of these are driven by or based on the three social cleavages described earlier: race/ethnicity, social class, and geography (Osypuk, 2013; Squires & Kubrin, 2005, p. 48). As such, the "choice" to reside in a given neighborhood reflects a decision made, not among the whole set of neighborhoods, but among a limited number of relatively similar neighborhoods defined by one's opportunities and resources. We now briefly review the historical context of racial/ethnic and socioeconomic residential segregation and inequality in the United States. This is crucial to understand because the question of "who goes where and why" is linked to how places come to be.

4.2 Neighborhood Patterning: Social Cleavages and the Stratification of Life Chances

Just as the Chicago School scholars observed that social problems are not randomly distributed across the city—but rather clustered in certain types of places—types of places themselves are not randomly distributed. The clustering of types of places is particularly characteristic of the United States. The physical separation of socially defined groups is inherently geographical (Massey, Rothwell, & Domina, 2009, p. 74). Indeed, geography itself is a marker of stratification and inequality (Lobao, 2004), although it remains frequently absent from studies of race/ethnicity and class. Neighborhoods reflect how groups are sorted and sifted according to their political and economic resources—that is, neighborhoods both define, and are defined by, persons' life chances (Fitzpatrick & LaGory, 2003). Individuals are differentially sorted into particular types of contexts (and not into others); contexts socialize individuals, who themselves modify their behavior in response to their environment (Mayer, 2004). Consequently, the concern with distinguishing the "unmeasured" characteristics that might lead individuals to "choose" certain neighborhoods (and thus may render a contextual effect "artifactual") stands in contrast with the argument that selection is not a statistical nuisance but is rather an important social process that requires explicit investigation (McLeod & Pavalko, 2008; Sampson & Sharkey, 2008).

4.2.1 Racial/Ethnic Stratification and Segregation

Race is a fundamental cleavage in the United States (Massey & Sampson, 2009) and a dominant organizational principle of housing and residential patterns (Massey & Denton, 1993). As a result, different racial/ethnic groups are exposed to vastly different spatial contexts, with varying degrees of risks and resources (Osypuk, 2013). Explanations for racial segregation generally revolve around three issues: (1) economic differences (e.g., class segregation, income differences); (2) preferences and prejudices of individuals and families (e.g., White avoidance of Black neighborhoods, racial differences in housing preferences); and (3) institutional discrimination (e.g., housing market discrimination; Quillian, 2002). For instance, segregation may result because groups with greater economic resources are able to translate those resources into better residential outcomes (i.e., access more desirable communities), while disadvantaged groups, lacking those same resources, are sorted into less desirable housing in separate neighborhoods.[b]

In terms of racial preferences, advantaged groups strive to put spatial distance between themselves and less-advantaged groups (South & Crowder, 1998). Studies confirm the desire among Whites for neighborhoods that are predominantly White, and the desire among Blacks for neighborhoods that have at least some presence of other Blacks (Quillian, 2002). Similarly, racial and ethnic biases may underlie institutional practices and barriers in housing markets. Although formal means of discrimination have been largely outlawed—as part of the Fair Housing Act—there is evidence that informal discriminatory practices remain (Yinger, 1995) and that fair housing enforcement is sporadic.[c]

---

[b] There is a great deal of debate about economic explanations of residential segregation, especially as they pertain to Black–White differences. Some evidence suggests that middle- and high-income Blacks live in neighborhoods not much more racially integrated than low-income Blacks (Quillian, 2002), while other recent research suggests that the segregation of middle-class Blacks has been decreasing (e.g., Iceland, Sharpe, & Steinmetz, 2005).

[c] Though much of the literature has focused on Black–White segregation, segregation between Blacks, Whites, Hispanics, or other racial/ethnic minorities is also important to consider, given the growing Hispanic population and the trend among both Hispanic and Asian households to live in suburban areas (Iceland & Nelson, 2008).

Racial discrimination (toward both individuals and neighborhoods) in lending practices has been singled out as having played a pivotal role in the subprime boom, housing market collapse, and financial crisis of the mid-2000s (Burd-Sharps & Rasch, 2015; Squires, Hyra, & Renner, 2009). As a consequence of the Great Recession, the racial wealth gap has widened, as White households have been rebounding but Black households have been struggling to recover. The foreclosure crisis had implications for communities too, as homeowners deferred maintenance on their homes and houses became vacant. These problems in turn contributed to declining property values and physical deterioration; to crime, social disorder, and population turnover; and to local government fiscal stress and the deterioration of services (Kingsley, Smith, & Price, 2009). Most notably, the fallout from the housing crisis occurred differentially across neighborhoods, affecting predominantly minority and low-SES neighborhoods most profoundly.

4.2.2 Class Stratification and Segregation

Prior to the 1970s, inequality was largely structured along race/ethnicity; thereafter, it became increasingly structured along social class lines—meaning that poor- and working-class Whites, as well as minorities, were (and are) confronted with similar social problems (Massey & Sampson, 2009). Indeed, neighborhood segregation is one of the most significant factors in raising consciousness of social class and class stratification (Giddens, 1980). Social stratification shapes land use (i.e., zoning), and land values are influential for which groups choose (or are chosen) to go where they do (Gans, 2002). Migration of residents away from moderately poor neighborhoods has been a key factor in the formation of high-poverty neighborhoods (Quillian, 1999), particularly in urban areas (Wilson, 1987). Historically, studies have shown the effect of race to be larger than that of class in driving migration and, accordingly, the bulk of segregation research focuses on racial segregation, not class segregation. Recent studies, however, have revealed that the effect of class is increasing (Massey & Sampson, 2009), and that segregation by class (particularly income) has risen sharply (Reardon, Fox, & Townsend, 2015).

Class stratification and segregation are persistent and upward socioeconomic mobility is differentially attainable. Recent work by Sharkey (2008), for example, illustrates the intergenerational influence of residential segregation by class. Children who grow up in poor neighborhoods are at a grave risk of living in poor neighborhoods as adults, and in turn pass that disadvantage onto their own children. Class segregation is particularly consequential for youth, since income segregation contributes to disparities in youth-serving resources, such as schools, parks, libraries, and recreation spaces (Bischoff & Reardon, 2014). Thus, *schools* are critical in the transmission process because the highest quality schools and best-prepared students are concentrated in resource-rich areas, while the lowest quality schools and worst-prepared students are concentrated in areas that are resource scarce, exacerbating class inequalities (Massey, 1996). Schools have traditionally been funded locally—by property taxes—further disadvantaging poorer communities, and although school finance reform addressed some of these challenges, notable disparities remain in school spending, educational opportunities, and outcomes (Rice, 2004). Continuing the example of educational attainment, class segregation can affect youth well-being and inequality in two distinct ways (Bischoff & Reardon, 2014). First, youth who grow up in poor neighborhoods may have fewer high-achieving adult role models. Second, high-income communities are better able to attract high-skilled teachers, leading to unequal school resources and inequalities in school success across neighborhoods.

Federal housing programs (e.g., Section 8) were designed to free families from public housing and therefore help poor families leave impoverished neighborhoods for more integrated ones. However, many voucher holders remain concentrated in poor segregated neighborhoods due to limited housing options, landlord practices/preferences, and aspects of the voucher program itself (e.g., time limits for locating housing; DeLuca, Garboden, & Rosenblatt, 2013). Further, the growth in income inequality in recent decades has largely been driven by "upper-tail inequality" (Reardon & Bischoff, 2011)—that is, "the rich got richer" while most other groups stayed the same or got worse, with the result being greater geographic concentration of *affluence* than poverty (Massey, 1996; Massey et al., 2009). The increasing isolation of rich and poor families has become visible in the declining number of middle-income communities (Squires & Hyra, 2010), paralleling the persistent lamentations about the "disappearing middle class" (Lazonick, 2015).

The recent foreclosure crisis has spurred increased attention to the impact of housing policy on child development, especially policies that address the features of housing units themselves. Housing features such as physical quality, crowding, homeownership, residential mobility, subsidized housing, and affordability are all theorized to affect development both directly (e.g., via exposure to toxins, such as lead paint) and indirectly (e.g., via a family's stress and resources; Leventhal & Newman, 2010).

Although most research focuses on the detrimental consequences of neighborhood disadvantage for youth, some research finds that concentrated *affluence* may also undermine well-being—as it, too, has been associated with unhappiness, depression, worse parent–child relationships, and substance use (Luthar & Sexton, 2004; see also Warner, 2016). It is therefore imperative that researchers probe the full range of types and consequences of class stratification and segregation for youth development and well-being.

4.2.3 Geographic Stratification and Segregation

Resources and services are differentially distributed across neighborhoods on the basis of geography. Some neighborhoods have more schools, churches, and libraries; others have more homeless shelters and group homes; and still others are completely lacking in services (Oakley & Logan, 2007). The differential geographic distribution of services and resources also has implications for residents' life chances and well-being across the life course, as disadvantage is consequential in *any* place that is plagued by risks and poor in resources and opportunities (Lobao & Hooks, 2007).

This is not simply a problem of variability among neighborhoods in more urban areas. Indeed, the economic transformation of rural America today has prompted dislocations similar to the urban dislocations of a few decades ago (Burton, Lichter, Baker, & Eason, 2013). Yet, due to a "nostalgic romanticization of agrarian society" (Tickameyer & Duncan, 1990, p. 69), rural residents have historically been characterized as more socially integrated and better regulated. Thus, the social problems of rural places are, in contrast to urban ones, relatively neglected. But the reality is that rural places are characterized by persistent concentrated poverty and high-income inequality (Lichter & Johnson, 2007). In impoverished rural areas, the poor are doubly disadvantaged, suffering from low income, a lack of institutional support and resources, and physical, cultural, and economic isolation from mainstream America (Jensen, McLaughlin, & Slack, 2003, p. 130)—creating what Burton et al. (2013) call "rural ghettos."

The housing crisis and Great Recession also affected the geographic patterning of people and places. The suburban poor now outnumber their central city counterparts, and it is these suburban poor residents who face particular challenges to maintain compliance with the rules and regulations of government assistance programs (e.g., mandatory participation in work preparation or community service, see Butz, 2016). Following the recession, poverty peaked in rural areas, and recovery has been slow. Most notably, increases in postrecession poverty rates were highest for rural children (United States Department of Agriculture et al., 2015).

Rural areas have experienced their own unique set of macrolevel social problems: the rise of agribusiness and big-box retailing that has undermined local businesses, the decline of unions and blue-collar wages, employers' increased reliance on (and exploitation of) undocumented workers, and the systemic underinvestment in young workers entering the labor force without college degrees (Carr & Kefalas, 2009). All of these contributed to what Carr and Kefalas (2009) call the "rural brain drain"—a "hollowing out" of rural places that occurs when areas lose their most talented/skilled/educated young people, who migrate to metropolitan areas in search of healthier labor markets and greater opportunities (possibly improving their life chances, but with devastating consequences for those left behind). Sherman and Sage (2011) noted that such brain drain has also led parents in rural communities to view education with ambivalence—recognizing it as their children's best hope for success, but also seeing the educational system as a catalyst that pushes the best and brightest young residents out of the area.

The detrimental consequences of racial/ethnic and class spatial segregation are therefore exacerbated when coupled with segregation by *type* of geography (e.g., rural, urban, suburban, exurban). The focus on urban/metropolitan areas in neighborhood research has limited the ability to fully understand the intersection of racial/ethnic, class, and geographic social cleavages, and how structural inequality plays out across types of places. Spatial boundaries and barriers mark social divisions, all of which have tangible effects on human development across the life course (Irwin, 2007).

4.3 Geographies of Opportunity: Neighborhoods as Springboards or Snares

As noted earlier, life course theory is attuned to issues of time, process, and context. It emphasizes the interplay between macrolevel influences—especially of history, demography, and policies—and individual-level biographies. It emphasizes the joint contribution of "agency" and "structure" in determining individuals' opportunities and outcomes. That is, individuals' opportunities and outcomes are, on one hand, due to their own efforts and capacities but also, on the other hand, due to social forces that systematically leave some people rewarded and others disadvantaged as a function of their location in society.

Disadvantage experienced early in life can set into motion a series of cascading socioeconomic and lifestyle events—"chains of risk" (Kuh, Ben-Shlomo, Lynch, Hallqvist, & Power, 2003) or "cumulative disadvantage" (Dannefer, 2003)—that have negative implications for development and trajectories of well-being (Sharkey, 2008; Wickrama & Noh, 2010). Of course, early advantage can accumulate in similar ways, furthering resources and protections as people grow up and older. The neighborhoods in which people live reflect these cumulative processes. Neighborhoods affect residents' possibilities for future success. They are landscapes of uneven risks, resources, hazards, and protections (Fitzpatrick & LaGory, 2003; O'Rand, 2001), where factors such as school quality, employment, crime, availability of health care and other services, and environmental conditions (e.g., pollution, toxins) influence health and well-being in childhood and adolescence (Leventhal & Newman, 2010) and beyond. This is important because, as Robert (1999) notes, empirical studies may find the independent effects of neighborhood context at any given moment are rather small, but the overall importance of neighborhoods is likely to be substantial when one accounts for the intertwined nature of neighborhood effects with those of families, schools, and peer groups; their cumulative effect over the lifetime; and their collective effect on large numbers of people.

As noted earlier, neighborhoods are major markers of social status. Status differences are expressed in where people live and in how whole social groups are sorted and even stigmatized on the basis of them. For instance, individuals tend to possess a cognitive hierarchical map of neighborhoods as good or bad, reflecting the social and economic characteristics of those residents (Semyonov & Kraus, 1983). Neighborhoods not only reinforce status hierarchies, but they engender in residents a place identity. Places "claim" people, and individuals view themselves relative to their surrounding environment—as Cheng, Kruger, and Daniels (2003, p. 90, emphasis in original) argue, "...to be some*where* is to be some*one*."

Neighborhoods affect individual outcomes through the channeling and concentration of certain types of individuals into certain types of neighborhoods, creating relatively homogeneous neighborhood groups. That is, the characteristics on which individuals are sorted into different types of neighborhoods represent social stratification processes. Thus, neighborhoods become a means for mediating the effects of individual factors on outcomes, and individual-level factors become a means for mediating the effects of neighborhoods on outcomes. Both are possibilities because neighborhoods are a *product of* and a *means for* social stratification. Yet, the usual methods of analysis and interpretation—"variable-centered" approaches examining neighborhood context via single items or indices related to composition—obscure these facts, which lead researchers to make conclusions based on the (unrealistic) premise of "all things being equal." Neighborhoods are rarely equal because they are both the *result of* and a *mechanism to reinforce* inequality.

5. A NEIGHBORHOOD-CENTERED APPROACH

Because race/ethnicity and social class covary so strongly in the United States, neighborhood effects research tends to discuss their effects in tandem (Sucoff & Upchurch, 1998, p. 573). For example, the percentage of Black residents in an area is often used as an indicator of socioeconomic disadvantage, or it is combined with other measures such as the poverty rate, because these measures are highly correlated (Land, McCall, & Cohen, 1990). Despite this, racial/ethnic and social class composition are not equivalent. Recent research on residential segregation suggests that their *intersection* is becoming increasingly important for the structuring of spatial inequality (Dwyer, 2010; Massey et al., 2009). As such, it will be useful to assess neighborhoods in ways that interrogate how race/ethnicity and class intersect to jointly and simultaneously (re)produce inequality (Choo & Ferree, 2010).

Treating compositional characteristics as independently modeled control variables obscures heterogeneity, "decontextualizes" data (Luke, 2005), and leads researchers to ignore the *meaning* behind particular contexts and the causes and consequences of patterns and constellations of compositional characteristics. For example, "percent Black," while associated with various negative outcomes, is not in and of itself a particularly meaningful construct (nor can "social structure" be captured in a single measure). Rather, "percent Black" is a proxy for a set of social forces and experiences (e.g., blocked opportunities, limited resources) that may be similarly applicable in places *not* characterized by a large proportion of Black residents (e.g., predominantly White poor rural areas) or not applicable in nonurban places with a high composition of Black residents (e.g., predominantly Black rural areas or middle-class Black areas).

Extending the focus on "variable-centered" methods to the intersection of the three key social cleavages described earlier—neighborhood race/ethnicity, social class, and geography—will allow us to bridge "ways of thinking about" neighborhoods with "ways of measuring" them (Burton,

Price-Spratlen, & Spencer, 1997, p. 132). It involves more nuanced considerations of neighborhoods as contexts that capture the challenges faced by, or resources available to, persons because of group memberships, socioeconomic positions, and spatial locations (Leung & Takeuchi, 2011; O'Rand, 2001; Williams, Mohammed, Leavell, & Collins, 2010).

A move in this direction calls for a multidimensional and relational approach, one that does not attribute causality to single independently operating independent variables (Abbott, 1998). Although advances in multilevel modeling techniques (e.g., HLM) have allowed the analytical recognition that individuals are embedded in larger contexts (Raudenbush & Bryk, 2002), these models nonetheless remain concerned with identifying the independent main effects of structural factors—attempting to explicate the effect of one factor "net of" others, which is a problem because nothing in the social world occurs "net of other variables" (Abbott, 1992, p. 6). Coulton and Spilsbury (2014, p. 1308) succinctly noted that much neighborhood effects research "has tended to reify neighborhoods as vessels floating in a vacuum at a point in time, relatively impervious to the social and economic processes that shape them." We must therefore explore how causal conditions *combine* to produce given outcomes; otherwise, resulting knowledge is both incomplete and biased (Cole, 2009, p. 173).

One way to continue advancing the study of neighborhoods for adolescent development in a manner that is consistent with the theoretical premise that neighborhoods are *socially defined* places is to seek inspiration from the "person-centered" approach in the field of human development (Cairns, Bergman, & Kagan, 1998). This approach identifies patterns or "constellations" among variables in the data, rather than relying on singular measures or linear relationships between a few variables. Just as person-centered approaches have been used to differentiate heterogeneity among individuals, these same approaches can be applied to the environments in which persons are nested (Bogat, 2009).

A "neighborhood-centered" approach would take the neighborhood as the key conceptual and analytical unit, emerging from the structural components that formulate it. Traditional multilevel modeling techniques treat each geographic unit (e.g., census tracts) as if it is distinct from the next, comparing average effects of compositional measures across a sample of tracts. A neighborhood-centered approach would instead treat tracts as groups, where a set of tracts share similar characteristics that are distinct from another set. Such an approach would take neighborhoods to be latent constructs that represent the nexus of social structural forces manifested in the primary interactive environments of daily life and that can be compared.

To capture fully the multidimensional intersections between race/ethnicity, class, and geography in linear models, one could theoretically compute several 3- and 4-way interactions. However, such higher order interaction terms are difficult to interpret and can imply combinations of variables that may not exist in reality or are infrequently observed in the data, which further undermines their utility (Weden et al., 2011). What is instead needed for a neighborhood-centered approach is a method that allows the emergence of neighborhood types represented in the data—classifying neighborhoods holistically (Plybon & Kliewer, 2002) and configurationally (Ragin, 2008). One such method is latent class analysis (LCA; Vermunt, 2008), which can be used to uncover and describe contextual patterns (Luke, 2005) and complex intersections among covarying measures (Dupéré & Perkins, 2007). A neighborhood-centered approach explicitly recognizes the social structural foundation of neighborhoods, allows for the exploration of neighborhood effects across *all* geographies, and facilitates comparative research (e.g., especially beyond comparisons of poor Black urban neighborhoods and White middle-class neighborhoods).

A neighborhood-centered approach using LCA can reveal unknown or previously unmeasured heterogeneity (Luke, 2005). Only a few prior studies have examined "types" of neighborhoods (e.g., Aneshensel & Sucoff, 1996; Gorman-Smith, Tolan, & Henry, 2000; Sucoff & Upchurch, 1998) and none have done so using data in which multiple geographies (urban, suburban, *and* rural) are represented—thus, geography has been absent. A finer-grained description of neighborhoods is needed to understand how the structural dimensions of neighborhood inequality are linked to human development in different life periods and over the life course.

6. AN EMPIRICAL DEMONSTRATION
6.1 Trajectories of Adolescent Violent Victimization Across Neighborhood Types

To more fully introduce a "neighborhood-centered" approach, we illustrate how LCA can embrace the *intersection* of race/ethnicity, class, and geography, and how a neighborhood-centered approach permits the exploration of neighborhood effects across *multiple* geographies. Specifically, we explore the extent to which adolescent violent victimization is embedded in and shaped by neighborhood context.

6.1.1 The Concentration and Consequences of Adolescent Violent Victimization

Adolescence is characterized by increasing autonomy, yet with this comes increased exposure to various risks. Particularly troubling is the increased risk of violent victimization, which is disproportionately concentrated among youth (Finkelhor, Turner, Ormrod, Hamby, & Kracke, 2009; Truman, Langton, & Planty, 2013). For instance, 2008 data from the National Survey of Children's Exposure to Violence (NatSCEV) show that 61% of children aged 17 and younger were exposed to or experienced violence in the past year, and 46% were assaulted. Violent victimization in adolescence is a risk factor for depressive symptoms (Latzman & Swisher, 2005), anger and aggression (Turner, Finkelhor, & Ormrod, 2006), fatalism (Warner & Swisher, 2014), substance abuse (DeMaris & Kaukinen, 2005), and suicidal thoughts and actions (Cleary, 2000).

Further, victims of violence are also at risk of experiencing subsequent victimization (Schreck, Stewart, & Osgood, 2008) and becoming violent perpetrators themselves (Menard, 2002). The 2008 NatSCEV data also show that as many as 39% of youth experienced two or more victimizations. Although research is limited, it does illustrate that victimization trajectories follow a similar pattern to the well-established age–crime curve: an increase during early adolescence, a peak around ages 15–17, and steady declines into young adulthood (Sullivan, Wilcox, & Osey, 2011). Many explanations for victim continuity are situational, pointing to lifestyles and routine activities that bring into contact potential victims and motivated offenders in environments that lack capable guardianship (i.e., social control). The environmental risks for victimization are particularly applicable to youth, who lack the autonomy to alter the neighborhoods environments that are "imposed" upon them (Sharkey, 2006). Within these imposed neighborhood environments, youth do have agency over their "selected" environments, although as Sharkey (2006) found, exposure to neighborhood disadvantage undermines adolescents' confidence in their ability to avoid violence, which in turn influences the types of environments they select for themselves.

Neighborhoods are therefore a crucial context for taking a developmental perspective on victimization, as they carry social and structural characteristics that heighten personal vulnerabilities to crime. In the remainder of this chapter, we address three specific objectives to: (1) develop a typology of neighborhoods based on multidimensional and intersecting characteristics of neighborhood racial/ethnic composition, socioeconomic class, and geography; (2) compare trajectories of risk across adolescent neighborhood types, considering the long-term consequences of neighborhood context for the violent victimization of adolescents and young adults; and (3) determine the extent to which neighborhood type affects trajectories of violent victimization through individual, peer, and family characteristics.

6.2 LCA of Neighborhood Types

We used data from the National Longitudinal Study of Adolescent to Adult Health (Add Health, a nationally representative school-based sample of adolescents in grades 7 through 12, first conducted between 1994 and 1995, with follow-up interviews in 1996 (Wave II), 2001–2002 (Wave III), and 2007–2008 (Wave IV, when respondents were aged 24–34 [detailed information about the design of Add Health can be found in Harris (2005)]). Respondents were sampled from schools that were (disproportionately) stratified by region, urbanicity, school type, racial/ethnic composition, and school size, resulting in a sample of students from a variety of geographic areas (e.g., urban, suburban, and rural).

6.2.1 Analytic Sample

Our analyses proceeded in two stages—the first addressing Objective 1 and the second addressing Objectives 2 and 3. The analytic samples, measures, and strategies differed for each stage. The first stage of the analytic plan used data from the Wave I Add Health in-home interview, along with data from the Wave I Contextual Database (containing demographic indicators from the 1990 US Census; Billy, Wenzlow, & Grady, 1998) and the Obesity and Neighborhood Environment (ONE) add-on (Harris & Udry, 2008), which provides built environment indicators. Analyses for Objective 1 used the 2366 Census tracts from the Wave I contextual data.[d]

6.2.2 Measures

Neighborhood class was measured via four indicators. The first was the tract-level *proportion of residents living below the poverty line*. An assumption of LCA is that continuous indicators are normally distributed (Collins & Lanza, 2010; McCutcheon, 1987); therefore, given the highly skewed distribution of this

---

[d] Because the addresses of Add Health respondents were deidentified in the restricted-use data, we were unable to append any additional Census measures beyond those contained in the Contextual Database or identify spatially contiguous tracts. Also, although an extensive literature debates the appropriateness of census tracts as measures of neighborhoods (Hipp, 2007; Sampson et al., 2002), the use of census tracts as proxies for neighborhoods remains the standard approach, particularly in analyses of nationally representative or other large-scale secondary data sources.

indicator (see Weden et al., 2011), this item was collapsed as: $0 = <0.03$ (affluent), $1 = 0.03–0.10$ (low poverty), $2 = 0.10–0.20$ (moderate poverty), $3 = 0.20–0.40$ (high poverty), $4 = >0.40$ (extreme poverty; see Jargowsky & Bane, 1991; Timberlake, 2007). Next, neighborhood educational composition was measured via two dummy variables: *low education* (=1 if the tract proportion of residents with less than a high school education was greater than the grand mean) and *high education* (=1 if the tract proportion of residents with a college degree was higher than the grand mean). Finally, we included tract-level *median household income* to differentiate better between neighborhoods falling along the socioeconomic continuum.[e]

Neighborhood ethnic diversity was assessed with two separate indicators of the *proportion of Hispanic residents* and *foreign-born residents* to distinguish predominately native-born Hispanic neighborhoods from predominately immigrant neighborhoods. *Neighborhood racial composition* was measured with three separate indicators of the *proportion of non-Hispanic White residents, non-Hispanic Black residents*, and *residents who are non-Hispanic Asian/Pacific Islander or other race*. Both sets of measures were also highly skewed; the proportion of White residents was therefore recoded as: $0 = <0.40$ White, $1 = 0.40–0.80$ White, and $2 = >0.80$ White. The proportion of residents non-Hispanic Black, Hispanic, non-Hispanic Asian/Pacific Islander/other, and proportion foreign born were recoded into the following categories: $0 = <0.05$, $1 = 0.05–0.10$, $2 = 0.10–0.20$, $3 = 0.20–0.50$, and $4 = >0.50$. Different thresholds were used for minorities to correspond better with their representation in the US population (Friedman, 2008).

Neighborhood geography was captured via five measures. *Urbanicity/rurality* was measured as the proportion of the tract that is urban (collapsed into $0 = 0$; $1 = 0.1–0.99$; $2 = 1.00$ [completely urban]). Because almost all new single-family construction since 1974 has taken place in the suburbs, and it is the availability of these new homes that distinguishes suburbs (and possibly "exurbs," Frey, 2012) from central cities (Gyourko & Linneman, 1993), the analyses included a measure of *median house age* as a proxy for suburbanicity (and following Nelson, Gordon-Larsen, Song, & Popkin, 2006). This was collapsed as follows: $0 = <15$ years, $1 = 15–25$, $2 = 25–35$, $3 = 35–50$, $4 = >50$. The *cylcomatic index* is the number of route alternatives between intersections (measured at a 3-km radius around respondents'

---

[e] This measure (which ranges from $4999 to $125,053) was also not normally distributed; based on the distribution of this measure in the data, this item was collapsed as follows: $0 = <\$10,000$, $1 = \$10,000–\$14,999$, $2 = \$15,000–\$19,999$, $3 = \$20,000–\$24,999$, $4 = \$25,000–\$29,999$, $5 = \$30,000–\$34,999$, $6 = \$35,000–\$39,999$, $7 = \$40,000–\$44,999$, $8 = \$45,000–\$59,999$, $9 = >\$59,999$.

homes, see Nelson et al., 2006); it ranges from 2 to 2947, where higher values indicate greater accessibility/connectivity. Although more often used by epidemiologists interested in "built environment" characteristics (than in traditional "neighborhood effects" research), we used the measure to further distinguish types of geographic areas (the measure was collapsed into quartiles). Finally, given documented regional differences in neighborhood types—for instance, the South and Midwest are considerably more "exurban"[f] (Berube et al., 2006)—dummy variables for *southern* and *western* regions were included.

6.2.3 Analytic Strategy

As a person-centered, model-based, probabilistic analytic strategy, LCA is a statistical method for identifying unmeasured class membership among observations. It estimates posterior probabilities (the probability of membership in a particular latent class [c]), and observations are assigned to the latent class for which the posterior probability is highest (Lanza, Collins, Lemmon, & Schafer, 2007). Such probabilistic strategies bring the risk of classification error, but in the case of these Add Health census tracts, the posterior probabilities resulting from our LCA were quite high. For instance, over 90% of the tracts in the Add Health data were assigned to a latent class with posterior probabilities at or above 0.90, which is much higher than the 0.70 criterion recommended for establishing reliable categorizations (Nagin, 2005) and increases our confidence in the rigor of these classifications. In the growth curve analyses (described later), *neighborhood type* was measured by c number of dummy variables (the number of latent classes identified).

6.3 Results

The number of potential neighborhood types, while unknown, is not infinite, and there are a sizeable number of possible combinations across these 13 measures in a large-scale dataset-like Add Health. To ascertain the best solution for capturing meaningful neighborhood types, we tested up to 15 classes. In order to balance model fit and parsimony, and provide

---

[f] The US Census does not delineate exurban (nor suburban) areas, and several studies have advanced a number of varying definitions (for a review, see Berube, Singer, Wilson, & Frey, 2006) involving combinations of housing density, population density, distance from metropolitan areas, and sociodemographic characteristics of the population. Given the lack of standardized definition(s), the limited availability of measures in the deidentified Add Health data, and the need for LCA model parsimony, the analyses included the fewest possible focal variables presumably needed to distinguish across types of geographic places.

adequate statistical power for comparing neighborhoods, our choice of model solution was guided by fit statistics (Akaike Information Criterion [AIC], Bayesian Information Criterion [BIC]), model comparison tests (likelihood-ratio statistic L^2), and an effort to ensure that each neighborhood type contained approximately 5% of census tracts. Based on these criteria, we chose a 10-class solution as most appropriate. Model fit statistics are displayed in Table 1, which shows a diminishing of the percent decrease in the L^2 statistic and an uptick in the Entropy R^2 (an indicator of classification certainty) around the 10-class solution.[g]

6.3.1 Labeling Neighborhood Types

The process of developing labels for the neighborhood types was guided by expectations grounded in theory, previous research, documented patterns of residential segregation, and, much like factor analysis, some subjective judgments. After selecting the 10-class solution, we reviewed the distributional patterns of the 13 indicators across each of the neighborhood types to construct meaningful labels to capture the intersections of the three social cleavages. We also reviewed the distributional patterns of additional contextual indicators not used in the LCA (e.g., proportion female-headed households, households receiving public income, population employed in occupational/managerial professions, proportion employed in farming/forestry/fishing occupations, etc.) to further facilitate the labeling of the emergent types.

We labeled the 10 neighborhood types as follows: (1) *Upper-Middle-Class White Suburban*, (2) *Poor Black Urban*, (3) *Working-Class Mixed Race Urban*, (4) *Working-Class White Rural*, (5) *Middle-Class Hispanic/Asian Suburban*, (6) *Middle-Class Black Urban*, (7) *Poor Hispanic/Immigrant Urban*, (8) *Poor White Urban*, (9) *Mixed-Class White Urban*, and (10) *Poor Black Rural*.[h]

---

[g] Ten (10) classes is larger than the number of neighborhoods extracted in some previous studies (e.g., Aneshensel & Sucoff, 1996; Gorman-Smith et al., 2000; Sucoff & Upchurch, 1998; Weden et al., 2011), yet this is to be expected since this study uses a nationally representative sample not limited to metropolitan areas, and distinguishes neighborhood types based on three key social structural cleavages.

[h] Because Add Health is not a neighborhood-based study, there are plausible combinations of the three social structural cleavages not represented (and not captured) in the current analysis. The current analysis is not intended to suggest that the 10 neighborhood types observed here represent the totality of neighborhood types in the United States. Rather, these types capture the general pattern of neighborhood contexts of the Add Health respondents. Analyses based on other samples or indicators may yield a different collection of neighborhood types. Our ultimate purpose here is to demonstrate the utility of a neighborhood-centered approach. However, we do note similarities between the neighborhood types we observe in Add Health and those observed in Weden et al. (2011) LCA of 1990 tract-level US Census data—using a 20% sample of US tracts, that analysis identified low SES rural, poor minority urban, high SES foreign born, and middle-class suburban neighborhood types.

Table 1 Model Fit Statistics for Latent Class Analysis of Neighborhood Types

	L^2	% Reduction in L^2	BIC (L^2)	AIC (L^2)	Entropy R^2
2-Class	31,236.26	12.89	13,274.44	26,612.26	0.87
3-Class	28,237.79	9.60	10,384.73	23,641.79	0.89
4-Class	26,487.35	6.20	8743.05	21,919.35	0.91
5-Class	24,978.07	5.70	7342.54	20,438.07	0.93
6-Class	23,977.94	4.00	6451.17	19,465.94	0.92
7-Class	23,048.01	3.88	5630.01	18,564.01	0.92
8-Class	22,288.84	3.29	4979.61	17,832.84	0.92
9-Class	21,707.28	2.61	4506.81	17,279.28	0.92
10-Class[a]	21,208.99	2.30	4117.23	16,808.99	0.93
11-Class	20,747.10	2.18	3764.17	16,375.10	0.93
12-Class	20,314.18	2.09	3440.01	15,970.18	0.93
13-Class	20,033.83	1.38	3268.43	15,717.83	0.94
14-Class	19,669.99	1.82	3013.35	15,381.99	0.93
15-Class	19,392.19	1.41	2844.32	15,132.19	0.93

[a]A $-2LL$ bootstrapping test was also used to assess the fit of the 10-class solution; compared to a 9-class solution, the test statistic ($-2LL$ difference $= 498.29$, $p = 0.0000$) indicates the 10-class solution provides a better fit than a solution with fewer classes.
Notes: L^2 is the likelihood-ratio Chi-square statistic, which indicates the amount of the association among the variables that remains unexplained after estimating the model; the lower the value, the better the fit of the model to the data.
Source: National Longitudinal Study of Adolescent to Adult Health, Wave I ($n = 2366$ census tracts).

Table 2 provides a subset of compositional characteristics for comparing the 10 neighborhood types and a portion of the data used for labeling neighborhood types. The neighborhoods designated as predominantly White had an average population that was almost entirely White (over 90% White), but readers may be confused as to why we labeled other neighborhoods as mixed race or minority neighborhoods when Whites still comprised a large share of the population. There is no standard definition for classifying the racial dominance of a neighborhood, but our assessment of neighborhood racial/ethnic composition was informed by Logan and Zhang (2010) 25% rule (that for a racial/ethnic groups to have a distinct presence it must cross a threshold of 25%) and other commonly employed racial cutoffs (e.g., Fischer & Massey, 2004; Friedman, 2008). In 1990, Whites comprised 80% of the US

Table 2 Select Descriptive Characteristics of Neighborhood Type Indicators, Means, and Standard Deviations (in Parentheses)

Neighborhood type[a]	Socioeconomic Class				Racial/Ethnic Composition/ Heterogeneity				Geography
	Poverty	Median Income (1000s)	<HS Degree	College Degree	NH White	NH Black	Hispanic	Foreign Born	Urban
Upper–Middle–Class White Suburb [18.3%]	0.046	42.928	0.120	0.386	0.912	0.038	0.028	0.042	0.770
	(0.027)	(12.437)	(0.049)	0.126	0.074	0.057	0.032	0.034	0.381
Middle–Class Hispanic/Asian Suburb [10.4%]	0.075	41.300	0.192	0.320	0.558	0.099	0.185	0.199	0.945
	(0.039)	(9.327)	(0.079)	0.118	0.190	0.161	0.114	0.141	0.210
Working–Class White Rural [11.1%]	0.140	25.666	0.306	0.157	0.952	0.022	0.018	0.013	0.193
	(0.083)	(6.584)	(0.103)	0.062	0.050	0.037	0.032	0.012	0.365
Poor Black Urban [12.1%]	0.391	14.968	0.467	0.096	0.124	0.807	0.060	0.048	0.999
	(0.135)	(5.538)	(0.089)	0.042	0.194	0.218	0.091	0.083	0.007
Poor Black Rural [4.4%]	0.275	19.449	0.377	0.153	0.529	0.448	0.016	0.013	0.148
	(0.118)	(6.123)	(0.120)	0.085	0.217	0.227	0.029	0.020	0.330

Poor White Urban [8.0%]	0.162	22.911	0.256	0.221	0.906	0.039	0.034	0.035	0.986
	(0.104)	(5.145)	(0.111)	0.143	0.070	0.041	0.042	0.037	0.106
Working-Class Mixed Race Urban [11.3%]	0.179	27.186	0.331	0.226	0.466	0.200	0.247	0.251	0.999
	(0.068)	(5.997)	(0.106)	0.114	0.235	0.240	0.123	0.137	0.010
Poor Hispanic/Immigrant Urban [8.6%]	0.278	20.838	0.546	0.124	0.177	0.078	0.713	0.437	0.995
	(0.107)	(6.154)	(0.107)	0.063	0.072	0.122	0.163	0.209	0.071
Middle-Class Black Urban [9.1%]	0.151	28.295	0.233	0.269	0.338	0.616	0.030	0.047	0.998
	(0.079)	(6.798)	(0.079)	0.123	0.286	0.303	0.037	0.066	0.013
Mixed-Class White Urban [6.8%]	0.054	38.696	0.257	0.288	0.912	0.012	0.052	0.136	1.000
	(0.031)	(11.984)	(0.092)	0.134	0.047	0.017	0.031	0.072	0.000

[a]Number in [] indicates percentage of study census tracts categorized into each type.

Source: National Longitudinal Study of Adolescent to Adult Health Wave I ($n = 2366$ census tracts).

population, Blacks 12%, and Asians/Pacific Islanders 3%; about 9% of the population identified as being of Hispanic ethnicity.

Following Fischer and Massey (2004), we defined predominantly Black neighborhood types as those with at least 60% Black residents, which matches the average proportion Black for *Poor Urban* and *Middle-Class Urban Black* neighborhoods, but does not for the neighborhood type we label *Poor Black Rural* (on average 45% Black); however, because 90% of the non-metropolitan population was White, it is very likely that 45% Black (on average) is a significant and noticeable presence of Black residents (also noteworthy, 99% of the tracts in this type were located in the South). The neighborhood type we designated *Hispanic/Asian Suburb* is distinguishable from the one labeled *Mixed Race* by their different Black populations (10% vs 20%, respectively) and Asian/Pacific Islander and other race populations (16% vs 9%, respectively [not shown]).

Designating neighborhood socioeconomic class is also challenging, as there is no standard definition of "social class" in general nor standardized distinctions between gradations within class categories (upper, middle, working, lower, etc.). Further, definitions of social class are relative, and commonly employed measures of class—such as median household income—vary by both race (highest among Whites) and geography (highest in suburban areas; U.S. Bureau of the Census, 1992). For instance, Whites live in very different types of neighborhoods than their non-White counterparts—where the poorest predominantly White neighborhood is not nearly as impoverished as the poorest non-White neighborhoods. This is also illustrated here. Recent work on residential segregation reveals that poor Whites tend to live in more affluent neighborhoods than even middle-class Blacks and Latinos (Reardon et al., 2015) and that the average affluent Black or Hispanic household is located in a poorer neighborhood than the average *low-income* White household (Logan & Zhang, 2010).

It is therefore important to be mindful of such pernicious effects of racial/ethnic residential segregation when attempting to label neighborhoods in a way most consistent with their composition. Following Jargowsky (2003), we defined neighborhoods with 40% or more of the population in poverty as poor/high poverty. We also used the 1990 race-specific household income distribution to inform the development of neighborhood type labels.[i]

---

[i] The median household income of White and Hispanic households in the United States in 1990 was $31,231 and $22,330, respectively, while median household income of Black households was considerably lower ($18,676) and Asian/Pacific Islander households considerably higher ($38,450) (U.S. Bureau of the Census, 1991).

No neighborhood type emerging in these data met the criteria for what might be considered "affluent" based on the top 5% of household income (Solari, 2012). Another designation (e.g., Massey et al., 2003) is to use the top fifth of the income distribution as an indicator of affluence, which was $55,205 in 1990. Thus, we labeled the "wealthiest" observed neighborhood type as *Upper-Middle Class* because its average median household income was $42,928. Education was also useful for making distinctions. For instance, the median household income for what we termed a *Mixed-Class* neighborhood was $38,696, but an average of 26% of tracts were above the median on the proportion of residents without a high school education (compared to only 12% of tracts in *Upper-Middle-Class* neighborhoods). Although we are unable to measure it in these data, we speculate that this *Mixed-Class White Urban* neighborhood—given its high-income and educational stratification, sizeable foreign-born population, and older house ages (not shown)—may be capturing gentrified neighborhoods, which are themselves controversial because gentrification may displace predominantly poor residents and further exacerbate class inequalities (Newman & Wyly, 2006).

The lower limit of median household income for the middle and fourth quintile in 1990 was $23,662 and $36,200, respectively, which we used—along with education and poverty—to inform our assessment of "middle-class" and "working-class" areas. Given the patterns of racial residential segregation discussed previously, our distinctions of neighborhood social class were done within race, which is why, for instance, the average median household income of *Poor Black Urban* neighborhoods is so much lower ($14,968) than that of *Poor White Urban* neighborhoods ($22,911), and the income of *Middle-Class Black Urban* neighborhoods ($28,295) only slightly higher than that of *Working-Class White Rural* neighborhoods ($25,666) (readers should also note the patterning of education across these types).

Finally, we relied on indicators of proportion urban, house age, region, and street connectivity to identify neighborhood geography, as (again) there is no standardized, universally accepted definition of urban, rural, or suburban. We labeled as urban those neighborhood types where, on average, the tracts were characterized as having 95% or more of its residents living inside an urbanized area (these neighborhoods also had high street connectivity measures). Of the remaining neighborhoods, house age and proportion rural residents informed labeling, where classes with over 50% of residents in rural areas classified as rural. Classes with average house ages of approximately 20 years or less were labeled suburban.

6.4 A Neighborhood-Centered Analysis of Violent Victimization Trajectories

6.4.1 Analytic Sample

The second stage of the analyses examined trajectories of violent victimization across adolescent neighborhood types. We used data from the in-home interviews of Waves I–IV. For parsimony, we do not detail the derivation of the sample here, but details are available upon request. The final sample consisted of 18,630 adolescents, distributed across 2288 census tracts at Wave I.

6.4.2 Outcome Measure

Violent victimization. Violent victimization was measured at each wave by four questions that asked how often, in the past year, respondents were (a) jumped or beaten up, (b) had a gun or knife pulled on them, (c) stabbed, or (d) shot. Respondents were coded as *victim* = 1 at each wave if they reported any of the four experiences (else = 0 if they did not experience any victimization).

Fig. 1 displays the percentage of youth victimized at age 15 by neighborhood type [we use age 15 to correspond with the peak of the age–crime curve described earlier (DeCamp & Zaykowski, 2015)]. This figure shows considerable variation across neighborhood types—for instance, 29% of 15 year olds from *Middle-Class Black Urban* neighborhoods had been violently victimized, compared to only 14% of 15 year olds from *Upper-Middle-Class White Suburbs.* This patterning is comparable to geographic trends in youth violent victimization for this same time

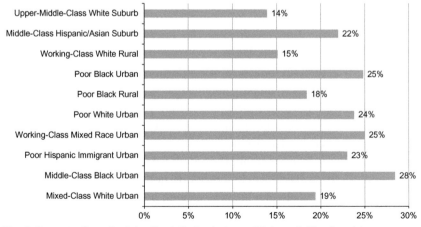

Fig. 1 Percent of youth violently victimized at age 15, by neighborhood type.

period, as reported in the *National Crime Victimization Survey* (Snyder & Sickmund, 2006).

We drew from extant literature to inform our modeling of the *indirect* effects of neighborhoods on victimization. As discussed earlier, neighborhood characteristics affect the availability and type of *peers* to whom youth are exposed (Haynie, 2001), and the amount of time they spend with those peers in unstructured activities (Osgood & Anderson, 2004). The *family* is another institution through which neighborhood characteristics influence behaviors, primarily because of the family's role in supervision and informal social control. Neighborhood disadvantage undermines parental efficacy, and ineffective, uninvolved, or even hostile parenting has detrimental consequences for youths' well-being that also makes adolescents more susceptible and/or vulnerable to delinquent peer influence and opportunity (Leventhal & Brooks-Gunn, 2000; Wickrama & Noh, 2010). Even *personal characteristics* such as self-control may mediate neighborhood effects, with recent studies suggesting that neighborhood disadvantage may contribute to low self-control and impulsivity (Teasdale & Silver, 2009).

Our final objective, therefore, explored how the effect of neighborhood type on trajectories of violent victimization operates through indicators of individual, family, and/or peer mediators. Details about these measures (including their coding) are listed in Table 3.

6.4.3 Analytic Strategy

We estimated a series of three-level models, with multiple observations over time (age [centered at 15]) nested within persons (respondents), who are in turn nested within census tracts. We conducted preliminary analyses (not shown) to determine the specification of fixed and random effects for change in victimization with age; comparisons of fit for models of increasing complexity indicated that a cubic model with random intercept and random linear slope provided the best fit.

6.5 Results

We ran a series of growth curve models exploring the role of neighborhood type in anchoring and shaping trajectories of violent victimization in adolescence and young adulthood. Analyses were stratified by gender because there are significant gender differences in overall risks for victimization (Lauritsen & Heimer, 2009). Figs. 2 through 5 illustrate the unadjusted (neighborhood type only) and adjusted (neighborhood type, plus all other covariates) models of the effects of adolescent neighborhood

Table 3 Independent Variables Measures and Coding for Analyses of Developmental Trajectories of Violent Victimization[a]

Construct[b]	Indicators and Response Options
Neighborhood accessibility	
Demographic characteristics	
Gender	Dummy variable for female (0/1)
Family characteristics	
Family socioeconomic status	Combined scale of parent's education and parent's occupational level (0–9; Bearman & Moody, 2004)
Family structure	Dummy variable for lived with both biological parents ($=1$; $0 =$ all other arrangements)
Mediators of neighborhood effects	
Individual mediators	
Relative pubertal development	Self-rated physical development compared to same-aged peers (range $-2 =$ "I look younger than most" to $2 =$ "I look older than most")
Low self-control	Scale of past year experiencing "trouble keeping your mind on what you were doing," "trouble getting your homework done," "difficulty paying attention in school," and the extent to which adolescents feel "like you are doing everything just about right"; higher scores represent *lower* self-control
School attachment	Likert scale of the extent to which respondents feel (a) close to people at school, (b) part of their school, and are (c) happy to be at their school (higher scores correspond to greater school attachment)
Academic aspirations	Measured from the question: "On a scale of 1–5, how likely is it that you will go to college?"
Life course transitions	Time varying (measured at each wave); three dichotomous indicators capturing whether the respondent was (a) in school, (b) working, and/or (c) married at each wave
Violent perpetration	4-item count of any past year perpetration (e.g., "been in a serious fight"; range 0–4)
Nonviolent delinquency	10-item scale of past year perpetration (e.g., vandalism, theft; range $0 =$ never to $3 = 5$ or more times)
Marijuana use	Any marijuana use in the past month ($1 =$ any; $0 =$ none)

Table 3 Independent Variables Measures and Coding for Analyses of Developmental Trajectories of Violent Victimization—cont'd

Construct	Indicators and Response Options
Family mediators	
Parental attachment	Mean of responses to the questions: "How close do you feel to your mother [father]?" and "How much do you feel that your mother [father] cares about you?" (responses range 0 = not at all to 4 = very much)
Family support	Scale of adolescents' reports about the extent to which they feel their family (a) understands them, (b) pays attention to them, and (c) they have fun together (response range 0 = not at all to 5 = very much)
Parental autonomy	Mean of two items asking whether parents let respondent make decisions (1 = yes, 0 = no) about "what time to be home on weekend" and "which friends you hang out with"
Peer mediators	
Unstructured socializing	Measured via the question: "During the past week, how many times did you just hang out with friends" (response range from 0 = not at all to 3 = 5 or more times)

[a]Unless otherwise noted, all indicators are measured at Wave I.
[b]Models also controlled for years lived in neighborhood at Wave I.

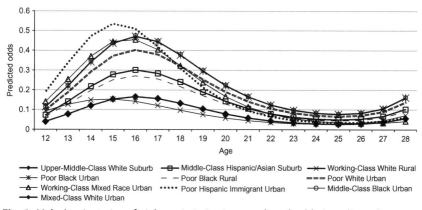

Fig. 2 Males' trajectories of violent victimization, predicted odds (unadjusted).

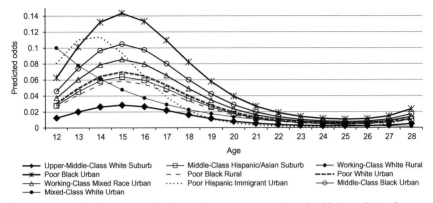

Fig. 3 Females' trajectories of violent victimization, predicted odds (unadjusted).

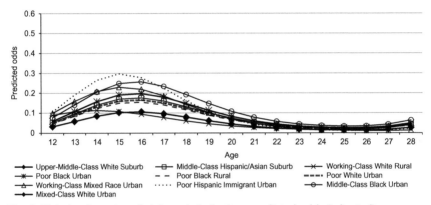

Fig. 4 Males' trajectories of violent victimization, predicted odds (adjusted).

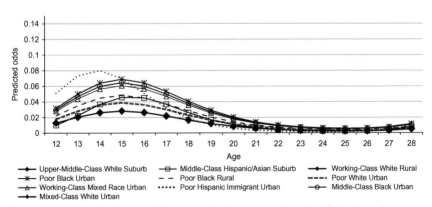

Fig. 5 Females' trajectories of violent victimization, predicted odds (adjusted).

type on victimization trajectories, with *Upper-Middle-Class White Suburb* as the reference category. To simplify our presentation, we display the results in figures rather than tables, although we do discuss some specific coefficients from multivariate tables which are available from the authors upon request.

We begin with the victimization trajectories for youth across the 10 neighborhood types, with males shown in Fig. 2 and females shown in Fig. 3. The figure for males shows a fairly consistent increase in victimization risk in early adolescence, peaking around age 15, and followed by a steady decline through age 29. However, the figure also illustrates considerable variation in the height of peak victimization risk, as well as variation in the rate at which it declines. For instance, odds of victimization at age 15 were highest for males from *Poor Hispanic Immigrant Urban* neighborhoods. Compared to their peers from *Upper-Middle-Class White Suburbs*, these youth were 78% more likely to be victimized. On the other hand, young men from *Working-Class White Rural* neighborhoods did not differ from their *UMC suburban* peers in risk at age 15, but their trajectories of risk declined more quickly between ages 15 and 22, such that they were actually less likely to be victimized during these years, a perhaps surprising finding given this rural neighborhood is more socioeconomically disadvantaged.

A neighborhood-centered approach allows us to observe variation among predominantly White neighborhoods (e.g., youth from *Poor White Urban* neighborhoods were 71% more likely than *UMC suburban* peers to have been victimized [at age 15]), and variation across neighborhoods with similar socioeconomic profiles (e.g., youth from *MC Hispanic and Asian suburbs* were 65% more likely than *UMC suburban* peers to have been victimized). The unadjusted models for young women display similar variation (Fig. 3), for instance, showing that females from *Poor Black Urban* neighborhoods were 83% and girls from *Mixed-Class White Urban* neighborhoods were 63% more likely to be victims (at age 15) than their *UMC White suburban* peers.

The adjusted models, which include a range of theorized mediators, are illustrated in Figs. 4 and 5. As both figures show, variation in victimization risk remained, although differences were minimized. For both young men and women, the effects of neighborhood type were partially mediated by individual characteristics, particularly involvement in risky behaviors, such as substance use and violent and delinquent behaviors. But it is important to note that the main effects of neighborhood type on victimization nonetheless remained statistically significant. The inclusion of these mediators helps answer the question not of whether neighborhoods matter, but *how* they matter—in this case, operating through neighborhood opportunity structures by differentially shaping youths' exposure to deviant/delinquent opportunities and to deviant/delinquent others.

In supplemental analyses not shown, we explored each set of mediators separately (individual, family, peer). An interesting finding emerged concerning the role of family characteristics. In a model with only the family measures (parental attachment, parental autonomy, family support) and neighborhood types, the disparities in victimization risk were actually exacerbated, especially for females. This is because, in multivariate models like these, the effect for neighborhood type reflects the effect at the grand mean of the other covariates. For instance, constraining the effect of *Poor Black* or *Poor Hispanic/Immigrant Urban* neighborhoods to the grand mean of parental autonomy makes the victimization risk for youth in those neighborhoods look worse than it actually is because parental autonomy in those poor neighborhoods is "lower" than the grand mean. That is, young women growing up in *Middle-Class Black Urban*, *Poor Hispanic/Immigrant Urban*, *Working-Class Mixed Race Urban*, *Poor Black Rural*, and *Poor Black Urban* neighborhoods, on average, experience *less* parental autonomy (thus, more parental monitoring/control) than all other youths—and this monitoring mitigates at least some of their victimization risk.

A similar pattern emerged for young men, particularly those from *Poor Hispanic/Immigrant Urban*, and *Poor Black Urban* and *Rural* neighborhoods. These youth had lower than average parental autonomy, and they also reported *higher* than average parental attachment and family support, and the effects of these latter two measures were stronger. Although we acknowledge the speculative nature of this interpretation, we believe these patterns suggest that parents—particularly those in "traditionally" disadvantaged neighborhoods—are employing strategies (emotional and behavioral regulation) that reduce their children's risk of victimization. That is, these parents may be aware of, and attempting to react to, the risks encapsulated in their immediate surroundings, and may be doing so differently for sons and daughters. We must temper these conclusions by noting that the analyses are based on the respondents (and caregivers) who participated in the Add Health study and, as such, the experiences and reactions of these youth may not be representative of all youth in a given neighborhood type.

6.6 Summary of Findings

The results revealed nuanced differences across neighborhood types for all four models of the trajectories of violent victimization in adolescence and young adulthood. The LCA exposed 10 distinct neighborhood types patterned along the dimensions of race/ethnicity, social class, and geography and their intersections. The analyses of victimization trajectories across neighborhood types showed variation that to date has not been observed in much of the "neighborhood effects" research.

Risks of violent victimization were fairly low for youth growing up in Upper-Middle-Class White suburbs and Working-Class White rural neighborhoods, but not all predominantly White neighborhoods were "safe" against victimization. Youth, and males in particular, who grew up in poor White urban neighborhoods had victimization risks rivaling their peers from poor Black urban neighborhoods, suggesting that victimization risk is shaped not only by race/ethnicity and class but also by geography.

Urban neighborhoods, however, were not similarly risky, nor were rural neighborhoods similarly protective for victimization (as one might expect, at least based on stereotypes from early urban sociology and criminology). Youth growing up in Poor Black rural neighborhoods were much more likely to be victimized than their peers from Working-Class White rural neighborhoods, but the difference cannot entirely be attributed to social class, as youth from Middle-Class Hispanic/Asian and Black neighborhoods had alarmingly high victimization risks (even though, on standard socioeconomic indicators [income, poverty], the Middle-Class Hispanic/Asian neighborhoods observed in these data looked almost "as good" as Upper-Middle-Class White suburbs).

Further, these neighborhood differences remained even after considering the effects of individual, family, and peer characteristics that may mediate the effect of neighborhoods on adolescents' experiences. Neighborhood effects were diminished when these correlates were considered, but much of the neighborhood effect on victimization could be attributed to youths' involvement with risky behaviors (substance use and delinquency), thereby illustrating *how* neighborhoods influence victimization. Neighborhoods differentially expose youth to and provide opportunities to be involved in both deviant/delinquent *and* prosocial institutions and behaviors. For instance, compared to peers from Upper-Middle-Class White suburban neighborhoods, youth from all other neighborhood types (except Mixed-Class White urban) had lower college expectations and were less likely to be working or in school at any point (analyses not shown).

7. DISCUSSION AND CONCLUSION

We introduced and advanced a "neighborhood-centered" approach to the study of adolescent development and behavior, integrating developmental perspectives with macrosociological theories of place stratification and the life course. This is an important endeavor, given the magnitude of influence of neighborhoods on adolescents, whose lives are geographically constrained, and given how entangled neighborhood effects are with family, school, and peer influences.

The neighborhood-centered approach developed and demonstrated here highlights the power of social structural forces—which intersect to create a finite set of neighborhood types—in anchoring trajectories of risk behaviors in adolescence. This approach is aimed at a level of analysis above the dominant focus on the mechanisms (intervening processes) through which neighborhoods are presumed to exert their influence, and instead underscores the need to first capture a more comprehensive universe of neighborhoods and their structural aspects. To do this, we leveraged ideas from person-centered psychological research to identify patterns among compositional and contextual variables, capturing neighborhoods in a way that reflects the nexus of social structural forces. This LCA approach is particularly germane to key tenets of the life course perspective, because it allows one to identify configurations of stratification that combine to pattern neighborhoods and their associated opportunity structures for the individuals and groups in them.

Using data from four waves of Add Health, we demonstrated the role of neighborhoods in defining trajectories of risk behavior in adolescence and young adulthood, applying this approach to youth victimization. Our analyses demonstrated the complex ways that three structural cleavages—neighborhood racial/ethnic composition, socioeconomic class, and geography—shape specific neighborhood contexts and result in stark variations in the lived experiences of youth. Such nuanced distinctions are not as easily visible in more traditional variable-centered approaches and/or studies focused on specific geographic areas (e.g., major metropolitan areas).

Conceptualizing neighborhoods in this way reveals considerable detail—and complex patterns of effects that are challenging to interpret, but nonetheless reflect the reality of the social world. We do not see this as a limitation but instead as a direct response to Bogat's (2009, p. 29) critique that "...developmental psychologists have over-simplified the measurement of contexts in which individuals live and work...[because individual variables] by themselves do not capture the dynamic systems in which individuals exist." That is, although developmental scholarship is theoretically attuned to dynamic systems, its data and measurement tend to rely on discrete contextual variables. Further, much scholarship has assumed that neighborhoods "work" by structuring individual, family, and peer processes, yet in a neighborhood-centered framework, we observe differences that are not statistically accounted for and therefore cannot be explained by these presumed mediating processes. There is a social structural reality to neighborhoods that must be understood above and beyond the more proximal processes that have long been the focus of research. In order to more meaningfully address place in developmental research, we must be willing to focus on the complexity of context, rather than attempting to reduce it to single indicators or a summary index. Taking into account the intersection of these social structural cleavages allows us to explore neighborhoods as spaces of developmental challenges and opportunities (Leung & Takeuchi, 2011).

Our findings, though complex, have implications for policy, particularly regarding targeted prevention and intervention efforts. As Antonishak and Reppucci (2008) note, a major challenge for intervention research is to extend into new communities programs that have demonstrated effectiveness elsewhere. However, the particular structural aspects of neighborhoods and outcomes of interest may undermine program success (Leventhal et al., 2009). For example, neighborhood SES is important for educational outcomes, but as the current analyses show, the implications of neighborhood SES are also shaped by its racial/ethnic and geographic aspects that affect how (and where) neighborhood SES manifests itself spatially. In their summary of the policy and programmatic approaches designed to reduce place-based disparities in child well-being, Coulton and Spilsbury (2014) note that these approaches—which they categorize as residential mobility programs, mixed-income developments, community change initiatives, and area-based services—all make varying assumptions about which elements of the neighborhood are important for different outcomes. Further, it appears that each approach is best tailored to address one problematic element of neighborhoods, but less equipped to address others and/or to address how a number of problems may interact. Multiple approaches may therefore be needed (simultaneously) to improve and optimize the development of children and youth. The neighborhood-centered approach illustrated here is useful for recognizing and addressing differences across types of communities.

A next step toward advancing a neighborhood-centered approach in youth research is to explore more fully how neighborhood types anchor and influence trajectories across adolescence and into young adulthood—for example, extending the analyses here to explore variations across neighborhood types in a host of health-risk and health-promoting behaviors (e.g., sexual behavior, high school drop-out, pregnancy, arrest or incarceration, academic aspirations and achievements, employment). Additional avenues for future applications of a neighborhood-centered approach include investigating interactions between individual- and family-level characteristics and neighborhood type, and exploring heterogeneity within neighborhood types.

The analyses presented here demonstrated how a neighborhood-centered approach can offer new insights into how various types of neighborhoods define life chances and shape trajectories of youth development and behavior. While the methods employed are not new, this approach begs for a reconceptualization of the meaning and consequences of neighborhoods as social categories (Cole, 2009). It demands a more comparative way of thinking, allowing investigators to test the extent to which seemingly well-established relationships can be found across various types of neighborhoods. By advancing an understanding of how the structural dimensions of neighborhood inequality matter for human development, we hope to have laid a foundation from which future research might leverage a neighborhood-centered approach to more thoroughly investigate why and how neighborhoods not only affect children and adolescents but also people in other periods of life.

ACKNOWLEDGMENTS

This research uses data from the National Longitudinal Study of Adolescent to Adult Health (Add Health), a program project directed by Kathleen Mullan Harris and designed by J. Richard Udry, Peter S. Bearman, and Kathleen Mullan Harris at the University of North Carolina at Chapel Hill, and funded by Grant P01-HD31921 from the Eunice Kennedy Shriver National Institute of Child Health and Human Development, with cooperative funding from 23 other federal agencies and foundations. Special acknowledgment is due Ronald R. Rindfuss and Barbara Entwisle for assistance in the original design. Information on how to obtain the Add Health data files is available on the Add Health website (http://www.cpc.unc.edu/addhealth). No direct support was received from Grant P01-HD31921 for this analysis.

REFERENCES

Abbott, A. (1992). Of time and place: The contemporary relevance of the Chicago School. In *Sorokin lecture delivered at the annual meeting of the Southern Sociological Society, New Orleans, LA*.
Abbott, A. (1998). The causal devolution. *Sociological Methods & Research, 27*(2), 148–181.
Anderson, E. (1999). *Code of the street: Decency, violence, and moral life of the inner city*. New York: Norton.

Anderson, E. (2013). *Streetwise: Race, class, and change in an urban community*. Chicago, IL: University of Chicago Press.

Aneshensel, C. S., & Sucoff, C. A. (1996). The neighborhood context of adolescent mental health. *Journal of Health and Social Behavior, 45*(3), 293–310.

Antonishak, J., & Reppucci, N. D. (2008). Ecological and community level influences on child development. In T. P. Gullotta & G. M. Blau (Eds.), *Handbook of childhood behavioral issues: Evidence-based approaches to prevention and treatment* (pp. 69–86). New York, NY: Routledge.

Bearman, P. S., & Moody, J. (2004). Suicide and friendships among American adolescents. *American Journal of Public Health, 94*, 89–95.

Berkman, L. F., Glass, T., Brissette, I., & Seeman, T. E. (2000). From social integration to health: Durkheim in the new millennium. *Social Science & Medicine, 51*, 843–857.

Berube, A., Singer, A., Wilson, J. H., & Frey, W. H. (2006). Finding exurbia: America's fast-growing communities at the metropolitan fringe. *Metropolitan policy program, living cities census series* . Washington, DC: The Brookings Institution.

Billy, J. O. G., Wenzlow, A. T., & Grady, W. R. (1998). *User documentation for the Add Health contextual database*. Seattle: Battelle.

Bischoff, K., & Reardon, S. F. (2014). Residential segregation by income, 1970–2009. In J. Logan (Ed.), *Diversity and disparities: America enters a new century* (pp. 208–233). New York: The Russell Sage Foundation.

Bogat, G. A. (2009). Is it necessary to discuss person-oriented research in community psychology? *American Journal of Community Psychology, 43*, 22–34.

Braveman, P. (2014). What is health equity: And how does a life-course approach take us further toward it? *Maternal and Child Health Journal, 18*, 366–372.

Bronfenbrenner, U. (1979). *The ecology of human development*. Cambridge: Harvard University Press.

Browning, C. R., Cagney, K. A., & Boettner, B. (2016). Neighborhood, place, and the life course. In J. M. Shanahan, T. J. Mortimer, & M. Kirkpatrick Johnson (Eds.), *Handbook of the life course: Vol. II*. (pp. 597–620). New York: Springer International Publishing.

Burd-Sharps, S., & Rasch, R. (2015). *Impact of the U.S. housing crisis on the racial wealth gap across generations*. Brooklyn, NY: Social Science Research Council.

Burgess, E. W. (1925). The growth of the city. In R. Park, E. W. Burgess, & R. D. McKenzie (Eds.), *The city: Suggestions of investigation of human behavior in the urban environment* (pp. 47–62). Chicago: University of Chicago Press.

Bursik, R. J. (1988). Social disorganization and theories of crime and delinquency. *Criminology, 26*, 515–552.

Burton, L. M., Lichter, D. T., Baker, R. S., & Eason, J. M. (2013). Inequality, family processes, and health in the "New" rural America. *American Behavioral Scientist, 57*(8), 1128–1151.

Burton, L. M., Price-Spratlen, T., & Spencer, M. B. (1997). On ways of thinking about measuring neighborhoods: Implications for studying context and development outcomes for children. In J. Brooks-Gunn, G. Duncan, & J. Aber (Eds.), *Policy implications in studying neighborhoods: Vol. 2. Neighborhood poverty* (pp. 132–144). New York: Russell Sage Foundation.

Butz, A. M. (2016). Theorizing about poverty and paternalism in suburban America: The case of welfare sanctions. *Poverty & Public Policy, 8*, 129–140.

Cairns, R. B., Bergman, L. R., & Kagan, J. (Eds.), (1998). *Methods and models for studying the individual*. Newbury Park, CA: Sage.

Cantillon, D. (2006). Community social organization, parents, and peers as mediators of perceived neighborhood block characteristics on delinquent and prosocial activities. *American Journal of Community Psychology, 37*(1), 111–127.

Carr, P. J., & Kefalas, M. J. (2009). *Hollowing out the middle: The rural brain drain and what it means for America*. Boston: Beacon Press.

Cheng, A. S., Kruger, L. E., & Daniels, S. E. (2003). "Place" as an integrating concept in natural resource politics: Propositions for a social science research agenda. *Society and Natural Resources, 16*(2), 87–104.

Choo, H. Y., & Ferree, M. M. (2010). Practicing intersectionality in sociological research: A critical analysis of inclusions, interactions, and institutions in the study of inequalities. *Sociological Theory, 28*, 129–149.

Cleary, S. D. (2000). Adolescent victimization and associated suicidal and violent behaviors. *Adolescence, 35*(140), 671–682.

Cole, E. R. (2009). Intersectionality and research in psychology. *American Psychologist, 64*(3), 170–180.

Collins, L. M., & Lanza, S. T. (2010). *Latent class and latent transition analysis with applications in the social, behavioral, and health sciences*. Hoboken, NJ: John Wiley & Sons, Inc.

Cook, T. D., Herman, M. R., Phillips, M., & Settersten, R. A., Jr. (2002). Some ways in which neighborhoods, nuclear families, friendship groups, and schools jointly affect changes in early adolescent development. *Child Development, 73*, 1283–1309.

Coulton, C. J., & Spilsbury, J. C. (2014). Community and place-based understanding of child well-being. In A. Ben-Arieh, F. Casas, I. Frønes, & E. J. Korbin (Eds.), *Handbook of child well-being: Theories, methods and policies in global perspective* (pp. 1307–1334). Dordrecht: Springer Netherlands.

Dannefer, D. (2003). Cumulative advantage/disadvantage and the life course: Cross-fertilizing age and social science theory. *The Journals of Gerontology Series B, Psychological Sciences and Social Sciences, 58*(6), S327–S337.

DeCamp, W., & Zaykowski, H. (2015). Developmental victimology. Estimating group victimization trajectories in the age–victimization curve. *International Review of Victimology, 21*(3), 255–272.

DeLuca, S., Garboden, P. M. E., & Rosenblatt, P. (2013). Segregating shelter how housing policies shape the residential locations of low-income minority families. *The ANNALS of the American Academy of Political and Social Science, 647*(1), 268–299.

DeMaris, A., & Kaukinen, C. (2005). Violent victimization and women's mental and physical health: Evidence from a national sample. *Journal of Research in Crime and Delinquency, 42*(4), 384–411.

Diez Roux, A. V., & Mair, C. (2010). Neighborhoods and health. *Annals of the New York Academy of Sciences, 1186*, 125–145.

Dupéré, V., Leventhal, T., Crosnoe, R., & Dion, E. (2010). Understanding the positive role of neighborhood socioeconomic advantage in achievement: The contribution of the home, child care, and school environments. *Developmental Psychology, 46*(5), 1227–1244.

Dupéré, V., & Perkins, D. D. (2007). Community types and mental health: A multilevel study of local environment stress and coping. *American Journal of Community Psychology, 39*, 107–119.

Dwyer, R. E. (2010). Poverty, prosperity, and place: The shape of class segregation in the age of extremes. *Social Problems, 57*, 114–137.

Elder, G. H., Shanahan, M. J., & Jennings, J. A. (2015). Human development in time and place. In M. H. Bornstein & T. Leventhal (Eds.), *Ecological settings and processes: Vol. 4. Handbook of child psychology and developmental science* (pp. 6–54). Hoboken, NJ: John Wiley & Sons, Inc.

Ferraro, K. F., Shippee, T. P., & Schafer, M. H. (2009). Cumulative inequality theory for research on aging and the life course. In V. L. Bengtson, D. Gans, N. M. Putney, & M. Silverstein (Eds.), *Handbook of theories of aging* (2nd ed., pp. 413–433). New York: Springer Publishing.

Finkelhor, D., Turner, H., Ormrod, R., Hamby, S., & Kracke, K. (2009). *Children's exposure to violence: A comprehensive national survey Juvenile Justice Bulletin*. Washington, DC: U.S.

Department of Justice, Office of Justice Programs, Office of Juvenile Justice and Delinquency Prevention.

Fischer, M. J., & Massey, D. S. (2004). The ecology of racial discrimination. *City & Community, 3*(3), 221–241.

Fitzpatrick, K. M., & LaGory, M. (2003). "Placing" health in an urban sociology: Cities as mosaics of risk and protection. *City & Community, 2*, 33–46.

Frey, W. H. (2012). *Population growth in metro America since 1980: Putting the volatile 2000s in perspective Metropolitan Policy Program.* Washington, DC: The Brookings Institution.

Friedman, S. (2008). Do declines in residential segregation mean stable neighborhood racial integration in metropolitan America? A research note. *Social Science Research, 37*(3), 920–933.

Galster, G. C., & Killen, S. P. (1995). The geography of metropolitan opportunity: A reconnaissance and conceptual framework. *Housing Policy Debate, 6*, 7–43.

Gans, H. J. (2002). The sociology of space: A use-centered view. *City & Community, 1*(4), 329–339.

Giddens, A. (1980). *The class structure of the advanced societies.* London: Hutchinson.

Gorman-Smith, D., Tolan, P. H., & Henry, D. B. (2000). A developmental-ecological model of the relation of family functioning to patterns of delinquency. *Journal of Quantitative Criminology, 16*, 169–198.

Gross, M. (2004). Human geography and ecological sociology: The unfolding of a human ecology, 1890 to 1930—and beyond. *Social Science History, 28*(4), 575–605.

Gyourko, J., & Linneman, P. (1993). The affordability of the American dream: An examination of the last 30 years. *Journal of Housing Research, 4*(1), 39–72.

Harris, K. M. (2005). *Design features of add health.* Chapel Hill, NC: Carolina Population Center, University of North Carolina.

Harris, K. M., & Udry, J. R. (2008). *National Longitudinal Study of Adolescent Health (Add Health) 1994–2002: Obesity and Neighborhood Environment Files (Restricted Use): Carolina Population Center.* Chapel Hill, NC: University of North Carolina-Chapel Hill.

Haynie, D. L. (2001). Delinquent peers revisited: Does network structure matter? *American Journal of Sociology, 106*(4), 1013–1057.

Hipp, J. R. (2007). Block, tract, and levels of aggregation: Neighborhood structure and crime and disorder as a case in point. *American Sociological Review, 72*, 659–680.

Iceland, J., & Nelson, K. A. (2008). Hispanic segregation in metropolitan America: Exploring multiple forms of spatial assimilation. *American Sociological Review, 73*(5), 741–765.

Iceland, J., Sharpe, C., & Steinmetz, E. (2005). Class differences in African American residential patterns in U.S. metropolitan areas: 1990–2000. *Social Science Research, 34*, 252–266.

Irwin, M. D. (2007). Territories of inequality: An essay on the measurement and analysis of inequality in grounded place settings. In L. M. Lobao, G. Hooks, & A. R. Tickamyer (Eds.), *The sociology of spatial inequality* (pp. 85–112). Albany, NY: State University of New York Press.

Jargowsky, P. A. (2003). *Stunning progress, hidden problems: The dramatic decline of concentrated poverty in the 1990s.* Washington, DC: The Brookings Institution.

Jargowsky, P. A., & Bane, M. J. (1991). Ghetto poverty in the United States, 1970–1980. In C. Jencks & P. Peterson (Eds.), *The urban underclass* (pp. 235–273). Washington, DC: The Brookings Institution.

Jencks, C., & Mayer, S. (1990). The social consequences of growing up in a poor neighborhood. In J. Lynn, E. Laurence, & M. G. H. McGeary (Eds.), *Inner city poverty in the United States* (pp. 111–186). Washington, DC: National Academy Press.

Jensen, L., McLaughlin, D. K., & Slack, T. (2003). Rural poverty: The persisting challenge. In D. L. Brown & L. E. Swanson (Eds.), *Challenges for rural America in the twenty-first century* (pp. 118–131). University Park, PA: Penn State University Press.

Kingsley, G. T., Smith, R., & Price, D. (2009). *The Impacts of Foreclosures on Families and Communities*. Report prepared for the Open Society Institute by The Urban Institute, Washington, DC.

Kohli, M. (2007). The institutionalization of the life course: Looking back to look ahead. *Research in Human Development, 4*(3–4), 253–271.

Kuh, D., Ben-Shlomo, Y., Lynch, J., Hallqvist, J., & Power, C. (2003). Life course epidemiology. *Journal of Epidemiology and Community Health, 57*, 778–783.

Land, K. C., McCall, P. L., & Cohen, L. E. (1990). Structural covariates of homicide rates: Are there any invariances across time and social space. *American Journal of Sociology, 95*, 922–963.

Lanza, S. T., Collins, L. M., Lemmon, D. R., & Schafer, J. L. (2007). PROC LCA: A SAS procedure for latent class analysis. *Structural Equation Modeling, 14*(4), 671–694.

Latzman, R. D., & Swisher, R. R. (2005). The interactive relationship among adolescent violence, street violence, and depression. *Journal of Community Psychology, 33*, 355–371.

Lauritsen, J. L., & Heimer, K. (2009). *Gender and violent victimization, 1973–2005*. Washington, DC: National Institute of Justice.

Lazonick, W. (2015). Labor in the twenty-first century: The top 0.1% and the disappearing middle-class. In C. E. Weller (Ed.), *Inequality, uncertainty, and opportunity: The varied and growing role of finance in labor relations* (pp. 143–196). Champaign, IL: Labor and Employment Relations Association, University of Illinois at Urbana-Champaign.

Leicht, K. T., & Jenkins, J. C. (2007). New and unexplored opportunities: Developing a spatial perspective for political sociology. In L. M. Lobao, G. Hooks, & A. R. Tickamyer (Eds.), *The sociology of spatial inequality* (pp. 63–84). Albany, NY: State University of New York Press.

Lerner, R. M., Lerner, J. V., & Benson, J. B. (2011). Positive youth development: Research and applications for promoting thriving in adolescence. *Advances in Child Development and Behavior, 41*, 1–17.

Leung, M., & Takeuchi, D. T. (2011). Race, place, and health. In L. M. Burton, S. P. Kemp, M. Leung, S. A. Matthews, & D. T. Takeuchi (Eds.), *Communities, neighborhoods, and health: Expanding the boundaries of place* (pp. 73–88). New York: Springer.

Leventhal, T., & Brooks-Gunn, J. (2000). The neighborhoods they live in: The effects of neighborhood residence on child and adolescent outcomes. *Psychological Bulletin, 126*(2), 309–337.

Leventhal, T., Dupéré, V., & Brooks-Gunn, J. (2009). Neighborhood influences on adolescent development. In R. M. Lerner & L. Steinberg (Eds.), *Handbook of adolescent psychology* (pp. 411–443). Hoboken, NJ: John Wiley & Sons, Inc.

Leventhal, T., & Newman, S. (2010). Housing and child development. *Children and Youth Services Review, 32*(9), 1165–1174.

Lichter, D. T., & Johnson, K. M. (2007). The changing spatial concentration of America's rural poor population. *Rural Sociology, 72*(3), 331–358.

Lobao, L. M. (2004). Continuity and change in place stratification: Spatial inequality and middle-range territorial units. *Rural Sociology, 69*(1), 1–30.

Lobao, L. M., & Hooks, G. (2007). Advancing the sociology of spatial inequality: Spaces, places, and the subnational scale. In L. M. Lobao, G. Hooks, & A. R. Tickamyer (Eds.), *The sociology of spatial inequality* (pp. 29–61). Albany, NY: State University of New York Press.

Logan, J. R., & Zhang, C. (2010). Global neighborhoods: New pathways to diversity and separation. *American Journal of Sociology, 115*(4), 1069–1109.

Luke, D. A. (2005). Getting the big picture in community science: Methods that capture context. *American Journal of Community Psychology, 35*, 185–199.

Luthar, S. S., & Sexton, C. C. (2004). The high price of affluence. In V. K. Robert (Ed.), *Advances in child development and behavior: Vol. 32.* (pp. 125–162). San Diego, CA: Elsevier.

Massey, D. S., & Fischer, M. J. (2003). The geography of inequality in the United States, 1950–2000. *Brookings-Wharton Papers on Urban Affairs*, 1–40.

Massey, D. S., & Denton, N. A. (1993). *American apartheid: The making of an underclass.* Cambridge, MA: Harvard University Press.

Massey, D. S., Fischer, M. J., Dickens, W. T., & Levy, F. (2003). The geography of inequality in the United States, 1950–2000. *Brookings-Wharton Papers on urban affairs* (pp. 1–40).

Massey, D. S., Rothwell, J., & Domina, T. (2009). The changing bases of segregation in the United States. *Annals of AAPSS, 626,* 74–90.

Massey, D. S., & Sampson, R. J. (2009). Moynihan redox: Legacies and lessons. *Annals of AAPSS, 621,* 6–27.

Mayer, K. U. (2004). Whose lives? How history, societies, and institutions define and shape the life course. *Research in Human Development, 1*(3), 161–187.

McBride Murry, V., Berkel, C., Gaylord-Harden, N. K., Copeland-Linder, N., & Nation, M. (2011). Neighborhood poverty and adolescent development. *Journal of Research on Adolescence, 21*(1), 114–128.

McCall, L. (2005). The complexity of intersectionality. *Signs, 30*(3), 1771–1800.

McCutcheon, A. L. (1987). *Latent class analysis.* Newbury Park, CA: Sage Publications.

McKenzie, R. D. (1924). The ecological approach to the study of the human community. *American Journal of Sociology, 30*(3), 287–301.

McLeod, J. D. (2013). Social stratification and inequality. In C. S. Aneshensel, J. C. Phelan, & A. Bierman (Eds.), *Handbook of the sociology of mental health* (2nd ed., pp. 229–253). New York: Springer.

McLeod, J. D., & Pavalko, E. K. (2008). From selection effects to reciprocal processes: What does attention to the life course offer? *Advances in Life Course Research, 13,* 75–104.

Menard, S. W. (2002). *Short and long-term consequences of adolescent victimization.* Washington, DC: US Department of Justice, Office of Justice Programs, Office of Juvenile Justice and Delinquency Prevention.

Merton, R. K. (1996). *On social structure and science.* Chicago: University of Chicago Press.

Nagin, D. (2005). *Group-based modeling of development over the life course.* Cambridge, MA: Harvard University Press.

Nelson, M. C., Gordon-Larsen, P., Song, Y., & Popkin, B. M. (2006). Built and social environments: Associations with adolescent overweight and activity. *American Journal of Preventative Medicine, 31,* 109–117.

Newman, K., & Wyly, E. K. (2006). The right to stay put, revisited: Gentrification and resistance to displacement in New York City. *Urban Studies, 43*(1), 23–57.

Oakley, D. A., & Logan, J. R. (2007). A spatial analysis of the urban landscape: What accounts for differences across neighborhoods? In L. M. Lobao, G. Hooks, & A. R. Tickamyer (Eds.), *The sociology of spatial inequality* (pp. 215–232). Albany, NY: State University of New York Press.

O'Rand, A. M. (2001). Stratification and the life course: The forms of life-course capital and their interrelationships. In R. H. Binstock & L. K. George (Eds.), *Handbook of aging and the social sciences* (5th ed., pp. 197–213). San Diego, CA: Academic Press.

Osgood, D. W., & Anderson, A. (2004). Unstructured socializing and rates of delinquency. *Criminology, 42,* 519–549.

Osypuk, T. L. (2013). Invited commentary: Integrating a life-course perspective and social theory to advance research on residential segregation and health. *American Journal of Epidemiology, 177*(4), 310–315.

Park, R. E. (1936). Human ecology. *American Journal of Sociology, 42,* 1–15.

Plybon, L. E., & Kliewer, W. (2002). Neighborhood types and externalizing behavior in urban school-age children: Tests of direct, mediated, and moderated effects. *Journal of Child and Family Studies, 10*, 419–437.

Quillian, L. (1999). Migration patterns and the growth of high-poverty neighborhoods, 1970–1990. *American Journal of Sociology, 105*(1), 1–37.

Quillian, L. (2002). Why is black-white residential segregation so persistent? Evidence on three theories from migration data. *Social Science Research, 31*, 197–229.

Ragin, C. C. (2008). *Redesigning social inquiry: Fuzzy sets and beyond.* Chicago: University of Chicago Press.

Raudenbush, S. W., & Bryk, A. S. (2002). *Hierarchical linear models: Applications and data analysis methods* (2nd ed.). . Thousand Oaks, CA: Sage Publications, Inc.

Reardon, S. F., & Bischoff, K. (2011). Income inequality and income segregation. *American Journal of Sociology, 116*(4), 1092–1153.

Reardon, S. F., Fox, L., & Townsend, J. (2015). Neighborhood income composition by household race and income, 1990–2009. *The Annals of the American Academy of Political and Social Science, 660*(1), 78–97.

Rice, J. K. (2004). Equity and efficiency in school finance reform: Competing or complementary goods? *Peabody Journal of Education, 79*(3), 134–151.

Robert, S. A. (1999). Socioeconomic position and health: The independent contribution of community socioeconomic context. *Annual Review of Sociology, 25*, 489–516.

Sampson, R. J. (1993). Linking time and place: Dynamic contextualism and the future of criminological inquiry. *Journal of Research in Crime and Delinquency, 30*, 426–444.

Sampson, R. J. (2012). *Great American city: Chicago and the enduring neighborhood effect.* Chicago, IL: University of Chicago Press.

Sampson, R. J., & Groves, W. B. (1989). Community structure and crime: Testing social-disorganization theory. *The American Journal of Sociology, 94*(4), 774–802.

Sampson, R. J., Morenoff, J. D., & Gannon-Rowley, T. (2002). Assessing "neighborhood effects": Social processes and new directions in research. *Annual Review of Sociology, 51*(1), 443–478.

Sampson, R. J., Raudenbush, S. W., & Earls, F. (1997). Neighborhoods and violent crime: A multi-level study of collective efficacy. *Science, 277*, 918–924.

Sampson, R. J., & Sharkey, P. (2008). Neighborhood selection and the social reproduction of concentrated racial inequality. *Demography, 45*(1), 1–29.

Schreck, C. J., Stewart, E. A., & Osgood, D. W. (2008). A reappraisal of the overlap of violent offenders and victims*. *Criminology, 46*(4), 871–906.

Semyonov, M., & Kraus, V. (1983). The social hierarchies of communities and neighborhoods. *Social Science Quarterly, 63*(4), 780–789.

Settersten, R. A., Jr., & Gannon, L. (2005). Structure, agency, and the space between: On the challenges and contradictions of a blended view of the life course. *Advances in Life Course Research, 10*, 35–55.

Sharkey, P. (2006). Navigating dangerous streets: The sources and consequences of street efficacy. *American Sociological Review, 71*(5), 826–846.

Sharkey, P. (2008). The intergenerational transmission of context. *American Journal of Sociology, 113*(4), 931–969.

Shaw, C. R., & McKay, H. D. (1942). *Juvenile delinquency and urban areas.* Chicago: University of Chicago Press.

Sherman, J., & Sage, R. (2011). Sending off all your good treasures: Rural schools, brain-drain, and community survival in the wake of economic collapse. *Journal of Research in Rural Education, 26*(11), 1.

Shinn, M., & Toohey, S. M. (2003). Community contexts of human welfare. *Annual Review of Psychology, 54*, 427–459.

Smetana, J. G., Campione-Barr, N., & Metzger, A. (2006). Adolescent development in interpersonal and societal contexts. *Annual Review of Psychology, 57*, 255–284.

Snell, P. (2010). From Durkheim to the Chicago school: Against the 'variables sociology' paradigm. *Journal of Classical Sociology, 10*(1), 51–67.

Snyder, H. N., & Sickmund, M. (2006). *Juvenile offenders and victims: 2006 National Report.* Washington, DC: U.S. Department of Justice, Office of Justice Programs, Office of Juvenile Justice and Delinquency Prevention.

Solari, C. D. (2012). Affluent neighborhood persistence and change in U.S. cities. *City & Community, 11*(4), 370–388.

South, S. J., & Crowder, K. (1998). Leaving the 'hood: Residential mobility between Black, White, and integrated neighborhoods. *American Sociological Review, 63*(1), 17–26.

Squires, G. D., & Hyra, D. S. (2010). Foreclosures—Yesterday, today, and tomorrow. *City & Community, 9*(1), 50–60.

Squires, G. D., Hyra, D. S., & Renner, R. N. (2009). Segregation and the subprime lending crisis. In *Paper presented at the 2009 Federal Reserve System Community Affairs Research Conference, Washington, DC, April 16, 2009.*

Squires, G. D., & Kubrin, C. E. (2005). Privileged places: Race, uneven development and the geography of opportunity in urban America. *Urban Studies, 42*(1), 47–68.

Sucoff, C. A., & Upchurch, D. M. (1998). Neighborhood context and the risk of childbearing among metropolitan-area black adolescents. *American Sociological Review, 63*(4), 571–585.

Sullivan, C. J., Wilcox, P., & Osey, G. C. (2011). Trajectories of victimization from early to mid-adolescence. *Criminal Justice and Behavior, 38*(1), 85–104.

Sundstrom, R. R. (2003). Race and place: Social space in the production of human kinds. *Philosophy & Geography, 6*(1), 83–95.

Teasdale, B., & Silver, E. (2009). Neighborhoods and self-control: Toward and expanded view of socialization. *Social Problems, 56*, 205–222.

Thomas, S. A., & Shihadeh, E. S. (2013). Institutional isolation and crime: The mediating effect of disengaged youth on levels of crime. *Social Science Research, 42*(5), 1167–1179.

Tickameyer, A. R., & Duncan, C. M. (1990). Poverty and opportunity structure in rural America. *Annual Review of Sociology, 16*, 67–86.

Timberlake, J. M. (2007). Racial and ethnic inequality in the duration of children's exposure to neighborhood poverty and affluence. *Social Problems, 54*(3), 319–342.

Truman, J., Langton, L., & Planty, M. (2013). *Criminal Victimization, 2012: NCJ 243389.* Washington, DC: U.S. Department of Justice, Office of Justice Programs, Bureau of Justice Statistics.

Turner, H. A., Finkelhor, D., & Ormrod, R. (2006). The effect of lifetime victimization on the mental health of children and adolescents. *Social Science and Medicine, 62*, 13–27.

U.S. Bureau of the Census. (1991). *Money income of households, families, and persons in the Unites States: 1990: Current Population Reports, Series P-60, No. 174.* Washington, DC: U.S. Government Printing Office.

U.S. Bureau of the Census. (1992). *Income, poverty, and wealth in the United States: A chartbook: Current Population Reports, Series P-60, No. 179.* Washington, DC: U.S. Government Printing Office.

United States Department of Agriculture, & Economic Research Service. (2015). Rural America at a glance: 2015 edition. *Economic information bulletin 145.* www.ers.usda.gov/media/1952235/eib145.pdf.

Vermunt, J. K. (2008). Latent class and finite mixture models for multilevel data sets. *Statistical Methods in Medical Research, 17*, 33–51.

Warner, T. D. (2016). Up in smoke: Neighborhood contexts of marijuana use from adolescence through young adulthood. *Journal of Youth and Adolescence, 45*(1), 35–53.

Warner, T. D., & Swisher, R. R. (2014). The effect of direct and indirect exposure to violence on youth survival expectations. *Journal of Adolescent Health, 55*(6), 817–822.

Weden, M. M., Bird, C. E., Escarce, J. J., & Lurie, N. (2011). Neighborhood archetypes for population health research: Is there no place like home? *Health & Place, 17*, 289–299.

Wickrama, K. A. S., & Noh, S. (2010). The long arm of community: The influence of childhood community contexts across the early life course. *Journal of Youth and Adolescence, 39,* 894–910.

Williams, D. R., Mohammed, S. A., Leavell, J., & Collins, C. (2010). Race, socioeconomic status, and health: Complexities, ongoing challenges, and research opportunities. *Annals of the New York Academy of Sciences, 1186,* 69–101.

Wilson, W. J. (1987). *The truly disadvantaged: The inner city, the underclass, and public policy.* Chicago: University of Chicago Press.

Wirth, L. (1945). Human ecology. *American Journal of Sociology, 50*(6), 483–488.

Yinger, J. (1995). *Closed doors, opportunities lost: The continuing cost of housing discrimination.* New York: Sage.

Yuval-Davis, N. (2006). Intersectionality and feminist politics. *European Journal of Women's Studies, 13*(3), 193–209.

CHAPTER FIVE

How Children Learn to Navigate the Symbolic World of Pictures: The Importance of the Artist's Mind and Differentiating Picture Modalities

M.L. Allen*[,1], E. Armitage[†]

*Lancaster University, Lancaster, United Kingdom
[†]AQA, Manchester, United Kingdom
[1]Corresponding author: e-mail address: melissa.allen@lancaster.ac.uk

Contents

Abstract

Pictures offer a unique and essential contribution to our lives, both in terms of aesthetic pleasure and links to symbolic thought. As such, psychologists have devoted significant time to investigating how children acquire an understanding of pictures. This chapter focuses on two particular facets of this development: the role of the artist and the importance of picture modality. First, we review work that has focused on tracking children's ability to (a) map the relationship between the mental state of the artist and their pictures, and (b) incorporate such considerations into their evaluations of pictures. Drawing these literatures together provides an up-to-date account of how children acquire a mentalistic understanding of pictures. Second, we argue that a mature theory of pictures must enable children to distinguish between different picture types (e.g., photographs vs drawings), and therefore that picture modality should be incorporated into existing theoretical accounts of pictorial development.

Advances in Child Development and Behavior, Volume 52
ISSN 0065-2407
http://dx.doi.org/10.1016/bs.acdb.2016.10.004

1. NAVIGATING THE SYMBOLIC WORLD OF PICTURES

Since the time of Plato and Aristotle, philosophers and psychologists alike have sought to understand the unique ability of the human race to communicate via symbols (Deacon, 1997; Ittelson, 1996). While language is our dominant symbol system, "pictorial perception has more immediacy than understanding of words" (Gibson, 1979, p. 34), and representational pictures (those that share a physical resemblance to their referents) are particularly ubiquitous symbols in everyday life. Freeman (2004) states, "lay people and experts of all ages often find themselves making many types of decisions about what a picture shows, how it shows it, and how well it shows it. These decisions are made on many types of pictures, photographs, road signs, artworks on a wall, quick sketches, text illustrations, and more" (p. 359), making the acquisition of pictorial understanding a crucial developmental milestone (DeLoache, 2002, 2004; Freeman, 2004; Jolley, 2010; Piaget, 1952).

Despite their importance, the complexity of pictures and our ability to comprehend them is often overlooked since, "most people think they know what a picture is, anything so familiar must be simple" (Gibson, 1980, p. xvii). In reality, the acquisition of pictorial understanding is a "protracted and multifaceted" (Liben, 1999, p. 307) process that unfolds over the first several years of a child's life. Significant attention has been devoted to pinpointing the key developmental milestones in the trajectory of this understanding, and to studying the factors that underpin it. This chapter focuses on a discussion of the importance of two of these factors. First, we highlight the critical role that an understanding of the artist's mind plays in children's pictorial development. By drawing together literature on how children map the relationship between artists' mental states and their pictures, with studies that document how this knowledge is incorporated into their evaluations of pictures, we attempt to create a more comprehensive account of how children acquire a mentalistic understanding of pictures. In doing so, we also highlight the benefits of broadening how we conceptualize the artist's mind, going beyond the traditional focus on the role of intention.

Second, we draw attention to an interesting but often overlooked factor in understanding pictures—picture modality (e.g., drawings vs photographs). In addition to the common properties most representational pictures share, there are properties unique to each picture modality. For instance, photographs are often characterized as reliable sources of information due to their, typically, causal relationship with their referents, while drawings are often appreciated as one artist's perspective. Consequently, we argue that in order to acquire a mature theory of pictures children need to be aware of these distinctions. To this end, we review existing literature on children's understanding of photographs and drawings to demonstrate how empirical comparisons of children's responses to different picture types provide scope for extending current theories of pictorial development to include picture modality. We concentrate here specifically on 2D photographs and drawings; however, we acknowledge the importance of understanding symbolic content from moving pictures such as video, which is covered in depth elsewhere in the literature (see Troseth, 2010). Alongside this, we highlight two cross-modal debates that arise from various psychological and philosophical perspectives on the nature of pictorial representation, as key topics for future research in this area.

2. FOUNDATIONS OF PICTORIAL UNDERSTANDING

Before children can appreciate the nuances of artists' influence over their pictures, or the differences in how various picture types relate to their referents and creators, they must acquire the building blocks of pictorial understanding. A general consensus has been reached among theorists regarding the steps this entails: first, children must learn to recognize the similarities and differences between pictures and their referents, and second, they must learn that pictures stand for their real-world referents, at which point they can begin to use pictures as sources of information about both generic and specific elements of the world (Liben, 1999).

Three-month-olds can recognize their mother's face in photographs and discriminate her face from that of a stranger (Barrera & Maurer, 1981), and by 5 months of age they can recognize the similarities between 2D photographs and their 3D referents (DeLoache, Strauss, & Maynard, 1979). Importantly, discrimination studies show that in addition to being aware of their perceptual similarities, infants also recognize that pictures and their referents are different entities. Slater, Rose, and Morison (1984) found that newborns look at 3D geometric figures of circles and crosses for significantly longer than they look at photographs of the same figures; in order to show a preference for one display over the other, it follows that the babies must have perceived a difference in the two stimuli. Other variables in these studies were held constant (e.g., same background color of the displays and familiarity of stimuli), confirming that differences were due to the discrimination of real vs 2D stimuli and not other extraneous factors.

Despite their early ability to visually distinguish pictures from their referents, infants do not always treat the two as dissimilar. Nine-month-old infants have a tendency to pick up objects from pictures, almost "as if" they were the objects themselves (DeLoache, Pierroutsakos, Uttal, Rosengren, & Gottlieb, 1998). However, this behavior appears to represent infants' attempts to ascertain the exact nature of the difference between pictures and their referents; they display more grasping behaviors toward objects when presented with picture–object pairs (DeLoache et al., 1998), and their hand and finger movements differ when they are grasping for real objects vs trying to "pick up" objects from pictures (Yonas, Granrud, Chov, & Alexander, 2005). By the time they are 18 months old infants' grasping behaviors are replaced by pointing behavior (DeLoache et al., 1998), marking the transition from viewing pictures as objects of action to viewing them as "objects of contemplation" (Werner & Kaplan, 1963, p. 18).

The successful "decoupling" of referential content from the pictorial surface (Ittelson, 1996) is insufficient to render children symbolic. For pictures to be useful to them, children need to know that pictures stand for, or refer to, their referents. Representational insight is the term used to describe children's recognition that pictures refer to something in the real world (DeLoache, 1995, 2002); a picture of a rabbit must be interpreted as referring to a real rabbit if it is to be utilized as a symbol. Preissler and Carey (2004) report one of the earliest demonstrations of representational insight. They taught 18- and 24-month-old children a label (e.g., "whisk") for a picture of a novel object (a whisk) by repeatedly pairing the two together. At test children were given a choice between the picture and the referent object (e.g., a real whisk) and the experimenter asked, "can you show me a whisk?" Remarkably, none of the children in either age group selected the picture alone, while 60% of 18-month-olds and 55% of 24-month-olds selected the real whisk, and 40% of 18-month-olds and 45% of 24-month-olds chose both the picture and the real whisk. Thus, despite the associative manner in which they were taught the pairing, children recognized that the picture was a representation of the real object, and thus extended the label from the picture to the object (see also Ganea, Allen, Butler, Carey, & DeLoache, 2009).

In reality of course, pictures serve as sources of information about very specific aspects of the world, for example, the location of a hidden toy in a particular room. This realization is imperative if children are to appropriately utilize the information provided in pictures. This issue has been tested rigorously by DeLoache (1987, 1991) using her classic search task, which involves asking children to use a picture of a room to locate a toy hidden in the corresponding real room. In a seminal series of experiments DeLoache and Burns (1994) conducted seven variations of this task to explore whether 24-, 27-, and 30-month-old children could extract the information about a toy's location from the picture and then use it to find the toy in the real room.

In Experiment 1, 24- and 30-month-olds were introduced to a Snoopy doll and the experimenter labeled each piece of furniture in the room, before presenting children with a photograph (or line drawing) of the room and pointing out the correspondence between the real and pictured items of furniture. After ensuring that they had understood the picture–room relationship, Snoopy was hidden in the pictured room and the experimenter pointed out his hiding place on the picture; children were then asked to find him. Success required children to treat the picture as a representation of reality, specifically, Snoopy's location. The age-related difference in performance was dramatic: 30-month-olds found Snoopy without error on 72% of trials, compared to only 13% of trials for 24-month-olds.

In the subsequent six experiments a series of modifications were made to the procedure in an effort to improve the performance of 24-month-old children. It was only when they were asked to place Snoopy in particular locations, rather than retrieve him, that 24-month-old children were successful, indicating a limited understanding of the picture–room relation. Success can be achieved at age 2 if children are asked to search different rooms, rather than the same room four times, since this prevents perseverative errors (Suddendorf, 2003).

This body of work clearly indicates that sometime between the age of 24 and 30 months children's representational insight encompasses an understanding that pictures refer to *general categories* (Ganea et al., 2009; Preissler & Carey, 2004), and also *specific realities*, and as such are useful sources of information about particular aspects of the world. However, children's success in using pictures as symbols in the studies reviewed thus far rest on a resemblance-based understanding of the picture–referent relationship— pictures represent their referents by virtue of the visual similarities they share. Iconicity bolsters children's ability to recognize the referential nature of the picture–referent relationship, and subsequently to transfer information from pictures to the real world (Callaghan, 2000; Ganea, Pickard, & DeLoache, 2008; Hartley & Allen, 2015; Simcock & DeLoache, 2006; Tare, Chiong, Ganea, & DeLoache, 2010). For example, in a picture-based word-learning task, Ganea et al. (2008) found that 15-month-old children's ability to extend novel labels from pictures to a novel target object was significantly better for photographs and drawings than static cartoons. Similarly, 3-year-old children learn more new facts about animals from a book filled with realistic photographs than a comparison book filled with drawings (Tare et al., 2010).

However, a resemblance-based theory of pictures is limited in two important ways. First, although pictures are often iconic, what a picture looks like is not always sufficient to identify its referent (Browne & Woolley, 2001; Myers & Liben, 2012), highlighting the need for additional, nonresemblance-based cues, with which to decode pictures. Second, the symbolic function of pictures as communicative vehicles is motivated and legitimized by an intentional, or human, component. Hence, in order to strengthen their understanding of pictures as symbols, children need to be aware of the role that the artist plays in constructing the picture–world relationship and recognize him or her as a useful source of information (Callaghan & Rochat, 2003; Freeman, 2000; Wollheim, 1987).

3. THE ROLE OF THE ARTISTS' MIND

3.1 Intention

Proponents of the intentional position argue that "if we are interested in...paintings, we must start with the artist" (Wollheim, 1987, p. 36), and indeed the role of the artist's intention in picture interpretation has garnered significant attention. Several theoretical accounts of pictorial development have posited that intention underlies our intuitions about pictures (Bloom, 1996, 2004; Callaghan, 2008; Freeman & Sanger, 1995; Wollheim, 1987). DeLoache (2004) argued that pictures only represent the world as a result of someone's intention to communicate information, making the ability to comprehend an artist's intention "both necessary and sufficient to establish a symbolic relation" (p. 67). While an artist's line drawing of a rabbit is taken to represent a rabbit, a similarly shaped, but naturally occurring, mud puddle is less likely to be perceived as a representation of a rabbit, since it was not created with that intention in mind (Bloom, 1996; Gelman & Ebeling, 1998).

In accordance with this viewpoint, Freeman and Sanger (1995) placed the artist at the heart of their "intentional net" framework, a theoretical model linking the artist, picture, world, and beholder. They state that in order to acquire a complete theory of pictures children must understand the role that artists play in defining what a picture represents, and bring this to bear on their interpretations of the pictures produced. With regard to precisely how children achieve these insights, Callaghan (2008) proposed that children rely on the social-cognitive skills of imitation and intention reading acquired in early infancy (Behne, Carpenter, & Tomasello, 2005; Meltzoff, 1995; Moore, Liebal, & Tomasello, 2013; Tomasello, 1999). In her view, children acquire knowledge of the referential function of pictures through interactions with others that involve the use of pictures to communicate information. These experiences equip them with the ability to produce their own representational pictures, which in turn affords them direct access to the way in which artists' intentions mediate the picture–referent relationship.

Indeed, it has been found that highlighting the communicative intent underlying a picture facilitates 30-month-old children's ability to use pictures to locate hidden objects (Salsa & Peralta de Mendoza, 2007), over and above highlighting the shared resemblance between the picture and the real toy. However, understanding that a picture is intended to communicate something about the world (i.e., the location of a hidden toy) is qualitatively different from understanding that artists' intentions underpin the representational status of pictures, and thus serves as a unique cue to precisely *what* a picture represents.

Children recognize the value of their own creative intentions from the age of 3. Bloom and Markson (1998) asked 3- and 4-year-old children to draw two pairs of pictures: a balloon and a lollipop, and the experimenter and him or herself. Unsurprisingly, the pairs of pictures were almost identical, which allowed the authors to investigate whether the children would disambiguate the pictures using their own referential intention, for instance, to depict a balloon, when asked to name them. They did, as 76% of the 3-year-olds and 87% of the 4-year-olds correctly named their pictures, indicating that resemblance, in this case shape, is not the only cue children can use to categorize pictures. They also recognize that artists play a role in defining what their pictures represent: a picture drawn with the intention of representing a balloon cannot be a lollipop. An alternative explanation, however, is that children relied on color rather than their intentions to discriminate between the pictures. A replication study showed that when color is held constant children perform at chance when labeling their drawings

(Callaghan & Rochat, 2008), and children with Autism Spectrum Disorder (ASD) also succeed in this task (Allen, 2009). Given that children with ASD have notable difficulties monitoring and utilizing the intentions of others, an associative strategy (see Hartley & Allen, 2014; Preissler, 2008) using perceptual cues (i.e., color) is a likely explanation, at least for this cohort of children.

Nonetheless, further support for the importance of intentionality can be derived from work by Gross and Hayne (1999), who found that 3- and 4-year-old children could identify and describe their own relatively abstract drawings of familiar events, such as birthdays, up to 3 months after they were drawn. Five- and six-year-old children could do so up to 6 months later. The lack of resemblance information children had to base their descriptions on suggests at least some reliance on their original picture conception, including what they intended to draw. Children could not have been relying on generic knowledge of birthdays, for instance, since they were also successful when they had to draw and later identify pictures of atypical events, such as a chocolate factory visit (Experiment 1b). Clearly, despite their non-representational appearance children assign symbolic content to their drawings via their referential intentions. However, while children are privy to their own intentions, they "do not have psychic access to the intentions of others" (Bloom, 1996, p. 7). This raises the question of whether they are equally competent at discerning other artist's intentions and using them to decode pictures.

From an early age children are aware of the importance of intentionality for various facets of social communication (Behne et al., 2005; Carpenter, Akhtar, & Tomasello, 1998; Gelman & Bloom, 2000; Meltzoff, 1995; Moore et al., 2013; Woodward, Sommerville, & Guajardo, 2001), and this includes pictures. For instance, 2-year-old children can use eye gaze to identify what an ambiguous drawing is intended to represent (Preissler & Bloom, 2008). In this task children were shown two similarly shaped novel objects, which were subsequently placed into two empty boxes. The key manipulation was whether children could follow the experimenter's eye gaze while she was drawing to identify which object she intended to draw. Eye gaze had a significant influence on children's generalization of the novel label, such that 62.5% chose the object that the experimenter had gazed at while drawing. In a second experiment where the drawing was "discovered" instead of drawn, only 17% of children chose the object the experimenter gazed at, confirming that the results from Experiment 1 were due to sensitivity to artist intention and not associative cues. Thus, from the age of 2 years children are capable of reflecting on the referential intentions of their creators to make picture–referent mappings.

Even more tellingly, Gelman and Ebeling (1998) report significant changes in children's picture naming depending on the presence or absence of referential intent. They asked 2- to 4-year-old children to name identical drawings, which were produced intentionally (John used some paint to make something for his teacher) or accidentally (John spilled some paint on the floor). Children in the intentional condition were significantly more likely to name the drawing according to its shape (i.e., the outline of a man was named "a man") than children in the accidental condition, who instead displayed a trend toward material-based naming (e.g., paint). Children are adept at identifying and labeling a picture's referent based on whether the creator acted intentionally or not. Accidentally resembling an object is insufficient for children to consider a picture a true representation of that object, which is testament to their awareness that intentionality is key to accurately decoding pictures (DeLoache, 2004; Wollheim, 1987). However, there is a caveat to this body of work. Thus far intention has only been shown to sway children's interpretation of visually ambiguous pictures, which leaves open the question of whether intention plays a lesser role when appearance provides a direct route to referent identification. That is, how do children decode iconic picture–referent relations? Hence, researchers began to design tasks in which appearance and intention are placed in direct conflict.

3.1.1 Appearance vs Intentional Cues

One such task was devised by Browne and Woolley (2001), who introduced 4-year-olds, 7-year-olds, and adults to a puppet who intended to draw, for instance, a bear, but whose final picture looked unequivocally like a rabbit. When asked what would be a better name for the picture—rabbit or bear— 84% of 4-year-olds, 94% of 7-year-olds, and 100% of adults preferred to name it according to what it looked like: a rabbit. Here, even adults prioritized appearance over intention. Similarly, in Richert and Lillard's (2002) study, 4- to 8-year-old children heard a story about Luna, a troll doll, who lives in a land without animals. The children then watched as Luna drew a picture resembling a fish. When asked, "is Luna drawing a fish?" the majority of children said that she was, indicating that they focused on the picture's appearance alone, without taking into account her knowledge state. However, there are alternative explanations. Perhaps, given the pictures' fish-like appearance, children simply could not think of an alternative name for it or thought Luna had drawn a fish by chance. Nevertheless, when considered in conjunction with Browne and Woolley's findings, it is entirely plausible that children and even adults consider appearance a more reliable cue to the identity of a picture than intention.

Taking a slightly different approach, Myers and Liben (2008) tested the limits of children's understanding that intention underpins pictorial symbolism, by using appearance as a confounding variable. In one of their tasks, 5- to 10-year-old children watched as two creators added colored dots to a map of a room. The first creator did so with the intention of representing the location of a series of hidden objects (symbolic), while the other did so with the intention of making the map more colorful (aesthetic). Crucially, for half of the children the color of the aesthetic dots (red) matched the hidden objects (red fire trucks) and for the other half they did not (yellow school bus). The experimenter then asked the children, "If you wanted to find a bunch of toy fire trucks [showing red toy fire truck] that were hidden in that room, whose drawing would help you do that?"

When the aesthetic dot and hidden object were the same color, only the 9- to 10-year-old children ignored the color match to select the symbolic map. When appearance-based responding was not an option, more children in all age groups selected the appropriate symbolic map; however, this was only significant for the 9- to 10-year-olds. When questioned, children in the younger two age groups knew why each creator had added the dots: to denote location or to make it prettier, yet they did not use this information to select the appropriate map. The 5- to 6-year-olds were seduced by the salience of the color match between the dot and the referent, and selected the red aesthetic map, while the 7- to 8-year-olds performed at chance, seemingly unsure whether to prioritize appearance or intention. It is evident from these findings that children's ability to infer and more importantly, use a creator's intentions, to interpret their depictions continues to evolve between the ages of 5 and 9, and is influenced by the presence of other factors, such as appearance. Table 1 summarizes the main age-related shifts thus far discussed in children's understanding of the role played by the artist's mind in pictorial representation.

Based on this review of current evidence, several open questions remain concerning the importance of intention when it is conflated with appearance. One possibility is that when the two cues conflict appearance usurps intention (Browne & Woolley, 2001; Richert & Lillard, 2002). Alternatively, intention may assume a more dominant role in older children's picture interpretation, while younger children are seduced by the salience of the perceptual similarity between pictures and their referents (Myers & Liben, 2008). Moreover, the level of iconicity may play a role

Table 1 Age-Related Trends in Children's Understanding of the Role Played by the Artist's Mind in Pictorial Representation

Age	Aspect of Pictorial Understanding	Relevant Empirical Work
2 Years	Children can use eye gaze to identify what an ambiguous drawing is intended to represent	Preissler and Bloom (2008)
	Children recognize that artist's intentions underpin the representational nature of pictures by assigning different names to identical pictures based on whether they were intentionally or accidentally created	Gelman and Ebeling (1998)
3 Years	Children show an appreciation that artist's intentions play a defining role in what a picture represents by demonstrating their ability to use their own intentions to disambiguate two identical pictures	Bloom and Markson (1998)
	Children can identify and describe their own abstract drawings after a delay, based on what they had intended to draw	Gross and Hayne (1998)
4 Years	Children and adults prioritize appearance over intention when naming ambiguous drawings	Browne and Woolley (2001)
	Children name pictures according to what they looked like, without taking into account the artist's knowledge state (lack of knowledge about the object pictured)	Richert and Lillard (2002)
5–6 Years	Children prioritize appearance over intention when the two cues conflict	Myers and Liben (2008)
7–8 Years	Children performed at chance and are unsure which cue to prioritize when the two cues conflict	Myers and Liben (2008)
9–10 Years	Children prioritize intention over appearance when the two cues conflict, indicating a shift toward a more robust mentalistic understanding of pictures	Myers and Liben (2008)

in mediating the interpretive power of these two cues (Browne & Woolley, 2001; Myers & Liben, 2008; Richert & Lillard, 2002). To date, only one study has addressed these questions.

In a series of three experiments, Armitage and Allen (2015) investigated children's use of appearance and intentional cues by systematically varying the level of conflict between the two cues. In Experiments 1 and 3, children aged 3–6 years and adults watched as the experimenter stated her intention to draw a particular referent (e.g., a blue duck) from a choice of three (e.g., a blue duck, a pink duck, and a teddy bear). In the color change condition the final picture clearly resembled a differently colored object from the one the experimenter intended to depict (e.g., a pink duck), thus creating a transparent picture–referent relationship that conflicted with the picture creator's intention. By contrast, in the black-and-white condition, the final picture was ambiguous (e.g., a gray duck), creating a much less transparent relation between the picture and the referent, which could be disambiguated using the artist's stated intention. When participants were asked to identify the picture's depicted referent (What is this?) they relied on the picture's appearance in the color change condition (pink duck), only deferring to intentional cues in the black-and-white condition (blue duck), when the pictures were ambiguous.

Using a modified version of the task, Experiment 2 confirmed that children's appearance-based responding in the color change condition reflected a genuine focus on what a picture looks like, rather than a disregard for the experimenter's intention. Together, these findings show that from the age of 3 children appreciate both the resemblance-based link pictures share with their referents, and the intentional relation they have to their creator. Critically, they reveal that children are selective in their use of these two cues when decoding picture–referent relations, as the route they follow is dependent on whether the picture is ambiguous or iconic. The similar performance of children and adults indicates that the use of appearance and intentional cues is not predicated upon age; children as young as 3 years switch flexibly between the two.

3.2 Knowledge and Ideas

The journey to understanding that pictures are "intentional manifestations of mind" (Freeman & Sanger, 1995) requires more than an appreciation of how artists' intentions affect their pictures. As Dutton states, "every work of art is an artifact, the product of human skills and techniques" (1979, p. 305); hence in order to fully comprehend the artist's role children must understand how other aspects of an artist's mind, such as their knowledge about the world and their ideas, mediate the picture–referent relationship (Dewey, 1958; Dutton, 1979). For instance, the assumption regarding knowledge is that if children recognize the intentional link between an artist's mind and their picture, then they should be able to reason that he or she could not draw a referent without *knowing* something about it.

This assumption was tested by Browne and Woolley (2001, Study 2, Task 2). They told their participants that the puppet who intended to depict a bear, but produced a picture that looked equally like a bear and a rabbit, did not know the difference between rabbits and bears. When asked, "Which animal do you think this picture looks like? Do you think it looks like a rabbit or a bear?" 7-year-olds said the picture looked like its intended referent 30% of the time, and adults 40% of the time, compared to a respective 94% and 100% in an earlier version of the task, in which intention was not devalued by a lack of artist knowledge. These findings indicate that by the age of 7 children understand how intentions are linked to knowledge, and how knowledge affects an artist's capacity to depict specific referents; without knowing what bears are, it is unlikely that one can intend to draw a bear. By contrast, artist knowledge had no effect on 4-year-old children's responding; they named the picture according to the puppet's intention more often than would be expected by chance.

In addition, when Richert and Lillard (2002) asked their 4- to 8-year-old participants "Does Luna *think* she is drawing a fish?" as well as the more objective, "Is Luna drawing a fish?" (see p. 13), the number of children who considered Luna's knowledge state, and said no, increased between the ages of 6 and 8. This suggests that while children may be predisposed to focus on the appearance of a picture (e.g., agreeing that Luna is drawing a fish), highlighting the salience of the artist's mind prompts older children to consider how her knowledge state, rather than appearance, determines the identity of her picture. This extends the findings of Browne and Woolley (2001) by showing that the capacity to map the relationship between an artist's knowledge and the identity of his or her subsequent depictions continues to gain sophistication until at least the age of 8.

As has been illustrated, children recognize that artists' intentions have a direct impact on the pictures they produce and that what an artist knows about the world defines, to some extent, the parameters of what he or she can draw. The consequence of these contributions is that pictures can be defined as "creative products of the [artist's] mind" (Olson & Shaw, 2011, p. 431), and valued accordingly. However, understanding the mechanisms via which artists translate their ideas into pictures does not necessarily mean children place value on those underlying ideas when evaluating an artist's contribution or the pictures themselves. It is possible to investigate this by asking how children react to the plagiarism of ideas, and whether they prefer pictures that contain their ideas over ones that they physically created.

The first of these questions has been addressed by Olson and Shaw (2011). They presented 7-year-olds, 9-year-olds, and adults with scenarios in which one person drew an original picture, and the second person deliberately or coincidentally drew the same thing, meaning the final pictures were identical. Participants were asked, "How much do you like [name of copier]?" All participants preferred the artists who drew unique pictures to the artists who copied intentionally or unintentionally, although those who drew the same picture unintentionally were liked more than those who copied intentionally. Thus, knowingly copying someone else's picture was worse than unwittingly doing so. A second study replicated these findings with 3- to 6-year-old children using a modified procedure. These children watched puppet shows, rather than hearing vignettes, and were asked to evaluate how good or bad the artist who copied was. Only the 5- to 6-year-old children evaluated the plagiarizer more negatively than the artist who drew a unique picture. To provide insight into children's rationale for their evaluations, a final study asked 3- to 6-year-old children to justify their responses, so after each trial they were simply asked "why?" Analyses revealed that 75% of 6-year-olds, compared to only 12.5% of 4-year-olds, mentioned copying in their justifications. Those children who referred to copying were also those who gave the most negative evaluations of plagiarizers. The robustness of these findings is evident in their replication across other cultures. Yang, Shaw, Garduno, and Olson (2014) reported that 5- and 6-year-olds, but not 4-year-olds from the United States, Mexico, and China, all evaluate plagiarizers more negatively than artists who draw unique pictures. Collectively, these findings reveal that not only do children recognize the intentional link between artists' and their pictures, but also that they prioritize the originality of the artist's ideas over the, more tangible, amount of time and effort invested in creation of the picture.

Extending these findings further, Li, Shaw, and Olson (2013) have shown that 6-year-olds place such high value on their own ideas that they would rather own a picture that contains their idea than one in which they invested physical labor. Conversely, 4-year-olds only wanted the picture containing their idea if the picture also contained their idiosyncratic preferences. The importance that 5- to 9-year-old children place on ideas may be indicative of their developing understanding that ideas originate in the mind, and as such are unique to individual artists and should be appropriately valued and guarded. More generally, research investigating the importance of artists' knowledge and ideas complements that conducted on the role of intention.

Together, these findings suggest a developmental progression in children's understanding of the artists' role in picture creation and their corresponding importance for interpreting pictures—initially, 24-month-old children learn that what an artist intends to draw determines what their picture represents, which in turn manifests itself in an awareness that much of the value in pictures stems from the artist's input. This is then supplemented by a growing appreciation, between the ages of 6 and 8 years, that what an artist knows about the world impacts what they can intentionally depict. The result is that by the age of 8 years children have escaped their reliance on resemblance as a way to map the referential relationship between pictures and their referents, toward a more sophisticated conception of pictures: as representations of both their referents and their artist, which is akin to the way in which adults approach the appraisal of artworks—by appealing to their knowledge of the interdependent relationships between pictures, their referents, and their artists.

4. PICTURE MODALITY

4.1 Theoretical Importance

It has been suggested that pictorial development does not necessarily follow the same trajectory for all types of pictures, particularly as they possess media-specific qualities and therefore share different relationships with the world and their creators. Philosophical and theoretical work on picture comprehension converges on the notion that the picture, the world it depicts, and the artist are crucial factors for developing a complete theory of pictures (Blumson, 2009; Freeman & Sanger, 1995; Hagen, 1974; Ittelson, 1996; Parsons, 1987; Wollheim, 1987). Although these factors are inextricably linked, they do not interact in the same way across different picture modalities (Beilin, 1991; Liben, 1999, 2003). In addition to the common properties most representational pictures share, such as their status as visual representations and function as social-communicative vehicles of meaning, there are properties unique to each picture modality. Each picture format is underpinned by a unique symbol–referent relationship (DeLoache & Burns, 1994; Troseth, 2010) and associated with distinctive rules (Beilin, 1999). For instance, photographs are often characterized as reliable sources of information due to their veridical relationship with the world, while drawings are often appreciated as one artist's perspective. Consequently, it has been suggested that children develop different expectations, and use different skill sets, to comprehend the various picture formats that exist (Barrett, 1986; Beilin, 1991). Thus, there is scope for broadening existing theories of pictorial development by comparing how children respond to assorted picture types (O'Connor, Beilin, & Kose, 1981; Seidman & Beilin, 1984).

To date, Liben (1999) is the only researcher to directly address the issue of modality. Levels five (correspondence mastery) and six (meta-representation) of her sequence theory posit that children must learn that the picture–referent relationship is not the same for all visual representations. That is, they are underpinned by unique rules and conventions and as such are suited to different tasks. For example, it would be unusual to see a drawing rather than a photograph used as evidence in a courtroom, since photographs are assumed to have more epistemic authority (Arnheim, 1974; Atencia-Linares, 2012; Cavedon-Taylor, 2014b) due to their causal relation to the referent it depicted. Furthermore, Liben, along with Barrett (1986) and Beilin (1983, 1991), proposes that knowledge of picture production will be linked to developmental changes in the understanding of pictorial representation. For instance, if children misunderstand how difficult it is to draw well, they might underestimate the age at which a child should be able to draw a recognizable picture. Likewise, if children do not grasp the mechanical nature of cameras, they may mistake an underexposed photograph for a dark room, or fail to recognize that photographs cannot depict fantasy creatures as readily as drawings can.

Just as Gibson (1980) pointed out that most people consider pictures simple, Liben (2003) asserts that photographs are often viewed as "very simple kinds of representations" (p. 2), since in their most amateurish form they are easily created, and the realism with which they recreate their referents allows beholders to bypass the representational surface with ease and focus on the depicted referent. However, Liben contends that there is more to photographs than meets the eye. Being able to take a canonical photograph of a panda is not the pinnacle of photography, nor is the recognition that a photograph shows a panda, without appreciating how the shot was set up to portray the panda in a specific light. She argues that despite the heightened perceptual similarity between photographs and their referents it is as important to look beyond photographic content, as it is to see past the subject matter of a painting. In particular, we need to appreciate the representational surface of the image, and the effort and skill the photographer invested in creating it.

4.2 Photographs vs Drawings

The comparison between photographs and handmade pictures, such as drawings, is particularly interesting for four reasons. First, the skills and tools required by artists to create drawings or paintings can be directly contrasted with those required by a photographer to take photographs. Most notably, while artists depend solely on their own motor skills to draw, photographers also rely on the causal–mechanical nature of cameras (Cavedon-Taylor, 2014a; Gooskens, 2012; Ross, 1982; Scruton, 1981). Second, and as a result of their differing processes of creation, photographs and drawings relate to their referents differently. Photographs are causally as well as intentionally related to their referents, and thus are typically confined to depicting physically present real-world referents, whereas drawings often depict fantasy as well as real referents since artists can draw from their imagination (Marriott, 2002; Woolley & Cox, 2007). Technology is eroding this boundary somewhat (Cavedon-Taylor, 2014b; Liben, 2003); advancing photograph manipulation and computer-generated imagery techniques mean children are being exposed to ever more realistic static, and animated, images of fantasy creatures and characters (Troseth, 2003, 2010), which adds a new variable to investigations of this cross-modal difference. Third, researchers have posited that knowledge of the aforementioned differences means viewers' subjective experience of photographs and drawings differs (Cavedon-Taylor, 2014a, 2014b; Gooskens, 2012; Pettersson, 2011; Walton, 1984). Last, the explosion of digital media means children are being exposed to photography at a younger age than ever before (Rideout, Saphir, Pai, Rudd, & Pritchett, 2013; Troseth, Casey, Lawver, Walker, & Cole, 2007), which might affect what, and how, children learn about this medium. Hence, this is a very fertile area of research with the potential to greatly enhance current theories of pictorial development, which tend to implicitly assume that children acquire a single global "picture concept," rather than individual concepts for different picture types. The key issues summarized here form the basis of research questions that could illustrate whether children do indeed distinguish drawings from photographs, and if so, whether the distinction is based on how they are produced, the content they depict, or both. Investigating these questions with children of various ages would provide insight into the developmental trajectory of such understanding, and cross-cultural work would shed light on the influence exerted by exposure to digital media.

4.3 Photograph Literature

Much less is known about how children interpret photographs compared to drawings, and how their conception of photographers compares to their understanding of artists (Liben, 2003; Szechter & Liben, 2007). Nevertheless, what research does exist provides some insight into the trajectory this developing understanding might follow, and also hints at places where cross-modal differences may arise. Research into the early referential understanding of pictures indicates that iconicity facilitates children's ability to transfer novel labels from pictures to their real-world referents (Ganea et al., 2008), use pictures to guide their actions (Callaghan, 2000), and learn new facts about animals (Tare et al., 2010). In short, the higher the level of visual similarity between a picture and its referent object, the easier it is for children to recognize that one refers to the other.

As the most iconic picture format, some have argued that photographs bear a transparent relation to their referent. That is we see only the referent and not the picture's surface (Currie, 1995; Freeman, 2004; Liben, 2003; Walton, 1984). Indeed, despite the advantages iconicity affords children in making the referential link between the symbolized content of a picture and its real-world referent, we also know that iconicity can to draw attention away from the representational surface of the picture. This was demonstrated in a simple behavioral task conducted by Liben (2003). She showed 3-, 5-, and 7-year-old children and college students pairs of photographs in which the subject matter was held constant, while angle or distance from the referent was manipulated. Participants were asked to state whether the pictures were different, and if they were, whether this was because something had happened to the referent or if it was attributable to something the photographer had done. The majority of 3- and 5-year-old children focused on referential content; 3-year-olds tended to make irrelevant comments about referential content, such as "I like tulips. My Mom likes tulips" (p. 15), whereas 5-year-olds tried to explain the difference by incorrectly claiming that a change had been made to the referential content, "this one [tulip] is open, and this one is closed" (p. 15). In contrast, the majority of the 7-year-old children and the college students correctly described how the photographer's use of angle had created the distinct appearance of the two tulips. By age 7 children in this study appear to acknowledge the photographer's ability to use technical manipulations to create a specific picture.

Dissimilar to handmade pictures, for children to understand photography it is necessary that they also recognize the mediating role cameras play in the photographer–picture relationship. When Kose (1985) asked 7- and 11-year-old children questions such as, "Are there things you can't take photographs of?" and "What makes a photograph good (or bad)?" 7-year-olds spontaneously referred to the camera's role in the production of a photograph with statements such as, "Sometimes cameras make things dark and fuzzy and you can't see them" (p. 376) and "You can't take a picture of the sun because there's too much light for the camera" (p. 377).

However, Wellman and Hickling (1994) exposed flaws in children's understanding of the *mechanical* nature of cameras up until age 8. They asked 6-, 8-, and 10-year-old children to explain how instant photographs were made. Approximately 70% of the 6-year-old children gave answers such as "The camera gets the idea of it and draws the picture" (p. 1572), which suggests they construe photography as an agentive, rather than a mechanical process, whereby the camera makes a conscious decision to "draw" something. In contrast, 8- and 10-year-old children described the physical or mechanical stages of photograph production. It is apparent from these studies that navigating the photograph–referent and photographer–picture relations is complicated by two photograph-specific characteristics: the involvement of a mechanical intermediary, in the form of a camera, and the subsequent reliance of photographs on real and physically present referents. It is these features around which two main cross-modal debates have arisen.

4.4 Cross-Modal Debates

First, researchers have posited that the mechanical production of photographs lessens the importance of the photographer for picture comprehension (Bloom, 2004; Browne & Woolley, 2001; Costello & Phillips, 2009). In contrast, others have argued that handmade pictures require that we understand the image as a realization of the artist's intentions (Scruton, 1981). This distinction is not absolute: it is not the case that photographers' have no influence over their pictures, or that we must always use an artist's intention to interpret handmade drawings. Nonetheless, photographers and artists are separated, to a greater or lesser degree, on the spectrum of intentionality. Perhaps this separation is best characterized by how easily children can track intention from the picture creator's mind to their pictures. While both artists' and photographers' intentions can be inferred from their choice of referent, beyond this photographers' intentions are evident in their use of angles, lighting, and shutter speed, to name just a few variables.

Photographs are also causally as well as intentionally related to their referents, due to the fact that cameras capture whatever is in their field of vision; a photograph of a monkey is always a photograph of a monkey regardless of whether it is underpinned by the intention to depict a monkey. By comparison, knowledge of the artist's intentions can sway children's interpretation of drawings (Gelman & Ebeling, 1998). Thus, familiarity with the photographic medium may lead children to disregard intention and focus instead on the photograph–referent relationship when naming and evaluating photographs. This possibility receives some support from a task conducted by Browne and Woolley (2001, Study 1, Task 3), in which they assessed children's use of intentional cues when naming a traced drawing. Here, 4-year-olds, 7-year-olds, and adults watched as a puppet announced his intention to draw a cow by tracing a picture he already had. The puppet then showed participants two drawings, one of a horse and one of a cow, before proceeding to "accidentally" trace the picture of the horse. Without seeing the puppet's finished drawing, participants were asked the test question: "What would be a good name for this picture—what do you think it's a picture of? A horse or a cow?" While 47% of the 4-year-old children named the drawing "a cow" in line with the puppet's intention, all of the 7-year-old children and adults named the drawing "a horse," according to what was underneath the tracing paper. The responses of the latter two groups led the authors to conclude that intention is disregarded when the picture concerned has been produced through a causal rather than an intentional process, like that of freehand drawing. However, these claims can be challenged on two main grounds.

First, tracing is not a causal process, and the testing paradigm used cued participants into this by showing them how tracing worked during a warm-up task. Second, just because participants were not shown the final drawing does not mean that they did not infer what it would look like (based on seeing the picture that had been traced), in which case their "causal" responses could be interpreted as "inferred appearance" responses. The latter explanation is particularly plausible given the importance of appearance cues for interpreting drawings (Browne & Woolley, 2001; DeLoache & Burns, 1994; Richert & Lillard, 2002). Although tracing does diminish an artist's input, the picture creator is still a human agent and therefore he or she retains ultimate control over the drawing. If we want to assess how children construe intentionality across the picture spectrum, a better comparison would be between artists and photographers. Photography relies partly on camera mechanics that reduces the photographer's input to a greater degree than in tracing. In addition, the causal link cameras forge between photographs and their real-world referents increases the relevance of appearance cues beyond that seen for traced pictures, thereby providing a stronger alternative cue to intention.

The relative importance of artists' and photographers' intentions was investigated by Armitage and Allen (2015). In addition to varying the level of conflict between appearance and intentional cues, as previously described, they also compared 3- to 6-year-old children's use of these two cues for interpreting photographs vs drawings. In the photograph task the experimenter took a picture of one of the referents and printed it out, rather than drawing it by hand. In the color change condition the printed picture clearly resembled a differently colored object to the one the experimenter intended to depict (e.g., a pink duck), while in the black-and-white condition the printed picture was ambiguous (e.g., a gray duck). Children were told the printer was not working very well to provide a plausible explanation for it printing the picture incorrectly.

When asked to identify the picture's referent, children in the photograph task gave fewer intentional responses, across both conditions, than children in the drawing task, suggesting that photographer's intentions were devalued relative to those of artists. This finding aligns with those of Browne and Woolley (2001), corroborating their claim that when pictures share a causal relationship to their referents, as they do in photography, children consider the creators' intention less important for interpreting the final picture. It may be that photographers' reliance on cameras to translate their intentions into pictures disrupts children's developing ability to map the intentional relation between the photographer and his or her picture, instead reinforcing the notion that photographs depend on cameras and their real-world referents. This explanation certainly fits with Wellman and Hickling's (1994) finding that 6-year-olds consider cameras capable of generating an idea as well as producing a photograph, while paying little attention to the photographer's input.

The insights these studies provide into how children differentially evaluate the importance of the creators' intentions in the mediums of photography and drawings indicate that this is a fruitful area for future research. Based on the studies reviewed, it will be important to establish whether, in photography, the use of a camera merely weakens the assumption that the creator's intention determines what a picture represents, or whether it facilitates the perception of photography as a causal process in which the creator's intention exerts minimal influence (Bazin & Gray, 1960; Black, 1979; Bloom, 1996; Browne & Woolley, 2001; Costello & Phillips, 2009; Schier, 1986). More broadly, it will be pertinent for researchers to investigate how the recent increase in young children's use of camera-enabled devices and photograph-related apps (Rideout et al., 2013) might influence their developing understanding of photography.

Aside from intention, the use of a camera also transforms the photographer's role in a broader sense. Photographers can produce photographs quickly and in rapid succession, yet can capture their referents in exquisite detail. By contrast, artists tend to draw relatively slowly, and although they too can include great detail in their pictures, they do not typically replicate the level of realism associated with photographs. Moreover, while photographers benefit from knowledge of angles and lighting, artists must master specialized motor skills to enable them to use pencils and paint to depict recognizable referents. In one of the only cross-modal studies to date, Seidman and Beilin (1984) explored how 4- to 10-year-old children perceive the roles of artists and photographers by asking them to talk aloud as they drew pictures or took photographs. Children's verbalizations were compared on four dimensions across the two conditions: "knowledge of their role in creating a picture," "knowledge of specific skills or techniques required to create pictures," "naming the visually depicted object," and "descriptions of ideas and events associated with drawing or photography." Two particularly interesting differences emerged.

Children of all ages were significantly more likely to describe what they were planning to draw than what they intended to photograph. In fact, the authors report that the youngest children, in particular, were focused on the camera and appeared eager to press the button, rather than to create a picture, suggesting less concern for the photographer's role, compared to the camera, in determining picture content. Furthermore, children in the photograph condition were more likely to comment on the technical aspects of picture creation than children in the drawing condition. For example, if their referent was moving, they knew to wait until it stopped before pressing the capture button. These findings provide some evidence that children do not necessarily approach picture creation in the same way across these two mediums. Specifically, they seem to show a greater regard for the artist's role in selecting and depicting a particular referent when drawing, compared to the camera-focused approach that is adopted when taking photographs.

Since this is the only cross-modal study on this topic, further research is necessary to elucidate how an understanding of the divergent roles of artists and photographers may feed into a theory of pictures that can account for differences across modality. One of the most important unanswered questions concerns how children use their knowledge of picture creation to reason about what artists and photographers can and cannot depict. For instance, are they equally capable of depicting a unicorn, or creating a picture of an absent referent, or is one more equipped to do so than the other?

A second cross-modal debate revolves around the fact that, as a result of cameras' reliance on real-world referents, photographs are typically constrained to depicting real and physically present referents. Some researchers have argued that, "the principal belief held in respect to photographs is their fidelity to reality" (Beilin, 1991, p. 46), which does not extend to handmade pictures, whose artists can distort reality or depict nonexistent referents using their imagination. Expanding upon this, Cavedon-Taylor (2014a, 2014b) states that as viewers we expect photographs to provide us with indisputable information about the world, largely as a function of how photographs are treated in society. Photographs, far more commonly than drawings or paintings, act as "evidence" that an event has occurred. Hoax photographs of spaceships or the Loch Ness monster cause a furor as a direct result of violating these expectations. Reports that adults experience an increase in electrodermal activity when cutting up a photograph of a sentimental possession compared to a control photograph (Hood, Donnelly, Leonards, & Bloom, 2010) confirm how closely we associate photographs with their real-world referents. This is reinforced by our tendency to find offensive content more disturbing when it is captured in a photograph, than when it is depicted in a drawing or a painting (Currie, 1999).

What about children? A task by O'Connor et al. (1981), which investigated 5- to 7-year-old children's belief in photographic fidelity, provides some empirical support for Beilin's (1991) argument. O'Connor and colleagues showed their participants a live demonstration of Piaget's liquid conservation task, and a series of photographs or drawings depicting the same task. Of most importance, the pictures showed either a logical ("unequal" fill levels in both glasses) or an illogical (equal fill levels in both glasses) outcome. To distinguish children who could and could not pass the conservation task, before presenting the outcome picture the experimenter asked the child to predict the amount of water that would be in each glass. Then, having seen the outcome picture children were asked whether they saw any difference between the picture and the level of water in the glasses from the live demonstration. Finally, in the illogical outcome condition children were asked the fidelity question: "Which is the way it really should look, should it be way down low as it is here, or should it be way up high as it is here?" (p. 860). Six-year-old children treated photographs of an illogical outcome (glass containing more liquid than it should) as the "correct" representation of the world, more often than the equivalent drawings. They did so in the presence of the physical conservation task materials in their logical final state (i.e., when the picture and the world contradicted each other), which supports the claim that at least until the age of 6 children adhere to some extent to the "fidelity-to-reality" principle.

Of course, due to the increasing popularity of photography—by the age of 2 most children in Western cultures have used a digital camera, and on average, 2- to 4-year-old children spend 1–2 h per day on some form of mobile media device, including camera-enabled tablets and smartphones (Rideout et al., 2013)—this expectation of veracity may be outdated (Troseth et al., 2007). Children growing up in a society dominated by technology might know far more about photographs from a young age, including that they can be manipulated to depict nonreal referents, than has previously been the case. This societal shift provides an excellent opportunity to examine children's understanding of how picture modality affects the content that can be depicted. However, if children pay insufficient attention to the representational surface of pictures, as Liben's (2003) findings suggest, they may fail to note whether a given picture is *a photograph* or *a drawing*, in the first instance, thereby inhibiting the activation of media-specific knowledge, such as "cameras take pictures of real things" or "drawings can depict imaginary creatures." This is potentially detrimental to children's ability to discriminate photographs from drawings on a richer conceptual, as well as a perceptual level. Table 2 summarizes the main age-related changes in children's understanding of picture modality.

5. CONCLUDING REMARKS

In this chapter we have provided an overview of how children acquire a mentalistic understanding of pictures. We specifically looked at how they construe the relationship between various facets of an artist's mind and their pictures, including: the role played by artists' intentions in defining what pictures represent, how their [lack of] knowledge of a referent affects their ability to draw it, and the extent to which their ideas define a picture as unique and therefore valuable. At the same time, we have highlighted the importance of picture modality which should be incorporated into theoretical accounts of pictorial development. Although Liben's (1999) theory specifically addresses possible cross-modal differences in pictorial understanding, at present there is scant extant research in this area to empirically support such claims.

Hence, going forward it will be important for researchers to build on the literature reviewed here to establish whether the foundations of pictorial understanding are the same for all picture types, and only later diverge to account for differences between, for instance, photographs and drawings, or alternatively if children perceive and respond differently to different types of picture from the outset. An assessment of how children respond to

Table 2 Summary of the Age-Related Trends in Children's Understanding of Picture Modality

Age	Aspect of Pictorial Understanding	Relevant Empirical Work
3 Years	Children cannot distinguish pictures of the same referent taken from different angles, indicating little awareness of a photographer's ability to influence a picture's appearance	Liben (2003)
	Children begin to evaluate the intentions of artists and photographers differently, signifying an awareness of the distinction between how pictures are created in these two modalities	Armitage and Allen (2015)
4 Years	When asked to describe taking a photograph vs drawing a picture, children begin to draw distinctions between picture creation in different mediums	Seidman and Beilin (1984)
6 Years	Children consider photography to be an agentive, rather than mechanical process, during which cameras "choose" what to depict	Wellman and Hickling (1994)
	Children think photographs represent the world more faithfully, even when faced with contradictory information, than drawings	O'Connor et al. (1981)
7 Years	Children can distinguish photographs of the same referent taken from different angles, and correctly attribute the difference to the photographer's use of angles	Liben (2003)
	Children still spontaneously focus on the camera's role in the production of photographs, to a greater extent than the role of the photographer	Kose (1985)
	Children name traced pictures according to what they resemble, rather than what they are intended to depict, indicating that they consider the picture creator's intention less important when the picture appears to share a "causal" relationship with its referent	Browne and Woolley (2001)
8 Years	Children begin to describe photography as a mechanical rather than agentive process	Wellman and Hickling (1994)

pictures taken with cell phones and tablets will be a crucial and timely area of research, given their prevalence in Western cultures and accessibility to young children. Focusing on the function of the role of creators' intentions and how children evaluate them across media types will also provide useful insights into the factors that drive the acquisition of cross-modal pictorial understanding.

These investigations would be complemented by work exploring the cognitive developments that underpin and facilitate pictorial development, since the existing literature has largely focused on how symbolic development progresses rather than *why* (Rochat & Callaghan, 2005). Several of the cognitive developments experienced in early childhood are highly relevant to children's ability to draw distinctions between the picture–world and picture–creator relationships within different picture modalities, and representational development more broadly (Rochat & Callaghan, 2005). One of the most important cognitive developments that occurs between the ages of 3 and 8 is the acquisition of theory of mind. Broadly speaking, this refers to the ability to recognize that people have mental states, such as desires, emotions, intentions, and beliefs, which govern their behavior (Astington, 1993; Flavell, 1999; Frye & Moore, 1991; Perner, 1991; Premack & Woodruff, 1978). Such mental state reasoning is fundamental to appreciating that pictures are the intentional products of artists' minds.

Traditionally, the false belief task has served as one of the core tests of theory of mind understanding. Callaghan, Rochat, and Corbit (2012) devised a pictorial version of this task in order to measure theory of mind in direct relation to pictorial representation. This task could prove useful in examining whether theory of mind drives children's ability to (a) recognize and map the picture–referent relationship using an artist or photographer's intention, and (b) why intention is perceived as less relevant for the interpretation of photographs than drawings (Armitage & Allen, 2015).

It has also been reported that the social context in which children experience and converse about pictures plays an important role in their representational development (Callaghan, 2000; Callaghan & Rankin, 2002; Callaghan, Rochat, MacGillivray, & MacLellan, 2004; Peralta de Mendoza & Salsa, 2003). In a cross-cultural comparison of the pictorial development of children from Canada, Peru, and India, Callaghan et al. (2012) found that while children from all three countries acquired social-cognitive skills such as intention reading, imitation, gaze following, communicative pointing, and joint attention, at approximately the same age, Peruvian and Indian children's picture comprehension and production was delayed relative to Canadian children. This was attributed to differences in the number and frequency of picture-based interactions with experienced symbol users, which were highest for Canadian children. Thus, in order to integrate the current findings with those of the broader literature it will be critical for future work to include measures of relevant cognitive skills and social-communicative understanding in order to explore how these developments are related to children's ability to distinguish photographs from drawings and artists from photographers.

It is clear that there is much to be gained, in terms of enhancing our understanding of children's pictorial development, from continuing to investigate how children map various facets of artist's minds to their pictures, and broadening existing theoretical accounts to include the role of picture modality. Moreover, simultaneous pursuit of these goals would yield a more comprehensive and unitary account of what constitutes a mature theory of pictorial understanding and how it is acquired by children.

REFERENCES

Allen, M. L. (2009). Brief report: Decoding representations: How children with autism understand drawings. *Journal of Autism and Developmental Disorders, 39*(3), 539–543. http://dx.doi.org/10.1007/s10803-008-0650-y.

Armitage, E., & Allen, M. L. (2015). Children's picture interpretation: Appearance or intention? *Developmental Psychology, 51*, 1201–1215. http://dx.doi.org/10.1037/a0039571.

Arnheim, R. (1974). On the nature of photography. *Critical Inquiry, 1*, 149–161. http://dx.doi.org/10.1086/447782.

Astington, J. W. (1993). *The child's discovery of the mind.* Cambridge, MA: Harvard University Press.

Atencia-Linares, P. (2012). Fiction, nonfiction, and deceptive photographic representation. *The Journal of Aesthetics and Art Criticism, 70*, 19–30. http://dx.doi.org/10.1111/j.1540-6245.2011.01495.x.

Barrera, M. E., & Maurer, D. (1981). Recognition of mother's photographed face by the three-month-old infant. *Child Development, 52*, 714–716. http://dx.doi.org/10.2307/1129196.

Barrett, T. (1986). A conceptual framework for understanding photographs. *Visual Arts Research, 12*, 68–77.

Bazin, A., & Gray, H. (1960). The ontology of the photographic image. *Film Quarterly, 13*, 4–9. http://dx.doi.org/10.1525/fr.1960.13.3.04a00030.

Behne, T., Carpenter, M., & Tomasello, M. (2005). One-year-olds comprehend the communicative intentions behind gestures in a hiding game. *Developmental Science, 8*, 492–499. http://dx.doi.org/10.1111/j.1467-7687.2005.00440.x.

Beilin, H. (1983). Development of photogenic comprehension. *Art Education, 36*, 28–33. http://dx.doi.org/10.2307/3192658.

Beilin, H. (1991). Developmental aesthetics and the psychology of photography. In R. M. Downs, L. S. Liben, & D. S. Palermo (Eds.), *Visions of aesthetics, the environment, and development: The legacy of Joachim F. Wohlwill* (pp. 45–86). Hillsdale, NJ: Lawrence Erlbaum Associates.

Beilin, H. (1999). Understanding the photographic image. *Journal of Applied Developmental Psychology, 20*, 1–30. http://dx.doi.org/10.1016/s0193-3973(99)80001-x.

Black, M. (1979). How do pictures represent? In W. Kennick (Ed.), *Art and philosophy: Readings in aesthetics* (pp. 257–286). New York: St. Martin's Press.

Bloom, P. (1996). Intention, history and artifact concepts. *Cognition, 60*, 1–29. http://dx.doi. org/10.1016/0010-0277(95)00699-0.

Bloom, P. (2004). *Descartes' baby: How the science of child development explains what makes us human.* New York: Basic Books.

Bloom, P., & Markson, L. (1998). Intention and analogy in children's naming of pictorial representations. *Psychological Science, 9*, 200–204. http://dx.doi.org/10.1111/ 1467-9280.00038.

Blumson, B. (2009). Images, intentionality and inexistence. *Philosophy and Phenomenological Research, 79*, 522–538. http://dx.doi.org/10.1111/j.1933-1592.2009.00292.x.

Browne, C. A., & Woolley, J. D. (2001). Theory of mind in children's naming of drawings. *Journal of Cognition and Development, 2*, 389–412. http://dx.doi.org/10.1207/ S15327647JCD0204_3.

Callaghan, T. C. (2000). Factors affecting children's graphic symbol use in the third year: Language, similarity, and iconicity. *Cognitive Development, 15*, 185–214. http://dx.doi. org/10.1016/S0855-2014(00)00026-5.

Callaghan, T. C. (2008). The origins and development of pictorial symbol functioning. In C. Milbrath & H. M. Trautner (Eds.), *Children's understanding and production of pictures, drawings, and art: Theoretical and empirical approaches* (pp. 21–32). Cambridge, MA: Hogrefe & Huber.

Callaghan, T. C., & Rankin, M. P. (2002). Emergence of graphic symbol functioning and the question of domain specificity: A longitudinal training study. *Child Development, 73*, 359–376. http://dx.doi.org/10.1111/1467-8624.00412.

Callaghan, T. C., & Rochat, P. (2003). Traces of the artist: Sensitivity to the role of the artist in children's pictorial reasoning. *British Journal of Developmental Psychology, 21*, 415–445. http://dx.doi.org/10.1348/026151003322277784.

Callaghan, T. C., & Rochat, P. (2008). Children's understanding of artist-picture relations: Implications for their theories of pictures. In C. Milbrath & H. M. Trautner (Eds.), *Children's understanding and production of pictures, drawings and arts: Theoretical and empirical approaches* (pp. 187–206). Gottingen, Germany: Hogrefe & Huber.

Callaghan, T. C., Rochat, P., & Corbit, J. (2012). Young children's knowledge of the representational function of pictorial symbols: Development across the preschool years in three cultures. *Journal of Cognition and Development, 13*, 320–353. http://dx.doi.org/ 10.1080/15248372.2011.587853.

Callaghan, T. C., Rochat, P., MacGillivray, T., & MacLellan, C. (2004). Modelling referential actions in 6- to 18-month-old infants: A precursor to symbolic understanding. *Child Development, 75*, 1733–1744. http://dx.doi.org/10.1111/j.1467-8624.2004.00813.x.

Carpenter, M., Akhtar, N., & Tomasello, M. (1998). Fourteen through 18-month-old infants differentially imitate intentional and accidental actions. *Infant Behavior and Development, 21*, 315–330. http://dx.doi.org/10.1016/S0163-6383(98)90009-1.

Cavedon-Taylor, D. (2014a). Photographically-based knowledge. *Episteme, 10*, 1–26. http:// dx.doi.org/10.1017/epi.2013.21.

Cavedon-Taylor, D. (2014b). Belief, experience and the act of picture making. *Philosophical Explorations, 17*, 1–14.

Costello, D., & Phillips, D. M. (2009). Automatism, causality and realism: Foundational problems in the philosophy of photography. *Philosophy Compass, 4*, 1–21. http://dx. doi.org/10.1111/j.1747-9991.2008.00193.x.

Currie, G. (1995). *Image and mind: Film, philosophy and cognitive science.* Cambridge: Cambridge University Press.

Currie, G. (1999). Visible traces: Documentary and the contents of photographs. *The Journal of Aesthetics and Art Criticism, 57*, 285–297. http://dx.doi.org/10.2307/432195.

Deacon, T. W. (1997). *The symbolic species: The co-evolution of language and the human brain.* London: W. W. Norton & Company Ltd.

DeLoache, J. S. (1987). Rapid change in the symbolic functioning of very young children. *Science, 238*, 1556–1557. http://dx.doi.org/10.1126/science.2446392.

DeLoache, J. S. (1991). Symbolic functioning in very young children: Understanding of pictures and models. *Child Development, 62*, 736–752. http://dx.doi.org/10.1111/j.1467-8624.1991.tb01566.x.

DeLoache, J. S. (1995). Early understanding and use of symbols: The model model. *Current Directions in Psychological Science, 4*, 109–113. http://dx.doi.org/10.1111/1467-8721.ep10772408.

DeLoache, J. S. (2002). The symbol-mindedness of young children. In W. W. Hartup & R. A. Weinberg (Eds.), *Child psychology in retrospect and prospect: In celebration of the 75th anniversary of the Institute of Child Development* (pp. 73–101). Mahwah, NJ: Lawrence Erlbaum Associates.

DeLoache, J. S. (2004). Becoming symbol-minded. *Trends in Cognitive Sciences, 8*, 66–70. http://dx.doi.org/10.1016/j.tics.2003.12.004.

DeLoache, J. S., & Burns, N. M. (1994). Early understanding of the representational function of pictures. *Cognition, 52*, 83–110. http://dx.doi.org/10.1016/0010-0277(94)90063-9.

DeLoache, J. S., Pierroutsakos, S. L., Uttal, D. H., Rosengren, K. S., & Gottlieb, A. (1998). Grasping the nature of pictures. *Psychological Science, 9*, 205–210. http://dx.doi.org/10.1111/1467-9280.00039.

DeLoache, J. S., Strauss, M. S., & Maynard, J. (1979). Picture perception in infancy. *Infant Behaviour and Development, 2*, 77–89. http://dx.doi.org/10.1111/j.1532-7078.2010.00038.x.

Dewey, J. (1958). *Art as experience*. New York: Capricorn.

Dutton, D. (1979). Artistic crimes: The problem of forgery in the arts. *The British Journal of Aesthetics, 19*, 302–341.

Flavell, J. H. (1999). Cognitive development: Children's knowledge about the mind. *Annual Review of Psychology, 50*, 21–45. http://dx.doi.org/10.1146/annurev.psych.50.1.21.

Freeman, N. H. (2000). Communication and representation: Why mentalistic reasoning is a lifelong endeavour. In P. Mitchell & K. Riggs (Eds.), *Children's reasoning and the mind* (pp. 349–366). Hove, England: Psychology Press.

Freeman, N. H. (2004). Aesthetic judgment and reasoning. In E. W. Eisner & M. D. Day (Eds.), *Handbook of research and policy art education* (pp. 359–377). Mahwah, NJ: Lawrence Erlbaum Associates.

Freeman, N., & Sanger, D. (1995). Commonsense aesthetics of rural children. *Visual Arts Research, 21*, 1–10.

Frye, D., & Moore, C. (1991). *Children's theories of mind: Mental states and social understanding*. East Sussex, UK: Psychology Press.

Ganea, P. A., Allen, M. L., Butler, L., Carey, S., & DeLoache, J. S. (2009). Toddlers' referential understanding of pictures. *Journal of Experimental Child Psychology, 104*, 283–295. http://dx.doi.org/10.1016/j.ecp.2009.05.008.

Ganea, P. A., Pickard, M. B., & DeLoache, J. S. (2008). Transfer between picture books and the real world. *Journal of Cognition and Development, 9*, 46–66. http://dx.doi.org/10.1080/15248370701836592.

Gelman, S. A., & Bloom, P. (2000). Young children are sensitive to how an object was created when deciding on what to name it. *Cognition, 76*, 91–103. http://dx.doi.org/10.1016/S0010-0277(00)00071-8.

Gelman, S. A., & Ebeling, K. S. (1998). Shape and representational status in children's early naming. *Cognition, 66*, B35–B47. http://dx.doi.org/10.1016/S0010-0277(98)00022-5.

Gibson, J. J. (1979). The information available in pictures. *Leonardo, 4*, 27–35. http://dx.doi.org/10.2307/1572214.

Gibson, J. J. (1980). Foreword: A prefatory essay on the perception of surfaces versus the perception of markings on a surface. In M. A. Hagen (Ed.), *The perception of pictures: Vol. 1* (pp. xi–xvii). New York: Academic Press.

Gooskens, G. (2012). Can digital pictures qualify as photographs? *American Society for Aesthetics Graduate E-Journal*, *4*, 1–7.

Gross, J., & Hayne, H. (1998). Drawing facilitates children's verbal reports of emotionally laden events. *Journal of Experimental Psychology: Applied*, *4*(2), 163.

Gross, J., & Hayne, H. (1999). Young children's recognition and description of their own and others' drawings. *Developmental Science*, *2*, 476–489. http://dx.doi.org/10.1111/1467-7687-00091.

Hagen, M. A. (1974). Picture perception: Toward a theoretical model. *Psychological Bulletin*, *81*, 471–497. http://dx.doi.org/10.1037/h0036801.

Hartley, C., & Allen, M. L. (2014). Brief report: Generalisation of word–picture relations in children with autism and typically developing children. *Journal of Autism and Developmental Disorders*, *44*(8), 2064–2071.

Hartley, C., & Allen, M. L. (2015). Iconicity influences how effectively minimally verbal children with autism and ability-matched typically developing children use pictures as symbols in a search task. *Autism*, *19*, 570–579. http://dx.doi.org/10.1177/1362361314536634.

Hood, B. M., Donnelly, K., Leonards, U., & Bloom, P. (2010). Implicit voodoo: Electrodermal activity reveals a susceptibility to sympathetic magic. *Journal of Cognition and Culture*, *10*, 391–399. http://dx.doi.org/10.1163/156853710X531258.

Ittelson, W. H. (1996). Visual perception of markings. *Psychonomic Bulletin & Review*, *3*, 171–187. http://dx.doi.org/10.3758/BF03212416.

Jolley, R. P. (2010). *Children and pictures: Drawing and understanding*. Oxford, UK: John Wiley & Sons.

Kose, G. (1985). Children's knowledge of photography: A study of the developing awareness of a representational medium. *British Journal of Developmental Psychology*, *3*, 373–384.

Li, V., Shaw, A., & Olson, K. R. (2013). Ideas versus labor: What do children value in artistic creation? *Cognition*, *127*, 38–45. http://dx.doi.org/10.1016/j.cognition.2012.11.001.

Liben, L. S. (1999). Developing an understanding of external spatial representations. In I. E. Sigel (Ed.), *Development of mental representation: Theories and applications* (pp. 297–321). Mahwah, NJ: Lawrence Erlbaum Associates Publishers.

Liben, L. S. (2003). Beyond point and shoot: Children's developing understanding of photographs as spatial and expressive representations. *Advances in Child Development and Behavior*, *31*, 1–42. http://dx.doi.org/10.1016/s0065-2407(03)31001-88624.2008.01150.x.

Marriott, S. (2002). Red in tooth and claw? Images of nature in modern picture books. *Children's Literature in Education*, *33*, 175–183. http://dx.doi.org/10.1023/A:1019677931406.

Meltzoff, A. N. (1995). Understanding the intentions of others: Re-enactment of intended acts by 18-month-old children. *Developmental Psychology*, *31*, 838–850. http://dx.doi.org/10.1037/0012-1649.31.5.838.

Moore, R., Liebal, K., & Tomasello, M. (2013). Three-year-olds understand communicative intentions without language, gestures, or gaze. *Interaction Studies*, *14*, 62–80. http://dx.doi.org/10.1075/is.14.1.05moo.

Myers, L. J., & Liben, L. S. (2008). The role of intentionality and iconicity in children's developing comprehension and production of cartographic symbols. *Child Development*, *79*, 668–684. http://dx.doi.org/10.1111/j.1467-8624.2008.01150.x.

Myers, L. J., & Liben, L. S. (2012). Graphic symbols as "the mind on paper": Links between children's interpretive theory of mind and symbol understanding. *Child Development*, *83*(1), 186–202.

O'Connor, J., Beilin, H., & Kose, G. (1981). Children's belief in photographic fidelity. *Developmental Psychology*, *17*, 859–865. http://dx.doi.org/10.1037/0012-1649.17.6.859.

Olson, K. R., & Shaw, A. (2011). 'No fair, copycat!': What children's response to plagiarism tells us about their understanding of ideas. *Developmental Science, 14*, 431–439. http://dx. doi.org/10.1111/j.1467-7687.2010.00993.x.

Parsons, M. J. (1987). Talk about a painting: A cognitive developmental analysis. *The Journal of Aesthetic Education, 21*, 37–55. http://dx.doi.org/10.2307/3332812.

Peralta de Mendoza, O. A., & Salsa, A. M. (2003). Instruction in early comprehension and use of symbol-referent relation. *Cognitive Development, 18*, 269–284. http://dx.doi.org/ 10.1016/S0885-2014(03)00024-8.

Perner, J. (1991). *Understanding the representational mind.* London, England: MIT Press.

Pettersson, M. (2011). Depictive traces: On the phenomenology of photography. *The Journal of Aesthetics and Art Criticism, 69*, 185–196. http://dx.doi.org/10.1111/j.1540-6245. 2011.01460.x.

Piaget, J. (1952). *The origin of intelligence in the child.* London: Routledge & Kegan Paul.

Preissler, M. A. (2008). Associative learning of pictures and words by low-functioning children with autism. *Autism, 12*(3), 231–248.

Preissler, M. A., & Bloom, P. (2008). Two year-olds use artist intention to understand drawings. *Cognition, 106*, 512–518. http://dx.doi.org/10.1016/j.cognition.2007.02.002.

Preissler, M. A., & Carey, S. (2004). Do both pictures and words function as symbols for 18- and 24-month old children? *Journal of Cognition and Development, 5*, 185–212. http://dx.doi.org/10.1207/s15327647jcd0502_2.

Premack, D., & Woodruff, G. (1978). Does the chimpanzee have a theory of mind? *Brain and Behavioral Sciences, 4*, 515–526. http://dx.doi.org/10.1017/S0150525X00076512.

Richert, R. A., & Lillard, A. S. (2002). Children's understanding of the knowledge prerequisites of drawing and pretending. *Developmental Psychology, 38*, 1004–1015. http://dx. doi.org/10.1037/0012-1649.38.6.1004.

Rideout, V., Saphir, M., Pai, S., Rudd, A., & Pritchett, J. (2013). *Zero to eight: Children's media use in America 2013.* Retrieved from https://www.commonsensemedia.org/ sites/default/files/research/zero-to-eight-2013.pdf.

Rochat, P., & Callaghan, T. (2005). What drives symbolic development? The case of pictorial comprehension and production. In L. L. Namy (Ed.), *Symbol use and symbolic representation: Developmental and comparative perspectives* (pp. 25–46). Mahwah, NJ: Erlbaum.

Ross, S. (1982). What photographs can't do. *The Journal of Aesthetics and Art Criticism, 41*, 5–17. http://dx.doi.org/10.2307/430819.

Salsa, A. M., & Peralta de Mendoza, O. (2007). Routes to symbolization: Intentionality and correspondence in early understanding of pictures. *Journal of Cognition and Development, 8*, 79–92. http://dx.doi.org/10.1207/s15327647jcd0801_4.

Schier, F. (1986). *Deeper into pictures: An essay on pictorial representation.* Cambridge, UK: Cambridge University Press.

Scruton, R. (1981). Photography and representation. *Critical Inquiry, 7*, 577–603. http://dx. doi.org/10.1086/448116.

Seidman, S., & Beilin, H. (1984). Effects of media on picturing by children and adults. *Developmental Psychology, 20*, 667–672. http://dx.doi.org/10.1037/0012-1649.20.4.667.

Simcock, G., & DeLoache, J. (2006). Get the picture? The effects of iconicity on toddlers' reenactment from picture books. *Developmental Psychology, 42*, 1352–1357. http://dx. doi.org/10.1037/0012-1649.42.6.1352.

Slater, A., Rose, D., & Morison, V. (1984). New-born infants' perception of similarities and differences between two- and three-dimensional stimuli. *British Journal of Developmental Psychology, 2*, 287–294. http://dx.doi.org/10.1111/j.2044-835X.1984.tb00936.x.

Suddendorf, T. (2003). Early representational insight: Twenty-four-month-olds can use a photo to find an object in the world. *Child Development, 74*, 896–904. http://dx.doi. org/10.1111/1467-8624.00574.

Szechter, L. E., & Liben, L. S. (2007). Children's aesthetic understanding of photographic art and the quality of art-related parent-child interactions. *Child Development, 78*, 879–894. http://dx.doi.org/10.1111/j.1467-8624.2007.01038.x.

Tare, M., Chiong, C., Ganea, P., & DeLoache, J. (2010). Less is more: How manipulative features affect children's learning from picture books. *Journal of Applied Developmental Psychology, 31*, 395–400. http://dx.doi.org/10.1016/j.appdev.2010.06.005.

Tomasello, M. (1999). *The cultural origins of human cognition.* Cambridge, MA: Harvard University Press.

Troseth, G. L. (2003). TV guide: Two-year-old children learn to use video as a source of information. *Developmental Psychology, 39*, 140–150. http://dx.doi.org/10.1037/0012-1649.39.1.

Troseth, G. L. (2010). Is it life or is it Memorex? Video as a representation of reality. *Developmental Review, 30*, 155–175. http://dx.doi.org/10.1016/j.dr.2010.03.007.

Troseth, G. L., Casey, A. M., Lawver, K. A., Walker, J. M. T., & Cole, D. A. (2007). Naturalistic experience and the early use of symbolic artifacts. *Journal of Cognition and Development, 8*, 309–331. http://dx.doi.org/10.1080/15248370701446772.

Walton, K. L. (1984). Transparent pictures: On the nature of photographic realism. *Critical Inquiry, 11*(2), 246–277. doi:1343394.

Wellman, H. M., & Hickling, A. K. (1994). The mind's "I": Children's conception of the mind as an active agent. *Child Development, 65*, 1564–1580. http://dx.doi.org/10.2307/1131281.

Werner, H., & Kaplan, B. (1963). *Symbol formation: An organismic–developmental approach to language and expression of thought.* New York: John Wiley & Sons.

Wollheim, R. (1987). *Painting as an art.* Princeton, NJ: Princeton University Press.

Woodward, A. L., Sommerville, J. A., & Guajardo, J. J. (2001). How infants make sense of intentional action. In B. Malle, L. Moses, & D. Baldwin (Eds.), *Intentions and intentionality: Foundations of social cognition* (pp. 149–169). Cambridge, MA: MIT Press.

Woolley, J. D., & Cox, V. (2007). Development of beliefs about storybook reality. *Developmental Science, 10*, 681–693. http://dx.doi.org/10.1111/j.146707687.2007.00612.x.

Yang, F., Shaw, A., Garduno, E., & Olson, K. R. (2014). No one likes a copycat: A cross-cultural investigation of children's response to plagiarism. *Journal of Experimental Child Psychology, 121*, 111–119. http://dx.doi.org/10.1016/j.jecp.2013.11.008.

Yonas, A., Granrud, C. E., Chov, M. H., & Alexander, A. J. (2005). Picture perception in infants: Do 9-month-olds attempt to grasp objects depicted in photographs? *Infancy, 8*, 147–166. http://dx.doi.org/10.1207/s15327078in0802_3.

CHAPTER SIX

Perspectives on Perspective Taking: How Children Think About the Minds of Others

S.A.J. Birch[*,1], V. Li[*], T. Haddock[*], S.E. Ghrear[*], P. Brosseau-Liard[†], A. Baimel[*], M. Whyte[*]
*University of British Columbia, Vancouver, BC, Canada
[†]École de Psychologie, Faculté des Sciences Sociales, Université d'Ottawa, Ottawa, ON, Canada
[1]Corresponding author: e-mail address: sbirch@psych.ubc.ca

Contents

Abstract

Perspective taking, or "theory of mind," involves reasoning about the mental states of others (e.g., their intentions, desires, knowledge, beliefs) and is called upon in virtually every aspect of human interaction. Our goals in writing this chapter were to provide an overview of (a) the research questions developmental psychologists ask to shed light on how children think about the inner workings of the mind, and (b) why such research is invaluable in understanding human nature and our ability to interact with, and learn from, one another. We begin with a brief review of early research in this field that culminated in the so-called litmus test for a theory of mind (i.e., false-belief tasks). Next, we describe research with infants and young children that created a puzzle for many researchers, and briefly mention an intriguing approach researchers have used to attempt to "solve" this puzzle. We then turn to research examining children's understanding of a much broader range of mental states (beyond false beliefs). We briefly discuss the value of studying individual differences by highlighting their important

Advances in Child Development and Behavior, Volume 52
ISSN 0065-2407
http://dx.doi.org/10.1016/bs.acdb.2016.10.005
185

implications for social well-being and ways to improve perspective taking. Next, we review work illustrating the value of capitalizing on children's proclivity for selective social learning to reveal their understanding of others' mental states. We close by highlighting one line of research that we believe will be an especially fruitful avenue for future research and serves to emphasize the complex interplay between our perspective-taking abilities and other cognitive processes.

1. A MULTIPURPOSE TOOL: THE MANY FUNCTIONS OF MENTAL STATE REASONING

Humans' capacity to reason about the unobservable inner workings of others' minds has fascinated philosophers and scientists for thousands of years. The wealth of interest in this capacity is not at all surprising when you consider that virtually all human behavior is driven by underlying mental states. As such, to make sense of another person's actions it is rarely sufficient to rely exclusively on observable aspects of the person's *external* environment. Instead, one must also make inferences about one's *internal* mental states, including, for example, his or her goals, intentions, desires, knowledge, beliefs, and emotional states. This concept is nicely illustrated in the kinds of stories developmental psychologists give to young children to see if they understand this important aspect of human behavior. Consider the following scenario: Henry has lost his pet rabbit. He hears a noise inside the shed in his backyard. He opens the shed door to find the neighbor's dog and tears begin to stream down his face. To make sense of Henry's actions of going to the shed, opening the door, and crying, it is necessary to make inferences about his mental states (italicized below for emphasis). For instance, one can infer that having lost his rabbit (a pet he presumably *likes*) he is motivated (*desires*) to find his rabbit. Having heard something in the shed he *thought or believed* his rabbit could be inside. Having found the neighbor's dog instead he *learned* (now *knows*) his *belief* was false, his *desire* to find his rabbit thwarted, and the tears streaming down his face were because he was *sad* as a result of his *unfulfilled desire*.[a] Impressively, even children as young as 2 years of age understand that a boy who is looking for his rabbit will be sad if he found a dog, whereas a boy who wanted to find a dog would be happy (Wellman, 1990). That is, even young children seem to understand

---

[a] Of course there are simpler explanations one could generate to account for Henry's behavior, such as "he is afraid of dogs or hates dogs" and, even though they might not be as accurate, they still involve positing mental states such as fear or hatred.

that it is not the *outcome*, or the physical reality of the situation, that matters most, but rather the person's mental states, such as their goals and desires toward that reality, that ultimately explain human behavior. In fact, the field of Psychology, the study of the mind and human behavior, rests upon this fundamental principle.

Of primary interest in this chapter, however, is not the formal discipline of Psychology but rather what has been called "naïve psychology": lay peoples' (i.e., nonpsychologists, typical children, and adults) capacity to explain and predict human behavior by inferring and reasoning about their mental states. This capacity has received a variety of names in the literature such as folk psychology, common sense psychology, mind-reading, mentalizing, mental state attribution, perspective taking, role-taking, and perhaps most commonly "theory of mind." For simplicity, we primarily use the terms theory of mind or perspective taking throughout, whereby we mean the processes involved in inferring, and reasoning about, the mental states of others. To be clear, this use of the term should be distinguished from its early use as an all or none concept that others possess minds (i.e., an understanding that people have mental representations that differ from reality), as in "Do chimpanzees (or young children) have '*a* theory of mind'?" (Premack & Woodruf, 1978; Wimmer & Perner, 1983).

In contrast, like many before us, we use the term more broadly to refer to the processes involved in reasoning about the *specific contents* of those minds, the particular thoughts, desires, or beliefs a person holds (not just the *presence* of *a* mind). Specifically, we contend that these processes (a) are partially innate, (b) develop over time and can be honed through experience, and (c) lie on a continuum with some individuals being better than others. Our goals in writing this chapter were to provide a skeletal review of the research questions developmental psychologists ask to shed light on children's understanding of the inner workings of the mind, and most importantly, why such research is so incredibly valuable in understanding human nature and our ability to interact with, and learn from, one another.

As the "lost rabbit" scenario illustrates, our theory of mind or perspective-taking abilities are vital to understanding human behavior. They do not just help us make sense of behavior *in retrospect* (as in the "lost rabbit" scenario) but they also assist us in making inferences about how someone will behave *in the future*. For example, if you know that Adam is unaware that the baseball game was canceled at the last minute, you can anticipate that he will still show up for the game. But the many functions of theory of mind do not stop there. For instance, our theory of mind also allows us to manipulate others, for better or for worse (e.g., we could tell Adam the game was canceled, even if it was not, so that he does not show up; or we could tell Vivian her Mom was not able to come to the game so she would be pleasantly surprised when she did). We also regularly deploy our theory of mind, particularly our ability to reason about what others will likely know and not know, to communicate effectively with others. Whether we are having a conversation with just one person, writing a manuscript, or giving a lecture, we routinely make inferences about what information is likely common knowledge to our audience (and does not need further explanation) and what information needs to be elaborated upon. Finally, we also use our theory of mind when learning from others. We do not passively absorb any and all information others provide, but are *selective* in our learning. Both adults and children use a variety of cues to make inferences about whether the information they encounter is from a knowledgeable source (e.g., who is knowledgeable and under what conditions).

In this chapter, we begin with an overview of the earliest research in the field of theory of mind that culminated in the birth of the classic false-belief tasks (often described as the best "litmus" tests for a theory of mind). Next, we describe research with infants and young children that created a puzzle for many developmental psychologists, and briefly mention an intriguing approach used by researchers to attempt to "solve" this puzzle. We then turn to the wealth of research on children's understanding of mental states that goes beyond false-belief reasoning to highlight the rich and complex set of processes involved in making inferences about the mental activities of others. We give a brief nod to the value of studying individual differences by highlighting their important implications for social functioning and social well-being and indicate ways to foster better perspective-taking abilities. Next, we review work illustrating the value of capitalizing on children's proclivity for selective social learning to shed light on their understanding of the mind. Finally, we close with a discussion of some open questions in the literature that we believe are especially fruitful avenues for future research and highlight the complex interplay between our perspective-taking abilities and other cognitive processes.

2. A HISTORICAL OVERVIEW OF RESEARCH LEADING TO THE BIRTH OF THE FALSE-BELIEF TASK

The question of how we develop the ability to reason about the mental states of others dates back to the beginning of developmental psychology. Often referred to as the founding father of cognitive development,

Jean Piaget proposed that young children are so fixated on their own point of view that they neglect other people's perspectives, making it difficult for them to effectively communicate or cooperate with others. In his famous three-dimensional "three-mountains" test of children's visual perspective-taking, it was not until 7 years of age that children could correctly identify another individual's visual perspective of the mountains; prior to that children routinely selected *their own view* of the mountains (Piaget & Inhelder, 1956). Piaget argued that young children's egocentrism prevents them from shifting from their point of view to reason about perspectives other than their own. For much of the 1960s and 1970s, the development of perspective taking was often viewed as the gradual decrease of egocentrism with age, despite challenges from Vygotsky and others who emphasized that children are very interested in the people around them and surprisingly attuned to them (Vygotsky, 1967; see also Flavell, Botkin, Fry, Wright, & Jarvis, 1968; Selman, 1971).

As research progressed, Piaget's late-onset approach to children's perspective taking, and ability to cooperate, began to lose support. An abundance of research showed that infants have a range of social abilities, including an inclination to cooperate with others (Trevarthen & Hubley, 1978), a capacity for joint attention (Scaife & Bruner, 1975), and a proclivity for imitation (Meltzoff, 1976; Meltzoff & Moore, 1977)—all abilities that require one to adopt perspectives different from their own. These findings suggested that infants are more in tune with other people than Piaget had surmised, and in some cases, were used to argue that infants are capable of making basic mental state inferences (e.g., infants realize that gaze indicates *interest*; Scaife & Bruner, 1975).

Around the same time, researchers took an interest in utilizing comparative psychology to better understand theory of mind. Vygotsky suggested that language and thought form a unique theory of mind understanding among humans that is not shared with other species that lack language. Yet, in what would become a landmark paper, Premack and Woodruf (1978) put forth a study suggesting that chimpanzees *do* understand that others have minds that govern behavior. Specifically, they examined a chimpanzee's inferences about the goals of another individual by showing a chimpanzee (Sarah) a series of clips of a human agent struggling to complete a goal (e.g., reaching for a banana). Subsequently, Sarah was prompted to indicate what the agent would do next by examining photographs. Interestingly, Sarah was able to indicate what the agent would do to complete the goal (e.g., use a stick to reach for the bananas). From Sarah's responses, the researchers suggested that chimpanzees can represent the goal of another agent, and predict what he or she will do next. However, in a subsequent set of commentaries, several researchers criticized their interpretation by suggesting that the chimpanzee's performance could be explained by general problem solving abilities, and did not necessitate mental state reasoning (Dennett, 1978).

Critics argued that Sarah was simply indicating what *she* would do next in that context (e.g., grab a stick to reach the bananas). Philosopher Dan Dennett suggested that to truly examine whether chimpanzees can reason about others' mental states, they must be able to predict an agent's action *even when it contradicts what the chimpanzee would do* him or herself. That is, if a chimpanzee can predict an action that he or she would not do (e.g., because it is inconsistent with reality), then the chimpanzee cannot simply be projecting his or her own actions but truly considering another individual's *belief*, or mental representation of reality. Dennett argued that to be certain that an individual can reason about mental states, one must show that they understand that mental states (or mental representations) can conflict with, or misrepresent, reality—as in the case of a *false* belief.

In response to this challenge, Wimmer and Perner (1983) gave birth to what is now often referred to as a classic false-belief task (also known as the "Maxi Task," the "unexpected transfer task," or the "Sally–Anne Task"). This task (see Fig. 1 for a depiction) was designed to examine whether

Fig. 1 A depiction of the Sally–Anne Task of false-belief reasoning (also referred to as the "unexpected transfer task" or "the Maxi Task") first developed by Wimmer and Perner (1983). In a typical variant of this task, children hear a short story about two characters, e.g., Sally and Anne (A). The story describes a scenario where the protagonist (e.g., Sally) leaves an object in one location (location X) and subsequently leaves the scene (B and C). Then, in the protagonist's absence, the second character moves the object from location X to location Y (D) and children are asked where the protagonist will look for the object upon her or his return (E). *This figure consists of original artwork courtesy of Carrie Cheung.*

human children understand that people can hold false beliefs. Here, children viewed a series of sketches outlining a scenario where a protagonist leaves an object in one location (location X) and subsequently leaves the scene. Then, in the protagonist's absence, the object is transferred from location X to location Y and children were asked where the protagonist would look for the object upon her or his return.

Using Dennett's logic, if children could predict that the protagonist would look for the object in location X, then they must understand that the mind can misrepresent reality. However, if children predicted that the protagonist would look for the object in location Y, so the argument went, then they did not understand that concept. Wimmer and Perner's results revealed that 3-year-old children inaccurately indicated that the protagonist would look for the object in its current location (location Y). Between 4 and 5 years of age, a little more than half responded accurately and by 6–9 years of age, they all responded accurately (see also Baron-Cohen, Leslie, & Frith, 1985).

This general pattern of results, where young preschoolers often fail to reason about false beliefs whereas older preschoolers pass, was subsequently observed in other experiments testing children's understanding of false beliefs, such as the Appearance–Reality Task (Gopnik & Astington, 1988) and the "Smarties" or "Unexpected Contents" Tasks (Perner, Leekam, & Wimmer, 1987). In an Appearance–Reality Task for instance, children are shown an object that looks like one thing (e.g., a rock) but is actually another thing (e.g., a sponge). After discovering the object's true identity (e.g., by touching it), children are asked what another person will think the object is. That is, children are asked to reason about the false belief of another individual who should mistake the object for something else because of its appearance (e.g., falsely believe the sponge is a rock; Gopnik & Astington, 1988). Impressively, the aforementioned pattern of results holds across nearly 200 different experiments using these three types of false-belief tasks (see Wellman, Cross, & Watson, 2001 meta-analyses and ensuing commentaries).

3. WHAT CAN WE INFER FROM THE RESULTS OF THE CLASSIC FALSE-BELIEF TASKS?

Why 3-year-old children consistently fail the classic false-belief tasks has been, and still is, a topic of great debate (Rubio-Fernández & Geurts, 2013; Wellman et al., 2001 and subsequent commentaries). Although several accounts of these findings have been put forth, two overarching views emerged. According to one view, sometimes referred to as the Conceptual Change view, 3-year-olds do not realize that the mind can misrepresent reality, but somewhere between ages 3 and 5 they experience a qualitative shift in their conceptual understanding of the mind (Perner, 1991; Wellman, 1990; Wellman et al., 2001). Another overarching view, sometimes referred to as a Processing Demands account, suggests that children cannot pass the task at 3 years of age because they have not fully developed *other* cognitive abilities required to pass the false-belief tasks (e.g., working memory, language, inhibitory control). According to this latter view, 5-year-olds' ability to pass these tasks could reflect the maturation of their general cognitive capacities rather than a *qualitative* conceptual change in their understanding of the mind (Bloom & German, 2000; Fodor, 1992; Zaitchik, 1990). For instance, Birch and Bloom (2003) emphasized that classic false-belief tasks pose the *unnecessary* demand of requiring children to ignore their own specific knowledge (see also Bernstein, Atance, Loftus, & Meltzoff, 2004; Royzman, Cassidy, & Baron, 2003).

In the Sally–Anne Task, for instance, children are not only told that Ann moved the object from Location A (a requirement to test their understanding of false beliefs) but they are also told *exactly where the object gets moved*. The latter is not required to test one's understanding of false beliefs, thereby making the task harder than it needs to be. This argument draws from an abundance of research with children and adults that shows that specific knowledge of an event, or fact, can bias one's ability to reason about a more naïve perspective (for reviews, see Birch & Bernstein, 2007; Ghrear, Birch, & Bernstein, 2016; Hawkins & Hastie, 1990; Pohl, Bender, & Lachmann, 2002). This bias, the tendency to be swayed by one's (current) knowledge when attempting to reason about a more naïve perspective, is referred to as the "curse of knowledge" (Birch & Bloom, 2003; Camerer, Loewenstein, & Weber, 1989). Importantly, this perspective-taking error occurs whether one is reasoning about someone else's perspective or one's own earlier perspective, although the latter manifestation is also referred to as "hindsight bias" or the "knew-it-all-along effect" (Bernstein et al., 2004; Fischhoff, 1977; Taylor, Esbensen, & Bennett, 1994; Sutherland & Cimpian, 2015; for a meta-analyses of 122 studies with adults see Christensen–Szalanski & Willham, 1991).

According to Birch and Bloom (2003), participants in the classic false-belief tasks not only have to make inferences about another individual's false belief, but they also have to overcome the curse of knowledge. Importantly, research suggests that overcoming the curse of knowledge is particularly challenging for young children compared to older children and adults (Bernstein et al., 2004; Epley, Morewedge, & Keysar, 2004; Lagattuta, Sayfan, & Blattman, 2010; Lagattuta, Sayfan, & Harvey, 2014; Mitchell & Taylor, 1999). That is, younger children are more likely to overattribute their own knowledge than older children when considering the perspectives of others. For instance, Birch and Bloom (2003) found a significant decrease in the bias between ages 3 and 5.

Taylor et al. (1994) observed a similar decline in the "knew-it-all-along" manifestation of the curse of knowledge between ages 4 and 5. They found that when 4-year-olds learned new information (e.g., the color chartreuse) they claimed they knew it all along and were unable to differentiate between knowledge that they had known for some time (e.g., the color red), and knowledge they acquired that day (see also Sutherland, Cimpian, Leslie, & Gelman, 2015). Interestingly, young children also seem to think that their peers, and even babies, will know the information they just learned (Taylor, Cartwright, & Bowden, 1991).

Critically, the curse of knowledge bias has been shown to influence even adults' false-belief performance—and few would question whether adults have a concept of false beliefs. Birch and Bloom (2007) presented adults with a variant of the classic false-belief task that used four containers instead of two. Participants read a story about Vicki who left her violin in the blue container. In Vicki's absence, the violin was moved to a different container. In a Knowledgeable (cursed) condition participants were told exactly where the violin was moved (e.g., "it was moved to the red container"), akin to the classic false-belief tasks. In the Ignorant condition, participants were not told where it was moved (e.g., "it was moved to another container"). Then, participants were asked, "What are the chances Vicki will first look for her violin in each of the containers?" (in percentages). Importantly, participants in both conditions needed to realize that Vicki would hold a false belief (i.e., she would falsely believe that the violin was still in the blue container where she left it). However, when participants knew the exact location where the violin was moved they were more likely (compared to those in the Ignorant condition) to predict she would look where *they* knew it was, and less likely to predict she would look in the false-belief location. That is, adults' specific outcome knowledge can interfere with their ability to predict that another person will act according to his or her false belief.[b]

Applying this same logic to understand the role the curse of knowledge plays in *children's* false-belief reasoning, Ghrear, Haddock, Li, and Birch (2016) found that 3- and 4-year-old children performed significantly better on false-belief tasks when they were not required to overcome the curse of knowledge (with the effect driven predominantly by 3-year-olds). Specifically, 3- and 4-year-old children were presented with four stories where a protagonist (e.g., Sally) hides an object in one of four containers (e.g., blue container). Then, in the protagonist's absence, another character placed the object in a different container (e.g., *When Sally was gone, Ryan hid Sally's ball in a different spot! He may have hid it here, or here, or here*). Half of the time children were told exactly which container (e.g., "we know he hid it here"), the rest of the time they were not (e.g., "we do not know where he hid it"). After each story, children were asked to predict where the protagonist would look for the object. Children were more likely to accurately infer the protagonist's false belief when they were not given specific information about where the object was moved, compared to when they were told exactly where the object was moved (the latter being most akin to the classic false-belief tasks[c]). Although these findings should be replicated across a range of different false-belief tasks, they suggest that the classic false-belief tasks are unnecessarily difficult for younger children, raising the question of how false-belief reasoning develops (in-and-of itself) without the added burden of the curse of knowledge. Or put another way, it is unclear how much of the earlier scholarship showing age-related changes in these tasks stemmed from age-related changes in the curse of knowledge rather than false-belief reasoning, per se.

To be clear, the aforementioned results do not preclude the possibility that children also undergo some conceptual change in their understanding of the mind during the preschool period. Importantly, we wish to emphasize that the curse of knowledge is believed to be *an inherent limitation on perspective taking* (a by-product of an otherwise adaptive learning mechanism; see Hoffrage, Hertwig, & Gigerenzer, 2000) that not only contributes to

---

[b] It is worth pointing out that in this study, among others, the curse of knowledge only occurs, or at least occurs to a greater degree, when the outcome makes sense or the participant can generate a plausible explanation for why it might be foreseeable to others (e.g., Pohl et al., 2002; Yopchick & Kim, 2012).

[c] Many real-world situations involving false-belief reasoning may also require overcoming the curse of knowledge.

children's difficulties with false-belief reasoning but also plays a significant role in a wide array of social perspective-taking "tasks" in children's and adults' everyday lives. As such, it warrants further investigation (see Section 8 for a discussion).

4. FALSE-BELIEF REASONING IN THE FIRST 2 YEARS OF LIFE?

In the past decade, a growing body of research emerged that further challenged the conceptual change view of the classic false-belief task. This research relying on an entirely different dependent variable (i.e., participants' looking time) suggested that even infants can reason about false beliefs (Onishi & Baillargeon, 2005; Scott & Baillargeon, 2009; Surian, Caldi, & Sperber, 2007). Specifically, researchers argued that infants have a conceptual understanding of how a protagonist *should behave* when he or she has a false belief. This understanding was investigated using a violation-of-expectation paradigm, wherein infants were shown an event and two opposing "outcomes" for the event. One outcome was meant to fit the infants' expectations and the other was meant to be incongruent with their expectations (if they understood false beliefs). Applying the logic that infants will look longer at an outcome that is inconsistent with their expectations (for a review, see Gweon & Saxe, 2013), the researchers measured participants' looking times (i.e., how long they looked) at each outcome. For example, Onishi and Baillargeon (2005) examined 15- to 18-month-old infants' looking time while observing a scenario where a protagonist leaves her toy in a hiding location and subsequently either leaves the scene or stays and observes. After a pause, the toy moves from one location to another. In one outcome the protagonist reaches for the toy at the original hiding location; in the other outcome she reaches to the new location. Critically, when infants viewed the scenario where the protagonist left before the toy moved, infants expected that the protagonist would behave according to a false belief. That is, infants looked longer when the protagonist reached for the new location rather than the original location where she had last seen it. The opposite pattern was observed when infants viewed the scenario where the protagonist stayed and observed the object move to the new location.

Again, how to interpret these data became a matter of great controversy. Some researchers suggested these data did not reflect false-belief reasoning but only that infants have certain expectations of behavioral rules

(De Bruin & Newen, 2012; Perner & Ruffman, 2005; Ruffman & Perner, 2005; Ruffman, Taumoepeau, & Perkins, 2012) or result from domain-general processes such as "low-level novelty" (Heyes, 2014). Moreover, violation-of-expectation tasks do not require participants to *predict* one's actions based on a false belief, but instead only require that they make sense of those actions *in retrospect* (in contrast to classic false-belief tasks). These criticisms opened the door for research designs to examine early false-belief reasoning without relying strictly on looking time data or retrospective analyses. For example, Buttelmann, Carpenter, and Tomasello (2009) tested toddlers' false-belief reasoning by capitalizing on their precocious helping tendencies (Warneken & Tomasello, 2006, 2007); here, one experimenter hid a toy inside one of two boxes and either stayed in the room or left. Then a second experimenter engaged the child and sneakily moved the toy from one box to the other and locked it. When the first experimenter returned, he tried (but failed) to open one of the boxes. The second experimenter encouraged the child to help. Wisely, instead of helping him open the box he was trying to open, children as young as 18 months appeared to recognize his goal (and his false belief about its location) and consistently helped the experimenter open the correct box.

These new types of designs that placed the participant in a much more active role harkened back to much earlier scholarship that similarly questioned the conceptual change interpretation of the false-belief tasks introduced in the 1980s (see Chandler & Birch, 2010 for review). For instance, Chandler, Fritz, and Hala (1989) demonstrated that 2.5-year-olds are capable of deceiving others, which appears to entail some appreciation that people can misrepresent reality (or hold false beliefs) as well as an understanding that the mental states of others can be manipulated. In their study, children were asked to help a puppet, named "Tony," hide a treasure from an experimenter. The problem was that when Tony moved the treasure, it left behind a trail that would lead the treasure-hunting experimenter right to its actual location. The trails, however, could be wiped away, which is something the children learned and practiced earlier in the study. Thus, when children were asked to help Tony hide the treasure, they had the opportunity to alter the physical state of the world (e.g., by removing the trails) in order to manipulate the mental state of the treasure-hunting experimenter. Their results demonstrated that 50% of their youngest participants (2-year-olds) were already capable of deceiving the experimenter and went so far as to create new false trails to false treasure locations.

The research suggesting that infants and young children (younger than those who passed the classic false-belief tasks) could reason about false beliefs posed an interesting puzzle for developmental psychologists. If the interpretation of these findings were correct and young children could understand false beliefs under some circumstances (or using some measures), then why did older children fail the classic false-belief tasks? To reconcile this apparent disparity some researchers have proposed a dual processing, or two-systems, account (Apperly & Butterfill, 2009; Low, 2010; Low, Apperly, Butterfill, & Rakoczy, 2016; Low & Perner, 2012; Penn & Povinelli, 2007; Sabbagh, Benson, & Kuhlmeier, 2013) of theory of mind. According to these two-systems accounts, humans have one evolutionarily "old" system that processes social information (such as eye-gaze direction) implicitly. This system processes information relatively quickly and effortlessly but has clear limitations and is somewhat inflexible. In contrast, humans have a second, slower but more flexible, system that involves explicit reasoning or deliberation. Apperly and Butterfill (2009) propose that the explicit system comes with the development of language and higher-order executive functions (i.e., cognitive processes including attentional control, inhibitory control, working memory, and cognitive flexibility, as well as reasoning, problem solving, and planning) and argue that infants and nonhuman animals are not yet capable of System 2 perspective taking, but may succeed in false-belief paradigms that do not necessitate explicit reasoning, via System 1.

Consistent with this approach, Rhodes and Brandone (2014) tested 3-year-old children's false-belief performance using both verbal and action-based responses. In their design, an experimenter (E1) left the room through one of two doors (curtains) and explained that they would ring the doorbell when they wanted to come back. On the way out, E1 placed a toy into a box in front of the door they were leaving through. Children completed two false-belief trials where another experimenter (E2) would engage the child and sneakily move the toy to the box in front of the other door. When the doorbell rang, the child was encouraged to open the door for E1; which door they opened served as a test of their action-based false-belief performance. To compare the child's action-based responses against their verbal responses, on one of the two test trials, the child was asked an explicit verbal question "where does E1 think the toy is?" The results revealed that 3-year-olds' *actions* suggested they understood another individual's false belief (by opening the correct door); however, they were not able to correctly answer the explicit question by pointing or verbally stating where E1 would think the toy was. By completing action-based and explicit measures in the same trial they were able to show the aforementioned discrepancy in children's responses *within the same task* (but see He, Bolz, & Baillargeon, 2012 for data suggesting that it is not specifically *verbal* demands that account for the differences in performance, and an alternative explanation for differences that emerge between what they refer to as "spontaneous" vs "elicited" measures).

These new theoretical accounts offer appealing solutions to the puzzle regarding the discrepancy between early false-belief competence and the later emerging ability to pass the classic false-belief tasks. At minimum they offer a novel approach to the study of theory of mind that goes far beyond their applications to false-belief understanding. They raise a multitude of questions for future research, such as: When and why, in the course of *evolution*, did "System 2" emerge? When and why, in the course of *development*, does System 2 emerge? How do these systems develop? How do they interact (e.g., Does System 2 build upon System 1)? Do they have different neuroanatomical loci? Are both systems domain-specific? What is the relationship between System 2 and metacognitive processes outside the domain of theory of mind? If they are *not* the result of two different systems, exactly what makes performance on "elicited" tasks different from performance on more spontaneous measures (see He et al., 2012)? In short, we still have a lot to learn about the processes involved in reasoning about others' mental states and how those processes develop. Consequently, there is much to be gained by comparing and contrasting the conditions under which children succeed and those under which they fail. However, to gain a comprehensive understanding of the processes involved in theory of mind and how they develop we must also "think outside the false-belief box."

5. THINKING OUTSIDE THE FALSE-BELIEF BOX: THEORY OF MIND IS MUCH, MUCH MORE THAN REASONING ABOUT FALSE BELIEFS

One needs only to consider the complexities of their own mental worlds to realize that when it comes to reasoning about another's mental activity there is much, much more than an understanding of false beliefs. Although the ontogeny of an explicit understanding of false beliefs (e.g., their ability to pass the classic false-belief tasks around age 4 or 5) has sometimes been considered the hallmark of children's "theory of mind," we suspect few would disagree that the parts of social cognition that children grasp earlier than 4, as well as those they grasp later, are just as important to our understanding of children's conceptions of the mind.

Well before children pass the classic false-belief tasks, they routinely make inferences about the mental worlds of other people. In a simple but clever study, for instance, Repacholi and Gopnik (1997) provided evidence that by 18 months children can differentiate their own preferences and desires from those of another person. In their study, an experimenter indicated that she preferred broccoli over crackers (i.e., a preference that differed from the child's preference for crackers). Afterward, the experimenter would hold his or her hand out as an indication of a desire for one of the snacks. The 18-month-olds tended to provide the experimenter with broccoli at rates above that expected by chance, but the 14-month-olds routinely offered the experimenter *their* preferred snack of crackers. Interestingly, Wellman and Liu (2004) demonstrated that children's later understanding of false beliefs is predicated by this earlier understanding that others have desires that can be different from one's own. Differentiating one's own desires from someone else's might seem like simply a necessary precondition; however, it raises the important question of how children come to carve up the world in terms of different mental states in the first place? Moreover, it highlights the importance of identifying exactly what processes are involved in making inferences about the various different kinds of mental states, such as goals, intentions, desires, emotions, knowledge, and false beliefs, not to mention other mental activity, such as forgetting, idea generation, speculating, and other mentalistic concepts, including bias, pretense, inference, opinion, and interpretation, to name just a few.

A full account of research that examines children's understanding of the full array of mentalistic concepts is clearly beyond the scope of the current chapter (see Harris, 2006 for an excellent review of more of this work). Instead, we briefly review a few examples to highlight the scope and richness of the mental activities children must understand in order to function in the complex social world in which we live. The consequences of a failure to understand mental activity are perhaps best exemplified by research with children diagnosed with an Autism Spectrum Disorder (ASD). Indeed, the pervasive impairments that individuals along the spectrum display in mental state reasoning have lent support to the notion of an early developing and specialized system for mental state reasoning (Baron-Cohen, 1997). There is ever-mounting evidence to suggest that children with Autism display a relatively specific deficit in mental state reasoning and its precursors, such as gaze-following (Baron-Cohen et al., 1985; Baron-Cohen, Tager-Flusberg, & Cohen, 1993; Perner, Frith, Leslie, & Leekam, 1989). Children with ASDs, even in the absence of general cognitive deficits, fail to reason about false beliefs (Baron-Cohen et al., 1985), and they fail to pay attention to subtle social cues, such as gaze direction that typically developing children use as indicators of others' mental states from an early age (Baron-Cohen, Campbell, Karmiloff-Smith, Grant, & Walker, 1995). Moreover, children with Autism have difficulty appreciating whether an action is accidental or deliberate (D'Entremont & Yazbek, 2007) unlike typically developing children (Dunfield & Kuhlmeier, 2010). Children diagnosed with ASDs tend to engage in virtually no spontaneous pretend (or fantasy) play (Sigman & Ungerer, 1981), they struggle with sarcasm (Happé, 1993), and they have difficulties with other pragmatic aspects of language (for a review, see Baron-Cohen, 1997).

According to some accounts, this specialized system responds to specific inputs and can be "tricked" into activation with cues that normally cooccur with minds (e.g., eyes and/or socially contingent behaviors). Such cues can lead even 12-month-old infants to treat inanimate objects as if they had mental states (Johnson, 2003; Kuhlmeier, Wynn, & Bloom, 2003). Even 5-month-old infants appear to recognize (presumably at an implicit level) that there is a fundamental distinction between the principles that govern inanimate objects (i.e., naïve physics) and the principles that govern human behavior (i.e., naïve psychology) (Kuhlmeier, Bloom, & Wynn, 2004; Spelke, Phillips, & Woodward, 1995). This specialized system for reasoning about *animate objects* is perhaps best exemplified by research that shows young children can infer that humans, but not inanimate mechanical agents, are goal directed. For example, Meltzoff (1995) demonstrated that 18-month-old children will *infer* the *intended* actions of a human target, and subsequently complete the intended outcome, but do not do so when a mechanical arm performs the same action as the adult human. This suggests that from an early age children treat humans and their mental states as "special" sources of information (see also Woodward, 1998).

With age children become increasingly able to apply their developing mental state reasoning skills (presumably in conjunction with other cognitive skills) for ever more complex purposes. For instance, although young children are capable of deception under at least some circumstances (Chandler et al., 1989 reviewed earlier), this does not mean they are master manipulators. Peskin (1992), for instance, demonstrated that children have some serious problems deceiving others, even when the potential for rewards are high. In this study, 3- to 5-year-old children were presented with stickers of varying desirability and asked to choose which ones they liked most and least. Afterward, children were introduced to a puppet that they were told would *always* take the sticker that the child wanted most.

Thus, for this malevolent puppet to not end up with the sticker the child wanted, he or she would have to lie about their true preferences and indicate a false preference for an unwanted sticker. Three-year-olds in this study persistently revealed their true preferences across repeated trials. Four- and 5- year-olds, however, were increasingly able to conceal their preferences to obtain their most desired stickers. These results are consistent with more recent scholarship that suggests that although 3-year-olds are capable of detecting the foundations of malicious intent (i.e., an individual's previous malevolence), it is not until ages 4 or 5 that children come to understand, and capitalize on, explicit references to deception (Mascaro & Sperber, 2009). Together, this work suggests that understanding that others can intend to deceive, figuring out how to avoid falling prey to those deceptions, and being able to manipulate others' mental states in order to deceive them are all important pieces in the development of theory of mind.

With development children's ability to reason about the mental states of others becomes increasingly complex and flexible (for reviews, see Astington & Baird, 2005; Doherty, 2009). For instance, Carpendale and Chandler (1996) argue that around age 7 or 8 children become aware that the mind *interprets* information and that two people can view *the exact same thing* and come to a different interpretation, sometimes referred to as an "interpretive theory of mind." Later developments also include the ability to appreciate ironic statements (Filippova & Astington, 2008), the ability to recognize how different kinds of knowledge are acquired through different senses (e.g., touch vs taste; see Robinson, 2000 for a review), and the ability to recognize that people's interpretations can result from various biases, including those stemming from self-interest or self-enhancement (Mills & Keil, 2005; see also Elashi & Mills, 2015), close personal relationships (Mills & Grant, 2009; Mills & Keil, 2008), or group membership (Bigler & Liben, 1993). As just one further example, by around 9–11 years of age, children demonstrate an understanding of *faux pas* (i.e., situations where one person unintentionally upsets another due to a lack of knowledge about some aspect of the situation; Baron-Cohen, O'Riordan, Stone, Jones, & Plaisted, 1999; Stone, Baron-Cohen, & Knight, 1998). For example, a friend bought new "retro" curtains to decorate her home, and upon visiting for the first time, you comment that the curtains look like they need to be updated. Detecting and understanding faux pas situations nicely illustrates the complexities of theory of mind reasoning because the child must not only detect that one person has upset another, but also that the violation occurred as a result of the offender's uninformed knowledge state, and that the resulting insult was unintended; it might also entail appreciating that the offender will likely be embarrassed by her mistake and the friend may be quite forgiving, and ultimately even amused, given the nature of the misunderstanding.

In sum, the ability to reason about the contents of other minds becomes increasingly sophisticated and nuanced across development. This development does not appear to have a clear end state, and even a so-called mature system is still remarkably error prone. Even adults' mental state reasoning is often inaccurate (Apperly, Warren, Andrews, Grant, & Todd, 2011; Birch, 2005; Royzman et al., 2003). Moreover, vast individual differences exist, in adults as well as in children, a subject we turn to next.

6. INDIVIDUAL DIFFERENCES IN THEORY OF MIND DEVELOPMENT, THEIR POSSIBLE ORIGINS, AND THE IMPLICATIONS FOR FOSTERING THEORY OF MIND

As reviewed throughout, several "milestones" mark the ontogeny of theory of mind. In addition to individual differences in the onset of these milestones, children (and adults) differ in the *degree* to which they can, and do, use theory of mind in their everyday lives (Cutting & Dunn, 1999; Repacholi & Slaughter, 2003). In other words, despite having the ability to explicitly reason about other minds, individuals can vary in the *frequency* with which they do so (sometimes related to their *motivation* to do so) and the *accuracy* with which they do so. As an extreme example of how individuals can vary along these dimensions, paranoid schizophrenia is argued to involve an *active* (noticing minds everywhere) but *inaccurate* (delusional) mental state reasoning system (Crespi & Badcock, 2008). Typically developing children's theory of mind abilities can also be scored along these two dimensions: propensities to attribute mental states (Severson & Lemm, 2016) vs accuracy in attributing mental states (Epley et al., 2004).

The individual differences approach to measuring theory of mind capacities has been especially fruitful at predicting children's social competencies (Walker, 2005). For instance, children who score higher on theory of mind measures (e.g., tasks that measure emotional understanding, perspective taking, and false-belief reasoning) are more likely to engage in prosocial behavior (Deković & Gerris, 1994; Denham, 1986; Lalonde & Chandler, 1995; Nelson & Crick, 1999; Watson, Nixon, Wilson, & Capage, 1999). A meta-analysis of 76 studies of children between the ages of 2 and 12 years suggests that individual differences in theory of mind are positively, albeit modestly, predictive of propensities for helping, sharing, comforting, and coordinating with others to achieve shared goals ($r = 0.19$; Imuta, Henry, Slaughter, Selcuk, & Ruffman, 2016). Moreover, links between better theory of mind performance and more positive peer relationships appear to be at least partially mediated by the relationship between early prosociality and peer acceptance (Caputi, Lecce, Pagnin, & Banerjee, 2012). Conversely, children who display poorer theory of mind performance are not as well regarded by their peers (Dunn, 1996; Slaughter, Dennis, & Pritchard, 2002) and are more likely to be involved in bullying behavior, either as bullies, victims, or "bully victims" (those who serve as both aggressor and victim; Renouf et al., 2010; Shakoor et al., 2012; Sutton, Smith, & Swettenham, 1999).

Interestingly, Banerjee, Watling, and Caputi (2011) found a bidirectional relationship between mental state understanding in the context of faux pas and peer rejection. In a longitudinal study of 210 children aged 5–6 and 8–9 at Time 1, who were followed up 1 year later and again 2 years later, revealed that earlier peer rejection impaired the acquisition of faux pas understanding. Additionally, difficulties in faux pas understanding in the older age group predicted increased peer rejection, highlighting the complex relations between mental state understanding and peer relationships.

Researchers study individual differences in theory of mind to illustrate the important function theory of mind serves in navigating our social worlds. In addition, researchers also want to account for what these differences may tell us about the *processes* involved in the development of theory of mind. This is likely to shed light on potential interventions to foster better perspective-taking abilities. Broadly speaking, research exploring individual differences in theory of mind has emphasized the contributions of *other* skills (e.g., language, memory, inhibitory control) and the importance of *environmental* scaffolding (e.g., mental state discourse, the role of siblings).

As just one example of the complex interplay between theory of mind and other cognitive skills, Hughes (1998) demonstrated a relationship between executive function and theory of mind performance, even when controlling for age and verbal ability. More specifically, there was a significant correlation between working memory and false-belief reasoning, and between inhibitory control, deception, and false-belief explanation tasks. Interestingly, these relationships can change with age and may interact in complex ways. One possible reason for individual differences in theory of mind is that some individuals have better language, memory, or inhibitory abilities that facilitate theory of mind, but that is unlikely the whole story. Precisely how these cognitive abilities interact with theory of mind is a matter of great interest and debate (Carlson & Moses, 2001; Carlson, Moses, & Claxton, 2004; Davis & Pratt, 1995; Flynn, 2007; Hala, Hug, & Henderson, 2003; Hughes, 1998; Landry, Miller-Loncar, Smith, & Swank, 2002; Moses & Carlson, 2004; Müller, Liebermann-Finestone, Carpendale, Hammond, & Bibok, 2012; Russell, 1996; Zelazo, Carter, Reznick, & Frye, 1997). For example, in considering the strong correlation between language and false-belief understanding, Jenkins and Astington (1996) suggest that theory of mind and language do not develop independently of one another, and show how early language abilities are extremely important to a child's social cognitive development. The opposite is also true; children's early theory of mind abilities (e.g., inferring intentions) are often critical for understanding the intended referents of word labels, as well as many pragmatic aspects of language, which may go a long way in explaining why children with ASD also have problems with language (see Bloom, 2000). Thus, individual variability in executive function and language abilities appear to account for some of the variability in theory of mind. However, precisely how these cognitive processes interact in producing measurable differences in mental state reasoning remains an important avenue for future research.

In twin studies, the similar performance on theory of mind measures between identical and fraternal twins suggests that environmental input is important for theory of mind development (Hughes et al., 2005). Interestingly, heritability estimates gradually decrease throughout the first decade of life (Hughes & Devine, 2015), emphasizing the increasing influence of environmental factors on theory of mind development. More specifically, the quantity and quality of language present in the child's environment (and specifically mental state language, e.g., terms like "want," "think," and "know") are important contributors to theory of mind development (Dunn, Brown, Slomkowski, Tesla, & Youngblade, 1991). This might explain why deaf children whose deafness went undetected for some time and were exposed to fewer conversations and less mental state discourse (whether in spoken or signed language) lag behind their typically developing counterparts in false-belief understanding (see Peterson & Siegal, 2000 for a review). In contrast, children with older siblings (and presumably greater exposure to intersibling and parent–child discourse) develop theory of mind somewhat earlier than those without older siblings (Lewis, Freeman,

Kyriakidou, Maridaki-Kassotaki, & Berridge, 1996; Ruffman, Perner, Naito, Parkin, & Clements, 1998).

Other kinds of experience, or practice, also appear helpful in improving one's social perspective taking abilities. For example, both the presence and richness of pretend play (imaginary friends, impersonation of imagined characters) positively predict later false-belief understanding (Taylor & Carlson, 1997; Youngblade & Dunn, 1995). The benefits of pretend play are compounded by *social* or interactive pretend play (e.g., with siblings or peers), arguably because it requires increasingly complex metarepresentational abilities (e.g., reasoning about how individuals can hold different beliefs or representations of the world at any given time, and practice "taking on the role" of different people or characters; Schwebel, Rosen, & Singer, 1999).

Beyond the child's immediate environment, one's broader sociocultural context appears to influence the developmental trajectory of mental state reasoning. For instance, American children come to understand that others can have diverse desires earlier than children from China (Wellman, Fang, Liu, Zhu, & Liu, 2006). Similar differences have been found between Australian and Iranian children (Shahaeian, Peterson, Slaughter, & Wellman, 2011). Research accounting for the origins of cultural differences in theory of mind development is still in its infancy and will surely be an important avenue of future research. However, recent work suggests that cultural differences in parent–child discourse and specifically the use of ostensive pedagogical cues in child–parent–object triangulation (e.g., eye gaze, pointing, verbal referents) may play an important role in accounting for some cultural differences in mental state reasoning (Little, Carver, & Legare, 2016).

Given the research supporting the importance of experiential factors, such as the quality and quantity of mental state language input on theory of mind development, it stands to reason that increasing children's exposure to mental state discourse can help foster theory of mind abilities. Training studies with younger children suggest that participating in mental state conversations causally advances theory of mind development. Ornaghi, Brockmeier, and Gavazzi (2011) randomly assigned 3- and 4-year-old children to a 2-month training program in which children either played language games and read stories containing mental state language (or to a control group that used the same time to engage in free play). They found that the former group showed significant improvement in emotion and false-belief understanding as well as metacognitive vocabulary compared to pretest performance (see also Dunn & Brophy, 2005;

Nelson, 2005). Lohmann, Tomasello, and Meyer (2005) conducted appearance–reality tasks with 3-year-old children and had them experience a deception (i.e., showing them a ball of soap that appears to be a golf ball). These researchers found that children who then engaged in a conversation about the deception using mental state terms performed better on subsequent theory of mind tasks compared with children who merely watched a discussion concerning the deceptive object.

Aside from training children directly, training studies with *their families* show that increasing mental state discourse in the child's environment can foster theory of mind. For instance, observations of parents of 2- and 6-year-old children showed that parents' use of mental state terms (e.g., think, know, believe) predicted individual differences in children's false-belief understanding 4 years later (Ensor, Devine, Marks, & Hughes, 2014; see also Meins et al., 2002). One experimental study showed that preschoolers who overheard characters in a video discussing another person's mental states improved their false-belief performance (Gola, 2012), impressively demonstrating that mental state discourse, even when it is not directed at the child, can help draw children's attention to others' perspectives and improve performance.

It is important to note that not all children may benefit similarly from the kind of training paradigms described in the aforementioned studies. In a training study of 3.5-year-old children who previously failed a false-belief task, researchers found that individual differences in executive function strongly predicted the degree to which children benefitted from theory of mind training (Benson, Sabbagh, Carlson, & Zelazo, 2013). Further research is needed to ascertain not only what other kinds of interventions can foster theory of mind (and which are *most* helpful), but also how individual differences in other skills can bolster or attenuate the benefits of different training strategies.

7. HOW SELECTIVE SOCIAL LEARNING CAN REVEAL CHILDREN'S UNDERSTANDING OF THE MIND

It should be no surprise that humans possess an array of cognitive abilities that seem tailored *for* reasoning about other minds as doing so has played an integral role in humans' success as a cultural species throughout our evolutionary history (Henrich, 2015). In addition to its usefulness for the interpretation of others' behavior, theory of mind comes in handy when using others' actions and words as information sources. Social learning (i.e., learning from others) is an efficient, relatively low-cost strategy to acquire information. However, people are sometimes poor sources of information, providing misleading information on purpose (lies, jokes), by accident (mistakes, ignorance, or misunderstandings), and because they frequently offer their *opinions* not just facts. Thus, theory of mind can render social information gathering more efficient by allowing one to consider others' knowledge, beliefs, and intentions, to gauge the reliability of the information they convey. A large body of research has demonstrated that children are *selective* in their social learning (see Chudek, Brosseau-Liard, Birch, & Henrich, 2013; Mills, 2013; Stephens, Suarez, & Koenig, 2015) and frequently capitalize on cues to others' mental states to guide their learning. For example, older preschoolers consider others' intentions, preferring to accept claims from a "helper" rather than a "tricky" individual (Vanderbilt, Liu, & Heyman, 2011). As another example, preschoolers are more likely to accept an individual's claim about a novel object if that individual claims familiarity with the object rather than ignorance, suggesting that they take a speaker's knowledge into account when deciding whether or not to trust his or her statements (Sabbagh & Baldwin, 2001).

The remainder of this section focuses on children's understanding of an individual's *knowledge* (or its counterpart, ignorance) in social learning. Knowledge can be conceptualized as a state or a trait: One may wonder whether a person possesses a specific piece of knowledge in a given situation (their knowledge *state*) or whether an individual is generally knowledgeable across a wide variety of situations (their *trait* knowledge). There is evidence that children use cues to both of these aspects of knowledge to facilitate social learning.

A valuable cue to knowledge as a state is a person's perceptual access to relevant information. Though preschoolers have an imperfect understanding of the relation between the different senses and different types of "knowing," they understand simple relations such as looking can lead to knowing—at least some types of knowing, such as knowing an object's visual identity (Pillow, 1989; Pratt & Bryant, 1990; Robinson, Champion, & Mitchell, 1999). In some situations they also distinguish informative from noninformative perception. For instance, 3- and 4-year-olds can infer whether they should trust an adult's claims about an object's identity depending on the *modality* of the adult's perceptual access: they are more likely to trust claims about texture if the adult has touched (but not seen) the object, and about color if the adult has seen (but not touched) the object (Whitcombe & Robinson, 2000). In the absence of information about an individual's perceptual access, children can use indirect cues to someone's knowledge state, such as markers of confidence. Preschoolers prefer to learn from people who currently appear confident rather than hesitant in their actions or statements, both when confidence (or lack thereof) is expressed verbally (Jaswal & Malone, 2007; Moore, Bryant, & Furrow, 1989) and nonverbally (Birch, Akmal, & Frampton, 2010).

There are also enduring individual differences in knowledge that can hold across many situations. Some people know a lot more than others about a broad variety of topics (e.g., they may be smarter or more educated); people also have specific niches of expertise that often generalize across a particular domain of knowledge (e.g., music, math, biology, pop culture). These individual differences depend on a combination of factors including the person's prior experience, interests, aptitudes, and so on, which may not be readily observable in a given situation. In the absence of other cues, one cue that is often readily available and can signal who has useful information is *who other people are observing*; indeed, children at least as young as 3 years of age take advantage of this cue to guide their learning (Chudek, Heller, Birch, & Henrich, 2012).

Another way to assess someone's credibility as a source of information is to track, over time, the *accuracy* of the information provided by an individual. All else being equal, someone who has repeatedly offered accurate information in the past is a safer bet for providing accurate information in the future over someone who has a history of being inaccurate. Impressively, children at least as young as 3 years of age appear to spontaneously track the accuracy of individuals (Birch, Vauthier, & Bloom, 2008) and prefer to learn new information from individuals who have repeatedly provided accurate information over those who have demonstrated inaccuracy or ignorance (Jaswal & Neely, 2006; Koenig, Clément, & Harris, 2004; Koenig & Harris, 2005). Older preschoolers demonstrate further sophistication by simultaneously tracking accuracy in different domains (Sobel & Corriveau, 2010). Preschoolers also take advantage of other cues such as age (Fitneva, 2010) or occupation (Lutz & Keil, 2002) to infer what someone is likely to know.

Even younger children appear sensitive to some cues to others' mental states when seeking information (for review, see Poulin-Dubois & Brosseau-Liard, 2016). At 18 months, toddlers prefer to learn from a previously reliable labeler, e.g., someone who correctly labels a bird, over someone who incorrectly labels a bird an "apple" (Brooker & Poulin-Dubois, 2013). By 24 months, children moderate their imitation of an adult's actions based on the nonverbal confidence cues demonstrated by that adult

(Brosseau-Liard & Poulin-Dubois, 2014). In terms of knowledge as a trait, 14-month-olds are more likely to imitate an individual's actions if that individual has previously demonstrated correct conventional actions (e.g., putting a shoe on one's foot) rather than incorrect ones (e.g., putting a shoe on a different body part; Zmyj, Buttelmann, Carpenter, & Daum, 2010). Precursors to these abilities may even be present in the first year of life (Tummeltshammer, Wu, Sobel, & Kirkham, 2014).

Although infants and children's selective learning preferences are now being used as a window into their understanding of the mind, there is still some controversy about the relation between some of the observed social learning preferences and theory of mind. Are children really engaging in mental state reasoning when deciding from whom to learn? Or could they be using more simplistic strategies (e.g., "stop listening to anyone who says weird things")? Research has tried to answer this question in a few different ways. One way is to examine correlations between children's theory of mind and their performance on selective learning tasks that appear to reflect some understanding, tacit or otherwise, of knowledge. If reasoning about knowledge does underlie children's learning strategies on these tasks, then we would expect children's theory of mind to predict more savvy selective learning.

A few studies have obtained moderate positive correlations between their preference to learn from a more knowledgeable individual and their performance on one or more theory of mind tasks (DiYanni & Kelemen, 2008; DiYanni, Nini, Rheel, & Livelli, 2012). In one such study by Brosseau-Liard, Penney, and Poulin-Dubois (2015), 3- and 4-year-olds' performance on Wellman and Liu's (2004) theory of mind scale correlated with a preference to learn new words from a previously accurate (rather than inaccurate) puppet, and as predicted no correlation was revealed between theory of mind task performance and their preference to learn from an individual demonstrating physical strength. This finding suggests that theory of mind may specifically predict selective social learning strategies involving reasoning about knowledge (as opposed to, for instance, a general tendency to be choosy about information sources).

Similarly, Lucas, Lewis, Pala, Wong, and Berridge (2013) investigated the impact of exposure to Turkish, a language that marks the source of one's knowledge with obligatory evidential markers. Turkish preschoolers were superior to children of the same age from England and Hong Kong on both theory of mind and selective word learning from an accurate individual. Moreover, across all three countries theory of mind performance predicted stronger selective learning from a previously accurate source. These studies suggest a potential relation between greater theory of mind skill and savvier social learning, but not all studies that have looked for such a correlation have found one (Pasquini, Corriveau, Koenig, & Harris, 2007). So far, the search for relations between savvy social learning and performance on theory of mind tasks has been mainly focused on 3- and 4-year-old children using only a few theory of mind tasks. More research is needed to fully understand the relation between theory of mind and selective social learning from the most knowledgeable sources (including, but not limited to, the use of tasks tapping other facets of theory of mind and the employment of experimental designs).

There are additional indications that children's selective learning preferences may constitute a demonstration of their knowledge understanding. For instance, by late in their preschool years (around age 5), children do not blindly apply simple rules (e.g., looking leads to knowing; ignore what previously inaccurate people say) when deciding from whom to learn. Instead, they appear to consider the situational relevance of the cues at hand. This is especially noticeable when children are put in a situation where multiple cues conflict. Older preschoolers seem to favor cues that are more objectively informative, such as one's prior accuracy, over less informative cues such as one's tendency to make confident claims (Brosseau-Liard, Cassels, & Birch, 2014). They also appear to correctly apply cues to state knowledge and trait knowledge in the situations where they are most relevant. As an example, imagine that one wants to find out what is inside an unmarked box. If one person makes a claim about the box's contents, that person's perceptual access to the contents (i.e., did they look inside?) is crucial to evaluating the accuracy of that person's claim; it does not matter how accurate that person has been in the past, if they have not seen inside the box they almost certainly will not know what the box contains.[d]

Furthermore, a person's knowledge of episodic information (e.g., one's knowledge of where your mother left her sunglasses) is not helpful for predicting that person's knowledge outside that situation—it is situation specific. Conversely, a person's accuracy about generic information, such as their knowledge of common facts or the labels for objects, is likely to be a better indicator of his or her knowledge in other situations. Although these may seem like complex notions, some research suggests that preschool-aged

---

[d] Barring, of course, situations where they were informed in some other way (e.g., someone told them) and were unable to infer the contents from the outward appearance of the box.

children recognize them. For example, preschoolers grant greater weight to a history of accuracy in providing semantic rather than episodic information (Stephens & Koenig, 2015), rely more heavily on information about a person's perceptual access over that person's prior accuracy in an episodic learning situation (Brosseau-Liard & Birch, 2011), and appreciate that someone with a history of accuracy is no more likely to know about situation-specific information than someone with a history of inaccuracy (Brosseau-Liard & Birch, 2010).

Overall, this body of work demonstrates the potential for capitalizing on children's selective social learning preferences to answer questions about their understanding of the mental states of others. Simultaneously, it serves to highlight the important role theory of mind plays in social learning—the type of learning that is critical for the cumulative transmission of information from one generation to the next, and arguably (see Henrich, 2015) what makes us unique from all other species.

8. FUTURE DIRECTIONS: THE VALUE IN UNDERSTANDING AN INHERENT LIMITATION ON PERSPECTIVE TAKING AND THE MECHANISMS INVOLVED

Throughout this chapter we have highlighted important areas for future research. Rather than reiterate them here, we chose to emphasize one particular line of research that we believe is key for a comprehensive understanding of the processes involved in perspective taking or theory of mind. In addition, by discussing other cognitive processes believed to influence perspective taking, we emphasize that to understand the development of theory of mind and its *deployment* in our everyday lives, we must consider its complex interplay with other cognitive processes.

To understand how humans reason about the minds of others, one needs to recognize an inherent cognitive limitation on perspective taking, namely the so-called curse of knowledge. As noted earlier, the curse of knowledge refers to the tendency to be biased by one's current knowledge state when attempting to reason about (or from) a more naïve perspective. This intrinsic limitation on perspective taking appears to stem from an otherwise adaptive learning mechanism: Our brains are geared toward *acquiring* knowledge, not ignoring it. Although humans are prone to forgetting, the act of *intentionally* "unknowing" something is inherently difficult, perhaps impossible (see Golding, Long, & MacLeod, 1994). When humans acquire new information, this information gets embedded into our knowledge structures, or mental representations, and these representations get updated rendering old information, or outdated perspectives, less accessible (Henriksen & Kaplan, 2003; Hoffrage et al., 2000). This knowledge updating is extremely adaptive, in fact critical, for learning and allows us to keep track of the most current state of affairs in an ever-changing environment (Hoffrage et al., 2000). The downside (the so-called curse): this learning mechanism, that is otherwise so adaptive, consequently interferes with our ability to reason *as if* we did not know that information, leading to biased perspective taking. Not surprisingly, this constraint on perspective taking is present cross-culturally (Heine & Lehman, 1996; Pohl et al., 2002), though the *magnitude* of the curse of knowledge bias may vary depending on cultural experience (McNamara, 2016).

Generally speaking, the curse of knowledge clouds our ability to predict what others know, and consequently, sometimes how they will feel or behave. Furthermore, given how much of communication rests upon making inferences about what one's audience knows (e.g., what information is common knowledge and what information needs to be explained) it can also interfere with our ability to communicate effectively (Hinds, 1999; Pinker, 2014). In fact, the consequences of this perspective-taking limitation have been demonstrated across a wide-range of disciplines including politics, behavioral economics, and education as well as in several applied settings, such as business, law, and medicine (for reviews, see Ghrear, Birch, et al., 2016; Hawkins & Hastie, 1990).

It is important to note, however, that this by-product of human learning cannot explain, in and of itself, why young children and aging adults tend to show the curse of knowledge bias to a greater degree than older children and young adults. To account for the U-shaped developmental trajectory in the magnitude of the bias (Bernstein, Erdfelder, Meltzoff, Peria, & Loftus, 2011) one needs to consider the developmental changes that occur in *other* cognitive processes that can reduce or accentuate its effects. To date, the specific cognitive processes that influence this bias are still a matter of great debate in the adult literature. According to an inhibitory control account, the bias can be partially overcome by *inhibiting the contents of one's knowledge* (Bayen, Pohl, Erdfelder, & Auer, 2007; Groß & Bayen, 2015). According to this account, if you know that Trump won the election and you want to recall what you thought *before* the election (e.g., how probable you thought it was that Trump would win) you must attempt to inhibit your newfound knowledge of the outcome. The same logic applies if you are reasoning about another person's perspective, rather than your own earlier perspective. In other words, one's ability to suppress the contents of one's current knowledge state influences the magnitude of the curse of knowledge. Consistent with the age-related changes in the magnitude of the bias, inhibitory control improves over development and declines in old age (Groß & Bayen, 2015). However in two studies by Bernstein, Atance, Meltzoff, and Loftus (2007), children's hindsight bias (or curse of knowledge) and theory of mind performance were correlated (i.e., the greater the bias, the worse one's theory of mind performance), but inhibitory control did not mediate that relationship. Of course, future work along these lines may shed additional light on the role of inhibitory control in perspective taking, and the curse of knowledge bias in particular, as inhibition appears to play some role in the successful deployment of one's theory of mind (as noted in Section 6).

A second mechanism that some have argued plays a role in the curse of knowledge is fluency misattribution (Harley, Carlsen, & Loftus, 2004). This account draws from a large body of research with adults that shows that people use (and sometimes misuse) the fluency with which information is processed (or comes to mind) to make a variety of perceptual, cognitive, and affective judgments (Bernstein, Whittlesea, & Loftus, 2002; Jacoby, Woloshyn, & Kelley, 1989; Sanna, Schwarz, & Small, 2002; Winkielman, Schwarz, Fazendeiro, & Reber, 2003; Zajonc, 1968). According to this account, the curse of knowledge is exaggerated when one *mis*attributes the source of the "fluency" or ease with which the information comes to mind (or with which the information is processed). The logic goes like this: instead of recognizing that the ease with which the information came to mind is due to our prior exposure to the information, we misinterpret that ease as resulting from the *objective* ease, foreseeability, or prevalence of the information. For example, if you know who won a recent election the information tends to come to mind quickly and easily and you can mistake that ease for it being easier, or more widely known, than it really is. In contrast to an inhibitory control account, it is not the ability to suppress the *content* of one's knowledge (who won the election) that influences the magnitude of the bias but rather one's ability to recognize, and correctly attribute, the source of the fluency with which it came to mind. In fact, fluency misattribution may be one type of source monitoring error.

Source monitoring includes tracking, encoding, and recalling the source of one's knowledge, such as how or when that knowledge was acquired (Johnson, Hashtroudi, & Lindsay, 1993). For example, source monitoring is involved in recalling *how and when you learned* that the capital of Syria is Damascus (i.e., your memory of the source of that knowledge). The potential role of source monitoring in perspective taking is somewhat intuitive. If you can remember, for instance, where and when you learned the location of the "Space Needle" (e.g., when you visited Seattle in high school) you are probably better positioned to gauge the likelihood that others shared a similar experience to acquire that knowledge. On the other hand, if you cannot recall how you learned the meaning of the word "confounded" you may have more difficulty gauging how well known the meaning of that word is, compared to words whose source you do recall (e.g., loquacious, studying for Scholastic Aptitude Tests, or SATs). As mentioned previously, fluency misattribution appears to be a failure to recognize the source of one's fluency (e.g., it is fluent because of your prior exposure rather than its objective frequency; Jacoby, Kelley, Brown, & Jasechko, 1989).

Young children are notoriously bad at source monitoring (Gopnik & Graf, 1988; Robinson, 2000). Substantial improvements in source monitoring occur across the preschool period in line with the age-related decline in the magnitude of the curse of knowledge (Birch & Bloom, 2003). Of course, to determine whether (or how) source monitoring, inhibition, and fluency misattribution contribute to the curse of knowledge one needs to go beyond correlations with age. Importantly, these processes may not be mutually exclusive but may work in tandem to ameliorate or compound the effects of the bias. They also may not represent the full set of processes that influence the curse of knowledge. We believe *experimentally* testing the roles of each of these mechanisms is a fruitful avenue for further research, especially given how pervasive the curse of knowledge bias is, and how profound its implications are for many real-world situations.

Ultimately, a better understanding of the development of theory of mind, and the processes that support it, will shed light on both the inner workings of the human mind and the ability to *reason about* those inner workings. This line of work is also key to identifying ways to improve perspective taking. This is an especially fruitful avenue of research considering the myriad of benefits associated with accurate perspective-taking abilities, including better social emotional health, greater academic success, and more satisfying relationships, to name just a few (see Repacholi & Slaughter, 2003 for review). To emphasize this point we quote Ickes (1997) referring to people with what he called "empathic accuracy" (i.e., accuracy at inferring the thoughts and feelings of others): "All else being equal, they are likely to be the most tactful advisors, the most diplomatic officials, the most effective negotiators, the most electable politicians, the most productive salespersons, the most successful teachers, and the most insightful therapists." (p. 2). His quote should also remind us that there is a myriad of work on perspective-taking abilities outside the field of developmental psychology (e.g., in social psychology, cognitive science, behavioral economics, philosophy, political science, education). Insights from those disciplines will prove valuable when researching the development of perspective-taking abilities (and vice versa). Developing techniques to improve perspective taking in early childhood may be particularly beneficial because early childhood is a time when cognitive malleability is high. Fortunately (or unfortunately as it *always depends on your perspective*), the mental lives of people are so incredibly rich and complex that there is no end in sight to our ability to hone our perspective-taking skills (or in the number of research questions we can ask).

ACKNOWLEDGMENTS

We would like to especially thank Janette B. Benson for her very helpful feedback on an earlier draft of this manuscript as well as the exceptionally helpful Research Assistants in the K.I.D. Studies Centre at the University of British Columbia who assisted with the literature reviews and editing the manuscript (in alphabetical order): Carrie Cheung, Gini Choi, Marisa Gagne, Nataly Kaufman, Parky Lau, Caitlin Mooney, and Janane Sri. A special thanks to Carrie Cheung for the artwork for Fig. 1.

REFERENCES

Apperly, I. A., & Butterfill, S. A. (2009). Do humans have two systems to track beliefs and belief-like states? *Psychological Review, 116*(4), 953–970.

Apperly, I. A., Warren, F., Andrews, B. J., Grant, J., & Todd, S. (2011). Developmental continuity in theory of mind: Speed and accuracy of belief-desire reasoning in children and adults. *Child Development, 82*(5), 1691–1703. http://doi.org/10.1111/j.1467-8624.2011. 01635.x.

Astington, J. W., & Baird, J. A. (Eds.), (2005). *Why language matters for theory of mind*. New York: Oxford University Press.

Banerjee, R., Watling, D., & Caputi, M. (2011). Peer relations and the understanding of faux pas: Longitudinal evidence for bidirectional associations. *Child Development, 82*(6), 1887–1905.

Baron-Cohen, S. (1997). *Mindblindness: An essay on autism and theory of mind*. Cambridge, MA: The MIT Press.

Baron-Cohen, S., Campbell, R., Karmiloff-Smith, A., Grant, J., & Walker, J. (1995). Are children with autism blind to the mentalistic significance of the eyes? *British Journal of Developmental Psychology, 13*(4), 379–398. http://doi.org/10.1111/j.2044-835X.1995. tb00687.x.

Baron-Cohen, S., Leslie, A. M., & Frith, U. (1985). Does the autistic child have a "theory of mind"? *Cognition, 21*(1), 37–46.

Baron-Cohen, S., O'Riordan, M., Stone, V., Jones, R., & Plaisted, K. (1999). Recognition of faux pas by normally developing children and children with Asperger syndrome or high-functioning autism. *Journal of Autism and Developmental Disorders, 29*(5), 407–418.

Baron-Cohen, S., Tager-Flusberg, H., & Cohen, D. (1993). *Understanding other minds: Perspectives from autism.* Oxford: Oxford University Press.

Bayen, U. J., Pohl, R. F., Erdfelder, E., & Auer, T. S. (2007). Hindsight bias across the lifespan. *Social Cognition, 25*, 83–97. http://dx.doi.org/10.1521/soco.2007.25.1.83.

Benson, J. E., Sabbagh, M. A., Carlson, S. M., & Zelazo, P. D. (2013). Individual differences in executive functioning predict preschoolers' improvement from theory-of-mind training. *Developmental Psychology, 49*(9), 1615.

Bernstein, D. M., Atance, C., Loftus, G. R., & Meltzoff, A. (2004). We saw it all along: Visual hindsight bias in children and adults. *Psychological Science, 15*(4), 264–267. http://dx.doi.org/10.1111/j.0963-7214.2004.00663.x.

Bernstein, D. M., Atance, C., Meltzoff, A. N., & Loftus, G. R. (2007). Hindsight bias and developing theories of mind. *Child Development, 78*(4), 1374–1394. http://dx.doi.org/10.1111/j.1467-8624.2007.01071.x.

Bernstein, D. M., Erdfelder, E., Meltzoff, A. N., Peria, W., & Loftus, G. R. (2011). Hindsight bias from 3 to 95 years of age. *Journal of Experimental Psychology-Learning Memory and Cognition, 37*(2), 378–391. http://dx.doi.org/10.1037/a0021971.

Bernstein, D. M., Whittlesea, B. W., & Loftus, E. F. (2002). Increasing confidence in remote autobiographical memory and general knowledge: Extensions of the revelation effect. *Memory & Cognition, 30*(3), 432–438. http://dx.doi.org/10.3758/BF03194943.

Bigler, R. S., & Liben, L. S. (1993). A cognitive-developmental approach to racial stereotyping and reconstructive memory in Euro-American children. *Child Development, 64*, 1507–1518. http://dx.doi.org/10.1111/j.1467-8624.1993.tb02967.x.

Birch, S. A. J. (2005). When knowledge is a curse children's and adults' reasoning about mental states. *Current Directions in Psychological Science, 14*(1), 25–29. http://dx.doi.org/10.1111/j.0963-7214.2005.00328.x.

Birch, S. A. J., Akmal, N., & Frampton, K. L. (2010). Two-year-olds are vigilant of others' non-verbal cues to credibility. *Developmental Science, 13*, 363–369. http://dx.doi.org/10.1111/j.1467-7687.2009.00906.x.

Birch, S. A. J., & Bernstein, D. M. (2007). What can children tell us about hindsight bias: A fundamental constraint on perspective-taking? *Social Cognition, 25*(1), 98–113. http://dx.doi.org/10.1521/soco.2007.25.1.98.

Birch, S. A. J., & Bloom, P. (2003). Children are cursed: An asymmetric bias in mental state attribution. *Psychological Science, 14*(3), 283–286. http://dx.doi.org/10.1111/1467-9280.03436.

Birch, S. A. J., & Bloom, P. (2007). The curse of knowledge in reasoning about false beliefs. *Psychological Science, 18*(5), 382–386. http://dx.doi.org/10.1111/j.1467-9280.2007.01909.x.

Birch, S. J., Vauthier, S. A., & Bloom, P. (2008). Three- and four-year-olds spontaneously use others' past performance to guide their learning. *Cognition, 107*, 1018–1034. http://dx.doi.org/10.10116/j.cognition.2007.12.008.

Bloom, P. (2000). *How children learn the meanings of words.* Cambridge, MA: The MIT Press.

Bloom, P., & German, T. P. (2000). Two reasons to abandon the false belief task as a test of theory of mind. *Cognition, 77*(1), 25–31.

Brooker, I., & Poulin-Dubois, D. (2013). Is a bird an apple? The effect of speaker labeling accuracy on infants' word learning, imitation, and helping behaviors. *Infancy, 18*, E46–E68. http://dx.doi.org/10.1111/infa.12027.

Brosseau-Liard, P. E., & Birch, S. A. J. (2010). 'I bet you know more and are nicer too!': What children infer from others' accuracy. *Developmental Science, 13*, 772–778.

Brosseau-Liard, P. E., & Birch, S. A. J. (2011). Epistemic states and traits: Preschoolers appreciate the differential informativeness of situation-specific and person-specific cues to knowledge. *Child Development*, *82*, 1788–1796. http://dx.doi.org/10.1111/j.1467-8624.2011.01662.x.

Brosseau-Liard, P., Cassels, T., & Birch, S. (2014). You seem certain but you were wrong before: Developmental change in preschoolers' relative trust in accurate versus confident speakers. *PLoS One*. *9*(9). e108308http://dx.doi.org/10.1371/journal.pone.0108308.

Brosseau-Liard, P., Penney, D., & Poulin-Dubois, D. (2015). Theory of mind selectively predicts preschoolers' knowledge-based selective word learning. *British Journal of Developmental Psychology*, *33*, 464–475. http://dx.doi.org/10.1111/bjdp.12107.

Brosseau-Liard, P. E., & Poulin-Dubois, D. (2014). Sensitivity to confidence cues increases during the second year of life. *Infancy*, *19*, 461–475. http://dx.doi.org/10.1111/infa.12056.

Buttelmann, D., Carpenter, M., & Tomasello, M. (2009). Eighteen-month-old infants show false belief understanding in an active helping paradigm. *Cognition*, *112*, 337–342.

Camerer, C., Loewenstein, G., & Weber, M. (1989). The curse of knowledge in economic settings: An experimental analysis. *Journal of Political Economy*, *97*(5), 1232–1254. Retrieved from http://www.jstor.org/stable/1831894.

Caputi, M., Lecce, S., Pagnin, A., & Banerjee, R. (2012). Longitudinal effects of theory of mind on later peer relations: The role of prosocial behavior. *Developmental Psychology*, *48*(1), 257–270. http://dx.doi.org/10.1037/a0025402. Retrieved from.

Carlson, S. M., & Moses, L. J. (2001). Individual differences in inhibitory control and children's theory of mind. *Child Development*, *72*(4), 1032–1053. http://dx.doi.org/10.1111/1467-8624.00333.

Carlson, S. M., Moses, L. J., & Claxton, L. J. (2004). Individual differences in executive functioning and theory of mind: An investigation of inhibitory control and planning ability. *Journal of Experimental Child Psychology*, *87*(4), 299–319. http://dx.doi.org/10.1016/j.jecp.2004.01.002.

Carpendale, J. I., & Chandler, M. J. (1996). On the distinction between false belief understanding and subscribing to an interpretive theory of mind. *Child Development*, *67*(4), 1686–1706. http://dx.doi.org/10.2307/1131725.

Chandler, M. J., & Birch, S. A. J. (2010). The development of knowing. In *Cognition, biology, and methods*: *Vol. 1. The handbook of life-pan development* (pp. 671–719). Hoboken, NJ: John Wiley & Sons Inc.

Chandler, M. J., Fritz, A. S., & Hala, S. (1989). Small-scale deceit: Deception as a marker of two-, three-, and four-year-olds' early theories of mind. *Child Development*, *60*(6), 1263–1277. http://dx.doi.org/10.2307/1130919.

Christensen-Szalanski, J. J., & Willham, C. F. (1991). The hindsight bias: A meta-analysis. *Organizational Behaviour and Human Decision Processes*, *48*(1), 147–168. http://dx.doi.org/10.1016/0749-5978(91)90010-Q. Retrieved from.

Chudek, M., Brosseau-Liard, P., Birch, S., & Henrich, J. (2013). Culture-gene coevolutionary theory and children's selective social learning. To appear in M. Banaji & S. Gelman (Eds.), *Navigating the Social World: The Early Years*. Oxford University Press.

Chudek, M., Heller, S., Birch, S., & Henrich, J. (2012). Prestige-biased cultural learning: Bystander's differential attention to potential models influences children's learning. *Evolution and Human Behaviour*, *33*, 46–56.

Crespi, B., & Badcock, C. (2008). Psychosis and autism as diametrical disorders of the social brain. *Behavioral and Brain Sciences*, *31*(03), 241–261.

Cutting, A. L., & Dunn, J. (1999). Theory of mind, emotion understanding, language, and family background: Individual differences and interrelations. *Child Development*, *70*(4), 853–865. http://dx.doi.org/10.1111/1467-8624.00061.

Davis, H. L., & Pratt, C. (1995). The development of children's theory of mind: The working memory explanation. *Australian Journal of Psychology, 47*(1), 25–31. http://dx.doi.org/10.1080/00049539508258765.

De Bruin, L. C., & Newen, A. (2012). An association account of false belief understanding. *Cognition, 123*(2), 240–259.

Deković, M., & Gerris, J. R. M. (1994). Developmental analysis of social cognitive and behavioural differences between popular and rejected children. *Journal of Applied Developmental Psychology, 15*(3), 367–386. http://dx.doi.org/10.1016/0193-3973(94)90038-8.

Denham, S. A. (1986). Social cognition, prosocial behavior, and emotion in preschoolers: Contextual validation. *Child Development, 57*(1), 194–201. http://dx.doi.org/10.2307/1130651.

Dennett, D. C. (1978). *Three kinds of intentional psychology. In Perspectives in the philosophy of language: A concise anthology* (pp. 163–186). Retrieved from: http://journals.cambridge.org/action/displayAbstract?fromPage=online&aid=7131756&fileId=S0140525X00076664.

D'Entremont, B., & Yazbek, A. (2007). Imitation of intentional and accidental actions by children with autism. *Journal of Autism and Developmental Disorders, 37*(9), 1665–1678.

DiYanni, C., & Kelemen, D. (2008). Using a bad tool with good intention: Young children's imitation of adults' questionable choices. *Journal of Experimental Child Psychology, 101*, 241–261. http://dx.doi.org/10.1016/j.jecp.2008.05.002.

DiYanni, C., Nini, D., Rheel, W., & Livelli, A. (2012). 'I won't trust you if I think you're trying to deceive me': Relations between selective trust, theory of mind, and imitation in early childhood. *Journal of Cognition and Development, 13*, 354–371. http://dx.doi.org/10.1080/15248372.2011.590462.

Doherty, M. J. (2009). *Theory of mind: How children understand other's thoughts and feelings.* New York: Psychology Press.

Dunfield, K. A., & Kuhlmeier, V. A. (2010). Intention-mediated selective helping in infancy. *Psychological Science, 21*, 523–527.

Dunn, J. (1996). Arguing with siblings, friends, and mothers: Developments in relationships and understanding. In D. I. Slobin, J. Gerhardt, A. Kyratzis, & J. Guo (Eds.), *Social interaction, social context, and language: Essays in honor of Susan Ervin-Tripp* (pp. 191–204). Hillsdale, NJ: Lawrence Erlbaum Associates.

Dunn, J., & Brophy, M. (2005). Communication, relationships, and individual differences in children's understanding of mind. In *Why language matters for theory of mind.* Toronto, ON: University of Toronto. This chapter originated from the aforementioned conference. Oxford University Press.

Dunn, J., Brown, J., Slomkowski, C., Tesla, C., & Youngblade, L. (1991). Young children's understanding of other people's feelings and beliefs: Individual differences and their antecedents. *Child Development, 62*(6), 1352–1366. Retrieved from http://www.jstor.org/stable/1130811.

Elashi, F. B., & Mills, C. M. (2015). Developing the bias blind spot: Increasing skepticism towards others. *PLoS One. 10*(11). http://dx.doi.org/10.1371/journal.pone.0141809.

Ensor, R., Devine, R. T., Marks, A., & Hughes, C. (2014). Mothers' cognitive references to 2-year-olds predict theory of mind at ages 6 and 10. *Child Development, 85*(3), 1222–1235.

Epley, N., Morewedge, C. K., & Keysar, B. (2004). Perspective taking in children and adults: Equivalent egocentrism but differential correction. *Journal of Experimental Social Psychology, 40*, 760–768.

Filippova, E., & Astington, J. W. (2008). Further development in social reasoning revealed in discourse irony understanding. *Child Development, 79*(1), 126–138.

Fischhoff, B. (1977). Perceived informativeness of facts. *Journal of Experimental Psychology: Human Perception and Performance, 3*, 349–358.

Fitneva, S. A. (2010). Children's representation of child and adult knowledge. *Journal of Cognition and Development*, *11*, 458–484. http://dx.doi.org/10.1080/15248371003700023.

Flavell, J. H., Botkin, P. T., Fry, C. L., Wright, J. W., & Jarvis, P. E. (1968). *The development of role-taking and communication skills in children*. New York: Wiley.

Flynn, E. (2007). The role of inhibitory control in false belief understanding. *Cognitive Development*, *16*(1), 53–69. http://dx.doi.org/10.1002/icd.500.

Fodor, J. (1992). A theory of the child's theory of mind. *Cognition*, *44*, 283–296.

Ghrear, S. E., Birch, S. A. J., & Bernstein, D. M. (2016). Outcome knowledge and false belief. *Frontiers in Psychology*, *7*, 118. http://doi.org/10.3389/fpsyg.2016.00118.

Ghrear, S. E., Haddock, T. B., Li, V., & Birch, S. A. J. (2016). The curse of knowledge and false belief reasoning. In *Poster presented at the 2016 meeting of the Human Behavior and Evolution Society, Vancouver, British Columbia, Canada.*

Gola, A. A. H. (2012). Mental verb input for promoting children's theory of mind: A training study. *Cognitive Development*, *27*(1), 64–76.

Golding, J. M., Long, D. L., & MacLeod, C. M. (1994). You can't always forget what you want: Directed forgetting of related words. *Journal of Memory and Language*, *33*(4), 493–510. http://dx.doi.org/10.1006/jmla.1994.1023.

Gopnik, A., & Astington, J. W. (1988). Children's understanding of representational change and its relation to the understanding of false belief and the appearance-reality distinction. *Child Development*, *59*, 26–37.

Gopnik, A., & Graf, P. (1988). Knowing how you know: Young children's ability to identify and remember the sources of their beliefs. *Child Development*, *59*(5), 1366–1371. http://dx.doi.org/10.2307/1130499.

Groß, J., & Bayen, U. J. (2015). Hindsight bias in younger and older adults: The role of access control. *Aging, Neuropsychology, and Cognition*, *22*(2), 183–200. http://dx.doi.org/10.1080/13825585.2014.901289.

Gweon, H., & Saxe, R. (2013). Developmental cognitive neuroscience of theory of mind. In J. Rubenstein & P. Rakic (Eds.), *Neural circuit development and function in the brain* (pp. 367–377). Cambridge, MA: Academic Press.

Hala, S., Hug, S., & Henderson, A. (2003). Executive function and false-belief understanding in preschool children: Two tasks are harder than one. *Journal of Cognition and Development*, *4*(3), 275–298. http://dx.doi.org/10.1207/S15327647JCD0403_03.

Happé, F. (1993). Communicative competence and theory of mind in autism: A test of relevance theory. *Cognition*, *48*(2), 101–119.

Harley, E. M., Carlsen, K. A., & Loftus, G. (2004). The "saw-it-all-along" effect: Demonstrations of visual hindsight bias. *Journal of Experimental Psychology. Learning, Memory, and Cognition*, *30*, 960–968.

Harris, P. L. (2006). Social cognition. In W. Damon, R. M. Lerner (Series Eds.) & D. Kunh, R. Siegler (Vol. Eds.), *Handbook of child psychology: Vol. 2. Cognition, perception, and language* (6th ed., pp. 811–858). New York: Wiley.

Hawkins, S. A., & Hastie, R. (1990). Hindsight: Biased judgments of past events after the outcomes are known. *Psychological Bulletin*, *107*(3), 311–327. http://dx.doi.org/10.1037/0033-2909.107.3.311.

He, Z., Bolz, M., & Baillargeon, R. (2012). 2.5-year-olds succeed at a verbal anticipatory-looking false-belief task. *British Journal of Developmental Psychology*, *30*(1), 14–29. http://dx.doi.org/10.1111/j.2044-835X.2011.02070.x.

Heine, S. J., & Lehman, D. R. (1996). Hindsight bias: A cross-cultural analysis. *The Japanese Journal of Experimental Social Psychology*, *35*(3), 317–323. http://dx.doi.org/10.2130/jjesp.35.317.

Henrich, J. (2015). *The secret of our success: How culture is driving human evolution, domesticating our species, and making us smarter*. Princeton, NJ: Princeton University Press.

Henriksen, K., & Kaplan, H. (2003). Hindsight bias, outcome knowledge and adaptive learning. *Quality & Safety in Health Care, 12*(2), 46–50. http://dx.doi.org/10.1136/qhc.12.suppl_2.ii46.

Heyes, C. (2014). False belief in infancy: A fresh look. *Developmental Science, 17*(5), 647–659. http://dx.doi.org/10.1111/desc.12148.

Hinds, P. J. (1999). The curse of expertise: The effects of expertise and debiasing methods on prediction of novice performance. *Journal of Experimental Psychology. Applied, 5*(2), 205–221. http://dx.doi.org/10.1037/1076-898X.5.2.205.

Hoffrage, U., Hertwig, R., & Gigerenzer, G. (2000). Hindsight bias: A by-product of knowledge updating. *Journal of Experimental Psychology. Learning, Memory, and Cognition, 26*(3), 566–581. http://dx.doi.org/10.1037/0278-7393.26.3.566.

Hughes, C. (1998). Executive function in preschoolers: Links with theory of mind and verbal ability. *British Journal of Developmental Psychology, 16*(2), 233–253. http://dx.doi.org/10.1111/j.2044-835X.1998.tb00921.x.

Hughes, C., & Devine, R. T. (2015). A social perspective on theory of mind. In M. E. Lamb & R. M. Lerner (Eds.), *Handbook of child psychology and developmental science: Socioemotional processes. Vol. 3.* (7th ed., pp. 564–609). John Wiley & Sons Inc.

Hughes, C., Jaffee, S. R., Happé, F., Taylor, A., Caspi, A., & Moffitt, T. E. (2005). Origins of individual differences in theory of mind: From nature to nurture? *Child Development, 76*(2), 356–370.

Ickes, W. J. (1997). *Empathic accuracy*. New York: Guilford Press.

Imuta, K., Henry, J. D., Slaughter, V., Selcuk, B., & Ruffman, T. (2016). Theory of mind and prosocial behavior in childhood: A meta-analytic review. *Developmental Psychology, 52*, 1192–1205. http://doi.org/10.1037/dev0000140.

Jacoby, L. L., Kelley, C., Brown, J., & Jasechko, J. (1989). Becoming famous overnight: Limits on the ability to avoid unconscious influences of the past. *Journal of Personality and Social Psychology, 56*(3), 326. http://dx.doi.org/10.1037/0022-3514.56.3.326.

Jacoby, L. L., Woloshyn, V., & Kelley, C. (1989). Becoming famous without being recognized: Unconscious influences of memory produced by dividing attention. *Journal of Experimental Psychology: General, 118*(2), 115–125. http://dx.doi.org/10.1037/0096-3445.118.2.115.

Jaswal, V. K., & Malone, L. S. (2007). Turning believers into skeptics: 3-year-olds' sensitivity to cues to speaker credibility. *Journal of Cognition and Development, 8*, 263–283. http://dx.doi.org/10.1080/15248370701446392.

Jaswal, V. K., & Neely, L. A. (2006). Adults don't always know best: Preschoolers use past reliability over age when learning new words. *Psychological Science, 17*, 757–758. http://dx.doi.org/10.1111/j.1467-9280.2006.01778.x.

Jenkins, J. M., & Astington, J. W. (1996). Cognitive factors and family structure associated with theory of mind development in young children. *Developmental Psychology, 32*(1), 70–78.

Johnson, S. C. (2003). Detecting agents. *Philosophical Transactions of the Royal Society of London. Series B, Biological sciences, 358*(1431), 549–559. http://doi.org/10.1098/rstb.2002.1237.

Johnson, M. K., Hashtroudi, S., & Lindsay, D. S. (1993). Source monitoring. *Psychological Bulletin, 114*(1), 3–28. http://dx.doi.org/10.1037/0033-2909.114.1.3.

Koenig, M., Clément, F., & Harris, P. (2004). Trust in testimony: Children's use of true and false statements. *Psychological Science, 15*, 694–699. http://dx.doi.org/10.1111/j.0956-7976.2004.00742.x.

Koenig, M. A., & Harris, P. L. (2005). Preschoolers mistrust ignorant and inaccurate speakers. *Child Development*, 76, 1261–1277. http://dx.doi.org/10.1111/j.1467-8624.2005.00849.x.

Kuhlmeier, V. A., Bloom, P., & Wynn, K. (2004). Do 5-month-old infants see humans as material objects? *Cognition*, 94, 95–103.

Kuhlmeier, V. A., Wynn, K., & Bloom, P. (2003). Attribution of dispositional states by 12-month-olds. *Psychological Science*, 14, 402–408.

Lagattuta, K. H., Sayfan, L., & Blattman, A. J. (2010). Forgetting common ground: Six- to seven-year-olds have an overinterpretive theory of mind. *Developmental Psychology*, 46(6), 1417–1432. http://dx.doi.org/10.1037/a0021062.

Lagattuta, K. H., Sayfan, L., & Harvey, C. (2014). Beliefs about thought probability: Evidence for persistent errors in mindreading and links to executive control. *Child Development*, 85(2), 659–674. http://dx.doi.org/10.1111/cdev.12154.

Lalonde, C. E., & Chandler, M. J. (1995). False belief understanding goes to school: On the social-emotional consequence of coming early or late to a first theory of mind. *Cognition and Emotion*, 9(2–3), 167–185. http://dx.doi.org/10.1080/02699939508409007.

Landry, S. H., Miller-Loncar, C. L., Smith, K. E., & Swank, P. R. (2002). The role of early parenting in children's development of executive processes. *Developmental Neuropsychology*, 21(1), 15–41. http://dx.doi.org/10.1207/S15326942DN2101_2.

Lewis, C., Freeman, N. H., Kyriakidou, C., Maridaki-Kassotaki, K., & Berridge, D. M. (1996). Social influences on false belief access: Specific sibling influences or general apprenticeship? *Child Development*, 67(6), 2930–2947. http://dx.doi.org/10.2307/1131760.

Little, E. E., Carver, L. J., & Legare, C. H. (2016). Cultural variation in triadic infant-caregiver object exploration. *Child Development*, 78(4), 1130–1145. http://dx.doi.org/10.1111/cdev.12513.

Lohmann, H., Tomasello, M., & Meyer, S. (2005). Linguistic communication and social understanding. In J. W. Astington & J. A. Baird (Eds.), *Why language matters for theory of mind* (pp. 245–265). Oxford University Press. It can also be found on Oxford Scholarship Online. http://dx.doi.org/10.1093/acprof:oso/9780195159912.003.0012.

Low, J. (2010). Preschoolers' implicit and explicit false-belief understanding: Relations with complex syntactical mastery. *Child Development*, 81(2), 579–615. http://dx.doi.org/10.1111/j.1467-8624.2009.01418.x.

Low, J., Apperly, I. A., Butterfill, S. A., & Rakoczy, H. (2016). Cognitive architecture of belief reasoning in children and adults: A primer on the two-systems account. *Child Development Perspectives*, 10, 1–6. http://dx.doi.org/10.1111/cdep.12183.

Low, J., & Perner, J. (2012). Implicit and explicit theory of mind: State of the art. *British Journal of Developmental Psychology*, 30, 1–13.

Lucas, A. J., Lewis, C., Pala, F. C., Wong, K., & Berridge, D. (2013). Social-cognitive processes in preschoolers' selective trust: Three cultures compared. *Developmental Psychology*, 49, 579–590. http://dx.doi.org/10.1037/a0029864.

Lutz, D. J., & Keil, F. C. (2002). Early understanding of the division of cognitive labor. *Child Development*, 73, 1073–1084. http://dx.doi.org/10.1111/1467-8624.00458.

Mascaro, O., & Sperber, D. (2009). The moral, epistemic, and mindreading components of children's vigilance towards deception. *Cognition*, 112(3), 367–380. http://dx.doi.org/10.1016/j.cognition.2009.05.012.

McNamara, R. A. (2016). Morality when the mind is opaque: Intent vs. outcome across the lifespan in Yasawa, Fiji. In *Paper presented at the University of British Columbia, Vancouver, Canada*.

Meins, E., Fernyhough, C., Wainwright, R., Das Gupta, M., Fradley, E., & Tuckey, M. (2002). Maternal mind-mindedness and attachment security as predictors of theory of mind understanding. *Child Development*, 73(6), 1715–1726.

Meltzoff, A. N. (1976). *Imitation in early infancy.* Unpublished doctoral dissertation England: Department of Experimental Psychology, University of Oxford.

Meltzoff, A. N. (1995). Understanding the intentions of others: Re-enactment of intended acts by 18-month-old children. *Developmental Psychology, 31*(5), 838–850. http://dx.doi.org/10.1037/0012-1649.31.5.838.

Meltzoff, A. N., & Moore, M. K. (1977). Imitation of facial and manual gestures by human neonates. *Science, 198,* 75–78.

Mills, C. M. (2013). Knowing when to doubt: Developing a critical stance when learning from others. *Developmental Psychology, 49,* 404–418. http://dx.doi.org/10.1037/a0029500.

Mills, C. M., & Grant, M. G. (2009). Biased decision-making: Developing an understanding of how positive and negative relationships may skew judgements. *Developmental Science, 12*(5), 784–797. http://dx.doi.org/10.1111/j.1467-7687.2009.00836.x.

Mills, C. M., & Keil, F. C. (2005). The development of cynicism. *Psychological Science, 16*(5), 385–390. http://dx.doi.org/10.1111/j.0956-7976.2005.01545.x.

Mills, C. M., & Keil, F. C. (2008). Children's developing notions of (im)partiality. *Cognition, 107*(2), 528–551. http://dx.doi.org/10.1016/j.cognition.2007.11.003.

Mitchell, P., & Taylor, L. M. (1999). Shape constancy and theory of mind: Is there a link? *Cognition, 70,* 167–190.

Moore, C., Bryant, D., & Furrow, D. (1989). Mental terms and the development of certainty. *Child Development, 60,* 167–171. http://dx.doi.org/10.2307/1131082.

Moses, L. J., & Carlson, S. M. (2004). *Self-regulation and children's theories of mind.* Mahwah, NJ: Lawrence Erlbaum Associates Publishers.

Müller, U., Liebermann-Finestone, D. P., Carpendale, J. I. M., Hammond, S. I., & Bibok, M. B. (2012). Knowing minds, controlling actions: The developmental relations between theory of mind and executive function from 2 to 4 years of age. *Journal of Experimental Child Psychology, 111*(2), 331–348. http://dx.doi.org/10.1016/j.jecp.2011.08.014.

Nelson, K. (2005). Language pathways into the community of minds. In J. W. Astington & J. A. Baird (Eds.), *Why language matters for theory of mind* (pp. 26–49). New York: Oxford University Press.

Nelson, D. A., & Crick, N. R. (1999). Rose-colored glasses: Examining the social information-processing of prosocial young adolescents. *The Journal of Early Adolescence, 19*(1), 17–38. http://dx.doi.org/10.1177/0272431699019001002.

Onishi, K. H., & Baillargeon, R. (2005). Do 15-month-old infants understand false beliefs? *Science, 308,* 255–258.

Ornaghi, V., Brockmeier, J., & Gavazzi, I. G. (2011). The role of language games in children's understanding of mental states: A training study. *Journal of Cognition and Development, 12*(2), 239–259.

Pasquini, E. S., Corriveau, K. H., Koenig, M., & Harris, P. L. (2007). Preschoolers monitor the relative accuracy of informants. *Developmental Psychology, 43,* 1216–1226. http://dx.doi.org/10.1037/0012-1649.43.5.1216.

Penn, D. C., & Povinelli, D. J. (2007). On the lack of evidence that non-human animals possess anything remotely resembling a 'theory of mind'. *Philosophical Transactions of the Royal Society of London. Series B, Biological sciences, 362,* 731–744. http://dx.doi.org/10.1098/rstb.2006.2023.

Perner, J. (1991). *Understanding the representational mind: Learning, development, and conceptual change.* Cambridge, MA: The MIT Press.

Perner, J., Frith, U., Leslie, A. M., & Leekam, S. R. (1989). Exploration of the autistic child's theory of mind: Knowledge, belief, and communication. *Child Development, 60*(3), 689–700.

Perner, J., Leekam, S. R., & Wimmer, H. (1987). Three-year-olds' difficulty with false belief: The case for a conceptual deficit. *British Journal of Developmental Psychology*, *5*(2), 125–137. http://dx.doi.org/10.1111/j.2044-835X.1987.tb01048.x.

Perner, J., & Ruffman, T. (2005). Infants' insight into the mind: How deep? *Science*, *308*(5719), 214–216.

Peskin, J. (1992). Ruse and representations: On children's ability to conceal information. *Developmental Psychology*, *28*(1), 84–89. http://dx.doi.org/10.1037/0012-1649.28.1.84.

Peterson, C. C., & Siegal, M. (2000). Insights into theory of mind from deafness and autism. *Mind & Language*, *15*(1), 123–145.

Piaget, J., & Inhelder, B. (1956). *The child's conception of space*. London: Routledge and Kegan Paul, Ltd.

Pillow, B. H. (1989). Early understanding of perception as a source of knowledge. *Journal of Experimental Child Psychology*, *47*, 116–129. http://dx.doi.org/10.1016/0022-0965(89) 90066-0.

Pinker, S. (2014). *The sense of style: The thinking person's guide to writing in the 21st century*. New York: Viking.

Pohl, R. F., Bender, M., & Lachmann, G. (2002). Hindsight bias around the world. *Experimental Psychology*, *49*(4), 270–282. http://dx.doi.org/10.1026//1618-3169.49.4.270.

Poulin-Dubois, D., & Brosseau-Liard, P. (2016). The developmental origins of selective social learning. *Current Directions in Psychological Science*, *25*, 60–64. http://dx.doi.org/ 10.1177/0963721415613962.

Pratt, C., & Bryant, P. (1990). Young children understand that looking leads to knowing (so long as they are looking into a single barrel). *Child Development*, *61*, 973–982. http://dx. doi.org/10.1111/j.1467-8624.1990.tb02835.x.

Premack, D., & Woodruf, G. (1978). Does the chimpanzee have a theory of mind? *Behavioral and Brain Sciences*, *1*, 515–526. Retrieved from: http://dx.doi.org/10.1017/ S0140525X00076512.

Renouf, A., Brendgen, M., Séguin, J. R., Vitaro, F., Boivin, M., Dionne, G., et al. (2010). Interactive links between theory of mind, peer victimization, and reactive and proactive aggression. *Journal of Abnormal Child Psychology*, *38*(8), 1109–1123.

Repacholi, B. M., & Gopnik, A. (1997). Early reasoning about desires: Evidence from 14- and 18-month olds. *Developmental Psychology*, *33*(1), 12–21. http://dx.doi.org/ 10.1037/0012-1649.33.1.12.

Repacholi, B. M., & Slaughter, V. (2003). *Individual differences in theory of mind: Implications for typical and atypical development*. New York: Psychology Press.

Rhodes, M., & Brandone, A. C. (2014). Three-year-olds' theories of mind in actions and words. *Frontiers in Psychology*, *5*(263), 1–8. http://doi.org/10.3389/fpsyg.2014.00263.

Robinson, E. J. (2000). Belief and disbelief: Children's assessments of the reliability of sources of knowledge about the world. In K. P. Roberts & M. Blades (Eds.), *Children's source monitoring* (pp. 355–381). Mahwah, NJ: Lawrence Erlbaum Associates.

Robinson, E. J., Champion, H., & Mitchell, P. (1999). Children's ability to infer utterance veracity from speaker informedness. *Developmental Psychology*, *35*(2), 535–546. http://dx. doi.org/10.1037/0012-1649.35.2.535.

Royzman, E. B., Cassidy, K. W., & Baron, J. (2003). 'I know, you know': Epistemic ego-centrism in children and adults. *Review of General Psychology*, *7*(1), 38–65. http://dx.doi. org/10.1037/1089-2680.7.1.38.

Rubio-Fernández, P., & Geurts, B. (2013). How to pass the false-belief task before your fourth birthday. *Psychological Science*, *24*(1), 27–33. http://dx.doi.org/ 10.1177/0956797612447819.

Ruffman, T., & Perner, J. (2005). Do infants really understand false belief? *Trends in Cognitive Science*, *9*, 462–463.

Ruffman, T., Perner, J., Naito, M., Parkin, L., & Clements, W. A. (1998). Older (but not younger) siblings facilitate false belief understanding. *Developmental Psychology, 34*(1), 161–174.

Ruffman, T., Taumoepeau, M., & Perkins, C. (2012). Statistical learning as a basis for social understanding in children. *British Journal of Developmental Psychology, 30*(1), 87–104.

Russell, J. (1996). *Agency: Its role in mental development.* Oxford: Erlbaum Taylor & Francis.

Sabbagh, M. A., & Baldwin, D. A. (2001). Learning words from knowledgeable versus ignorant speakers: Link between preschoolers' theory of mind and semantic development. *Child Development, 72*, 1054–1070. http://dx.doi.org/10.1111/1467-8624.00334.

Sabbagh, M. A., Benson, J. E., & Kuhlmeier, V. A. (2013). False-belief understanding in infants and preschoolers. In M. Legerstee, D. W. Haley, & M. H. Bornstein (Eds.), *The infant mind: Origins of the social brain* (pp. 301–323). New York: Guilford Press.

Sanna, L. J., Schwarz, N., & Small, E. M. (2002). Accessibility experiences and the hindsight bias: I knew it all along versus it could never have happened. *Memory & Cognition, 30*(8), 1288–1296. http://dx.doi.org/10.3758/BF03213410.

Scaife, M., & Bruner, J. S. (1975). The capacity for joint visual attention in the infant. *Nature, 253*(5489), 265–266. http://dx.doi.org/10.1038/253265a0.

Schwebel, D. C., Rosen, C. S., & Singer, J. L. (1999). Preschoolers' pretend play and theory of mind: The role of jointly constructed pretence. *British Journal of Developmental Psychology, 17*, 333–348.

Scott, R. M., & Baillargeon, R. (2009). Which penguin is this? Attributing false beliefs about object identity at 18 months. *Child Development, 80*(4), 1172–1196.

Selman, R. L. (1971). The relation of role taking to the development of moral judgment in children. *Child Development, 42*(1), 79–91. http://dx.doi.org/10.2307/1127066.

Severson, R. L., & Lemm, K. M. (2016). Kids see human too: Adapting an individual differences measure of anthropomorphism for a child sample. *Journal of Cognition and Development, 17*(1), 122. http://dx.doi.org/10.1080/15248372.2014.989445.

Shahaeian, A., Peterson, C. C., Slaughter, V., & Wellman, H. M. (2011). Culture and the sequence of steps in theory of mind development. *Developmental Psychology, 47*(5), 1239.

Shakoor, S., Jaffee, S. R., Bowes, L., Ouellet-Morin, I., Andreou, P., Happé, F., et al. (2012). A prospective longitudinal study of children's theory of mind and adolescent involvement in bullying. *Journal of Child Psychology and Psychiatry, 53*(3), 254–261.

Sigman, M., & Ungerer, J. (1981). Sensorimotor skills and language comprehension in autistic children. *Journal of Abnormal Child Psychology, 9*(2), 149–165. http://dx.doi.org/10.1007/BF00919111.

Slaughter, V., Dennis, M., & Pritchard, M. (2002). Theory of mind and peer acceptance in preschool children. *British Journal of Developmental Psychology, 20*(4), 545–564. http://dx.doi.org/10.1348/026151002760390945.

Sobel, D. M., & Corriveau, K. H. (2010). Children monitor individuals' expertise for word learning. *Child Development, 81*, 669–679. http://dx.doi.org/10.1111/j.1467-8624.2009.01422.x.

Spelke, E. S., Phillips, A., & Woodward, A. L. (1995). *Infants' knowledge of object motion and human action.* New York: Clarendon Press/Oxford University Press.

Stephens, E., & Koenig, M. A. (2015). Varieties of testimony: Children's selective learning in semantic and episodic domains. *Cognition, 137*, 182–188.

Stephens, E., Suarez, S., & Koenig, M. A. (2015). Early testimonial learning: Monitoring speech acts and speakers. *Advances in Child Development and Behavior, 48*, 151–183.

Stone, V. E., Baron-Cohen, S., & Knight, R. T. (1998). Frontal lobe contributions to theory of mind. *Journal of Cognitive Neuroscience, 10*, 640–656.

Surian, L., Caldi, S., & Sperber, D. (2007). Attribution of beliefs by 13-month-old infants. *Psychological Science, 18*, 580–586.

Sutherland, S. L., & Cimpian, A. (2015). Children show heightened knew-it-all-along errors when learning new facts about kinds: Evidence for the power of kind representations in children's thinking. *Developmental Psychology*, *51*(8), 1113–1130. Retrieved from: http://internal.psychology.illinois.edu/~acimpian/reprints/SutherlandCimpianDP.pdf.

Sutherland, S. L., Cimpian, A., Leslie, S., & Gelman, S. A. (2015). Memory errors reveal a bias to spontaneously generalize to categories. *Cognitive Science*, *39*(5), 1021–1046. http://dx.doi.org/10.1111/cogs.12189.

Sutton, J., Smith, P. K., & Swettenham, J. (1999). Social cognition and bullying: Social inadequacy or skilled manipulation? *British Journal of Developmental Psychology*, *17*(3), 435–450.

Taylor, M., & Carlson, S. M. (1997). The relation between individual differences in fantasy and theory of mind. *Child Development*, *68*(3), 436–455. Retrieved from http://www.jstor.org/stable/1131670.

Taylor, M., Cartwright, B. S., & Bowden, T. (1991). Perspective taking and theory of mind: Do children predict interpretive diversity as a function of differences in observers' knowledge? *Child Development*, *62*, 1334–1351.

Taylor, M., Esbensen, B. M., & Bennett, R. T. (1994). Children's understanding of knowledge acquisition: The tendency for children to report that they have always known what they have just learned. *Child Development*, *65*(6), 1581–1604. http://dx.doi.org/10.2307/1131282.

Trevarthen, C., & Hubley, P. (1978). Secondary intersubjectivity: Confidence, confiding and acts of meaning in the first year. In A. Lock (Ed.), *Action, gesture, and symbol* (pp. 183–229). London: Academic Press.

Tummeltshammer, K. S., Wu, R., Sobel, D. M., & Kirkham, N. Z. (2014). Infants track the reliability of potential informants. *Psychological Science*, *25*, 1730–1738. http://dx.doi.org/10.1177/0956797614540178.

Vanderbilt, K. E., Liu, D., & Heyman, G. D. (2011). The development of distrust. *Child Development*, *82*, 1372–1380.

Vygotsky, L. S. (1967). Play and its role in the mental development of the child. *Soviet Psychology*, *5*, 6–18.

Walker, S. (2005). Gender differences in the relationship between young children's peer-related social competence and individual differences in theory of mind. *The Journal of Genetic Psychology*, *166*(3), 297–312.

Warneken, F., & Tomasello, M. (2006). Altruism helping in human infants and young chimpanzees. *Science*, *311*(5765), 1301–1303. http://dx.doi.org/10.1126/science.1121448.

Warneken, F., & Tomasello, M. (2007). Helping and cooperation at 14 months of age. *Infancy*, *11*(3), 271–294. http://dx.doi.org/10.1111/j.1532-7078.2007.tb00227.x.

Watson, A. C., Nixon, C. L., Wilson, A., & Capage, L. (1999). Social interaction skills and theory of mind in young children. *Developmental Psychology*, *35*(2), 386–391. http://dx.doi.org/10.1037/0012-1649.35.2.386.

Wellman, H. (1990). *Children's theories of mind*. Cambridge, MA: MIT Press.

Wellman, H. M., Cross, D., & Watson, J. (2001). Meta-analysis of theory-of-mind development: The truth about false belief. *Child Development*, *72*(3), 655–684.

Wellman, H. M., Fang, F., Liu, D., Zhu, L., & Liu, G. (2006). Scaling of theory-of-mind understandings in Chinese children. *Psychological Science*, *17*(12), 1075–1081. http://dx.doi.org/10.1111/j.1467-9280.2006.01830.x.

Wellman, H. M., & Liu, D. (2004). Scaling of theory-of-mind tasks. *Child Development*, *75*(2), 523–541. http://doi.org/10.1111/j.1467-8624.2004.00691.x.

Whitcombe, E. L., & Robinson, E. J. (2000). Children's decisions about what to believe and their ability to report the source of their belief. *Cognitive Development*, *15*, 329–346.

Wimmer, H., & Perner, J. (1983). Beliefs about beliefs: Representation and constraining function of wrong beliefs in young children's understanding of deception. *Cognition*, *13*, 103–128.

Winkielman, P., Schwarz, N., Fazendeiro, T., & Reber, R. (2003). The hedonic marking of processing fluency: Implications for evaluative judgment. In J. Musch & K. C. Klauer (Eds.), *The psychology of evaluation: Affective processes in cognition and emotion* (pp. 189–217). Mahwah, NJ: Lawrence Erlbaum.

Woodward, A. L. (1998). Infants selectively encode the goal object of an actor's reach. *Cognition*, *69*(1), 1–34. http://dx.doi.org/10.1016/S0010-0277(98)00058-4.

Yopchick, J. E., & Kim, N. S. (2012). Hindsight bias and causal reasoning: A minimalist approach. *Cognitive Processing*, *13*(1), 63–72. http://dx.doi.org/10.1007/s10339-011-0414-z.

Youngblade, L. M., & Dunn, J. (1995). Individual differences in young children's pretend play with mother and sibling: Links to relationships and understanding of other people's feelings and beliefs. *Child Development*, *66*, 1472–1492.

Zaitchik, D. (1990). When representations conflict with reality: The preschooler's problem with false beliefs and 'false' photographs. *Cognition*, *35*(1), 41–68. http://dx.doi.org/10.1016/0010-0277(90)90036-J.

Zajonc, R. B. (1968). Attitudinal effects of mere exposure. *Journal of Personality and Social Psychology*, *9*(2p2), 1–27. http://dx.doi.org/10.1037/h0025848.

Zelazo, P. D., Carter, A., Reznick, J. S., & Frye, D. (1997). Early development of executive function: A problem-solving framework. *Review of General Psychology*, *1*(2), 198–226.

Zmyj, N., Buttelmann, D., Carpenter, M., & Daum, M. M. (2010). The reliability of a model influences 14-month-olds' imitation. *Journal of Experimental Child Psychology*, *106*, 208–220. http://dx.doi.org/10.1016/j.jecp.2010.03.002.

CHAPTER SEVEN

The Development of Tactile Perception

A.J. Bremner*,[1], C. Spence[†]

*Goldsmiths, University of London, London, United Kingdom
[†]University of Oxford, Oxford, United Kingdom
[1]Corresponding author: e-mail address: a.bremner@gold.ac.uk

Contents

Abstract

Touch is the first of our senses to develop, providing us with the sensory scaffold on which we come to perceive our own bodies and our sense of self. Touch also provides us with direct access to the external world of physical objects, via haptic exploration. Furthermore, a recent area of interest in tactile research across studies of developing children and adults is its social function, mediating interpersonal bonding. Although there are a range of demonstrations of early competence with touch, particularly in the domain of haptics, the review presented here indicates that many of the tactile perceptual skills that we take for granted as adults (e.g., perceiving touches in the external world as well as on the body) take some time to develop in the first months of postnatal

Advances in Child Development and Behavior, Volume 52
ISSN 0065-2407
http://dx.doi.org/10.1016/bs.acdb.2016.12.002

life, likely as a result of an extended process of connection with other sense modalities which provide new kinds of information from birth (e.g., vision and audition). Here, we argue that because touch is of such fundamental importance across a wide range of social and cognitive domains, it should be placed much more centrally in the study of early perceptual development than it currently is.

1. INTRODUCTION

Tactile sensations are pervasive in how they determine our experiences and behavior in everyday life. Perhaps the first thing which comes to mind when thinking about touch is how we actively bring our skin into contact with objects (usually with our hands or other limbs) in order to encode and recognize objects and their features. This is commonly known as haptics or haptic touch. Tactile receptors can also passively transduce information presented directly to the skin. This function is especially pertinent in the context of conveying the social/interpersonal aspects of touch which in turn bring about strong affective/emotional responses (indeed, these are thought to be particularly important in early life; Field, 2001).

But touch is not just used to perceive, understand, and respond to the external world. Events in the external world can also give rise to tactile sensations on the self, on the body (Martin, 1993). In this way, touch also plays a fundamental role in framing our mental representations of our own bodies and the disposition of our limbs with respect to ourselves and the external environment. The way in which the brain decides to attribute self-ownership to the portion of space that the body currently happens to occupy—what is fundamentally a tactile spatial representation—determines the perceptual basis of our sense of self.

Touch has a very clear precedence over vision and hearing in prenatal development (see Bremner, Lewkowicz, & Spence, 2012; Gallace & Spence, 2014, for reviews; see Fig. 1A). The first sensations we experience are tactile. Cutaneous and trigeminal somatosensory receptors mature at around 4–7 weeks of gestation (Humphrey, 1964), and somatosensory function follows soon thereafter. At 7 weeks of gestation, the fetus will move if its lips are touched (Hooker, 1952). Grasping and rooting reflex responses are reported to have been observed from as early as 12 weeks of gestation (Fifer & Moon, 2003; Humphrey, 1964). Although this early emergence of tactile (somatosensory) anatomy and function is very quickly followed by vestibular and chemosensory functioning, auditory and visual

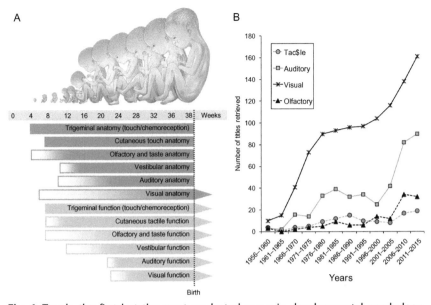

Fig. 1 Touch, the first but the most neglected sense in developmental psychology. (A) The emergence of the anatomy and function of multiple sensory systems during human gestation. *Dark gray bars* indicate the emergence and maturation of the senses (usually provided by histological evidence). *Shading* of the *dark gray bars* indicates the time between the first observation of sensory apparatus and its full anatomical maturation. *Light gray bars* indicate the onset of function of the senses. *Shading* of the *light gray bars* indicates the uncertainty in the literature concerning the first age at which function is observable. *Arrows* pointing beyond birth indicate continued postnatal development. (B) The number of articles retrieved by PsycINFO for searches on sensory development restricted to 5-year time windows from 1956 to 2015. Numbers of retrieved items with conjunctions of words indicating consideration of tactile, visual, auditory, and olfactory development are compared. All items contained the word "development" in the title as well as "visual" to retrieve items related to visual development, "auditory" to retrieve items related to auditory development, "olfactory" to retrieve items related to olfactory development. For tactile development, any titles containing any of the following words in conjunction with "development" were retrieved: "tactile," "tactual," "haptic," and "touch." Since 1956, articles retrieved under these searches indicating consideration of tactile development have not exceeded 20 per 5-year period. Even despite the specification of fewer search terms for visual, auditory, and olfactory development, tactile development is the least considered of these four. Since 2006, around twice as many titles related to olfactory development than tactile development are retrieved. Titles indicating studies of both tactile and olfactory development are dwarfed by titles considering visual and auditory development which underwent exponential increases in research in the late 1960s to early 1970s, and again in the opening years of the 21st century. The early surges in interest in these sense modalities are presumably due to the advent of new methods for investigating infants' and children's abilities in vision and audition (e.g., Fantz, 1961), and perhaps also the popularity of Piaget's sensorimotor theory of development in the 1970s. *(A) Reproduced from (i) Moore, K. L., & Persaud, T. V. N., The developing human: Clinically oriented embryology, 8th ed., Philadelphia, PA: Saunders Elsevier © Elsevier 2008 with permission and (ii) Bremner. A. J., Lewkowicz, D. J., & Spence, C. (Eds.). (2012).* Multisensory development. *Oxford, UK: Oxford University Press © OUP 2012 with permission*

functioning are first observed much later in prenatal development. Given the primacy of touch in early development, it is reasonable to assume that tactile perception has great importance to the developing (and also the mature) organism. Indeed, some have argued that the differential timing of these separate sensory systems facilitates perceptual development by reducing, in the initial stages, the amount of sensory information that the developing fetus has to assimilate and combine in a coherent way (Kenny & Turkewitz, 1986; Turkewitz, 1994; Turkewitz & Kenny, 1982). Accepting this, touch might well be seen as the sensory scaffold on which multisensory perceptual development is constructed! And yet, as we shall see next, touch has largely been ignored by those psychologists interested in perceptual development. In this chapter, we argue that touch should, in contrast, be placed at the *center* of the study of perceptual development.

2. STUDYING MULTIPLE SENSES IN DEVELOPMENT

How do you perceive yourself and the world around you? A folk psychology response to this question would probably tend to appeal to a range of sense modalities. We concurrently touch, taste, smell, hear, and see the world, ourselves, and the things that we are doing. It is intuitive that these multiple sense modalities provide us with rich and complementary sources of perceptual information. While some overlap (or redundancy) in the content conveyed by our multiple senses is desirable for enhancing perceptual accuracy and precision (multiple sources of information help us, as adults at least, to refine our perceptual estimates and overcome noise in each separate system; Alais & Burr, 2004; Ernst & Banks, 2002), different sense channels also convey different kinds of information. For instance, touch is a relatively unambiguous source of information about the world as it impinges on the body. And what we hear gives us important clues to communicative content, whereas taste helps us to figure out whether something is going to be good for us to ingest.

Given these considerations, it is surprising to note a significant lack of diversity in developmental psychologists' consideration of perceptual development. Fig. 1B displays the findings of a small literature survey of the article titles that have mentioned visual, auditory, olfactory, and tactile development from 1956 to 2015. Whereas around 64% of the retrieved articles consider visual development, auditory development is mentioned in about 21% of titles, and olfactory and tactile development are considered in only about

7% and 8% of titles, respectively, even with a methodology biased in favor of retrieving articles on tactile development. It is, of course, important to acknowledge the substantial contributions of researchers investigating the development of multisensory (also sometimes known as crossmodal or intersensory) perception (see, for example, Bahrick & Lickliter, 2012; Bremner et al., 2012; Lewkowicz & Lickliter, 1994). However, even the majority of studies in this area tend to stick to the more well-trodden path of audiovisual perceptual interactions.

So what are we missing? The focus of this particular chapter is to consider the development of tactile perception and so we will discuss the particular contributions of tactile sensory information and how these develop.[a] We will consider, in turn, the development of what we think are three key contributions of touch: (i) haptics (i.e., active tactile sensing of the external environment), (ii) self/body sensing (i.e., the role of cutaneous touch and proprioception in specifying the body's shape and layout in space), and (iii) affective touch (i.e., the role tactile input plays in social/interpersonal contexts). It is also useful to indicate here two further themes considered throughout the chapter. First, we will highlight where the literature bears on the important questions of whether touch and tactile experience play special causal roles in development more generally. Second, we will not consider touch in isolation. Even if we might tend to introspect that we *see*, *hear*, *touch*, *taste*, and *smell* the world around us in separate sensory acts (Auvray & Spence, 2008; Gibson, 1966; see also Spence & Bayne, 2015), experimental psychology and cognitive neuroscience have revealed, particularly over the last 20 years, the numerous ways in which our various senses interact to give rise to multisensory percepts (i.e., percepts of objects or events which are informed by information arriving through more than one sense modality; Calvert, Spence, & Stein, 2004; Stein, 2012). Despite its primacy in development, touch is no exception to this principle. Our sense of touch is substantially affected by visual, auditory, and olfactory information (see Gallace & Spence, 2014), and so a consideration of the development of such multisensory interactions is going to be crucial to our understanding of the development of tactile perception (Bremner et al., 2012).

---

[a] For a consideration of the development of olfaction and taste and their multisensory interactions, see Schaal (2006), Schaal and Durand (2012), and Spence (2012).

3. TOUCH: A PRIMER

In the mature adult, less is known about the sense of touch than about either of the other spatial senses (vision or audition). Why? One possible reason is that touch is more difficult to study experimentally in a controlled manner. Nonetheless, it is odd that the sense which occupies a greater extent of our bodies (the skin, our organ of cutaneous touch, is thought to account for 16–18% of body mass; Montagu, 1978) than all other senses put together should be so relatively neglected in experimental psychology (Gallace & Spence, 2014). Nonetheless, perhaps spurred on by this neglect, a growing number of researchers, across a range of disciplines, are becoming increasingly interested in touch as shown by a clear increase in the scientific literature since the beginning of the 21st century (Gallace & Spence, 2014).

What are the defining features of touch? As previously discussed, touch can certainly be considered *the* bodily sense, being distributed not just in our haptic organs (typically our hands: see Radman, 2013), but throughout and covering our bodies. Other aspects of touch have been summarized by Gallace and Spence (2014): despite its greater coverage, the number of tactile sensors and afferent neurons are somewhat comparable to those used by the auditory and visual systems. Eleven and a half percent of neocortex responds to tactile stimulation (compared to 55% for visual stimuli and 3.5% for auditory). Strikingly, however, the tactile system has much lower bandwidth than vision and hearing when it comes to transducing information for perception (Zimmerman, 1989; see Gallace, Ngo, Sulaitis, & Spence, 2012, for a review). Nonetheless, as Gallace and Spence (2014) have pointed out, it would be an error to rate the importance of a sense modality purely on the basis of how much information that it can carry; the type and salience of that information surely matters just as much.

What kinds of receptors do we mean when we refer to touch? The broad definition of touch includes not just cutaneous sensation, but also interoception and proprioception. Interoceptors are located in the internal organs and provide information (typically unconscious) that is used to maintain organ function, homeostasis, digestion, and respiration (for a review of what we know about interoception in adults, see Craig, 2009). Proprioception provides information about how our body and limbs are arrayed, or moving, in space (the latter is sometimes also referred to as kinaesthesis), and is mediated by receptors that are found in the muscles, tendons, and joints.

To limit the scope of this chapter, we will not discuss the development of the more interoceptive aspects of touch. Little is known in fact, despite much interest in interceptive processes in regard to the characterization of certain developmental disorders (e.g., Miller, Fuller, & Roetenberg, 2014; Quattrocki & Friston, 2014). However, this is not to suggest that the development of interoception is of limited interest. As any parent will testify, some interoceptive processes involved in digestion are striking in the extent to which they are both absorbing for young infants, and under-developed in terms of the control exerted over them! We will cover propri-oceptive aspects of touch, particularly in Section 5. For now, suffice to say that proprioceptive inputs play a crucial role in the formation of repres-entations[b] of the body and limbs. They are also integrated with cutaneous stimulation to better interpret our tactile environments through haptics.

Cutaneous tactile sensations are determined by the activation of several different classes of receptors scattered throughout the skin surface including Meissner's corpuscles, Merkel's disks, Pacinian corpuscles, Ruffini's end organs, and free nerve endings (McGlone & Spence, 2010). These various receptor types are differentially sensitive to different kinds of stimulus, including pressure (low, high, sustained), temperature, pain, itch, vibration, and so on. As with the eyes, tactile sensitivity and acuity is certainly not uni-form across the receptor (body) surface with higher levels in some areas compared to others (Weinstein, 1968). For instance, the lips are particularly sensitive to pressure, and the finger tips have particularly high spatial reso-lution. The lower leg is not really well known for either of these skills. Pro-prioceptive tactile sensations are transduced by proprioceptors: muscle spindles provide information about muscle length, and Golgi tendon organs in the tendons provide information about muscle stretch. Tactile signals are transmitted to the primary somatosensory cortex where areas on the body with greatest tactile innervation (and typically greatest tactile sensitivity and acuity) are represented across greater portions of the cortex, giving rise to the somatosensory homunculus made famous by Penfield and Rasmussen (1950).

However, not everything we feel and would identify as touch is deter-mined by signals entering our brain in somatosensory cortex, or even signals arising from the stimulation of the tactile receptors. As is now well

---

[b] We are using the term "representation" to denote a particular pattern of neural firing corresponding to (an aspect of) a sensory stimulus. This is meant to encompass a wide range of possibilities, but we will try to be as precise as we can in distinguishing between different types of representation where appropriate.

established across all sense modalities, numerous crossmodal interactions influence tactile perception (for a review, see Gallace & Spence, 2014). For example, the perceived dryness of our skin can be greatly altered by changing the sound that we hear when running our hands together (this is known as the "parchment skin illusion"; Guest, Catmur, Lloyd, & Spence, 2002; Jousmäki & Hari, 1998). In perhaps the most famous of all multisensory illusions, the "rubber hand illusion" (RHI) (Botvinick & Cohen, 1998; Cowie, Makin, & Bremner, 2013; Ehrsson, Spence, & Passingham, 2004; Tsakiris & Haggard, 2005), seeing a fake hand being stroked in synchrony with felt touches on the real (hidden hand) induces powerful feelings of ownership over the fake hand. Here, visual information about a hand and strokes applied to it, fool us by overriding the veridical information about hand position coming from proprioception. Researchers have even demonstrated that olfactory cues influence tactile perception: What a person smells while touching fabric influences their perception of its softness (Churchill, Meyners, Griffiths, & Bailey, 2009; Demattè, Sanabria, Sugarman, & Spence, 2006).

4. THE DEVELOPMENT OF HAPTICS

When we use touch to encode and recognize objects, this is typically an active "haptic" process. Consider, for example, the situation in which your eyes are closed and an object is placed in your outstretched hand. The near-immediate response (a reflex in the newborn baby) is to enclose the object with the fingers—helping to determine the shape and size of that which we hold. Thus, we do not simply feel these properties as presented to the skin—we use proprioceptive information from our hand in order to infer the shape of the object (see Lederman & Klatzky, 2009, for a review). In this way, haptic perception allows us to gain information about objects and surfaces; information concerning both their substance (hardness, weight, temperature, texture, etc.) and structural properties (size, shape, and volume; Kahrimanovic, Bergmann Tiest, & Kappers, 2010).

In delivering haptic perception, touch often works together with vision and the other senses. Intuition indicates that touch is also particularly useful when we want to verify the material properties of what we are seeing or hearing. For instance, when looking at items to buy in a shop, we often want to get our hands on them. It is as if we use touch to determine whether what vision is telling us is not fooling us into a rash purchase of some inferior product (see Spence & Gallace, 2011). This intuitive precedence of touch in helping us to identify the "real" (material) properties of objects is also present in early childhood. Flavell and colleagues' classic work on children's understanding of the appearance/reality distinction (Flavell, Flavell, & Green, 1983; Flavell, Green, & Flavell, 1986) showed 3-year-old children deceptive objects in which "appearance" conflicted with "reality" (e.g., a sponge with the visual appearance of a rock). Three year olds will not only identify such objects in accordance with their real (felt) properties, but will even go so far as to insist that they also have the appearance of (that they look like) their real felt identities (i.e., like a rock rather than a sponge). Next, in Sections 4.1 and 4.2, we discuss what is known about the development of haptic abilities in early life.

4.1 Haptic Abilities in Early Infancy

When an object is placed in the hand, newborns will press down on it with their fingers (the palmar grasp reflex). This also happens with the toes when objects are presented to the soles of the feet (the plantar grasp reflex). And yet, some of the earliest studies of haptics in young infants have tended to avoid the hands and feet in preference for another organ of touch not typically thought of as such by adults: the mouth (Gibson & Walker, 1984; Meltzoff & Borton, 1979; see Section 4.2 for discussion). In the first 6 months of life, there is a strong tendency to use the hand to bring objects to the mouth for exploration, although this declines substantially in preference for manual exploration thereafter (e.g., Ruff, 1984; see Rochat & Senders, 1991, for a review of oral exploration and manual-oral coordination in newborn behavior, and Jacobs, Serhal, & van Steenberghe, 1998, for a discussion of similar sensing behaviors known as "oral stereognosis" in adults).

Nevertheless, it turns out that newborns are able to encode some tactile properties of objects with their hands, even if the active processes which they use (the palmar grasp reflex) are fairly limited. For instance, Jouen and Molina (2005) demonstrate that the palmar grasp reflex is modulated by the textural properties of objects placed in the hand. Streri, Lhote, and Dutilleul (2000) have used haptic habituation to show that newborns can discriminate objects on the basis of their shapes (prism vs cylinder). After habituating to one of these objects held in the hand (habituation was identified by a decline in manual inspection of the object below a certain criterion—i.e., earlier release of the object from the hand), newborns would then show a novelty preference for the object which had not been presented in habituation. A similar ability has also been demonstrated more recently in preterm infants as young as 28 gestational weeks (Marcus, Lejeune, Berne-Audéoud, Gentaz, & Debillon, 2012).

Despite these early competencies, it is clear that newborns are more limited in the active aspects of haptic perception. With only the grasp reflex and mouthing at their disposal, it seems likely that they will be more limited in the aspects of objects which they can encode at this stage, and the development of manual exploratory abilities across infancy should bootstrap the emergence of more sophisticated haptic perceptual abilities. Just such a proposal has been made by Bushnell and Boudreau (1993) who undertook a literature survey of the development of both manual exploratory abilities and haptic perceptual competencies. Referring to Lederman and Klatzky's (e.g., Lederman & Klatzky, 2009) classification of optimal "exploratory procedures" for haptic perception of certain object properties (e.g., enclosure of the object with the hands for extracting size/volume, unsupported holding of the object to extract weight, or contour following to extract shape; see Fig. 2), they argue that there is a close developmental link between the ability to produce a given exploratory procedure, and the ability to differentiate an object haptically according to the properties which that exploratory procedure yields.

One study has found some evidence for Bushnell and Boudreau's (1993) proposal within individual children. Beyond infancy, exploratory procedures for haptic perception are largely developed and adult like by 3 years of age (Kalagher & Jones, 2011a). However, shape perception is one of the last skills to develop haptically according to Bushnell and Boudreau (1993) and Kalagher and Jones (2011b) report that children under 5 years of age were less likely to produce the enclosure exploratory procedures required for shape encoding (as according to Lederman & Klatzky, 2009). Those children who produced these behaviors were more likely to be able to match the haptically felt shape to a corresponding visual shape in a crossmodal matching task.

So haptic perception (and exploratory procedures) seems to be fairly well developed by early childhood. But to what extent are the representations formed through haptic exploration available or transferable to other representational modalities. This question has been addressed as part of a larger body of work concerned with how and when we come to be able to transfer our perceptions or representations of objects between senses (typically touch and vision).

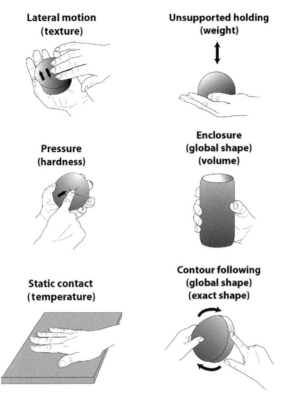

Fig. 2 Exploratory procedures in haptics (Lederman & Klatzky, 2009). Six different exploratory procedures are pictured with the associated object properties which they transduce named in parentheses. Bushnell and Boudreau (1993) propose that the acquisition of the motor skills required to execute these procedures is causal in the development of haptic perception and present a review of the literature which is consistent with this proposal. Kalagher and Jones (2011b) present some limited evidence of a correlation between abilities with exploratory procedures and haptic object recognition in 3-year-old children.

4.2 The Origins of Visual–Haptic Coordination

Can the newborn infant make a crossmodal match concerning an object between touch and vision? This is a form of a paradigmatic question that has fascinated philosophers and psychologists since the 17th century. Locke reported (in 1688) that Molyneux queried whether an adult born blind, if restored to sight, might be able to identify and distinguish, with vision alone, objects that he/she had previously only experienced through touch. Molyneux, Locke, and a little later George Berkeley (1685–1753) were agreed that the answer was "no." Berkeley, in particular, was of the view that the senses were quite distinct in nature, providing completely different forms of information that were irreconcilable without the construction of crossmodal associations through experience.

There have been a number of attempts to address "Molyneux's question" through the restoration of sight to the congenitally blind, the first one being made by Chesselden (1728) and more recently by Held et al. (2011). But the first empirical attempts to discern the development of crossmodal transfer in infancy and childhood did not emerge until Birch and Lefford (1963) reported that the accuracy of children's crossmodal matching of stimuli between vision and touch increases from 5 to 11 years of age. However, their conclusion, that the crossmodal integration of these senses undergoes extended development across childhood, rightly received robust criticism. In particular, Bryant and his colleagues (Bryant, 1974; Bryant, Jones, Claxton, & Perkins, 1972; Hulme, Smart, Moran, & Raine, 1983) showed that Birch and Lefford's (1963) findings of age-related developments in crossmodal matching were fully explained by corresponding developments in unimodal perceptual matching.

Subsequently to this debate, it is now clear that haptic–visual crossmodal matching is available rather early in postnatal development. Rose and her colleagues confirmed in a series of studies that bidirectional crossmodal transfer between touch and vision is present at 6 months of age (Rose, Gottfried, & Bridger, 1981), but they also demonstrated that between 6 and 12 months infants become progressively more efficient at this kind of crossmodal encoding and recognition (for a review, see Rose, 1994). Even more remarkably, some studies have demonstrated an ability to perceive commonalities between touch and vision from soon after birth in both man-ual (Sann & Streri, 2007; Streri, 2012) and oral (Meltzoff & Borton, 1979) haptic exploratory contexts. And while there has been some difficulty rep-licating oral-visual transfer at 1 month (Maurer, Stager, & Mondloch, 1999), the weight of evidence for manual-visual transfer in newborns is now strong (see Streri, 2012, for a review).

But how does evidence of visual–haptic transfer at birth relate to work on the congenitally blind who have been restored to sight? This is currently unclear, as findings from Held et al.'s (2011) recent study of crossmodal transfer following the removal of congenital cataracts conflict directly with the findings of Streri and colleagues (reviewed in Streri, 2012). Held et al. (2011) found that an ability to make visual–tactile crossmodal matches is not available straight away (despite abilities to make visual–visual and tactile–tactile matches), but is learned over a period of several days following the onset of visual experience. Could it be that newborns learn the correspondences they are successful at very quickly? More research is needed.

Visual–haptic coordination can develop in more subtle ways than the straightforward improvement in crossmodal matching and memory. Gori, Del Viva, Sandini, and Burr (2008) have worked with young children to investigate the development of the ability to integrate visual and haptic information about objects which are simultaneously seen and felt. They asked children and adults to identify which of two successively presented objects (which the children both observed visually and felt with their hands at the same time) was larger. When adults are presented with multiple cues to the same stimulus dimension their estimates tend to combine estimates from the component modalities which are weighted according to their relative reliabilities (Alais & Burr, 2004; Ernst & Banks, 2002). For instance, in one particular experimental scenario which Gori et al. used, visual size was the most reliable cue to the size of the object, and so adults tend to weight it more highly than haptic cues. And because this optimal weighting of touch and vision determines the combined estimate, adults perform significantly better when *both* visual and haptic cues are presented. However, prior to 8 years of age, children did not show this multisensory advantage (Gori et al., 2008)—they were not able to optimally integrate haptics and vision according to their relatively reliabilities. Furthermore, when haptic and visual cues were set in conflict, young children's estimates appeared to be dominated by haptics, even though that was not the most reliable cue for them.

Gori et al. (2008) propose an interesting explanation for why the development of optimal multisensory integration may take so long; they suggest that the optimal weighting of the senses is delayed so as to provide a point of reference against which to calibrate the senses in multisensory tasks. Because the body and limbs continue to grow over the course of childhood and adolescence, this recalibration is constantly required, and so, according to Gori et al. (2008), optimal weighting does not take place until the body has stopped growing substantially. Although there is no direct support as yet for the idea of multisensory integration being delayed for this reason, a number of studies have backed up the idea that crossmodal calibration is an important aspect of multisensory development during childhood. Gori, Sandini, Martinoli, and Burr (2010) have shown than congenitally blind children show poor haptic orientation discrimination relative to their sighted peers. What might explain this counterintuitive finding? Gori et al. (2010) argue that congenitally blind children are poorer at haptic orientation discrimination because they have not been availed of visual orientation cues during development which would have otherwise calibrated their perception of haptic orientation.

As well as being calibrated by vision in development, more recent findings from Gori, Giuliana, Sandini, and Burr (2012) suggest that in some contexts haptics help calibrate our visual discriminations. Gori et al. (2012) presented visual size discrimination tasks to adults and children at different distances. They found that inside the reaching space, visual size discriminations were fairly accurate, whereas outside of reaching space, children were biased to underestimate size, and adults were biased to overestimate size. This suggests that haptic cues to size are able to recalibrate visual cues to the same when visual stimuli are close enough to the body to be able to receive both haptic and visual estimates. Gori et al. (2008) point out that haptic cues provide "direct" size information, rather than the "indirect" cues provided by vision which have to be interpreted. This may be why haptic cues play this calibrating role.

In summary, haptic perception is a key skill at our disposal from early in postnatal development and even before. Indeed, the ability to make links between what we sense about objects with our hands and what we see appears to be something which develops early with fairly minimal experience (Held et al., 2011; Streri, 2012). As infants' and children's motor skills progress, their ability to explore objects haptically and form more accurate and transferable representations of them also improves (Kalagher & Jones, 2011b). Later in development, children continue to improve not only in both haptic perception but also in their coordination of haptics with vision (Gori et al., 2012, 2010). In particular, crossmodal calibration processes in which vision helps improve the estimates we make with haptics and vice versa appear to be an important aspect of early-to-mid-childhood. However, after 8 years or so, children start to integrate separate sensory cues in order to achieve an optimal multisensory estimate concerning objects (Gori et al., 2008).

5. THE DEVELOPING ROLE OF TOUCH IN PERCEPTION OF THE BODY

Studies of "deafferented" patients who have lost their ability to process proprioceptive and tactile signals (see Cole & Paillard, 1995) highlight the fundamental role that touch plays in self-perception; such patients can report the sensation of not having a body or that their body seems to be "floating."

This fundamental role of touch in body phenomenology may be due, as suggested earlier, to touch acting as the preeminent scaffold on which perceptual development is constructed. What do we know about the development of tactile body representations?

5.1 Tactile "Reflexes," Their Modification, and Spatial Specificity

A substantial proportion of the "neonatal reflexes" are triggered by specific tactile stimuli. The spatial specificity of the stimuli required to elicit such responses can tell us a little about the early origins of spatial tactile representations of the body. In the palmar grasp reflex, for instance, the newborn's fingers clamp down on the specific palm to which tactile pressure is applied. Some have even argued that the human fetus produces such movements as early as the 11th week of gestation (Fifer & Moon, 2003). Other spatially specific tactile responses include the crossed-extension reflex (Sherrington, 1910; Zappella & Simopoulos, 1966): If a newborn infant is touched close to the inguinal canal at the top of the leg they will flex and extend their other leg (Fényes, Gergely, & Tóth, 1960). Moreau, Helfgott, Weinstein, and Milner (1978) have observed the habituation of neonatal head turning to tactile stimulation, and Kisilevsky and Muir (1984) have demonstrated that sleeping neonates will habituate to a brush stroke on either the lips or ear and then dishabituate to brushing at the novel one of these two locations.

Of course, given that reflexes and habituation can, in theory at least, be mediated subcortically, or even spinally, we might question whether the spatial specificity of the various behaviors just described could be relevant to the kind of tactile spatial map of the body feeding into body representations in adults (and resident in somatosensory cortex, at least in part). However, there is increasing consensus that neonatal reflexes are not simply automatic (spinal) sensorimotor loops, but are subject to somewhat more control (with some even arguing that such behaviors are intentional or goal directed; von Hofsten, 2007). We have already noted the modification of the grasp reflex as a function of the texture of an object (Jouen & Molina, 2005). As another example, rooting (the orienting of the mouth in response to touch on the cheek which helps the infant suckle), does not occur with the same frequency when the newborn is hungry (Prechtl, 1958). In any case, it would seem reasonable that such neonatal tactile behaviors, by providing a spatial structure to early sensorimotor experience (at least in the first months of life; see Thelen & Fisher, 1982), will play an important role in the postnatal development of tactile spatial representations.

5.2 The Development of Tactile Body Maps

We know relatively little about how the brain develops spatial maps of the body such as the sensory homunculus in early life (see Marshall & Meltzoff, 2015, for a review). Saby, Meltzoff, and Marshall (2015) reported that somatosensory evoked potentials (SEPs) in 7 month olds occupy distinct scalp sites depending on whether their feet or hands receive the tactile stimulus, with hand stimulation eliciting stronger responses more laterally, and foot stimulation more medially, consistent with such SEPs being generated by activity in the somatosensory homunculus. In fact, Milh et al. (2007) have reported a similar spatial differentiation of "delta-brush" EEG oscillatory signals in response to tactile foot and hand stimulation in premature neonates (~30 weeks gestational age). These signals were apparent both when the hands and feet were stimulated by touch, and following spontaneous fetal movements that resulted in somatosensory feedback. On this basis, Milh et al. (2007) proposed that spontaneous fetal motor activity may lead to the differentiation of somatosensory body maps in the infant brain (see also Nevalainen, Lauronen, & Pihko, 2014), although we might also consider whether experience-independent somatosensory differentiation of feet and hand areas in the brain might particularly encourage movements of these limbs due to the somatosensory feedback that results therefrom.

Irrespective of the differentiation of body parts in somatosensory cortex, we can also ask how infants and children come to perceive their body parts as separate or distinct. Brownell, Nichols, Svetlova, Zerwas, and Ramani (2010) investigated 20- to 30-month-old children's knowledge of the layout of their own body parts. The children were asked to place stickers on specified body parts, copying an experimenter, and to imitate meaningless gestures aimed at a specified site. The younger children were able to accurately locate two or three common body parts (e.g., hand and foot). By 30 months, almost twice as many body parts were located, including less salient sites such as the neck, but still the children were by no means perfect (only ~35% correct).

This work by Brownell et al. (2010) has revealed that there is a rudimentary knowledge of the layout of body parts by the second birthday which seems likely to be supported by a representational map of the body. But to what extent do young children perceive their body parts as distinct entities? Studies in adults demonstrate that there are category boundary effects in tactile spatial perception indicating that tactile spatial perception is structured around a topology of body parts. De Vignemont, Majid, Jola, and Haggard

(2009) and also Le Cornu Knight, Longo, and Bremner (2014) have shown that pairs of tactile stimuli that cross the boundary between arm and hand (the wrist) are perceived as more distant than if those same tactile distances are presented within either the hand or the forearm. Thus, the topology of body parts appears to structure tactile spatial perception of distance on the body surface. Le Cornu Knight, Cowie, and Bremner (2016) have recently demonstrated this tactile category boundary effect in children as young as 5 years of age. If future investigations can examine this effect in younger children or even infants, it will be fascinating to probe developmental relationships between the acquisition of various behaviors that might lead children to differentiate body parts and thus to this categorical perception of the body. The acquisition of body part names and differentiated articulation of body parts are two such candidates for investigation.

5.3 The Early Development of Proprioception: Newborn Hand–Mouth Coordination

Hand-to-mouth movements are an important feature of the early oral-manual behavior of the prenatal and newborn infant (Blass, Fillion, Rochat, Hoffmeyer, & Metzger, 1989; Butterworth & Hopkins, 1988; De Vries, Visser, & Prechtl, 1984). That a newborn's mouth will open in anticipation of the arrival of the hand at the mouth or the perioral region has been cited as evidence of the intentionality of movement (Butterworth & Hopkins, 1988), and an innate ability to represent the posture of the limbs for this particular behavior (Gallagher, 2005; Rochat, 2010). For our purposes, it is clear that touch plays an important role in hand–mouth coordination, both in providing proprioceptive information about limb position (relative to the mouth), and presumably also in terms of the goal of the action which is likely largely tactile in-and-of-itself (i.e., tactile cutaneous contact between the hand and oral area).

One immediate query concerning hand–mouth coordination in newborns is whether the tactile representations underlying this behavior are underpinned by a more general ability to perceive the posture of the limbs across a wider range of contexts (Gallagher, 2005, does not think so). It is also important to consider whether hand–mouth behaviors could in fact be learned, rather than preprogrammed as many authors have argued (Gallagher, 2005). The newborn has already had significant experience of hand-to-mouth movements prenatally. De Vries et al. (1984) report that hand–face contact occurs in the fetus 50–100 times an hour from as early as 12 weeks gestation. In the restricted environment of the uterus, this may be due, at least in part, to the proximity of the hands to the face and may also be encouraged by the rich somatosensory innervation of the hands and face/mouth. Thus, claims about innate proprioceptive schemas for hand–mouth coordination should be balanced against the possibility that such seemingly complex and functionally relevant behaviors may result from the complex interaction of a range of factors during the ample opportunities for learning in utero (indeed, see Castiello et al., 2010, for some striking claims about how prenatal cosharing twins have opportunities to learn about each other in an interpersonal sense through touch).

5.4 Self-Touch and Early Body Representations

Self-touch is thought to be an important sensory context for learning about the body (see also Bolanowski, Verrillo, & McGlone, 1999). Rochat and Hespos (1997) examined whether newborns would perceive self-touch in a distinct manner to other kinds of touch. They compared newborns' and 1-month-old infants' rooting responses to touches delivered to their cheeks, specifically examining whether there was any difference in response when that touch was self-applied vs applied by the experimenter. Rochat and Hespos found greater rooting to self-touch in the 1 month olds, but no statistically reliable difference in rooting for newborns. This is an ingenious test of an ability to differentiate self vs other touch, but this study has a number of limitations (also discussed extensively elsewhere by Bremner, in press).

One of the most interesting proposals made by Rochat and Hespos (1997) is that a sensitivity of infants to double touch might be a special diagnostic sign for a coherent own body representations, demonstrating that the touch is perceived *in a single place in external space*. But whether young infants do perceive touch in this way remains to be seen. In Rochat and Hespos's study, the differential rooting response in the 1 month olds might be due to either the proprioceptive difference (the infants might root more when the hand is near the face), the tactile difference (the infants might root more when they feel a double touch than when they feel a single touch), or to the combination of the two (the infants might root more when they know that their hand is near their face and they feel a double touch). Rochat and Hespos prefer the latter explanation, inferring a spatial representation that encompasses a coordination of proprioception and touch. However, either of the other alternatives would seem to be just as likely, and neither of them need rest on a representation of external space in which touch and proprioception are coordinated. Furthermore, the simpler interpretations are more commensurate with our own recent work that we describe next and which indicates that external spatial coding of touch does not emerge until 6 months of age (Begum Ali, Spence, & Bremner, 2015; Bremner, Mareschal, Lloyd-Fox, & Spence, 2008).

5.5 Coming to Represent the Body in the Outside World

Arriving in the outside world, the newborn infant has to determine how the tactile sensory stimulation experienced in utero relates to an entirely new external spatial environment. Proprioception and touch continue to provide the same kinds of information about the limbs and touches to the body, although being less enclosed will certainly enable the body to get into a new range of postures. Although recent modeling indicates that there is not an insignificant amount of visual stimulation that reaches the fetus (Del Giudice, 2011), at birth vision provides, for the first time, information about objects and events that are taking place beyond immediate personal space. Sights, sounds, and even smells now offer up a much richer array of information about the external world than the newborn has been presented with before. He or she has to learn to make sense of how the tactile stimulation which they know about fits into the new visual (and auditory) environment.

In the first few months after birth, a casual observation of infants' behavior with respect to their own hands suggests significant limitations in their appreciation of the relationship of their tactile bodies to the externally sensed environment. For instance, the following anecdotal observation of a 4-month-old infant suggests difficulties in appreciating the relationship between his or her own seen and felt hands: "Sometimes the hand would be stared at steadily, perhaps with growing intensity, until interest reached such a pitch that a grasping movement followed as if the infant tried by an automatic action of the motor hand to grasp the visual hand, and it was switched out of the center of vision and lost as if it had magically vanished" (Hall, 1898, p. 351). The picture given by this observation is reminiscent of Merleau-Ponty's (1964) proposal that the development of body perception is characterized by learning how sensations arising from one's own body (what Merleau-Ponty calls "interoceptivity," not to be confused with interoception discussed as a subcategory of touch; see earlier, and Craig, 2009) relate in space and time to the new sensations regarding the external world (exteroceptivity). It is also supported by recent studies examining tactile spatial perception in infants, children, and blind people that indicate that external spatial coding of cutaneous touch takes some time to develop in early life.

We can trace the emergence of the external spatial coding of touch by examining the effects of body posture on tactile localization. For instance, under certain circumstances, when adults are asked to localize touches on their hands, they make more mistakes when their hands are crossed than when they are uncrossed (Schicke & Röder, 2006; Shore, Spry, & Spence, 2002; Yamamoto & Kitazawa, 2001). This "crossed-hands deficit" (CHD) arises because adults are obliged to encode the location of tactile events in the external world.

Work with blind adults demonstrates that external spatial coding of touch arises out of visual experience. Congenitally blind participants show no CHD even though blindfolded sighted and late blind adults (even those with only a few years of visual experience in early life) show the same CHD as sighted adults (Röder, Rösler, & Spence, 2004). More recently, a study reported no CHD in an individual who was born congenitally blind, but whose sight was restored at the age of 2 years through the removal of congenital cataracts (Ley, Bottari, Shenoy, Kekunnaya, & Röder, 2013). Thus, visual experience, seemingly at some point in the first 2 years of life, is important for the typical development of the external spatial coding of touch. Similarly, crossed-hands effects are not always found in those parts of space which we do not have extensive visual experience of (e.g., in the space behind the back; Kóbor, Füredi, Kovács, Spence, & Vidnyánszky, 2006).

When does external spatial coding of touch (as demonstrated through the CHD) develop? Two studies have found the CHD in early childhood (Begum Ali, Cowie, & Bremner, 2014; Pagel, Heed, & Röder, 2009) via verbal responses in which the participants had to identify which of two hands was touched (or which was touched first) across crossed and uncrossed postures. Studies with infants have tackled this question by examining the accuracy of infants' orienting responses to touches, particularly infants' orienting of their eyes, hands, and feet toward the site of tactile stimulation. Bremner et al. (2008) found that 6 month olds' first manual responses following a tactile stimulus were more likely to occur on the touched hand in the uncrossed- than in the crossed-hands posture, indicating a CHD, and thus external coding of touch, in this age group.

Recently, with our colleague Jannath Begum Ali (Begum Ali et al., 2015), we investigated whether the external spatial coding of touch emerges in the first 6 months of postnatal life, comparing 4- and 6-month-old infants. Due to difficulties inherent in crossing 4-month-old infants' arms, we examined the accuracy of their orienting responses to tactile stimuli on the feet across both crossed- and uncrossed-feet postures (see Fig. 3A). Crossed-feet effects have been observed in adults (Schicke & Röder, 2006). As shown in Fig. 3B, the 6-month-olds demonstrated the usual crossed-limb deficit with

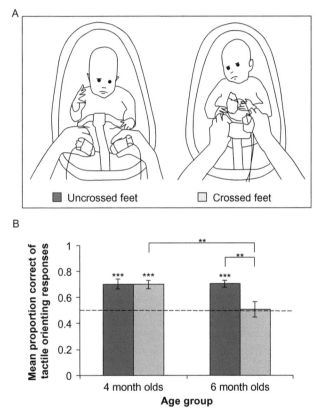

Fig. 3 The development of the crossed-limb deficits in tactile localization (Begum Ali et al., 2015). (A) An infant participating in the uncrossed- and crossed-feet postures. The tactors, attached to the infants' feet using a cohesive bandage, were controlled remotely. The experimenter held the infant's feet in the assigned posture during tactile stimulation. (B) Mean proportion of correct first unilateral foot movements to vibrotactile stimuli (error bars indicate the standard error of the mean). The 6-month-olds showed a crossed-feet effect whereas the 4-month-olds performed equivalently across conditions, matching the best performance of the 6-month-olds. Significant comparisons are indicated (*$p < 0.05$, **$p < 0.01$, ***$p < 0.001$). *Figure reprinted with permission from Begum Ali, J., Spence, C., & Bremner, A. J. (2015). Human infants' ability to perceive touch in external space develops postnatally.* Current Biology, 25, R978–R979.

~70% accuracy in the uncrossed posture, and chance (50%) performance in the crossed posture. In striking contrast, the 4-month-olds showed no crossed-feet deficit, matching the performance of the 6-month-olds in the uncrossed-feet posture and outperforming them in the crossed-feet posture.

Given that a crossed-feet deficit emerges between 4 and 6 months of age, we (Begum Ali et al., 2015) concluded that external spatial coding of touch develops between 4 and 6 months of age. This conclusion is commensurate with findings concerning tactile spatial coding in blind adults mentioned previously (Ley et al., 2013; Röder et al., 2004), and in combination with this work indicates that visual experience somehow plays a role in bringing about the development external coding of touch between 4 and 6 months of age.

Our current explanation of the mediating effects of visual experience on the development of external coding of touch is that the onset of successful reaching at around 4–5 months of age brings with it experiences of synchronous multisensory (visual–tactile) stimuli. Similar experiences are likely across hands and feet as the infants' first reaches are made with both sets of limbs (Galloway & Thelen, 2004). Infants may well build up an expectation that tactile stimuli on the right hand (or foot) typically occur in right visual (or multisensory) space, and tactile stimuli on the left hand (or foot) typically occur in left visual (or multisensory) space (Bremner & Van Velzen, 2015; Yamamoto & Kitazawa, 2001). Thus, multisensory interactions between vision and touch may be the developmental mechanism by which infants come to represent the relation between their body and external space. Indeed, as we demonstrate next (in Section 5.6), recent behavioral findings (Freier, Mason, & Bremner, 2016) indicate that infants can perceive visual–tactile spatial relations from at least 6 months of age.

5.6 The Development of Multisensory Interactions With Touch Underlying Body Representations

We have argued that the most direct sensory information concerning the body arises from cutaneous touch and proprioception. Signals from the vestibular system also provide direct information about the body's positioning with respect to the environment. Nonetheless, as adults, our representations of limb and body position result from the combination and integration of information from these direct (and largely somatosensory) receptors with the visual and even auditory information that is more particularly suited to providing information about the external world (Holmes & Spence,

2004; cf. Merleau-Ponty, 1964). The multisensory nature of body representations gives rise to a number of computational challenges for the developing
child. Not only do the senses convey information about the body and limbs
in different neural codes and reference frames, but the spatial and temporal
relations between sensory modalities can vary dramatically from one
moment to the next. For instance, each time our arm changes posture,
the relations between tactile coordinates on the hands and locations in
the external environment are realigned.

While adults dynamically and automatically remap spatial correspondences between touch and vision across changes in the posture of the limbs
(Holmes & Spence, 2004; although not perfectly; Yamamoto & Kitazawa,
2001; Zampini, Harris, & Spence, 2005), we cannot necessarily infer that the
same is the case earlier in development. In fact, the computational problems
surrounding multisensory spatial perception are amplified during infancy
and childhood. Consider the increasing number and variety of postural
changes that an infant makes across the first years of life. Furthermore,
the spatial distribution of the limbs and the body also changes profoundly.
Such physical and behavioral changes necessitate the continuous adaptation
of multisensory body representations in early life (Adolph & Avolio, 2000;
Burr, Binda, & Gori, 2011).

Several studies using infants' looking preferences have investigated an
early ability to make crossmodal links between cues about the body coming
from touch (both proprioception and cutaneous touch) and vision. These
studies typically examine infants' preferences for visual movements of limbs
projected on a screen that are either congruent or incongruent with their
own limb movements perceived proprioceptively (see Fig. 4; Bahrick &
Watson, 1985; Rochat, 1998). From as early as 3 months of age, infants'
looking behavior demonstrates that they are able to differentiate multisensory bodily events on the basis of visual–proprioceptive (temporal and spatial) congruency. More recently, researchers have examined whether infants
can detect whether a visually observed stroke to the skin occurs at the same
time as a felt (tactile) stroke (Filippetti, Lloyd-Fox, Longo, Farroni, &
Johnson, 2014; Zmyj, Jank, Schütz-Bosbach, & Daum, 2011). Even newborn infants are able to do this (Filippetti et al., 2013), and more recent data
also indicate an ability to code spatial congruence between touches felt on
the skin and seen on a video screen in newborns (Filippetti, Orioli,
Johnson, & Farroni, 2015). Early crossmodal competencies of this kind
provide fuel for speculation that an ability to perceive the bodily self is well
specified from birth (e.g., Rochat, 2010).

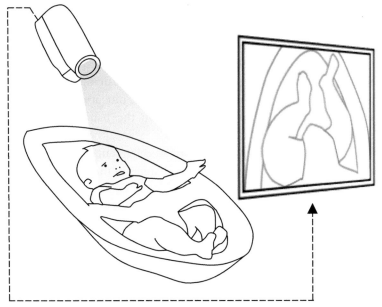

Fig. 4 Crossmodal matching studies of multisensory body perception in infancy. Researchers have measured infants' looking preferences for visual movements of limbs projected on a screen which are either congruent or incongruent with their own limb movements perceived proprioceptively (Bahrick & Watson, 1985; Filippetti, Johnson, Lloyd-Fox, Dragovic, & Farroni, 2013; Rochat, 1998). Differentiation of congruent and incongruent displays is typically demonstrated by a looking preference for the incongruent presentation, but preferences for the congruent presentation are also observed under some circumstances, and are just as diagnostic of differentiation. *Figure reprinted with permission from Bremner, A. J. (2016). Developing body representations in early life: Combining somatosensation and vision to perceive the interface between the body and the world. Developmental Medicine & Child Neurology, 58(Suppl. 4), 12–16.*

One key question which arises from these studies is exactly how infants achieve a perception of visual–tactile (or visual–proprioceptive) simultaneity. This problem here is particularly difficult in the domain of touch, given the latency of the tactile signal relative to the visual signal varies as a function of the distance of the relevant tactile receptors from multisensory convergence zones in the brain (see Bergenheim, Johansson, Granlund, & Pedersen, 1996; Harris, Harrar, Jaekl, & Kopinska, 2010). Tactile signals from the legs arrive much later than signals from the hands or face, whereas visual cues to the same events arrive at the same time irrespective of the limbs involved. One possibility is that infants recalibrate simultaneity perception across different body parts. Another scenario is that young infants use a wider temporal window for multisensory integration to achieve this goal. The fact that the temporal window for audiovisual integration narrows with development (Lewkowicz, 1996; Lewkowicz & Flom, 2014) suggests that this latter solution is the more likely.

One important limitation of the crossmodal matching studies just described (see Fig. 4) is that they present visual bodily information on a screen well outside of personal space (sometimes as far as 1 m away). Thus, any crossmodal links that infants make in this context are necessarily abstracted from spatial frames of reference centered on the body and limbs. This prompts the question of whether an ability to link this screen-based visual information to somatosensory input is of relevance to spatial representations of the body and limbs that could provide the basis for sensorimotor coordination, and body representations more generally (Bremner & Cowie, 2013).

Recently, Freier et al. (2016) attempted to overcome some of these spatial shortcomings of the crossmodal matching methods discussed earlier in order to determine whether young infants can register crossmodal colocation with respect to the body (see Fig. 5). Six- and 10-month-old infants were presented with visual (flashes) and tactile (vibrotactile) stimuli on their hands either colocated on one hand or spread across two hands (a touch on one hand and a light on the other). In contrast to the studies described earlier, in the congruent condition, the bimodal stimuli only occupied one single place in both external and anatomical (bodily) space. Both age groups preferred to look at the incongruent displays. Thus, infants are sensitive to visual–tactile colocation from at least 6 months of age, and before they are able to orient visually to tactile stimuli presented in isolation (Bremner et al., 2008).

This multisensory perceptual skill obviously plays an important role in forming representations of spatial relationships between the body and our external surroundings (Eilan, 1993). We are currently undertaking further studies to examine the origins of this ability prior to 6 months of age. Further questions that also remain to be addressed concern what kind of multisensory representation underlies this ability to perceive visual–tactile colocation. Do the infants perceive a unified (integrated) multisensory stimulus, or the colocation of two quite separate unisensory cues? The current work addressing the development of integration in multisensory perception more broadly (largely in the audiovisual domain) is quite limited, but points to an extended developmental trajectory later in infancy (Neil, Chee-Ruiter, Scheier, Lewkowicz, & Shimojo, 2006) and even into childhood (Burr et al., 2011).

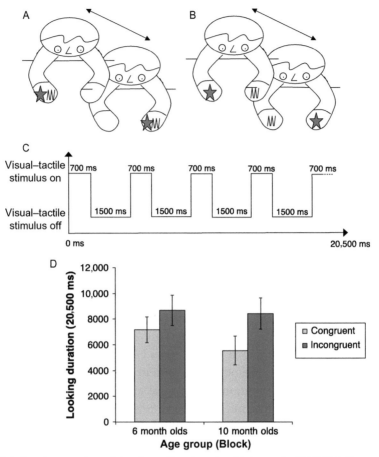

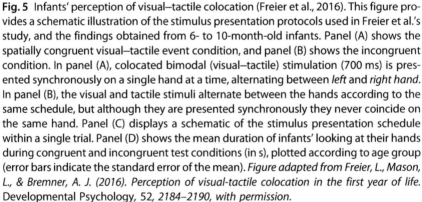

Fig. 5 Infants' perception of visual–tactile colocation (Freier et al., 2016). This figure provides a schematic illustration of the stimulus presentation protocols used in Freier et al.'s study, and the findings obtained from 6- to 10-month-old infants. Panel (A) shows the spatially congruent visual–tactile event condition, and panel (B) shows the incongruent condition. In panel (A), colocated bimodal (visual–tactile) stimulation (700 ms) is presented synchronously on a single hand at a time, alternating between *left* and *right hand*. In panel (B), the visual and tactile stimuli alternate between the hands according to the same schedule, but although they are presented synchronously they never coincide on the same hand. Panel (C) displays a schematic of the stimulus presentation schedule within a single trial. Panel (D) shows the mean duration of infants' looking at their hands during congruent and incongruent test conditions (in s), plotted according to age group (error bars indicate the standard error of the mean). *Figure adapted from Freier, L., Mason, L., & Bremner, A. J. (2016). Perception of visual-tactile colocation in the first year of life. Developmental Psychology, 52, 2184–2190, with permission.*

Even once infants or children learn to colocate touches with visual stimuli in the external environment, a further hurdle involves the development of an ability to update the location of a touch (and a limb) when the body moves into unfamiliar postures. The data from Freier et al. (2016) only pertain to a scenario in which the hands occupy fairly canonical positions with respect to the body. At 6 months of age, we know that when infants are locating touches presented in isolation, they do not take account of current limb position and seemingly fall back on a reliance that the body is in a canonical posture (as evidenced by their crossed-hands and crossed-feet deficits; Begum Ali et al., 2015; Bremner et al., 2008). However, by 10 months of age, infants maintain a consistent level of accuracy in their orienting responses across both familiar and unfamiliar postures. It seems that an ability to incorporate sensory information about current limb posture into representations of the external location of tactile events (referred to here as "postural remapping") develops significantly during the second half-year of life.

What processes underlie the development of postural remapping? One question here is whether development reflects a process of multisensory perceptual gains or whether instead we are seeing improvements in the infants' coordination of their crossmodal orienting responses. A second question concerns what sensory information infants are making use of to update their representations of limb position and remap their behavioral responses. A recent physiological study of tactile processing in infancy from our lab helps to address both of these issues.

Rigato, Begum Ali, van Velzen, and Bremner (2014) investigated the modulatory effects of arm posture on SEPs recorded from the scalp in 6- and 10-month-old infants. When presented with tactile stimuli, the 6-month-old infants showed no reliable effect of posture on their SEPs. Thus, it was as if these younger infants processed tactile events in the same way regardless of the posture of their limbs. However, the older 10-month-old infants, just like adults (Rigato et al., 2013; Soto-Faraco & Azañón, 2013), showed significant postural modulations of somatosensory processing. Thus, improvements in tactile localization across limb posture may well be underpinned by the increased role of postural information in somatosensory processing seen in the SEPs. Importantly, the modulatory effects of posture seen at 10 months occur (as they do in adults) early in somatosensory processing ($\sim$60–120 ms). In answer to the first question raised above, this suggests that improvements in somatosensory processing and postural remapping at 10 months of age occur largely at the early feed-forward (perceptual) end of neural processing in somatosensory cortex, rather than in terms of the responses to touches.

In addressing the second question, we conducted a further study to investigate what sensory information concerning limb position drives the postural modulation of somatosensory processing seen at 10 months (Rigato et al., 2014). Tactile stimuli were again presented, but this time the infants' arms were obscured from their view by a cloak. In this case, the 10-month-old infants showed no effect of posture on their SEPs. Therefore, it seems that, at this point in development, visual cues to hand posture are required to remap tactile space.

Thus, by 10 months of age, infants appear to be able not just to represent the location of touches in the external environment but also to dynamically update tactile localization across changes in posture. However, it is likely that the neural mechanisms underlying multisensory body representations continue to develop beyond infancy. Children's representations of the layout of their tactile receptor surface and their limbs from proprioception would need to be tuned and retuned throughout development in order to cope with physical changes in the disposition, sizes, and movements of the limbs which continue even beyond adolescence.

Some classic and more recent studies have indicated that the multisensory processes involved in representations of the hands and arms may change substantially in early childhood. For instance, a number of researchers have asserted that, across early childhood to adolescence, children come to rely more on vision relative to touch and hearing in localizing multisensory events (Renshaw, 1930; Warren & Pick, 1970). Certainly, visual guidance of reaching movements of the hand increases from infancy into childhood (e.g., Carrico & Berthier, 2008). Using a "mirror hand illusion" task, with young children, Holmes, Crozier, and Spence (2004) found a ~20% increase between 5 and 6 years of age in the extent to which visual (illusory) cues to the hand biased proprioceptively perceived hand position measured by subsequent reaches with that hand (Bremner, Hill, Pratt, Rigato, & Spence, 2013).

However, developmental changes in visual determinants of tactile experience in childhood do not seem to be characterized by a straightforward increase across the board. In contrast to adults and older children, 4-year-old children are actually worse at determining which hand felt a vibrotactile stimulus when they can see their hands (Begum Ali et al., 2014), whereas sight of the hands does not influence accuracy in older children. It would seem that as well as increasingly biasing perceived limb position with age in some situations (Bremner et al., 2013; Carrico & Berthier, 2008), visual cues to hand position also undergo a developmental decline in the extent to which they interfere with the process of localizing touches in early childhood. More research is clearly needed to yield a coherent picture of how interactions of vision and touch change in early childhood.

5.7 The Developing Role of Touch in Determining a Sense of Self

Developing tactile and multisensory representations of the body and its movements are intrinsically tied-up with emerging representations of the self, and many researchers have derived conclusions concerning the emerging self-concept from studies investigating infants' and children's use of multisensory information about the body (see, e.g., Rochat, 2010). The apparently early ability of infants to detect multisensory synchrony between proprioceptive and visual stimuli concerning the limbs has led some researchers to propose that multisensory contingency detection is an innate predisposition in humans which allows them to develop a "primary representation of the bodily self" (Gergely & Watson, 1999).

However, the precise relationship between multisensory body (or hand) perception and perceptions of the self have been a subject of recent scrutiny by researchers studying body representations in mature adults. Specifically, researchers have investigated the perceptual basis of our experience of body ownership in adults and its neural correlates, often using the RHI (Botvinick & Cohen, 1998), already mentioned above. Body-ownership is defined as the "feelings" of ownership of, e.g., a hand, which can be considered separately from the perception of it (see Tsakiris, 2010).

A particular controversy in this debate has been whether body- or limb-ownership is derived—in a so-called "bottom-up" fashion—from current spatiotemporal correlations between synchronous multisensory stimulation (e.g., the synchronous proprioceptive, tactile, auditory, and visual sensations which might arise when a baby bangs a hand or toy on a table; Armel & Ramachandran, 2003; Botvinick & Cohen, 1998; see also Makin, Holmes, & Ehrsson, 2008), or whether additional sources of information picked out by an internal mental body model are used to derive experience of body ownership in a "top-down" fashion (see Tsakiris, 2010; Tsakiris & Haggard, 2005): In the RHI, the extent to which the fake hand resembles a real hand (Tsakiris & Haggard, 2005), the similarity of the fake hand's texture to that of the real hand (Haans, Ijsselsteijn, & de Kort, 2008), or the congruency of its posture with that of the real hand (Costantini & Haggard, 2007; Lloyd, 2007; Pavani, Spence, & Driver, 2000), have all been shown to influence feelings of ownership.

Perhaps the most obvious implication of RHI research is that infants' early abilities to detect the multisensory correlations between proprioception, touch, and vision from early in life may not, by necessity, imply that they experience limb or body ownership under ecological conditions. Developmental researchers have considered whether young infants also respond to some of the cues which are purported to be used by the internal body model (Morgan & Rochat, 1997; Zmyj et al., 2011; for a discussion, see Bremner & Cowie, 2013). However, the studies in question used the experimental paradigm discussed above in which visual cues to the limbs were presented well outside of personal space (sometimes at a distance of as much as 1 m). This is well outside the bounds within which adults experience ownership over illusory limbs (Lloyd, 2007). Thus, although it seems very likely that young infants are able to perceive the multisensory synchrony cues which specify the layout of one's own body, it would seem premature to conclude that they perceive ownership of their limbs via the top-down influence of an internal body representation.

Given the difficulties of evaluating the subjective sense of self or ownership in preverbal infants, Cowie and her colleagues (Cowie et al., 2013; Cowie, Sterling, & Bremner, 2016) have examined whether changes in this are evident across early to mid-childhood. Using the RHI, Cowie et al. (2013, 2016) found that synchronous visual–tactile stroking of the fake and real hands induced a sense of ownership over the fake hands and the fake touches to a similar extent from 4 to 5 years through to adulthood. However, the effects of the RHI on perceived hand position (as measured by the illusion's "drift" influence on estimations of the proprioceptive hand position) declined steeply between 4 and 5 years of age and 10 and 11 years of age, at which point the extent of the illusion resembled that seen in adults. Interestingly, this decline is seen irrespective of the synchrony of visual–tactile stroking, suggesting that we are seeing a developmental reduction in the effect of the visual appearance of the fake hand (i.e., the so-called "top-down" cues rather than the "bottom-up" multisensory synchrony cues) on proprioception. And so, echoing the findings discussed in Section 5.6, it seems that there are considerable changes in the ways in which visual cues influence a proprioceptive sense of hand position in early childhood (although note that, yet again, there is no consistent picture emerging as to how such crossmodal interactions change). Second, the sense of ownership which children experience over the hand in the RHI is similar to that experienced by adults, but does not change with these changes in the effect of the illusion on perceived hand position. This suggests a clear distinction to be drawn between the development of the multisensory determinants of the perceived layout of the body and the development of a sense of self. This is, in fact, commensurate with some recent claims that such processes are distinct in the mature adult (Rohde, Di Luca, & Ernst, 2011).

It is clear that further research is needed in order to determine how a sense of the bodily self develops in early life. The current picture indicates that there is not a consistent relationship between multisensory determinants of the perceived body and limbs and a sense of ownership and self. The clearest determinant of body ownership across all age groups tested appears to be multisensory synchrony between visual and tactile stroking. The sensitivity of young infants, and even newborns, to such cues (Filippetti et al., 2014; Rochat, 1998) could be used to conclude that feelings of ownership over the body are an early acquisition which is substantially supported by multisensory cues to the body. However, changes in the way in which the body is perceived in infancy and childhood (e.g., Begum Ali et al., 2015; Cowie et al., 2013) could mean that the content of a sense of ownership (i.e., what kind of body we feel ownership over, and the spatial and temporal characteristics of that body) could be very different at various points in development.

6. INTERPERSONAL TOUCH PERCEPTION IN EARLY LIFE

Early *social* touch has been argued to occur between twin fetuses in the womb (Castiello et al., 2010). Amazingly, Castiello and his colleagues documented the occurrence of movements that they argued were aimed at touching the cotwin starting from the 14th week of gestation. In line with this observation, researchers studying touch in adults are coming to consider the possibility that touch, and the skin surface, should really be considered as social organs (Field, 2001; Gallace & Spence, 2010, 2014; Morrison, Löken, & Olausson, 2009).

The very first examples of pleasant and comforting sensations are mediated by touch. Given that the human baby is, from a functional and anatomical point of view, critically undeveloped with respect to other mammals (and thus requires a much higher level of parental care), it is natural that these early forms of interaction must be social in nature. The automatic hand closure response seen in babies in response to those objects that are placed in their palm is certainly an important mechanism for helping the developing newborn to develop haptic perception. However, the fact that this behavior can also be observed when the feet of a newborn baby are touched (e.g., Zappella, 1967), would seem to suggest a somewhat different evolutionary role: That is, that this behavior might also carry an important social function. Baby primates use grasping behavior in order to cling on to their mother's fur. Thus, maintaining physical contact with the caregiver (and the level of comfort mediated by that) can probably be seen as one of the most important functions of touch in the early stages of human development, and is likely foundational in the establishment of reciprocal interactions and attachment between infant and caregiver (see, e.g., Harlow & Zimmerman, 1959). In this instance, touch-triggered neonatal grasping might encourage the parent to reciprocally respond and perhaps wrap his or her arms around the infant as a further means of protection and social contact.

One of the most intriguing areas of research in relation to the sense of touch concerns the relatively recent discovery of a new class of tactile fibers in humans, known as C-Tactile (CT) afferents (e.g., see Löken, Wessberg, Morrison, McGlone, & Olausson, 2009; McGlone & Spence, 2010). These fibers, which are found in the hairy, but not in the glabrous skin, respond optimally when the skin is stroked at a speed of about 1–10 cm/s, a stimulation that can resemble a caress (e.g., Morrison, Björnsdotter, & Olausson, 2011; Sailer et al., 2016). These fibers are associated with the perception of the more pleasant and social aspects of tactile stimulation. It has even been suggested that the CT fibers constitute part of a neural system responsible of the maintenance of physical and social well-being in humans (e.g., Morrison et al., 2009).

Tiffany Field is perhaps most well known for her research investigating the role of interpersonal touch in human development. One of her key arguments over the years has been that as adults and even as infants and children we are not provided with as much interpersonal touch as we require, and that modern society prevents or prohibits touch to such an extent that many of us may be "touch hungry." This is clearly a highly theoretical argument, but certainly one to take seriously given the apparently evolved social role which touch plays mediated by the CT afferent system, not to mention of course the studies of Harlow and Zimmerman (1959) demonstrating that newborn rhesus monkeys prefer a surrogate mother that provided tactile comfort as compared to one which provides nutrition. However, one key question is the extent to which infants and children are able to identify and respond differentially to social touch of the kind mediated by the CT afferent system.

Fairhurst, Löken, and Grossmann (2014) recently examined whether 7-month-old infants would show a differentiated response to tactile stroking within the velocity range which the CT afferent system is sensitive to (1–10 cm/s). They found that the infants' heart-rates declined more to strokes of 3 cm/s, with trends for increased heart rate following slower (0.3 cm/s) or faster (30 cm/s) stroking. The infants also showed greater interest in the 3 cm/s stroking than the slow or fast stroking (as indexed by a composite measure of interest gleaned from measures of longer durations of looking), and more gaze shifts toward the 3 cm/s stroking. Of course, 7 months make up a reasonable length of time in which infants could learn about which kinds of touch are particularly associated with interpersonal scenarios, so it is difficult to be completely sure that this specific response is related to an innate physiology for processing interpersonal touch. Indeed, a study by Kida and Shinohara (2013) indicates that there are at least some developments in the brain networks involved in processing pleasant touch, showing, using functional near-infrared spectroscopy (fNIRS), that there is greater activation of anterior prefrontal areas in response to pleasant touch (in this case operationalized as touch from a piece of velvet fabric, as opposed to a wooden rod) in 10-month-old infants as compared to 3- to 6 month olds. More research is needed though if we are to understand the developmental origins of sensitivity to social touch.

Many studies have investigated the benefits which touch can bestow on the developing infant. The question of whether physical handling is important for preterm babies is somewhat controversial with some indicating that it is crucial for good developmental outcomes (e.g., Ang et al., 2012; Diego, Field, & Hernandez-Reif, 2005; Lee, 2005; Lipsitt, 2002), and others pointing out evidence of increased risk of hypoxia due to handling (e.g., Norris, Campbell, & Brenkert, 1981). However, it is now fairly clear that pain-related responses can be decreased by parental touch. Pain during medical procedures (specifically, the heel lance procedure) is significantly reduced if the baby is held in skin-to-skin contact (sometimes known as "kangaroo care"), both for preterm (Johnston et al., 2003; Ludington-Hoe & Hosseini, 2005) and full term neonates (Gray, Watt, & Blass, 2000). In Gray et al.'s (2000) study of full term babies, crying and grimacing were reduced by skin-to-skin contact by 82% and 65%, respectively!

Field and her colleagues also argue that touch can have more long term benefits. Field and Hernandez-Reif (2001) show that parents' evaluations of the quality of their infants' sleep improves more when they are receiving routine massage than when read to in a control group. Benefits of massage on cognitive performance are also thought to be present beyond infancy. Hart, Field, Hernandez-Reif, and Lundy (1998) have demonstrated that a session of massage led to improved cognitive performance and increased alertness and attentiveness in 4 year olds relative to a control group who had a story read to them.

7. SUMMARY

Touch is the first of our senses to develop, providing us with the sensory scaffold on which we come to perceive our own bodies and selves. Touch also provides us with direct access to the physical external world of objects, via haptic exploration. Furthermore, recent research suggests that our tactile perceptual systems are sensitive from at least 7 months (Fairhurst et al., 2014) to interpersonal social touch (or caressing). How is it that this profoundly important sense modality which tells infants so much about themselves, their physical and social environments, can be the subject of so little research compared to vision, hearing and even olfaction?

One possible explanation is that touch is profoundly crossmodal in the way in which it functions. As well as providing the developmental scaffold or foundations of the other senses, there are a number of ways in which, as adults, children and even as infants, what we feel in touch is determined by stimuli arriving through other sense modalities. Maybe because touch plays second fiddle so often to vision in the adult state, researchers have not found it so immediately appealing to investigate. However, that is certainly changing in the literature on adult tactile perception (Gallace & Spence, 2014), and what we have reviewed in this chapter indicates a number of promising new directions in developmental research into touch perception across infancy and childhood. One key message is that although there are some connections between touch and the other senses (particularly vision) early in postnatal development, there are some fundamental ways in which our perceptions of touch and our bodies functions more separately from our (visual) perceptions of the external world in early infancy (Begum Ali et al., 2015).

Despite a number of recent advances in our understanding of the development of touch as a haptic sense (e.g., Gori et al., 2012), as a bodily sense (e.g., Cowie et al., 2013), and as a social sense (e.g., Fairhurst et al., 2014; Morrison et al., 2009), there is clearly a great deal more to be done, particularly in the realm of understanding the development of interpersonal touch. We look forward to the touch being placed where it belongs in the developmental psychology literature: at the center of research in perceptual development.

ACKNOWLEDGMENTS

The authors would like to acknowledge helpful discussions with J. Begum Ali, Jo Johnston, Dorothy Cowie, Fran Le Cornu Knight, Silvia Rigato, Rhiannon Thomas, and José van Velzen.

REFERENCES

Adolph, K. E., & Avolio, A. M. (2000). Walking infants adapt locomotion to changing body dimensions. *Journal of Experimental Psychology: Human Perception and Performance, 26,* 1148–1166.

Alais, D., & Burr, D. (2004). The ventriloquist effect results from near-optimal cross-modal integration. *Current Biology, 14,* 257–262.

Ang, J. Y., Lua, J. L., Mathur, A., Thomas, R., Asmar, B. I., Savasan, S., et al. (2012). A randomized placebo-controlled trial of massage therapy on the immune system of preterm infants. *Pediatrics, 130,* e1549–e1558.

Armel, K. C., & Ramachandran, V. S. (2003). Projecting sensations to external objects: Evidence from skin conductance response. *Proceedings of the Royal Society of London: Biological, 270,* 1499–1506.

Auvray, M., & Spence, C. (2008). The multisensory perception of flavor. *Consciousness and Cognition, 17,* 1016–1031.

Bahrick, L. E., & Lickliter, R. (2012). The role of intersensory redundancy in early perceptual, cognitive, and social development. In A. J. Bremner, D. J. Lewkowicz, & C. Spence (Eds.), *Multisensory development* (pp. 183–205). Oxford, UK: Oxford University Press.

Bahrick, L. E., & Watson, J. S. (1985). Detection of intermodal proprioceptive-visual contingency as a potential basis of self-perception in infancy. *Developmental Psychology, 21,* 963–973.

Begum Ali, J., Cowie, D., & Bremner, A. J. (2014). Effects of posture on tactile localization by 4 years of age are modulated by sight of the hands: Evidence for an early acquired external spatial frame of reference for touch. *Developmental Science, 17,* 935–943.

Begum Ali, J., Spence, C., & Bremner, A. J. (2015). Human infants' ability to perceive touch in external space develops postnatally. *Current Biology, 25,* R978–R979.

Bergenheim, M., Johansson, H., Granlund, B., & Pedersen, J. (1996). Experimental evidence for a sensory synchronization of sensory information to conscious experience. In S. R. Hameroff, A. W. Kaszniak, & A. C. Scott (Eds.), *Toward a science of consciousness: The first Tuscon discussions and debates* (pp. 303–310). Cambridge, MA: MIT Press.

Birch, H. G., & Lefford, A. (1963). Intersensory development in children. *Monographs of the Society for Research in Child Development, 28*(5), 1–48.

Blass, E. M., Fillion, T. J., Rochat, P., Hoffmeyer, L. B., & Metzger, M. A. (1989). Sensorimotor and motivational determinants of hand-mouth coordination in 1–3-day-old human infants. *Developmental Psychology, 25,* 963–975.

Bolanowski, S. J., Verrillo, R. T., & McGlone, F. (1999). Passive, active and intra-active (self) touch. *Somatosensory & Motor Research, 16,* 304–311.

Botvinick, M., & Cohen, J. (1998). Rubber hands 'feel' touch that eyes see. *Nature, 391,* 756.

Bremner, A. J. (in press). The origins of body representations in early life. In A. Alsmith & F. De Vignemont (Eds.), *The body and the self, revisited.* Cambridge, MA: MIT Press.

Bremner, A. J., & Cowie, D. (2013). Developmental origins of the hand in the mind and the role of the hands in the development of the mind. In Z. Radman (Ed.), *The hand, an organ of the mind: What the manual tells the mental* (pp. 27–55). Cambridge, MA: MIT Press.

Bremner, A. J., Hill, E. L., Pratt, E., Rigato, S., & Spence, C. (2013). Bodily illusions in young children: Developmental change in the contribution of vision to perceived hand position in early childhood. *PloS One, 8*. e51887.

Bremner, A. J., Lewkowicz, D. J., & Spence, C. (Eds.), (2012). *Multisensory development.* Oxford, UK: Oxford University Press.

Bremner, A. J., Mareschal, D., Lloyd-Fox, S., & Spence, C. (2008). Spatial localization of touch in the first year of life: Early influence of a visual code, and the development of remapping across changes in limb position. *Journal of Experimental Psychology: General, 137*, 149–162.

Bremner, A. J., & Van Velzen, J. (2015). Sensorimotor control: Retuning the body–world interface. *Current Biology, 25*, R159–R161.

Brownell, C. A., Nichols, S. R., Svetlova, M., Zerwas, S., & Ramani, G. (2010). The head bone's connected to the neck bone: When do toddlers represent their own body topography? *Child Development, 81*, 797–810.

Bryant, P. E. (1974). *Perception and understanding in young children.* London, UK: Methuen.

Bryant, P. E., Jones, P., Claxton, V., & Perkins, G. H. (1972). Recognition of shapes across modalities by infants. *Nature, 240*, 303–304.

Burr, D., Binda, P., & Gori, M. (2011). Multisensory integration and calibration in adults and in children. In J. Trommershauser, K. Kording, & M. S. Landy (Eds.), *Sensory cue integration* (pp. 173–194). Oxford, UK: Oxford University Press.

Bushnell, E. W., & Boudreau, J. P. (1993). Motor development and the mind: The potential role of motor abilities as a determinant of aspects of perceptual development. *Child Development, 64*, 1005–1021.

Butterworth, G., & Hopkins, B. (1988). Hand-mouth coordination in the new-born baby. *British Journal of Developmental Psychology, 6*, 303–314.

Calvert, G. A., Spence, C., & Stein, B. E. (Eds.), (2004). *The handbook of multisensory processes.* Cambridge, MA: MIT Press.

Carrico, R. L., & Berthier, N. E. (2008). Vision and precision reaching in 15-month-old infants. *Infant Behavior & Development, 31*, 62–70.

Castiello, U., Becchio, C., Zoia, S., Nelini, C., Sartori, L., Blason, L., et al. (2010). Wired to be social: The ontogeny of human interaction. *PloS One, 5*. e13199.

Chesselden, W. (1728). An account of some observations made by a young gentleman, who was born blind, or lost his sight so early, that he had no remembrance of ever having seen, and was couch'd between 13 and 14 years of age. *Philosophical Transactions (1683–1775), 35*, 447–450.

Churchill, A., Meyners, M., Griffiths, L., & Bailey, P. (2009). The cross-modal effect of fragrance in shampoo: Modifying the perceived feel of both product and hair during and after washing. *Food Quality & Preference, 20*, 320–328.

Cole, J., & Paillard, J. (1995). Living without touch and peripheral information about body position and movement: Studies with deafferented subjects. In J. L. Bermudez, A. Marcel, & N. Eilan (Eds.), *The body and the self* (pp. 245–266). Cambridge, MA: MIT Press.

Costantini, M., & Haggard, P. (2007). The rubber hand illusion: Sensitivity and reference frame for body ownership. *Consciousness & Cognition, 16*, 229–240.

Cowie, D., Makin, T., & Bremner, A. J. (2013). Children's responses to the rubber hand illusion reveal dissociable pathways in body representations. *Psychological Science, 24*, 762–769.

Cowie, D., Sterling, S., & Bremner, A. J. (2016). The development of multisensory body representation and awareness continues to 10 years of age: Evidence from the rubber hand illusion. *Journal of Experimental Child Psychology, 142*, 230–238.

Craig, A. D. (2009). How do you feel—Now? The anterior insula and human awareness. *Nature Reviews. Neuroscience, 10*, 59–70.

De Vignemont, F., Majid, A., Jola, C., & Haggard, P. (2009). Segmenting the body into parts: Evidence from biases in tactile perception. *The Quarterly Journal of Experimental Psychology, 62*, 500–512.

De Vries, J. I. P., Visser, G. H. A., & Prechtl, H. F. R. (1984). Fetal motility in the first half of pregnancy. *Clinics in Developmental Medicine, 94*, 46–64.

Del Giudice, M. (2011). Alone in the dark? Modeling the conditions for visual experience in human fetuses. *Developmental Psychobiology, 53*, 214–219.

Demattè, M. L., Sanabria, D., Sugarman, R., & Spence, C. (2006). Cross-modal interactions between olfaction and touch. *Chemical Senses, 31*, 291–300.

Diego, M. A., Field, T., & Hernandez-Reif, M. (2005). Vagal activity, gastric motility, and weight gain in massaged preterm neonates. *The Journal of Pediatrics, 147*, 50–55.

Ehrsson, H. H., Spence, C., & Passingham, R. E. (2004). That's my hand! Activity in premotor cortex reflects feeling of ownership of a limb. *Science, 305*, 875–877.

Eilan, N. (1993). Molyneux's question and the idea of an external world. In N. Eilan, R. McCarthy, & B. Brewer (Eds.), *Spatial representation: Problems in philosophy and psychology* (pp. 236–255). Oxford, UK: Oxford University Press.

Ernst, M. O., & Banks, M. S. (2002). Humans integrate visual and haptic information in a statistically optimal fashion. *Nature, 415*, 429–433.

Fairhurst, M. T., Löken, L., & Grossmann, T. (2014). Physiological and behavioral responses reveal 9-month-old infants' sensitivity to pleasant touch. *Psychological Science, 25*, 1124–1131.

Fantz, R. L. (1961). The origin of form perception. *Scientific American, 204*, 66–72.

Fényes, I., Gergely, C., & Tóth, S. (1960). Clinical and electromyographic studies of "spinal reflexes" in premature and full-term infants. *Journal of Neurology, Neurosurgery & Psychiatry, 23*, 63–68.

Field, T. (2001). *Touch*. Cambridge, MA: MIT Press.

Field, T., & Hernandez-Reif, M. (2001). Sleep problems in infants decrease following massage therapy. *Early Child Development & Care, 168*, 95–104.

Fifer, W. P., & Moon, C. (2003). Prenatal development. In A. Slater & G. Bremner (Eds.), *An introduction to developmental psychology* (pp. 95–114). Oxford, UK: Blackwell Publishing.

Filippetti, M. L., Johnson, M. H., Lloyd-Fox, S., Dragovic, D., & Farroni, T. (2013). Body perception in newborns. *Current Biology, 23*, 2413–2416.

Filippetti, M. L., Lloyd-Fox, S., Longo, M. R., Farroni, T., & Johnson, M. H. (2014). Neural mechanisms of body awareness in infants. *Cerebral Cortex, 25*, 3779–3787.

Filippetti, M. L., Orioli, G., Johnson, M. H., & Farroni, T. (2015). Newborn body perception: Sensitivity to spatial congruency. *Infancy, 20*, 455–465.

Flavell, J. H., Flavell, E. R., & Green, F. L. (1983). Development of the appearance-reality distinction. *Cognitive Psychology, 15*(1), 95–120.

Flavell, J. H., Green, F. L., & Flavell, E. R. (1986). Development of knowledge about the appearance-reality distinction. *Monographs of the Society for Research in Child Development, 51*(1), 1–87.

Freier, L., Mason, L., & Bremner, A. J. (2016). Perception of visual-tactile colocation in the first year of life. *Developmental Psychology, 52*, 2184–2190.

Gallace, A., Ngo, M. K., Sulaitis, J., & Spence, C. (2012). Multisensory presence in virtual reality: Possibilities & limitations. In G. Ghinea, F. Andres, & S. Gulliver (Eds.), *Multiple sensorial media advances and applications: New developments in MulSeMedia* (pp. 1–40). Hershey, PA: IGI Global.

Gallace, A., & Spence, C. (2010). The science of interpersonal touch: An overview. *Neuroscience & Biobehavioral Reviews, 34*, 246–259.

Gallace, A., & Spence, C. (2014). *In touch with the future: The sense of touch from cognitive neuroscience to virtual reality*. Oxford, UK: Oxford University Press.

Gallagher, S. (2005). *How the body shapes the mind*. Oxford, UK: Oxford University Press.

Galloway, J. C., & Thelen, E. (2004). Feet first: Object exploration in young infants. *Infant Behavior & Development*, *27*, 107–112.

Gergely, G., & Watson, J. S. (1999). Early socio-emotional development: Contingency perception and the social-biofeedback model. In P. Rochat (Ed.), *Early social cognition: Understanding others in the first months of life* (pp. 101–136). Mahwah, NJ: Lawrence Erlbaum Associates.

Gibson, J. J. (1966). *The senses considered as perceptual systems*. Oxford, UK: Houghton-Mifflin.

Gibson, E. J., & Walker, A. S. (1984). Development of knowledge of visual-tactual affordances of substance. *Child Development*, *55*, 453–460.

Gori, M., Del Viva, M. M., Sandini, G., & Burr, D. C. (2008). Young children do not integrate visual and haptic form information. *Current Biology*, *18*, 694–698.

Gori, M., Giuliana, L., Sandini, G., & Burr, D. (2012). Visual size perception and haptic calibration during development. *Developmental Science*, *15*, 854–862.

Gori, M., Sandini, G., Martinoli, C., & Burr, D. (2010). Poor haptic orientation discrimination in nonsighted children may reflect disruption of cross-sensory calibration. *Current Biology*, *20*, 223–225.

Gray, L., Watt, L., & Blass, E. M. (2000). Skin-to-skin contact is analgesic in healthy newborns. *Pediatrics*, *105*, e14.

Guest, S., Catmur, C., Lloyd, D., & Spence, C. (2002). Audiotactile interactions in roughness perception. *Experimental Brain Research*, *146*, 161–171.

Haans, A., Ijsselsteijn, W. A., & de Kort, Y. A. (2008). The effect of similarities in skin texture and hand shape on perceived ownership of a fake limb. *Body Image*, *5*, 389–394.

Hall, G. S. (1898). Some aspects of the early sense of self. *American Journal of Psychology*, *9*, 351–395.

Harlow, H. F., & Zimmerman, R. R. (1959). Affectional response in the infant monkey. *Science*, *130*, 421–431.

Harris, L. R., Harrar, V., Jaekl, P., & Kopinska, A. (2010). Mechanisms of simultaneity constancy. In R. Nijhawan (Ed.), *Space and time in perception and action* (pp. 232–253). Cambridge, UK: Cambridge University Press.

Hart, S., Field, T., Hernandez-Reif, M., & Lundy, B. (1998). Preschoolers' cognitive performance improves following massage. *Early Child Development & Care*, *143*, 59–64.

Held, R., Ostrovsky, Y., de Gelder, B., Gandhi, T., Ganesh, S., Mathur, U., et al. (2011). The newly sighted fail to match seen with felt. *Nature Neuroscience*, *14*, 551–553.

Holmes, N. P., Crozier, G., & Spence, C. (2004). When mirrors lie: "Visual capture" of arm position impairs reaching performance. *Cognitive, Affective, & Behavioral Neuroscience*, *4*, 193–200.

Holmes, N. P., & Spence, C. (2004). The body schema and multisensory representation(s) of peripersonal space. *Cognitive Processing*, *5*, 94–105.

Hooker, D. (1952). *The prenatal origin of behavior*. Lawrence, KS: University of Kansas Press.

Hulme, C., Smart, A., Moran, G., & Raine, A. (1983). Visual kinaesthetic and cross-modal development: Relationships to motor skill development. *Perception*, *12*, 477–483.

Humphrey, T. (1964). Some correlations between the appearance of human fetal reflexes and the development of the nervous system. *Progress in Brain Research*, *4*, 93–135.

Jacobs, R., Serhal, C. B., & van Steenberghe, D. (1998). Oral stereognosis: A review of the literature. *Clinical Oral Investigations*, *2*, 3–10.

Johnston, C. C., Stevens, B., Pinelli, J., Gibbins, S., FIllon, F., Jack, A., et al. (2003). Kangaroo care is effective in diminishing pain response in preterm neonates. *Archives of Pediatrics & Adolescent Medicine*, *157*, 1084–1088.

Jouen, F., & Molina, M. (2005). Exploration of the newborn's manual activity: A window onto early cognitive processes. *Infant Behavior & Development, 28*, 227–239.

Jousmäki, V., & Hari, R. (1998). Parchment-skin illusion: Sound-biased touch. *Current Biology, 8*, R190–R191.

Kahrimanovic, M., Bergmann Tiest, W. M., & Kappers, A. M. (2010). Haptic perception of volume and surface area of 3-D objects. *Attention, Perception, & Psychophysics, 72*, 517–527.

Kalagher, H., & Jones, S. S. (2011a). Young children's haptic exploratory procedures. *Journal of Experimental Child Psychology, 110*, 592–602.

Kalagher, H., & Jones, S. S. (2011b). Developmental change in young children's use of haptic information in a visual task: The role of hand movements. *Journal of Experimental Child Psychology, 108*, 293–307.

Kenny, P., & Turkewitz, G. (1986). Effects of unusually early visual stimulation on the development of homing behaviour in the rat pup. *Developmental Psychobiology, 19*, 57–66.

Kida, T., & Shinohara, K. (2013). Gentle touch activates the prefrontal cortex in infancy: an NIRS study. *Neuroscience Letters, 541*, 63–66.

Kisilevsky, B. S., & Muir, D. W. (1984). Neonatal habituation and dishabituation to tactile stimulation during sleep. *Developmental Psychology, 20*, 367–373.

Kóbor, I., Füredi, L., Kovács, G., Spence, C., & Vidnyánszky, Z. (2006). Back-to-front: Improved tactile discrimination performance in the space you can't see. *Neuroscience Letters, 400*, 163–167.

Le Cornu Knight, F., Cowie, D., & Bremner, A. J. (2016). Part-based representations of the body in early childhood: Evidence from perceived distortions of tactile space across limb boundaries. *Developmental Science*. http://dx.doi.org/10.1111/desc.12439.

Le Cornu Knight, F., Longo, M., & Bremner, A. J. (2014). Categorical perception of tactile distance. *Cognition, 131*, 254–262.

Lederman, S. J., & Klatzky, R. L. (2009). Haptic perception: A tutorial. *Attention, Perception, & Psychophysics, 71*, 1439–1459.

Lee, H. K. (2005). The effect of infant massage on weight gain: Physiological and behavioral responses in premature infants. *Taehan Kanho Hakhoe Chi, 35*, 1451–1460.

Lewkowicz, D. J. (1996). Perception of auditory–visual temporal synchrony in human infants. *Journal of Experimental Psychology: Human Perception & Performance, 22*, 1094–1106.

Lewkowicz, D. J., & Flom, R. (2014). The audiovisual temporal binding window narrows in early childhood. *Child Development, 85*, 685–694.

Lewkowicz, D. J., & Lickliter, R. (Eds.), (1994). *The development of intersensory perception: Comparative perspectives*. Hillsdale, NJ: Lawrence Erlbaum Associates.

Ley, P., Bottari, D., Shenoy, B. H., Kekunnaya, R., & Röder, B. (2013). Partial recovery of visual–spatial remapping of touch after restoring vision in a congenitally blind man. *Neuropsychologia, 51*, 1119–1123.

Lipsitt, L. P. (2002). The newborn as informant. In J. W. Fagen & H. Hayne (Eds.), *Progress in infancy research: Vol. 2* (pp. 1–24). Mahwah, NJ: Lawrence Erlbaum Associates.

Lloyd, D. M. (2007). Spatial limits on referred touch to an alien limb may reflect boundaries of visuo-tactile peripersonal space surrounding the hand. *Brain and Cognition, 64*, 104–109.

Locke, J. (1688). An essay concerning human understanding. London.

Löken, L. S., Wessberg, J., Morrison, I., McGlone, F., & Olausson, H. (2009). Coding of pleasant touch by unmyelinated afferents in humans. *Nature Neuroscience, 12*, 547–548.

Ludington-Hoe, S. M., & Hosseini, R. B. (2005). Skin-to-skin contact analgesia for preterm infant heel stick. *American Association of Critical Care Nurses Clinical Issues, 16*, 373–387.

Makin, T. R., Holmes, N. P., & Ehrsson, H. H. (2008). On the other hand: Dummy hands and peripersonal space. *Behavioural Brain Research, 191*, 1–10.

Marcus, L., Lejeune, F., Berne-Audéoud, F., Gentaz, E., & Debillon, T. (2012). Tactile sensory capacity of the preterm infant: Manual perception of shape from 28 gestational weeks. *Pediatrics, 130*, e88–e94.

Marshall, P. J., & Meltzoff, A. N. (2015). Body maps in the infant brain. *Trends in Cognitive Sciences, 19*, 499–505.

Martin, M. G. F. (1993). Sense modalities and spatial properties. In N. Eilan, R. McCarthy, & B. Brewer (Eds.), *Spatial representation: Problems in philosophy and psychology* (pp. 206–218). Oxford, UK: Oxford University Press.

Maurer, D., Stager, C. L., & Mondloch, C. J. (1999). Cross-modal transfer of shape is difficult to demonstrate in one-month-olds. *Child Development, 70*, 1047–1057.

McGlone, F. P., & Spence, C. (2010). Editorial: The cutaneous senses: Touch, temperature, pain/itch, and pleasure. *Neuroscience & Biobehavioural Reviews, 34*, 145–147.

Meltzoff, A. N., & Borton, R. W. (1979). Intermodal matching by human neonates. *Nature, 282*, 403–404.

Merleau-Ponty, M., (Ed. J. M. Edie). (1964). The primacy of perception: And other essays on phenomenological psychology, the philosophy of art, history, and politics. Evanston, IL: Northwestern University Press.

Milh, M., Kaminska, A., Huon, C., Lapillonne, A., Ben-Ari, Y., & Khazipov, R. (2007). Rapid cortical oscillations and early motor activity in premature human neonate. *Cerebral Cortex, 17*, 1582–1594.

Miller, L. J., Fuller, D. A., & Roetenberg, J. (2014). *Sensational kids: Hope and help for children with sensory processing disorder (SPD)*. London, UK: Penguin.

Montagu, A. (1978). *Touching: The human significance of the skin*. New York, NY: Harper & Row.

Moreau, T., Helfgott, E., Weinstein, P., & Milner, P. (1978). Lateral differences in habituation of ipsilateral head-turning to repeated tactile stimulation in the human newborn. *Perceptual & Motor Skills, 46*, 427–436.

Morgan, R., & Rochat, P. (1997). Intermodal calibration of the body in early infancy. *Ecological Psychology, 9*, 1–23.

Morrison, I., Björnsdotter, M., & Olausson, H. (2011). Vicarious responses to social touch in posterior insular cortex are tuned to pleasant caressing speeds. *Journal of Neuroscience, 31*, 9554–9562.

Morrison, I., Löken, L. S., & Olausson, H. (2009). The skin as a social organ. *Experimental Brain Research, 204*, 305–314.

Neil, P. A., Chee-Ruiter, C., Scheier, C., Lewkowicz, D. J., & Shimojo, S. (2006). Development of multisensory spatial integration and perception in humans. *Developmental Science, 9*, 454–464.

Nevalainen, P., Lauronen, L., & Pihko, E. (2014). Development of human somatosensory cortical functions—What have we learned from magnetoencephalography: A review. *Frontiers in Human Neuroscience, 8*, 158.

Norris, S., Campbell, L. A., & Brenkert, S. (1981). Nursing procedures and alterations in transcutaneous oxygen tension in premature infants. *Nursing Research, 31*, 330–336.

Pagel, B., Heed, T., & Röder, B. (2009). Change of reference frame for tactile localization during child development. *Developmental Science, 12*, 929–937.

Pavani, F., Spence, C., & Driver, J. (2000). Visual capture of touch: Out-of-the-body experiences with rubber gloves. *Psychological Science, 11*, 353–359.

Penfield, W., & Rasmussen, T. (1950). *The cerebral cortex of man: A clinical study of localization*. Oxford, UK: MacMillan.

Prechtl, H. F. R. (1958). The directed head turning response and allied movements of the human baby. *Behaviour, 13*, 212–242.

Quattrocki, E., & Friston, K. (2014). Autism, oxytocin and interoception. *Neuroscience & Biobehavioral Reviews, 47*, 410–430.

Radman, Z. (2013). *The hand, an organ of the mind: What the manual tells the mental.* Cambridge, MA: MIT Press.

Renshaw, S. (1930). The errors of cutaneous localization and the effect of practice on the localizing movement in children and adults. *Journal of Genetic Psychology, 28,* 223–238.

Rigato, S., Begum Ali, J., van Velzen, J., & Bremner, A. J. (2014). The neural basis of somatosensory remapping develops in human infancy. *Current Biology, 24,* 1222–1226.

Rigato, S., Bremner, A. J., Mason, L., Pickering, A., Davis, R., & van Velzen, J. (2013). The electrophysiological time course of somatosensory spatial remapping: Vision of the hands modulates effects of posture on somatosensory evoked potentials. *European Journal of Neuroscience, 38,* 2884–2892.

Rochat, P. (1998). Self-perception and action in infancy. *Experimental Brain Research, 123,* 102–109.

Rochat, P. (2010). The innate sense of the body develops to become a public affair by 2–3 years. *Neuropsychologia, 48,* 738–745.

Rochat, P., & Hespos, S. J. (1997). Differential rooting response by neonates: Evidence for an early sense of self. *Early Development & Parenting, 64,* 153–188.

Rochat, P., & Senders, S. J. (1991). Active touch in infancy: Action systems in development. In M. J. S. Weiss & P. R. Zelazo (Eds.), *Newborn attention: Biological constraints and the influence of experience* (pp. 412–442). Westport, CT: Ablex.

Röder, B., Rösler, F., & Spence, C. (2004). Early vision impairs tactile perception in the blind. *Current Biology, 14,* 121–124.

Rohde, M., Di Luca, M., & Ernst, M. O. (2011). The rubber hand illusion: Feeling of ownership and proprioceptive drift do not go hand in hand. *PloS One, 6,* e21659.

Rose, S. A. (1994). From hand to eye: Findings and issues in infant cross-modal transfer. In D. J. Lewkowicz & R. Lickliter (Eds.), *The development of intersensory perception: Comparative perspectives* (pp. 265–284). Hillsdale, NJ: Lawrence Erlbaum Associates.

Rose, S. A., Gottfried, A. W., & Bridger, W. H. (1981). Cross-modal transfer in 6-month-old infants. *Developmental Psychology, 17,* 661–669.

Ruff, H. A. (1984). Infants' manipulative exploration of objects: Effects of age and object characteristics. *Developmental Psychology, 20,* 9–20.

Saby, J. N., Meltzoff, A. N., & Marshall, P. J. (2015). Neural body maps in human infants: Somatotopic responses to tactile stimulation in 7-month-olds. *NeuroImage, 118,* 74–78.

Sailer, U., Triscoli, C., Häggblad, G., Hamilton, P., Olausson, H., & Croy, I. (2016). Temporal dynamics of brain activation during 40 minutes of pleasant touch. *NeuroImage, 139,* 360–367.

Sann, C., & Streri, A. (2007). Perception of object shape and texture in human newborns: Evidence from cross-modal transfer tasks. *Developmental Science, 10,* 399–410.

Schaal, B. (2006). The development of flavor perception from infancy to adulthood. In A. Voilley (Ed.), *Flavour in food* (pp. 401–436). Cambridge, UK: Woodhead Publishing.

Schaal, B., & Durand, K. (2012). The role of olfaction in human multisensory development. In A. J. Bremner, D. Lewkowicz, & C. Spence (Eds.), *Multisensory development* (pp. 29–62). Oxford, UK: Oxford University Press.

Schicke, T., & Röder, B. (2006). Spatial remapping of touch: Confusion of perceived stimulus order across hand and foot. *Proceedings of the National Academy of Sciences of the United States of America, 103,* 11808–11813.

Sherrington, C. S. (1910). Flexion-reflex of the limb, crossed extension-reflex, and reflex Stepping and standing. *Journal of Physiology, 40,* 28–121.

Shore, D. I., Spry, E., & Spence, C. (2002). Confusing the mind by crossing the hands. *Cognitive Brain Research, 14,* 153–163.

Soto-Faraco, S., & Azañón, E. (2013). Electrophysiological correlates of tactile remapping. *Neuropsychologia, 51,* 1584–1594.

Spence, C. (2012). The development and decline of multisensory flavour perception. In A. J. Bremner, D. Lewkowicz, & C. Spence (Eds.), *Multisensory development* (pp. 63–87). Oxford, UK: Oxford University Press.

Spence, C., & Bayne, T. (2015). Is consciousness multisensory? In D. Stokes, M. Matthen, & S. Biggs (Eds.), *Perception and its modalities* (pp. 95–132). Oxford, UK: Oxford University Press.

Spence, C., & Gallace, A. (2011). Multisensory design: Reaching out to touch the consumer. *Psychology & Marketing, 28*, 267–308.

Stein, B. E. (Ed.), (2012). *The new handbook of multisensory processes*. Cambridge, MA: MIT Press.

Streri, A. (2012). Crossmodal interactions in the human newborn: New answers to Molyneux's question. In A. J. Bremner, D. J. Lewkowicz, & C. Spence (Eds.), *Multisensory development* (pp. 88–112). Oxford, UK: Oxford University Press.

Streri, A., Lhote, M., & Dutilleul, S. (2000). Haptic perception in newborns. *Developmental Science, 3*, 319–327.

Thelen, E., & Fisher, D. M. (1982). Newborn stepping: An explanation for a "disappearing" reflex. *Developmental Psychology, 18*, 760–775.

Tsakiris, M. (2010). My body in the brain: A neurocognitive model of body-ownership. *Neuropsychologia, 48*, 703–712.

Tsakiris, M., & Haggard, P. (2005). The rubber hand illusion revisited: Visuotactile integration and self-attribution. *Journal of Experimental Psychology: Human Perception & Performance, 31*, 80–91.

Turkewitz, G. (1994). Sources of order for intersensory functioning. In D. J. Lewkowicz & R. Lickliter (Eds.), *The development of intersensory perception: Comparative perspectives* (pp. 3–18). Hillsdale, NJ: Lawrence Erlbaum Associates.

Turkewitz, G., & Kenny, P. A. (1982). The role of developmental limitations of sensory input on perceptual development: A preliminary theoretical statement. *Developmental Psychobiology, 15*, 357–368.

von Hofsten, C. (2007). Action in development. *Developmental Science, 10*, 54–60.

Warren, D. H., & Pick, H. L., Jr. (1970). Intermodality relations in blind and sighted people. *Perception & Psychophysics, 8*, 430–432.

Weinstein, S. (1968). Intensive and extensive aspects of tactile sensitivity as a function of body part, sex, and laterality. In D. R. Kenshalo (Ed.), *The skin senses* (pp. 195–222). Springfield, IL: Thomas.

Yamamoto, S., & Kitazawa, S. (2001). Reversal of subjective temporal order due to arm crossing. *Nature Neuroscience, 4*, 759–765.

Zampini, M., Harris, C., & Spence, C. (2005). Effect of posture change on tactile perception: Impaired direction discrimination performance with interleaved fingers. *Experimental Brain Research, 166*, 498–508.

Zappella, M. (1967). Placing and grasping of the feet at various temperatures in early infancy. *Pediatrics, 39*, 93–96.

Zappella, M., & Simopoulos, A. (1966). The crossed-extension reflex in the newborn. *Annales Paediatriae Fenniae, 12*, 30–33.

Zimmerman, M. (1989). The nervous system in the context of information theory. In R. F. Schmidt & G. Thews (Eds.), *Human physiology* (2nd Complete ed., pp. 166–173). Berlin: Springer-Verlag.

Zmyj, N., Jank, J., Schütz-Bosbach, S., & Daum, M. M. (2011). Detection of visual-tactile contingency in the first year after birth. *Cognition, 120*, 82–89.

CHAPTER EIGHT

The Development of Body Image and Weight Bias in Childhood

S.J. Paxton[1], S.R. Damiano

School of Psychology and Public Health, La Trobe University, Melbourne, VIC, Australia
[1]Corresponding author: e-mail address: susan.paxton@latrobe.edu.au

Contents

Abstract

Negative body image attitudes are related to the onset of disordered eating, poor self-esteem, general mental health problems, and obesity. In this chapter, we will review the nature of body image attitudes in girls and boys in early (approximately 3–7 years old) and later childhood (approximately 8–11 years old). The body image attitudes explored in this chapter include body image attitudes related to the *self*, with a focus on body dissatisfaction, and body image attitudes related to *others*, with a focus on weight bias. Issues of measurement of body image and weight bias will first be explored. In light of measurement considerations, the prevalence and predictors of body dissatisfaction and related concerns, and weight bias will be examined. The chapter will conclude with a review of promising directions in the prevention of body dissatisfaction and weight bias in children.

Advances in Child Development and Behavior, Volume 52
ISSN 0065-2407
http://dx.doi.org/10.1016/bs.acdb.2016.10.006

1. UNDERSTANDING BODY IMAGE ATTITUDES

Body image is a broad term that is used to encompass thoughts, feelings, perceptions, and behaviors related to one's body, and thus may be considered a multidimensional concept (Thompson, Heinberg, Altabe, & Tantleff Dunn, 1999). Body image may relate to the physical experiences of the body or more holistically to the experience of embodiment, that is, the positive connection to the body and attunement with inner states (Piran, 2016). However, in the Western world, body image research has largely focused on attitudes, emotions, and perceptions that relate to one's physical appearance (Thompson et al., 1999). The main reason for this is because appearance concerns, in particular, have been shown to predict a range of mental health problems, described further later. Consequently, although recognizing the breadth of body image attitudes and experiences, the focus of this chapter will be on body image as it relates to attitudes about, and experiences of, physical appearance.

1.1 Body Dissatisfaction

Body image has frequently been conceptualized along a dimension of body satisfaction to body dissatisfaction; that is, from positive thoughts and feelings about one's body, especially in relation to weight and shape, to negative thoughts and feelings that may range from mild dissatisfaction to intense loathing and rejection of one's body (Paxton & McLean, 2010). Body satisfaction (also described as body esteem) or dissatisfaction may be directed toward appearance in general, but is often directed toward a specific aspect of the body (such as weight and shape) or specific body parts (such as the stomach). Body dissatisfaction in girls tends to focus on weight and shape dissatisfaction, but may also relate to other physical features, such as facial characteristics or skin appearance (Wertheim & Paxton, 2011). However, even in 5- to 8-year-old boys, muscularity, strength, and speed are associated with the ideal masculine image (Drummond, 2012), and body dissatisfaction in boys typically takes on the form of a drive for lean muscularity with boys wishing to be leaner, stronger, and more muscular than they are (Ricciardelli & McCabe, 2011). In a related way, concerns about sporting performance and a desire to have greater height, speed, strength, fitness, and endurance may be a focus of body dissatisfaction in boys (Ricciardelli & McCabe, 2011). Body dissatisfaction and concerns may focus on perceived rather than actual physical appearance and becomes particularly problematic when a person places a high value or investment on weight and shape in females, or leanness and muscularity in males (Cash, 2002).

Body dissatisfaction has become a focus of research as it is not only an immediate source of unhappiness but has also been shown to have serious negative consequences. Research has shown that body dissatisfaction in early adolescence is a risk factor for low self-esteem and depressive symptoms (Goldschmidt, Wall, Choo, Becker, & Neumark-Sztainer, 2016; Paxton, Eisenberg, & Neumark-Sztainer, 2006), unsafe sexual behaviors (Schooler, 2013), smoking onset (Kaufman & Augustson, 2008), disordered eating, including unhealthy dieting or muscle building behaviors (Neumark-Sztainer, Paxton, Hannan, Haines, & Story, 2006; Pope, Kanayama, & Hudson, 2012), overweight and obesity (Loth, Watts, van den Berg, & Neumark-Sztainer, 2015), and clinical eating disorders (Stice, Marti, & Durant, 2011). Until recently there has been relatively little research in children that explores the long-term consequences of body dissatisfaction in childhood. However, one important study of girls conducted by Davison, Markey, and Birch (2003) found that high weight concerns at 5 and 7 years predicted higher dietary restraint, more maladaptive eating attitudes, and a greater likelihood of dieting at 9 years, independent of body mass index (BMI). These findings are consistent with those in adolescents and suggest there are likely to be other negative consequences of body dissatisfaction in childhood that have yet to be identified.

1.2 Weight Bias

Body image attitudes may also be held in relation to the appearance of others. In particular, individuals may hold stereotypical attitudes about others with particular physical features. This has long been recognized in relation to skin pigment and racial features, but in Western societies, body-related stereotypes have become strongly associated with weight and fatness. These attitudes have been described as weight bias (Puhl & Heuer, 2009; Spiel et al., 2016), weight stereotypes (Holub, Tan, & Patel, 2011), or weight stigma (Latner, Simmonds, Rosewall, & Stunkard, 2007; Puhl & Suh, 2015). In this chapter, weight bias will be used to capture all these terms. Weight bias typically takes the form of positive attitudes about individuals with thinner body sizes, such as the belief that thinner people are intelligent, friendly, successful, and strong-willed, and negative attitudes about fatter people, including that fatter people are unintelligent, unhappy, unsuccessful, lazy, and weak-willed (Damiano, Gregg, et al., 2015; Latner et al., 2007).

These externalized body image attitudes are important to understand for two reasons. First, holding these attitudes may result in the discrimination of individuals with larger body sizes, and this effect is well documented (Puhl & Heuer, 2009). In children, this discrimination frequently results in children with larger body sizes being teased, isolated, bullied, or victimized with resulting low self-esteem, body dissatisfaction, disordered eating, and mental health problems as the target of this discrimination (Eisenberg, Neumark-Sztainer, & Story, 2003; Jendrzyca & Warschburger, 2016; Latner & Schwartz, 2005; Strauss & Pollack, 2003). Cooley, Elenbaas, and Killen (2016) suggest that children who are socially excluded due to biases are at risk for elevated mental health problems and decreased academic motivation; and those being excluded as well as those who are excluding their peers, are likely to miss out on positive social development through interactions with diverse peers.

Second, weight bias attitudes, first held in relation to others, may then be internalized and used as a measure to judge the self. Thus, internalized weight bias is the belief that weight-based stereotypes and prejudices are accurate and apply to the self (Durso & Latner, 2008). In adolescents and adults internalization of weight bias has been found to be associated with greater body dissatisfaction and more negative mental and physical health outcomes in overweight adolescents and adults (Latner, Durso, & Mond, 2013).

Research is demonstrating that preschool-aged children are beginning to report weight biases, such that they are favoring thinner bodies (Musher-Eizenman, Holub, Edwards-Leeper, Persson, & Goldstein, 2003) and attributing negative qualities to overweight bodies and positive qualities to thin bodies (Damiano, Gregg, et al., 2015; Spiel et al., 2016). Additionally, 5–8 year olds appear to be endorsing the importance of thinness (Dittmar, Halliwell, & Ive, 2006). Although children are presenting with such attitudes, to date, very little research has explored whether weight bias is internalized in children or what effects weight bias internalization may have, and it would not be surprising that this parallels the negative impacts observed in adolescents and adults.

2. MEASUREMENT OF BODY IMAGE ATTITUDES IN CHILDREN

In the current literature, it is difficult to identify at what age children begin to experience body satisfaction and dissatisfaction in the same way this has been described in the adolescent and adult literature. By 9 months infants are able to discriminate their own image from another child's in photographs and by 2 years can label their own image (Lewis & Brooks-Gunn, 1979). However, it has been difficult to gain a sense of at what point children start to evaluate their body. As discussed further later (Section 3.2.4), children frequently start to engage in social comparisons in preschool years (Smolak, 2011) and this may include social comparison and subsequent evaluation of their body. One reason, little is known about this early developmental stage is the lack of longitudinal research from early childhood; however, limited longitudinal data are largely due to the difficulty in assessing body image in very young children using reliable and valid measures. Similarly, the assessment of weight bias in children is a relatively new endeavor with comparable measurement concerns. Herein, we will describe the current tools used to assess child body image and weight bias and the evidence for their use.

2.1 Measuring Children's Body Dissatisfaction

A commonly used method for assessing body image (i.e., body satisfaction or dissatisfaction) in children has been the use of a figure rating scale in an interview situation whereby children are shown age- and gender-matched pictorial representations of an array of body sizes ranging from very thin to very large. Children are then asked to select the image they perceive they currently look like (current) and the image they would most like to look like (ideal). A current-ideal discrepancy score is then calculated by subtracting the current figure minus ideal figure.

Although this method has been commonly reported for the assessment of body dissatisfaction in younger (Damiano, Gregg, et al., 2015; Damiano, Paxton, Wertheim, McLean, & Gregg, 2015; Lowes & Tiggemann, 2003; Musher-Eizenman et al., 2003) and older (Harrison, 2000; Truby & Paxton, 2002) children, the figure rating scale methodology has varied across researchers in terms of pictorial representation and the number of figures included. With some exceptions, researchers tend to use fewer figures with young children to simplify the task. The Children's Body Image Scale (CBIS) is a 7-figure scale of computer-modified photographs of children used in interviews with 7–12 year old (Truby & Paxton, 2002), while the children's figure rating scale (Tiggemann & Pennington, 1990) is a 9-figure scale of silhouette drawings used with young children aged 5–8 years (Lowes & Tiggemann, 2003). Musher-Eizenman et al. (2003) used a 7-figure scale of silhouette drawings as an age-modified version from the scale originally developed by Collins (1991), that assessed body image in children aged 4–6. Spiel, Paxton, and Yager (2012) later modified the display of Tiggemann and Pennington's (1990) scale by creating 2D felt dolls wearing a bathing suit to depict the different body sizes to assess weight biases in 3- to 5-year-old children, in which children were required to select a hair color close to theirs. More recently, a 5-figure version of the felt dolls used by Spiel et al. (2012) that was adapted from Tiggemann and Pennington's (1990) scale was employed to assess body image in children as young as four (Damiano, Gregg, et al., 2015) and a 5-figure silhouette version was used with 5-year-old children (Damiano, Paxton, et al., 2015) (see Figs. 1 and 2).

Interestingly, despite the common use of the current-ideal discrepancy score to assess body image in children, only a few researchers have assessed the reliability and validity of the tool. Truby and Paxton (2002) demonstrated construct validity of the CBIS and adequate test–retest reliability of the discrepancy score (2008) in 7- to 12-year-old children. Damiano, Gregg, et al. (2015) reported adequate test–retest reliability of the 5-figure rating scale used to assess body image in 4-year-old children. Thus, there is some evidence to support the use of the discrepancy score in older and younger children as a measure of body dissatisfaction.

Other commonly used measures of body dissatisfaction include questionnaire measures, in particular, the Body Esteem Scale (BES) (Mendelson & White, 1982) and the Body Satisfaction Scale (BSS) (Slade, Dewey, Newton, Brodie, & Kiemle, 1990). The BES asks children to respond yes or no to 24 statements about their satisfaction with their body or some aspect of their appearance, with high scores indicating higher body esteem

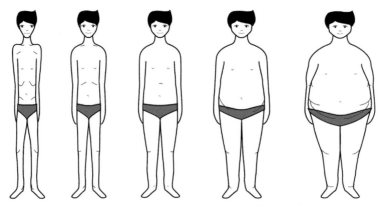

Fig. 1 The Children's Body Image Development Study silhouette figure rating scale for boys who chose *black hair*.

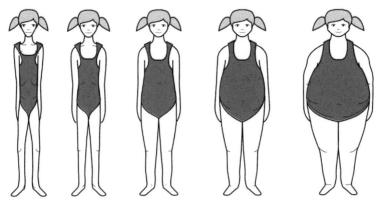

Fig. 2 The Children's Body Image Development Study silhouette figure rating scale for girls who chose *blonde hair*.

(e.g., "I'm pretty happy about the way I look"). The BES has shown to have good internal reliability ($\alpha = 0.73$) in younger age groups of 4- to 6-year-old children (Davison & Birch, 2001) and good split-half reliability ($r = 0.85$, $p < 0.002$) and concurrent validity in 7- to 12-year-old children (Mendelson & White, 1982).

The BSS is designed to assess an individual's satisfaction with 16 body parts or aspects of their body (e.g., height, weight, body shape, thighs, stomach, and face) on a 7-point Likert scale of satisfaction (Slade et al., 1990). Variations of the BSS have been used by numerous researchers who have explored the effects of a body image prevention program for older children (ranging from 4th to 7th grades) using a written questionnaire (Haines, Neumark-Sztainer, Perry, Hannan, & Levine, 2006; McVey, Tweed, & Blackmore, 2007; Neumark-Sztainer, Sherwood, Coller, & Hannan, 2000). In these studies the composite scale of body dissatisfaction showed good internal reliability.

There are, however, a number of important considerations when attempting to assess body image in children at a time when their attitudes are still forming. In relation to the current-ideal discrepancy score it is unknown if there is an ideal number of body figures to appropriately assess body dissatisfaction as the scales used in previous research have included a 5-, 7-, or 9-figure rating scale. Another potential challenge with the use of the discrepancy score is determining whether a child wanting to be larger (i.e., selection of a larger ideal than current figure) is an indication of actual body dissatisfaction or young children's common desire to grow or wanting to be more muscular. To better understand the true meaning of such a score longitudinal data may be required that can assess the changes in children's preferences over time, and qualitative data may be necessary to triangulate the extent to which children are concerned with their current body size when they are choosing a different ideal size. It will also be important for future research to identify whether a desire to be larger is measuring fat or muscle size.

2.2 Measuring Children's Weight Bias

Various measures currently exist to assess weight bias in children. For example, Latner and Stunkard (2003) assessed weight bias in fifth and sixth grade children using illustrations from Richardson, Goodman, Hastorf, and Dornbusch (1961), whereby children were shown six same-sex images: a "healthy" child (with no visible disability), a child holding crutches with one leg in a brace, a child sitting in a wheelchair, a child with no left hand, a child with a facial disfigurement to the mouth, and a child who was obese. Children were asked to select their preference from most to least liked of the six drawings. No validity or reliability information is available for this scale.

Increasingly, attempts have been made to assess weight bias in children using interview protocols, particularly from the preschool years. Early work by Cramer and Steinwert (1998) in 3- to 5-year-old children explored the presence of weight bias by reading children two short stories about girls and two about boys in which one character was considered mean and one nice based on their behavior in the story. Children were asked to select from a thin figure or a chubby figure the one that was mean and nice. Cramer and Steinwert (1998) also used an Adjective Attribution Task in which children were presented with 12 positive (e.g., smart) and 12 negative (e.g., stupid) adjectives, and with each word were asked to select between a thin, average, and overweight figure to represent the adjective presented. No information on the psychometric properties of these scales are available as predominantly frequency type information was reported.

A similar method was described by Musher-Eizenman, Holub, Miller, Goldstein, and Edwards-Leeper (2004), whereby during an interview children were presented with adjective pairs. In each pair, children were presented with a positive adjective (e.g., nice) and a negative adjective (e.g., mean), and were asked to place a very thin, average weight, and overweight silhouette drawing of a child, using Collins (1991) drawings, on a 7-point scale between the two polar adjectives (Musher-Eizenman et al., 2004). This was repeated for six adjective pairs and three scores were calculated (average for overweight figure, average for thin figure, and difference between the average and overweight figure) to demonstrate weight bias. The overweight scale score has shown adequate reliability in 4- to 6-year-old children (Holub, 2008; Musher-Eizenman et al., 2004).

Birbeck and Drummond (2005) used the nine silhouette figures developed by Tiggemann and Pennington (1990) and presented each figure on a standard sheet of paper and allowed children to place the images in any order they chose. Children were then asked to select three of the figures they would invite to their birthday party and were asked to provide reasons for their choices. The qualitative information collected validated the data.

Spiel et al. (2012) measured weight bias in 3–5 year olds using the nine felt figures introduced earlier ranging from (1) very thin to (9) obese. Children were asked two lines of questioning to assess weight bias. First, similar to Birbeck and Drummond's (2005) interview procedure children were asked four social questions, including which figure they: (1) would invite to their birthday party, (2) would not invite to their birthday party, (3) has the most friends, and (4) has the least friends. Second, children were read eight stories from an illustrated gender-matched storybook designed for the research that asked children to identify which of the nine figures they thought represented the child in the story. The characteristics assessed included naughty/good, happy/sad, mean/nice, and active/lazy. The story helped to place each adjective in context, which was thought to be particularly useful for such young children. Spiel et al. (2012) subjected child responses to these questions to a principal components analysis, and subsequently a 3-item scale for negative characteristics and a 3-item scale for positive characteristics were examined and yielded adequate internal consistency.

Subsequently, Damiano, Gregg, et al. (2015) reported on the Children's Body Size Attitudes Scale, for which the questions asked of 4-year-old children in an interview setting were an adaptation of the measures described by Spiel et al. (2012), Cramer and Steinwert (1998), and Birbeck and Drummond (2005). Following pilot testing of measures, reported in Damiano, Gregg, et al. (2015), to assess negative body size attitudes children were asked four social questions (who: they would not invite to their birthday; has no friends to play with; plays by him/herself; other children do not like); and were read three illustrated stories of a child who was mean, naughty, and rude. To assess positive body size attitudes children were asked two social questions (who: they would invite to their birthday; has lots of friends to play with) and were read four illustrated stories of a child who was good, happy, fun, and clever. For each question, children were asked to select a figure from the figure rating scale described previously, which included five felt figures placed on a board from thinnest to largest. Mean scores for each scale were calculated with higher scores on the negative attitudes scale indicating children attribute negative qualities to larger figures, and lower scores on the positive attitudes scale indicating children attribute positive qualities to thinner figures. Damiano, Gregg, et al. (2015) reported adequate internal reliability for both scales in the study sample, as well as providing information from a pilot study with children (mean age 4.65 years) supporting the internal reliability, test–retest reliability, and construct validity of the scales.

Evidently there are a small number of measures that have been developed to assess children's weight bias. These measures have typically involved the use of body figures to assess children's attitudes and have been shown to be valid and reliable for young children. There is, however, a dearth of measures that may assist in evaluating how children may internalize such weight biases to apply to their own bodies; tools to assess children's internalization of weight bias are needed.

3. BODY DISSATISFACTION IN CHILDREN

3.1 Prevalence of Body Dissatisfaction in Children

Body dissatisfaction appears to increase across childhood, but in the early years children are usually free of these concerns. As described earlier, measurement of body image concerns in very young children has not proved easy and few studies have been conducted in this area. However, we know that at 4 years the majority of children are satisfied with their current body size. Damiano, Gregg, et al. (2015) noted that with 4-year-old girls, using a 5-figure rating scale from very thin (1) to very large (5), the mean current figure size selected was 2.13, while the mean ideal figure size selected was a little larger at 2.31. Of girls, 13.3% selected a thinner ideal figure, 62.3% desired the same figure size (i.e., satisfaction), and 24.4% selected a larger figure. A similar pattern was observed in 4-year-old boys for whom the mean current figure size selected was 2.09, while the mean ideal figure size selected was a little larger at 2.36. For boys, 6.4% selected a thinner ideal figure, 72.2% desired the same figure size (i.e., satisfaction), and 21.4% selected a larger desired figure. Thus, even at this young age children generally perceive themselves as thin and if they wish to have a different body size they are more likely to select a slightly larger one; notably the desired figure is still below the average sized figure (3).

To date, very few studies have quantified body dissatisfaction in 5- to 8-year-old boys. However, research with 5- to 8-year-old girls shows a pattern of increasing desire for a thinner body size. In one cross-sectional study using a 9-point figure rating scale, Dohnt and Tiggemann (2006a) found that 32.3% of 5 year olds wished to be thinner, 19.4% wished to be the same size, and 48.4% wished to be larger. However, at age 6 years, this balance had changed and 46.7% wished to be thinner, 36.7% wished to be the same size, and 16.7% wished to be larger. By 8 years, although the proportion wishing to be thinner did not change greatly, only 9.4% desired a larger body. The authors concluded that 6 years is likely to be an important time for the development of a desire to be thinner in girls. Using questionnaire measures, Davison et al. (2003) observed a different pattern from 5- to 7- to 9-year-old girls with declines in weight concerns and body dissatisfaction with age. Although the reason for this is not clear, assessment techniques were different and as questionnaire measures assess emotional intensity to a greater extent than figure rating scales, it may be that emotions around body image concerns do not significantly increase across this age period.

As dieting is widely viewed in the Western world to be an appropriate response to body dissatisfaction, especially weight concerns, research has also explored the emergence of dietary restraint or reported changes in eating to avoid getting fat and knowledge of the dieting concept. One study found that of 5-year-old girls, 37% reported moderate levels of dietary restraint (Damiano, Paxton, et al., 2015). At 5 years, a small proportion of children have an awareness that diets are associated with food (Rodgers, Wertheim, Damiano, Gregg, & Paxton, 2015) but by 6 years old, over 40% of girls are aware of dieting as a means of controlling weight (Dohnt & Tiggemann, 2006a).

Between 7 and 12 years, research consistently shows that close to a half of girls wish to be thinner. Clark and Tiggemann (2006) found that 49% of girls in this age range selected a thinner body ideal than current figure, although less than 15% could be considered overweight. Also using a figure rating scale, Truby and Paxton (2002) found that 48% of girls wished to have a smaller figure, 42% wanted to stay the same, 10% wanted a larger body, and in a different sample, 52% of girls wished to have a smaller figure, 39% wanted to stay the same, and 9% wanted a larger body (Truby & Paxton, 2008). Schur, Sanders, and Steiner (2000) observed a slightly lower desire for another body figure size, with 41.9% selecting a thinner ideal than current body size, 51.6% desiring no change, and 6.5% selecting a larger ideal than current body size. Although when using figure rating scales little difference in the proportion of girls in grades 4–7 who select a thinner ideal than current figure was found by Clark and Tiggemann (2006), they did observe that there was a significant decline in body esteem across these grades suggesting that the intensity of body image concerns increases in girls during later childhood.

In a review of nine studies of body image in preadolescent boys using figure rating scales, Ricciardelli, McCabe, Mussap, and Holt (2009) found estimates of the desire to be thinner to range between 27% and 47%, and estimates of the number of boys who desired to be larger ranged between 15% and 44%. The authors note that the proportion of boys desiring a thinner body had increased since an earlier review (Ricciardelli & McCabe, 2001) at which time the estimate ranged between 17% and 30%. However, it is important to note that body figure rating scales typically used in this assessment do not examine a desire to be both leaner and more muscular, and thus may miss an important aspect of body image concerns in boys as the majority of boys have been found to rate both their weight (58.5%) and muscles (59.5%) as important (Ricciardelli, McCabe, Lillis, & Thomas, 2006).

3.2 Correlates and Predictors of Body Dissatisfaction
3.2.1 Theoretical Models of Predictors of Body Image
Ways to help conceptualize the development of sense of self and sense of body in infancy have largely drawn on psychoanalytic and attachment theories and have been very well described by Knafo (2016) who highlights that the very early development of one's sense of body is associated with development of autonomy, cognition, and self-recognition, and is closely linked to the development of self-esteem. Care and attention to an infant's body and bodily needs is proposed to influence development of self-worth and body esteem. As Knafo (2016) points out, these early experiences are likely to be very influential in the development of body image; however, they do not lend themselves easily to investigation. In relation to children, research that has recently focused on correlates and predictors of body image and body dissatisfaction has largely been guided by theoretical models of the development of body dissatisfaction used widely with adolescent samples. Sociocultural theories have been particularly influential in this respect.

A leading sociocultural theory, the Tripartite Influence Model (Thompson et al., 1999), proposes that three sociocultural factors, media, family, and peer pressures to conform to social appearance ideals, influence the development of body dissatisfaction. The influence of these risk factors is mediated by two cognitive processes, internalization of social appearance or media ideals (i.e., the extent to which an individual subscribes to social appearance ideals as their personal standard) and body comparison (i.e., the tendency to compare one's appearance with the appearance of another) (Thompson et al., 1999).

There is substantial support for this model in adolescents based on cross-sectional and prospective studies (e.g., Keery, van den Berg, & Thompson, 2004; Rodgers, Chabrol, & Paxton, 2011; Rodgers, McLean, & Paxton, 2015). This model has been extended by a number of authors to include additional variables within a biopsychosocial model of risk factors for body dissatisfaction (e.g., Mitchell, Petrie, Greenleaf, & Martin, 2015; Rodgers, Paxton, & McLean, 2014). Biopsychosocial models not only include the influence of sociocultural variables but also propose that body size and psychological predisposition (including low self-esteem and depressive symptoms) play a role. This model also has cross-sectional and prospective support in adolescents (e.g., Mitchell et al., 2015; Rodgers, McLean, et al., 2015; Rodgers et al., 2014). Although these models have not been fully tested with children, they have informed research examining correlates and predictors of body image in children.

3.2.2 Correlates and Predictors in Young Children

Consistent with the biopsychosocial model, a small number of studies of young girls have found that greater weight concerns are associated with higher weight status (Davison et al., 2003) and higher BMI predicts the development of body dissatisfaction (Dohnt & Tiggemann, 2006b). Although the reason for this has not been confirmed, it is clear that from a very young age children are exposed to sociocultural influences that endorse weight stigmatizing attitudes. For example, a content analysis of popular children's videos and books found many videos, though relatively few books, emphasized the importance of physical appearance and portrayed body stereotypes (Herbozo, Tantleff-Dunn, Gokee-Laros, & Thompson, 2004). Interestingly, although exposure to children's television did not predict the development of body dissatisfaction in 5- to 8-year-old girls at a 1-year follow-up, it did predict heightened dieting awareness (Dohnt & Tiggemann, 2006b). Further, media exposure was a cross-sectional predictor of dietary restraint in 5-year-old girls (Damiano, Paxton, et al., 2015). These findings suggest that children's media are likely to provide information about appearance ideals and their relation to actual body size, which may be internalized at a later age.

Peer factors have also been proposed to influence the development of body image attitudes in sociocultural and biopsychosocial models, and there is support for the role of peer influences in young girls. In a longitudinal study of 5- to 8-year-old girls, perceived peer body dissatisfaction predicted the development of body dissatisfaction 1 year later (Dohnt & Tiggemann, 2006b), and in a cross-sectional study of 5-year-old girls, peer appearance conversations (e.g., about clothes and hair) predicted dietary restraint (Damiano, Paxton, et al., 2015).

Two experimental studies also implicate sociocultural influences in the development of body image concerns in young children. Dittmar and colleagues (2006) found that 5- to 8-year-old girls who were exposed to images of Barbie then reported lower body esteem and greater desire for thinness compared to those who were exposed to Emme (a US size 16 doll) or no doll. This effect was already evident in 5.5- to 6.5-year-old girls, but was more pronounced in 6.5- to 7.5-year-old girls. Interestingly, in the older age group, exposure to Emme resulted in an increased desire to be thinner when an adult. The authors propose that for these older girls who may already have internalized the thin ideal, this doll may represent a possible but feared future self.

Parents are the third proposed sociocultural influence on development of body image. A recent experimental study by Perez, Kroon Van Diest, Smith, and Sladek (2016, early view) provides support for a relation between mother's body dissatisfaction and body dissatisfaction in their 5- to 7-year-old daughters. Both girls and their mothers completed an interview assessment of a number of body image attitudes. In addition, both girls and their mothers were randomly assigned to either (a) a mirror activity in which they were asked only to give positive comments about their body, or (b) a mirror activity in which there were no instructions about what to say, and their comments during this activity were recorded. Mothers and daughters completed the mirror activity independently. As an index of body satisfaction, the number of positive (i.e., satisfaction) and negative (i.e., dissatisfaction) body comments were counted. In the next phase of the study, mothers and daughters engaged in the mirror activity together and mothers were given the same instructions they received in the first phase. They found that daughters' internalization of the thin ideal was significantly correlated with mothers' body dissatisfaction and self-objectification, and daughters' self-objectification was associated with mothers' self-objectification. In the joint mirror condition, Perez et al. (2016) observed that when mothers talked positively about her own body, daughters were also more likely to talk favorably about their body. They found that girls changed their positive and negative comments after being exposed to their mother's comments to be more in line with their mothers' responses. The authors concluded that their study provided evidence that young girls modeled their body image attitudes after their mothers' attitudes.

Psychological variables, in particular low self-esteem and depressive symptoms, have also been proposed to contribute to the development of body dissatisfaction in biopsychosocial models of the development of body dissatisfaction (Rodgers, McLean, et al., 2015). These factors have been found to predict the later development of body dissatisfaction in adolescents girls and boys (e.g., Paxton et al., 2006). In addition, perfectionistic traits have been implicated in the development of risk factors for eating disorders, including weight and shape concerns in adolescent girls (e.g., Wade, Wilksch, Paxton, Byrne, & Austin, 2015). However, there has been little research that has explored relations between these variables in young children. In recent research, however, Nichols et al. (2016) found that in 6-year-old girls and boys, lower child reported self-esteem was associated with lower body esteem. In addition, higher children's self-reported socially prescribed and self-oriented perfectionism was associated with lower body esteem, and greater dietary restraint in boys and girls. Although these findings are based on cross-sectional data, they suggest that relations among these variables should be explored further in young children.

Taken together, the findings from these studies suggest that there is growing support for relations among child BMI, social environment variables (media, peer, and parent), and psychological variables and body dissatisfaction in young children. Further research is required to identify the relative roles of these variables and the direction of relations.

3.2.3 Correlates and Predictors in Older Children
A larger body of research has examined correlates and predictors of body dissatisfaction in older children compared to younger children, and a greater number of studies have examined pathways to the development of body dissatisfaction, along with possible mediators and mechanisms of action. Research also substantially supports a biopsychosocial model of the development of body image problems.

As in younger children and adolescents, larger body size has typically been found to predict greater body dissatisfaction, desire to be thinner, and strategies to lose weight in older girls and boys in both cross-sectional and prospective studies (e.g., Anschutz, Kanters, Van Strien, Vermulst, & Engles, 2009; Clark & Tiggemann, 2008; Field et al., 2001; Holt & Ricciardelli, 2002; Jendrzyca & Warschburger, 2016; Lunde, Frisén, & Hwang, 2007; Ricciardelli et al., 2006; Sands & Wardle, 2003; Schur et al., 2000). In older children, actual and perceived body size are fairly closely matched so they appear to be aware that they have a larger body size (Truby & Paxton, 2002). In addition, as described further in Section 4, weight bias attitudes are strongly held by older children and consequently larger children are frequently teased and stigmatized for their larger weight from many sources in their environment including peers, parents, and educators (Puhl & Latner, 2007). Not surprisingly, body dissatisfaction is one of the numerous negative mental health consequences of weight bias (Puhl & Latner, 2007).

Exploration of sociocultural correlates of body dissatisfaction and related behaviors such as dieting (particularly in girls) or weight change strategies (particularly in boys) has also focused on media exposure, and peer and family influences. For example, cross-sectional relations have been observed in children between greater exposure to appearance focused magazines (Sands & Wardle, 2003), and more frequently watching soaps and music videos, and higher body dissatisfaction (Anschutz, Engels, Van Leeuwe, & van Strien, 2009). There is also support for both direct and indirect parental influences on children's body dissatisfaction in children with a mean age of 10.1 years (Haines, Neumark-Sztainer, Hannan, & Robinson-O'Brien, 2008). Haines et al. (2008) observed that when children reported that their parents commented about their weight or encouraged them to diet, they were more likely to have higher body dissatisfaction, regardless of actual BMI, and when children reported that their parents dieted or commented on their own weight, they were more likely to experience body dissatisfaction; although there was no relationship between when parents reported dieting or making comments about their own weight and children's body dissatisfaction. Consistent with these findings, Anschutz, Kanters, et al. (2009a) found that children's perception of higher levels of maternal encouragement to be thin was associated with greater body dissatisfaction and restrained eating.

Of particular interest in this age group, however, are the more extensive prospective studies that enhance our understanding of risk factors, as well as more cross-sectional and longitudinal studies that have examined pathways to the development of body dissatisfaction with particular attention to potential mediating variables. Prospective studies have not yielded consistent longitudinal support for relations between sociocultural factors and body image outcomes. Field et al. (2001) followed up 9- and 14-year-old girls and boys, and found that children who reported making a lot of effort to look like same-sex figures in the media at 9 years predicted becoming very concerned with their weight by age 14. Further, when children reported that thinness was important to fathers they were more likely to become constant dieters at 14. However, neither peer concern about weight nor peer or adult teasing predicted the development of body image concerns. Similarly, in a sample of 9- to 12-year-old girls in a 1-year follow-up study, no prospective relationships were observed between exposure to appearance-related television and magazines, and peer appearance conversations assessed at Time 1 and body esteem assessed at Time 2 (Clark & Tiggemann, 2008). The authors suggest that it is possible that these sociocultural variables may have had an influence prior to the assessment period.

In one of the few longitudinal studies of boys aged between 8- and 11-years old, Ricciardelli et al. (2006) found that although initial BMI was the only prospective predictor of body dissatisfaction, perceived pressure to modify weight and muscles from parents, peers, and media prospectively predicted use of body change strategies. Further research with boys in this age group is clearly required.

3.2.4 Mediators of Sociocultural Influences in Older Children

A number of studies with older children support roles for internalization of social appearance ideals and body comparison tendencies as mediators between sociocultural influences and body dissatisfaction. In girls, cross-sectional studies indicate that internalization of appearance ideals mediates relations between: perceptions of maternal and peer concerns about weight and eating; exposure to appearance-related magazines and body dissatisfaction (Sands & Wardle, 2003); and watching soaps and music videos and body dissatisfaction and restrained eating (Anschutz, Engels, et al., 2009b). A further cross-sectional study of 9- to 12-year-old girls found that appearance media exposure predicted peer appearance conversations, which predicted internalization of thin ideals, which in turn, predicted body dissatisfaction (Clark & Tiggemann, 2006).

Prospective studies have not provided as strong support for a mediating role for internalization between sociocultural influences and body dissatisfaction (e.g., Clark & Tiggemann, 2008). However, in a study of girls with an average age of 8.72 years in a follow-up after 1 year, Harrison and Hefner

(2006) found that television viewing predicted a thinner future body ideal 1 year later and also predicted greater eating disorder symptomatology. Further longitudinal research, especially with data collected at more than two time points, is required to clarify the role of internalization in the development of body dissatisfaction. It is notable that no studies, of which we are aware, have examined these relations in boys.

Despite body comparison having been identified as an important contributor to body dissatisfaction in adolescents and adults (Myers & Crowther, 2009; Rodgers, McLean, et al., 2015), little research has explored the role of body comparison in children. Smolak (2011) proposes that preschoolers can compare themselves to another child and by 8 years of age compare themselves to many other children in a number of domains including physical appearance. Holt and Ricciardelli (2002) explored body comparison in 8- to 10-year-old girls and boys, and found that 30% engaged in body comparison. However, body comparison did not predict body dissatisfaction but rather was a unique predictor of concerns about muscles and exercising in boys. More recently, Tatangelo and Ricciardelli (2016) examined peer- and media-related comparisons in 8- to 10-year-old children and found that peers were more important targets for comparison than media figures. Girls were most likely to make appearance-related social comparisons, often resulting in self-criticism, while boys were more likely to make sport and abilities-related social comparisons. It would be valuable to further explore the emergence of body comparisons and their role in body image attitudes in children.

4. WEIGHT BIAS IN CHILDREN

4.1 Prevalence of Weight Bias in Children

Research indicates that weight bias against overweight-children has become greater over recent decades with one study of 10–11 year olds showing that an obese child was liked significantly less in 2003 than 1961 (Latner & Stunkard, 2003). Further, it is clear that weight bias starts very early in life. In one of the earliest studies of weight bias in young children, Cramer and Steinwert (1998) found that weight bias was clearly present in 3-year-old children. Subsequent studies support this finding. In a cross-sectional study, Spiel et al. (2012) found that 3-year-old children selected thinner figures to illustrate positive characteristics in children than negative characteristics, and that this difference was significantly more marked in 5 year olds. In a further sample of 3 year olds followed-up after 1 year, weight bias was already present at 3 years of age, and at 1-year follow-up, weight bias had increased such that figures selected for positive characteristics were thinner and figures selected for negative characteristics were fatter than a year earlier (Spiel et al., 2016). In addition, in a large sample of 6- to 11-year-old children, indicative of the presence of weight bias, 12.2% of children reported being teased about their weight and higher proportions of obese- and overweight-children than normal-weight children reported experiencing weight stigma (Jendrzyca & Warschburger, 2016). Interestingly, children who perceive themselves as heavier were found to hold fewer antifat attitudes (Holub, 2008). Although research in this area is not extensive, it is clear that weight bias is widespread in young children and that this continues through childhood.

4.2 Predictors of Weight Bias

As with body dissatisfaction, sociocultural influences have been proposed to contribute to the learning of weight bias in children. In particular, parental modeling of weight bias attitudes and transmission through negative portrayal of overweight people in media have been proposed (Latner & Schwartz, 2005). Research examining sociocultural predictors of weight bias in children has focused on the relation between parent weight bias and body image attitudes and weight bias in their children. Although not consistently observed (e.g., Davison & Birch, 2004), relations between mothers' attitudes and their daughters' attitudes have been found, and fathers' attitudes and their sons' attitudes have frequently been found.

In one small study of both young girls and boys, mothers' fear of fat was found to predict children's negative stereotypes toward overweight peers (Holub et al., 2011). In larger studies that have examined young girls and boys separately in relation to attitudes of both their parents a gender transmission of weight bias attitudes appears to be apparent. For example, in relation to 4-year-old girls, attributing positive characteristics to thinner figures, indicative of a greater positive weight bias, has been shown to be cross-sectionally associated with greater maternal dieting (Damiano, Gregg, et al., 2015) and also predicted by maternal dieting assessed 1 year previously (Spiel et al., 2016). Relationships between young boys' attitudes and father's attitudes were more consistent at this age. In 4-year-old boys, positive weight bias (i.e., attributing positive qualities to thinner figures) was cross sectionally associated with greater paternal negative attitudes toward obese people and more paternal dieting, while greater negative weight bias (i.e., attributing negative qualities to larger figures) was associated with greater paternal negative attitudes about obese people (Damiano, Gregg, et al., 2015). Furthermore, paternal negative attitudes about obese people assessed a year earlier predicted both positive and negative weight bias in boys (Spiel et al., 2016).

To date, little research has examined predictors of weight bias in older children. It might be expected that peer attitudes and behaviors become greater determinants of weight bias as children enter school.

5. APPROACHES TO PREVENTION OF BODY DISSATISFACTION AND WEIGHT BIAS IN CHILDREN

In light of research that demonstrates that weight bias, and in some instances body dissatisfaction, emerge during childhood, many authors have highlighted the need for interventions that promote positive body image attitudes in children (e.g., Clark & Tiggemann, 2006, 2008; Perez et al., 2016; Sands & Wardle, 2003; Tiggemann & Slater, 2014). Consequently, a number of prevention interventions have been conducted. These have typically aimed to reduce risk factors for body dissatisfaction while enhancing potential protective factors. The ecological model of prevention purports that given the diverse external factors influencing children's body size attitudes, efforts for preventing body dissatisfaction, and weight bias must include not only enhancing children's critical skills and knowledge but also attempt to make changes to peer and school environments, family attitudes and behaviors, and societal body attitudes often conveyed through the media (Levine & McVey, 2012). Prevention interventions in children have aimed to achieve this in different ways.

Prevention programs for children have typically been universal programs, that is, they involve all children in a group rather than those who are particularly at risk of developing body image problems, or holding weight bias attitudes. Universal programs are considered ideal as they attempt to prevent body dissatisfaction during its formative stages and before it becomes part of a child's life. Selective or indicated interventions that are specifically for children at risk have not been used, partly because the measurement challenges described in Section 2 makes it difficult to accurately and confidently identify which children are at significant risk of body dissatisfaction. In addition, as weight bias is so widespread it is likely that encouraging appreciation of diversity in all children will be beneficial. As body dissatisfaction is frequently present in late adolescence and adulthood, indicated programs that address existing body image problems and its risk factors are more frequently implemented for these age groups (Watson et al., 2016). However, as the research described earlier shows, universal interventions for these older age groups may often be too late to prevent the development of body image concerns.

5.1 Prevention in Young Children

There are no prevention interventions designed for delivery to young children to prevent body dissatisfaction and weight bias. There is, however, recognition that parents can play an important role in preventing body dissatisfaction and other eating disorder risk factors in their young children (Hart, Cornell, Damiano, & Paxton, 2015). Despite the role that parents play in the development of body image attitudes, many parents do not have an accurate concept of body image and there is a lack of resources available to guide parents in ways to provide a positive body image environment for their young children (Hart, Damiano, Cornell, & Paxton, 2015). Recently, Hart, Damiano, Chittleborough, Paxton, and Jorm (2014) developed guidelines for parents of 2- to 6-year-old children to promote a positive body image and healthy eating patterns, based on expert consensus. Subsequently the "Confident Body, Confident Child" resource was developed for parents of young children, aged 2–6 years, to guide parents in creating an environment that fosters positive body image attitudes (Hart, Damiano, & Paxton, 2016). Results from a randomized controlled trial of the program have shown that at 6 weeks postintervention significant improvements in parenting variables associated with childhood risk for body dissatisfaction were found for parents who received the Confident Body, Confident Child program, including parenting intentions to implement positive body image behaviors and knowledge of child body image and healthy eating patterns (Hart et al., 2016). Outcomes for the children are not yet available, and future translation and cross-cultural research is required.

As mentioned, no specific program exists to target body image attitudes in young children. However, Dohnt and Tiggemann (2008) evaluated the effects of reading the children's book "Shapesville," which encourages body acceptance and appreciation of diversity in appearance, to 5- to 9-year-old girls. Following reading of the book, improvements were found in appearance satisfaction and stereotyping on the basis of shape and weight was reduced, and weight reduction was maintained at a 6-week follow-up (Dohnt & Tiggemann, 2008). Trend level changes were found for reductions in weight stigma (Dohnt & Tiggemann, 2008).

5.2 Prevention in Older Children

Despite attempts at incorporating a parent component in body dissatisfaction or eating disorder prevention programs for older children, little prevention research with older children has successfully included parents in programs, with small sample sizes and lack of parent engagement being considered as major hurdles (Hart, Cornell, et al., 2015). Universal prevention programs aimed at older children have typically been delivered in primary school environments.

Internalization of appearance ideals has been considered an important target for body dissatisfaction prevention programs for older children by a number of researchers (e.g., Clark & Tiggemann, 2008; Sands & Wardle, 2003). Media exposure and peer variables, such as peer appearance conversations, that promote internalization of appearance ideals have particularly been identified as suitable targets for preventions programs aimed at improving body image (Clark & Tiggemann, 2006). Examples of programs that have aimed to improve body image and have been empirically evaluated in older boys and girls include "ACE kids" (McCabe, Ricciardelli, & Salmon, 2006), "Beautiful from the inside out" (Norwood, Murray, Nolan, & Bowker, 2011), and an adapted version of "Happy Being Me" (Bird, Halliwell, Diedrichs, & Harcourt, 2013), while programs only targeting older girls include "Free to Be Me" (Neumark-Sztainer et al., 2000), and "Y's girl" (Ross, Paxton, & Rodgers, 2013). A number of programs resulted in improvements in body satisfaction and appearance ideal internalization (Bird et al., 2013; Norwood et al., 2011; Ross et al., 2013), as well as improvements in appearance comparisons and appearance conversations (Bird et al., 2013; Ross et al., 2013). However, other programs showed no effects on body image (McCabe et al., 2006; Neumark-Sztainer et al., 2000).

Similar to those for body image, programs that have targeted weight bias have also typically incorporated a peer component with the aim of reducing appearance-based teasing, rather than appearance comparisons or appearance conversations (e.g., Haines et al., 2006). Weight bias prevention programs also typically aim to teach children about size acceptance. Unlike the body image programs, fewer programs appear to exist that aim to reduce weight bias in children. One such program, "The EDAP Puppet Program" was shown to reduce stereotypes about larger body sizes in fifth grade girls. However, these were preliminary results and data from only a small sample were analyzed (Irving, 2000). Another program, "Very Important Kids" was found to reduce the frequency of teasing about appearance and weight (Haines et al., 2006). Although both program evaluations showed promising results by reducing the primary outcomes variables of weight bias (Irving, 2000) and appearance and weight teasing (Haines et al., 2006), both interventions incorporated a theatrical component, which would make broad dissemination of the program challenging.

In summary, few prevention programs targeting body image attitudes in young children exist, despite this being a time in which the foundations for these attitudes are formed. For young children, more prevention efforts are required to prevent body dissatisfaction and weight biases from forming. In the current literature, it is evident that attempts to prevent body dissatisfaction and weight bias in older children have been made and that a number of these programs have shown promise to improve such outcomes for children in the short term. Nonetheless, a number of important considerations remain for future prevention efforts in older children. Longer term follow-up is required and replication of promising interventions would be valuable in establishing support for specific interventions. In addition, school-based interventions need to be easy for teachers to deliver, rather than delivery required by psychologists or research staff (Yager & O'Dea, 2015). Finally, very few programs in older children have been designed with the aim to reduce weight bias, despite the prevalence of such attitudes reported earlier in this chapter, and the effects of weight bias on body image; thus, future programs may also aim to target both body dissatisfaction and weight bias in children.

6. CONCLUDING COMMENTS ON CHILDREN'S BODY DISSATISFACTION AND WEIGHT BIAS

Understanding factors that influence the development of body image attitudes toward the self (i.e., body satisfaction or dissatisfaction) and toward others (i.e., weight bias) is important for informing prevention efforts with the aim to mitigate the long-term implications of negative body image attitudes, including disordered eating, low self-esteem, mental health issues, and obesity. In recent years, significant progress has been made to understand the factors that are related to the development of body dissatisfaction in young girls, in particular in relation to understanding and testing theoretical models. The investigation of the development of weight bias in children is a far newer area of research. Less is known about the predictors of weight bias, despite the increasing evidence for the presence of such attitudes in early childhood. Improving our understanding about how weight bias fits into the theoretical models leading to body dissatisfaction and disordered eating in children is needed. In addition, further research is needed to understand the predictors of body dissatisfaction and weight bias for boys, especially in later childhood. Boys have been shown to respond well to prevention efforts that have mostly been developed based on the literature of girls, but identifying the most suitable targets for boys (e.g., importance of muscularity rather than thinness) is likely to aid in better long-term outcomes. Finally, future prevention programs that aim to reduce body dissatisfaction and weight bias in children may benefit from an ecological approach in which parent, peer, and school environments are targeted.

REFERENCES

Anschutz, D., Engels, R., Van Leeuwe, J., & van Strien, T. (2009). Watching your weight? The relations between watching soaps and music television and body dissatisfaction and restrained eating in young girls. *Psychology and Health, 24,* 1035–1050.

Anschutz, D. J., Kanters, L. J. A., Van Strien, T., Vermulst, A. D., & Engles, R. C. M. E. (2009). Maternal behaviors and restrained eating and body dissatisfaction in young children. *International Journal of Eating Disorders, 42,* 54–61.

Birbeck, D., & Drummond, M. (2005). Interviewing, and listening to the voices of, very young children on body image and perceptions of self. *Early Child Development and Care, 175*(6), 579–596. http://dx.doi.org/10.1080/03004430500131379.

Bird, E. L., Halliwell, E., Diedrichs, P. C., & Harcourt, D. (2013). Happy being me in the UK: A controlled evaluation of a school-based body image intervention with pre-adolescent children. *Body Image, 10*(3), 326–334. http://dx.doi.org/10.1016/j.bodyim.2013.02.008.

Cash, T. F. (2002). Cognitive behavioral perspectives on body image. In T. F. Cash & T. Pruzinsky (Eds.), *Body image: A handbook of theory, research, and clinical practice* (pp. 38–46). New York: Guilford Press.

Clark, L. A., & Tiggemann, M. (2006). Appearance culture in nine- to 12-year-old girls: Media and peer influences on body dissatisfaction. *Social Development, 15*(4), 628–643. http://dx.doi.org/10.1111/j.1467-9507.2006.00361.x.

Clark, L. A., & Tiggemann, M. (2008). Sociocultural and individual psychological predictors of body image in young girls: A prospective study. *Developmental Psychology, 44*(4), 1124.

Collins, M. E. (1991). Body figure perceptions and preferences among preadolescent children. *International Journal of Eating Disorders, 10*(2), 199–208. http://dx.doi.org/10.1002/1098-108X(199103)10:2<199::AID-EAT2260100209>3.0.CO;2-D.

Cooley, S., Elenbaas, L., & Killen, M. (2016). Chapter four—Social exclusion based on group membership is a form of prejudice. In M. D. R. Stacey, S. Horn, & S. L. Lynn (Eds.), *Advances in child development and behavior: Vol. 51* (pp. 103–129). Greenwich, USA: JAI Press.

Cramer, P., & Steinwert, T. (1998). Thin is good, fat is bad: How early does it begin? *Journal of Applied Developmental Psychology, 19*(3), 429–451. http://dx.doi.org/10.1016/S0193-3973(99)80049-5.

Damiano, S. R., Gregg, K. J., Spiel, E. C., McLean, S. A., Wertheim, E. H., & Paxton, S. J. (2015). Relationships between body size attitudes and body image of four-year-old boys and girls, and attitudes of their fathers and mothers. *Journal of Eating Disorders*, *3*, 16. http://dx.doi.org/10.1186/s40337-015-0048-0.

Damiano, S. R., Paxton, S. J., Wertheim, E. H., McLean, S. A., & Gregg, K. J. (2015). Dietary restraint of 5-year-old girls: Associations with internalization of the thin ideal and maternal, media, and peer influences. *International Journal of Eating Disorders*, *48*, 1166–1169. http://dx.doi.org/10.1002/eat.22432.

Davison, K. K., & Birch, L. L. (2001). Weight status, parent reaction, and self-concept in five-year-old girls. *Pediatrics*, *107*(1), 46–53. http://dx.doi.org/10.1542/peds.107.1.46.

Davison, K. K., & Birch, L. L. (2004). Predictors of fat stereotypes among 9-year-old girls and their parents. *Obesity Research*, *12*, 86–94.

Davison, K. K., Markey, C. N., & Birch, L. L. (2003). A longitudinal examination of patterns in girls' weight concerns and body dissatisfaction from 5 to 9 years. *International Journal of Eating Disorders*, *33*, 320–332.

Dittmar, H., Halliwell, E., & Ive, S. (2006). Does Barbie make girls want to be thin? The effect of experimental exposure to images of dolls on the body image of 5- to 8-year-old girls. *Developmental Psychology*, *42*, 283–292.

Dohnt, H. K., & Tiggemann, M. (2006a). Body image concerns in young girls: The role of peers and media prior to adolescence. *Journal of Youth and Adolescence*, *35*, 141–151.

Dohnt, H. K., & Tiggemann, M. (2006b). The contribution of peer and media influences to the development of body satisfaction and self-esteem in young girls: A prospective study. *Developmental Psychology*, *42*, 929–936.

Dohnt, H. K., & Tiggemann, M. (2008). Promoting positive body image in young girls: An evaluation of 'Shapesville'. *European Eating Disorders Review*, *16*, 222–233.

Drummond, M. (2012). Boy's bodies in early childhood. *Australasian Journal of Early Childhood*, *37*, 107–114.

Durso, L. E., & Latner, J. D. (2008). Understanding self-directed stigma: Development of the weight bias internalization scale. *Obesity*, *16*, S80–S86.

Eisenberg, M. E., Neumark-Sztainer, D., & Story, M. (2003). Association of weight-based teasing and emotional well-being among adolescents. *Archives of Pediatrics and Adolescent Medicine*, *157*, 733–738.

Field, A. E., Camargo, C. A., Taylor, C. B., Berkey, C. S., Roberts, S. B., & Colditz, G. A. (2001). Peer, parent, and media influences on the development of weight concerns and frequent dieting among preadolescent and adolescent girls and boys. *Pediatrics*, *107*, 54.

Goldschmidt, A. B., Wall, M., Choo, T.-H. J., Becker, C., & Neumark-Sztainer, D. (2016). Shared risk factors for mood-, eating-, and weight-related health outcomes. *Health Psychology*, *35*, 245–252. http://dx.doi.org/10.1037/hea0000283. Advance online publication.

Haines, J., Neumark-Sztainer, D., Hannan, P., & Robinson-O'Brien, R. (2008). Child versus parent report of parental influences on children's weight-related attitudes and behaviors. *Journal of Pediatric Psychology*, *33*, 783–788.

Haines, J., Neumark-Sztainer, D., Perry, C. L., Hannan, P. J., & Levine, M. P. (2006). V.I.K. (very important kids): A school-based program designed to reduce teasing and unhealthy weight-control behaviors. *Health Education Research*, *21*(6), 884–895. http://dx.doi.org/10.1093/her/cyl123.

Harrison, K. (2000). Television viewing, fat stereotyping, body shape standards, and eating disorder symptomatology in grade school children. *Communication Research*, *27*, 617–640. http://dx.doi.org/10.1177/009365000027005003.

Harrison, K., & Heffner, V. (2006). Media exposure, current and future body ideals, and disordered eating among preadolescent girls: A longitudinal panel study. *Journal of Youth and Adolescence*, *35*, 153–163. http://dx.doi.org/10.1007/s10964-005-9008-3.

Hart, L. M., Cornell, C., Damiano, S. R., & Paxton, S. J. (2015). Parents and prevention: A systematic review of interventions involving parents that aim to prevent body dissatisfaction or eating disorders. *International Journal of Eating Disorders*, *48*, 157–169. http://dx.doi.org/10.1002/eat.22284.

Hart, L. M., Damiano, S. R., Chittleborough, P., Paxton, S. J., & Jorm, A. F. (2014). Parenting to prevent body dissatisfaction and unhealthy eating patterns in preschool children: A Delphi consensus study. *Body Image*, *11*(4), 418–425. http://dx.doi.org/10.1016/j.bodyim.2014.06.010.

Hart, L. M., Damiano, S. R., Cornell, C., & Paxton, S. J. (2015). What parents know and want to learn about healthy eating and body image in preschool children: A triangulated qualitative study with parents and early childhood professionals. *BMC Public Health*, *15*, 596. http://dx.doi.org/10.1186/s12889-015-1865-4.

Hart, L. M., Damiano, S. R., & Paxton, S. J. (2016). Confident body, confident child: A randomized controlled trial evaluation of a parenting resource for promoting healthy body image and eating patterns in 2- to 6-year old children. *The International Journal of Eating Disorders*, *49*(5), 458–472. http://dx.doi.org/10.1002/eat.22494.

Herbozo, S., Tantleff-Dunn, S., Gokee-Laros, J., & Thompson, J. K. (2004). Beauty and thinness messages in children's media: A content analysis. *Eating Disorders*, *12*, 21–34. http://dx.doi.org/10.1080/10640260490267742.

Holt, K. E., & Ricciardelli, L. A. (2002). Social comparisons and negative affect as indicators of problem eating and muscle preoccupation among children. *Journal of Applied Developmental Psychology*, *23*, 285–304.

Holub, S. C. (2008). Individual differences in the anti-fat attitudes of preschool-children: The importance of perceived body size. *Body Image*, *5*, 317–321. http://dx.doi.org/10.1016/j.bodyim.2008.03.003.

Holub, S. C., Tan, C. C., & Patel, S. L. (2011). Factors associated with mothers' obesity stigma and young children's weight stereotypes. *Journal of Applied Developmental Psychology*, *32*, 118–126.

Irving, L. M. (2000). Promoting size acceptance in elementary school children: The EDAP puppet program. *Eating Disorders: The Journal of Treatment & Prevention*, *8*(3), 221–232.

Jendrzyca, A., & Warschburger, P. (2016). Weight stigma and eating behaviors in elementary school children: A prospective population-based study. *Appetite*, *102*, 51–59. http://dx.doi.org/10.1016/j.appet.2016.02.005.

Kaufman, A. R., & Augustson, E. M. (2008). Predictors of regular cigarette smoking among adolescent females: Does body image matter? *Nicotine and Tobacco Research*, *10*, 1301–1309. http://dx.doi.org/10.1080/14622200802238985.

Keery, H., van den Berg, P., & Thompson, J. K. (2004). An evaluation of the tripartite influence model of body dissatisfaction and eating disturbance with adolescent girls. *Body Image*, *1*, 237–251. http://dx.doi.org/10.1016/j.bodyim.2004.03.001.

Knafo, H. (2016). The development of body image in school-aged girls: A review of the literature from sociocultural, social learning, psychoanalytic, and attachment theory perspectives. *The New School Psychology Bulletin*, *13*, 1–16.

Latner, J. D., Durso, L. E., & Mond, J. M. (2013). Health and health-related quality of life among treatment seeking overweight and obese adults: Associations with internalized weight bias. *Journal of Eating Disorders*, *1*, 3.

Latner, J. D., & Schwartz, M. B. (2005). Weight bias in a child's world. In K. D. Brownell, R. M. Puhl, M. B. Schwartz, & L. Rudd (Eds.), *Weight bias: Nature, consequences and remedies* (pp. 54–67). New York: The Guilford Press. Chapter 4.

Latner, J. D., Simmonds, M., Rosewall, J. K., & Stunkard, A. J. (2007). Assessment of obesity stigmatization in children and adolescents: Modernizing a standard measure. *Obesity*, *15*, 3078–3085.

Latner, J. D., & Stunkard, A. J. (2003). Getting worse: The stigmatization of obese children. *Obesity Research, 11*(3), 452–456. http://dx.doi.org/10.1038/oby.2003.61.

Levine, M. P., & McVey, G. L. (2012). Prevention, prevention science, and an ecological perspective: A framework for programs, research, and advocacy. In G. L. McVey, M. P. Levine, N. Piran, & H. B. Ferguson (Eds.), *Preventing eating-related and weight-related disorders: Collaborative research, advocacy, and policy change*. Waterloo, ON: Wilfrid Laurier University Press.

Lewis, M., & Brooks-Gunn, J. (1979). *Social cognition and the acquisition of self*. New York, NY: Plenum Press.

Loth, K. A., Watts, A. W., van den Berg, P., & Neumark-Sztainer, D. (2015). Does body satisfaction help or harm overweight teens? A 10-year longitudinal study of the relationship between body satisfaction and body mass index. *Journal of Adolescent Health, 57,* 559–561. http://dx.doi.org/10.1016/j.jadohealth.2015.07.008.

Lowes, J., & Tiggemann, M. (2003). Body dissatisfaction, dieting awareness and the impact of parental influence in young children. *British Journal of Health Psychology, 8,* 135–147. http://dx.doi.org/10.1348/135910703321649123.

Lunde, C., Frisén, A., & Hwang, P. C. (2007). Ten-year-old girls' and boys' body composition and peer victimization experiences: Prospective associations with body satisfaction. *Body Image, 4,* 11–28.

McCabe, M. P., Ricciardelli, L. A., & Salmon, J. (2006). Evaluation of a prevention program to address body focus and negative affect among children. *Journal of Health Psychology, 11*(4), 589–598. http://dx.doi.org/10.1177/1359105306065019.

McVey, G. L., Tweed, S., & Blackmore, E. (2007). Healthy schools-healthy kids: A controlled evaluation of a comprehensive universal eating disorder prevention program. *Body Image, 4*(2), 115–136. http://dx.doi.org/10.1016/j.bodyim.2007.01.004.

Mendelson, B. K., & White, D. (1982). Relation between body esteem and self-esteem of obese and normal children. *Perceptual and Motor Skills, 54,* 899–905.

Mitchell, S. H., Petrie, T. A., Greenleaf, C. A., & Martin, S. B. (2015). A biopsychosocial model of dietary restraint in early adolescent boys. *Journal of Early Adolescence, 1–25.* http://dx.doi.org/10.1177/0272431615619232.

Musher-Eizenman, D. R., Holub, S. C., Edwards-Leeper, L. A., Persson, A. V., & Goldstein, S. E. (2003). The narrow range of acceptable body types of preschoolers and their mothers. *Journal of Applied Developmental Psychology, 24,* 259–272. http://dx.doi.org/10.1016/S0193-3973(03)00047-9.

Musher-Eizenman, D. R., Holub, S. C., Miller, A. B., Goldstein, S. E., & Edwards-Leeper, L. (2004). Body size stigmatization in preschool children: The role of control attributions. *Journal of Pediatric Psychology, 29,* 613–620. http://dx.doi.org/10.1093/jpepsy/jsh063.

Myers, T. A., & Crowther, J. H. (2009). Social comparison as a predictor of body dissatisfaction: A meta-analytic review. *Journal of Abnormal Psychology, 118,* 683–698. http://dx.doi.org/10.1037/a0016763.

Neumark-Sztainer, D., Paxton, S. J., Hannan, P. J., Haines, J., & Story, M. (2006). Does body satisfaction matter? Five-year longitudinal associations between body satisfaction and health behaviors in adolescent females and males. *Journal of Adolescent Health, 39,* 244–251.

Neumark-Sztainer, D., Sherwood, N. E., Coller, T., & Hannan, P. J. (2000). Primary prevention of disordered eating among preadolescent girls: Feasibility and short-term effect of a community-based intervention. *Journal of the American Dietetic Association, 100*(12), 1466–1473.

Nichols, T. E., Paxton, S. J., Gregg, K. J., Daminao, S. R., Alexander, M., & Wertheim, E. H. (2016). Body image attitudes are related to perfectionism and self-esteem in six-year old children. In *Paper presented at the 7th appearance matters conference, London*.

Norwood, S. J., Murray, M., Nolan, A., & Bowker, A. (2011). Beautiful from the inside out: A school-based programme designed to increase self-esteem and positive body image among preadolescents. *Canadian Journal of School Psychology*, *26*, 263–282. http://dx.doi.org/10.1177/0829573511423632.

Paxton, S. J., Eisenberg, M. E., & Neumark-Sztainer, D. (2006). Prospective predictors of body dissatisfaction in adolescent girls and boys: A five year longitudinal study. *Developmental Psychology*, *42*, 888–899.

Paxton, S. J., & McLean, S. (2010). Body image treatment. In C. Grilo & J. Mitchell (Eds.), *The treatment of eating disorders* (pp. 471–486). New York: The Guilford Press. Chapter 28.

Perez, M., Kroon Van Diest, A. M., Smith, H., & Sladek, M. R. (2016). Body dissatisfaction and its correlates in 5- to 7-year-old girls: A social learning experiment. *Journal of Clinical Child and Adolescent Psychology*, 1–13. http://dx.doi.org/10.1080/15374416.2016.1157758.

Piran, N. (2016). Embodied possibilities and disruptions: The emergence of the experience of embodiment construct from qualitative studies with girls and women. *Body Image*, *18*, 43–60.

Pope, H. G., Jr., Kanayama, G., & Hudson, J. I. (2012). Risk factors for illicit anabolic-androgenic steroid use in male weightlifters: A cross-sectional cohort study. *Biological Psychiatry*, *71*, 254–261. http://dx.doi.org/10.1016/j.biopsych.2011.06.024.

Puhl, R. M., & Heuer, C. A. (2009). The stigma of obesity: A review and update. *Obesity*, *17*, 941–964.

Puhl, R. M., & Latner, J. (2007). Stigma, obesity and the health of the nation's children. *Psychological Bulletin*, *133*, 557–580.

Puhl, R., & Suh, Y. (2015). Health consequences of weight stigma: Implications of obesity prevention and treatment. *Current Obesity Reports*, *4*, 182–190.

Ricciardelli, L. A., & McCabe, M. P. (2001). Children's body image concerns and eating disturbance: A review of the literature. *Clinical Psychology Review*, *21*, 325–344.

Ricciardelli, L. A., & McCabe, M. P. (2011). Body image development in adolescent boys. In T. Cash & L. Smolak (Eds.), *Body image: A handbook of science, practice and prevention* (2nd ed., pp. 85–92). New York: Guilford Press. Chapter 10.

Ricciardelli, L. A., McCabe, M. P., Lillis, J., & Thomas, K. (2006). A longitudinal investigation of the development of weight and muscle concerns among preadolescent boys. *Journal of Youth and Adolescence*, *35*, 177–187.

Ricciardelli, L. A., McCabe, M. P., Mussap, A. J., & Holt, K. (2009). Body image in preadolescent boys. In L. Smolak & J. K. Thompson (Eds.), *Body image, eating disorders and obesity in youth* (2nd ed., pp. 77–95). Washington, DC: American Psychological Association. Chapter 4.

Richardson, S., Goodman, N., Hastorf, A. H., & Dornbusch, S. M. (1961). Cultural uniformity in reaction to physical disabilities. *American Sociological Review*, *26*(2), 241–247. http://dx.doi.org/10.2307/2089861.

Rodgers, R., Chabrol, H., & Paxton, S. J. (2011). An exploration of the tripartite influence model of body dissatisfaction and disordered eating among Australian and French college women. *Body Image*, *8*(3), 208–215.

Rodgers, R. F., McLean, S. A., & Paxton, S. J. (2015). Longitudinal relationships among internalization of the media ideal, peer social comparison, and body dissatisfaction: Implications for the tripartite influence model. *Developmental Psychology*, *51*, 706–713.

Rodgers, R. F., Paxton, S. J., & McLean, S. A. (2014). A biopsychosocial model of body image concerns and disordered eating in early adolescent girls. *Journal of Youth and Adolescence*, *43*, 814–823.

Rodgers, R. F., Wertheim, E. H., Damiano, S. R., Gregg, K. J., & Paxton, S. J. (2015). "Stop eating lollies and do lots of sports": A prospective qualitative study of the development of children's awareness of dietary restraint and exercise to lose weight. *International Journal of Behavioral Nutrition and Physical Activity*, *12*, 155. http://dx.doi.org/10.1186/s12966-015-0318-x.

Ross, A., Paxton, S. J., & Rodgers, R. F. (2013). Y's Girl: Increasing body satisfaction among primary school girls. *Body Image*, *10*(4), 614–618. http://dx.doi.org/10.1016/j.bodyim.2013.06.009.

Sands, E. R., & Wardle, J. (2003). Internalization of ideal body shapes in 9–12-year-old girls. *International Journal of Eating Disorders*, *33*, 193–204. http://dx.doi.org/10.1002/eat.10121.

Schooler, D. (2013). Early adolescent body image predicts subsequent condom use behavior among girls. *Sexuality Research and Social Policy*, *10*, 52–61. http://dx.doi.org/10.1007/s13178-012-0099-9.

Schur, E. A., Sanders, M., & Steiner, H. (2000). Body dissatisfaction and dieting in young children. *International Journal of Eating Disorders*, *27*, 74–82.

Slade, P. D., Dewey, M. E., Newton, T., Brodie, D., & Kiemle, G. (1990). Development and preliminary validation of the body satisfaction scale (BSS). *Psychology & Health*, *4*, 213–220. http://dx.doi.org/10.1080/08870449008400391.

Smolak, L. (2011). Body image development in childhood. In T. Cash & L. Smolak (Eds.), *Body Image: A handbook of science, practice and prevention* (2nd ed., pp. 67–75). New York: Guilford Press. Chapter 8.

Spiel, E. C., Paxton, S. J., & Yager, Z. (2012). Weight attitudes in 3- to 5-year-old children: Age differences and cross-sectional predictors. *Body Image*, *9*(4), 524–527. http://dx.doi.org/10.1016/j.bodyim.2012.07.006.

Spiel, E., Rodgers, R. F., Paxton, S. J., Wertheim, E. H., Damiano, S. D., Gregg, K. J., & McLean, S. A. (2016). "He's got his father's bias": Parental influence on weight bias in young children. *British Journal of Developmental Psychology*, *34*, 198–211, http://dx.doi.org/10.1111/bjdp.12123.

Stice, E., Marti, C. N., & Durant, S. (2011). Risk factors for onset of eating disorders: Evidence of multiple risk pathways from an 8-year prospective study. *Behaviour Research and Therapy*, *49*, 622–627. http://dx.doi.org/10.1016/j.brat.2011.06.009.

Strauss, R. S., & Pollack, H. A. (2003). Social marginalization of overweight children. *Archives of Pediatrics and Adolescent Medicine*, *157*, 746–752.

Tatangelo, G. K., & Ricciardelli, L. A. (2016). Children's body image and social comparisons with peers and the media. *Journal of Health Psychology*, http://dx.doi.org/10.1177/1359105315615409.

Thompson, J. K., Heinberg, L. J., Altabe, M., & Tantleff Dunn, S. (1999). *Exacting beauty: Theory, assessment, and treatment of body image disturbance*. Washington, DC: American Psychological Association.

Tiggemann, M., & Pennington, B. (1990). The development of gender differences in body-size dissatisfaction. *Australian Psychologist*, *25*, 306–313. http://dx.doi.org/10.1080/00050069008260025.

Tiggemann, M., & Slater, A. (2014). NetTweens: The Internet and body image concerns in preteenage girls. *Journal of Early Adolescence*, *34*, 606–620.

Truby, H., & Paxton, S. J. (2002). Development of the children's body image scale. *British Journal of Clinical Psychology*, *41*, 185–203. http://dx.doi.org/10.1348/014466502163967.

Truby, H., & Paxton, S. J. (2008). The children's body image scale: Reliability and use with international standards for body mass index. *British Journal of Clinical Psychology*, *47*, 119–124. http://dx.doi.org/10.1348/014466507X251261.

Wade, T. D., Wilksch, S. M., Paxton, S. J., Byrne, S. M., & Austin, S. B. (2015). How perfectionism and ineffectiveness influence growth of eating disorder risk in young adolescent girls. *Behaviour Research and Therapy*, *66*, 56–63.

Watson, H. J., Joyce, T., French, E., Willan, V., Kane, R. T., Tanner-Smith, E. E., … Egan, S. J. (2016). Prevention of eating disorders: A systematic review of randomized, controlled trials. *The International Journal of Eating Disorders*, *49*, 833–862. http://dx.doi. org/10.1002/eat.22577.

Wertheim, E. H., & Paxton, S. J. (2011). Body image in adolescent girls. In T. Cash & L. Smolak (Eds.), *Body image: A handbook of science, practice and prevention* (2nd ed., pp. 76–84). New York: Guilford Press. Chapter 9.

Yager, Z., & O'Dea, J. (2015). School-based prevention. In M. P. Levine & L. Smolak (Eds.), *The Wiley-Blackwell handbook of eating disorders* (pp. 569–581): London: Wiley-Blackwell. Chapter 42.

Edwards Brothers Malloy
Ann Arbor MI. USA
May 9, 2017